MOURNING THE PRESIDENTS

Miller Center Studies on the Presidency
GUIAN A. MCKEE AND MARC J. SELVERSTONE, EDITORS

Mourning the Presidents

→ • ←

LOSS AND LEGACY IN AMERICAN CULTURE

Edited by Lindsay M. Chervinsky

and Matthew R. Costello

UNIVERSITY OF VIRGINIA PRESS

Charlottesville and London

Published in association with the
University of Virginia's Miller Center of Public Affairs
and in collaboration with the White House Historical Association
and the Center for Presidential History

University of Virginia Press
© 2023 by the Rector and Visitors of the University of Virginia
All rights reserved
Printed in the United States of America on acid-free paper

First published 2023

1 3 5 7 9 8 6 4 2

Library of Congress Cataloging-in-Publication Data

Names: Chervinsky, Lindsay M., editor. | Costello, Matthew (Matthew R.), editor. |
White Burkett Miller Center.
Title: Mourning the presidents : loss and legacy in American culture /
edited by Lindsay M. Chervinsky and Matthew R. Costello.
Other titles: Loss and legacy in American culture
Description: Charlottesville : University of Virginia Press, 2023. | Series: Miller Center
studies on the presidency | "Published in association with the University of Virginia's
Miller Center of Public Affairs and in collaboration with the White House Historical Association
and the Center for Presidential History." | Includes bibliographical references and index.
Identifiers: LCCN 2022042568 (print) | LCCN 2022042569 (ebook) | ISBN 9780813949284
(hardcover) | ISBN 9780813949291 (paperback) | ISBN 9780813949307 (ebook)
Subjects: LCSH: Presidents—United States—Death. | Presidents—United States—
Biography. | Funeral rites and ceremonies—United States—History. | Collective memory—
United States. | United States—Social life and customs.
Classification: LCC E176.1 .M935 2023 (print) | LCC E176.1 (ebook) |
DDC 973.09/9—dc23/eng/20220915
LC record available at https://lccn.loc.gov/2022042568
LC ebook record available at https://lccn.loc.gov/2022042569

Cover art: Franklin D. Roosevelt's funeral procession, Pennsylvania Avenue, Washington, DC,
April 14, 1945 (Prints and Photographs Division, Library of Congress, LC-USZ62-67439);
detail images, Chinnapong/Shutterstock.com, In-Finity/Shutterstock.com

CONTENTS

FOREWORD

Grief drives men into habits of serious reflection, sharpens the
understanding, and softens the heart; it compels them to arouse
their reason, to assert its empire over their passions, propensities and
prejudices; to elevate them to a superiority over all human events. . . .
—John Adams to Thomas Jefferson, May 6, 1816

I N THIS EXCHANGE BETWEEN two former presidents, John Adams provided an answer to a question underlying this volume. As citizens of
the United States, why do we mourn presidents? This tradition began
with the passing of the nation's first chief executive, George Washington.
Since then, the rituals surrounding the deaths of presidents have intensified, with more attention, time, resources, and ceremonial pomp devoted to
commemorating their lives.

In his poignant response to Jefferson, Adams argues that grief is not
simply an emotional or psychological reaction. Instead, Adams views grief
as utilitarian. Grief forces humans to engage in deep contemplation. In
fact, grief "arouses" reason, providing clarity that might not have existed
otherwise. In this sense, Adams connects the concepts of grief and mourning to lasting memory and legacy. The only way we can grasp memory is to
mourn and grieve. It is a necessary first step in the process of considering
historical legacy. Each of the essays in this book illustrates the connection

between the ritualistic act of mourning and how presidents are eventually remembered and memorialized, by both the American public and professional historians alike.

The idea for this volume arose soon after the funeral of President George H. W. Bush, in 2018. The public response to Bush's death was considerable, with thousands of mourners lined up to pay their respects to the former president at the United States Capitol and in Texas. Such an outpouring of grief opened the door for a longitudinal, comprehensive examination concerning the history of presidential mourning and memory.

This project brought together the White House Historical Association (WHHA) and Southern Methodist University's Center for Presidential History (CPH). The WHHA and CPH decided to hold a workshop for invited book chapter authors immediately preceding the 2020 Presidential Sites Summit, a biannual conference organized by WHHA to gather leadership from historic presidential sites across the country. Unfortunately, the pandemic intervened, preventing the summit and the edited volume workshop from taking place. Additionally, most archives, presidential libraries, and repositories were closed to researchers. The editors of the volume, Dr. Lindsay M. Chervinsky and Dr. Matthew R. Costello, postponed the workshop until August 2021, thus giving authors more time to gain access to needed materials and complete their research. Due to the unpredictability of COVID-19 and the emergence of new variants, the 2021 workshop was held virtually.

Despite considerable challenges, the contributors of this volume persisted, producing an array of essays that accomplished the original stated goal of the project: to provide a comprehensive historical understanding of presidential mourning and its role in American political history. As I listened to the presentations at the virtual workshop, several arguments surfaced as worthy of further reflection.

First, as suggested by Adams in his letter to Jefferson, these essays demonstrate a distinction between presidential mourning and presidential memory. Mourning refers to the immediate period after a president's death. It is often ritualistic, with recent presidential funerals lasting at least a week and spanning several locations across the country. There is remarkable consistency in presidential mourning rituals over time. Funerals for deceased presidents are uniformly respectful, even when an administration has been viewed unfavorably by historians or the American electorate. Criticism or disagreement is not emphasized in the immediate mourning period after a president dies. Most recently, President Donald J. Trump attended the funeral of former President George H. W. Bush. No love was lost between the two men, yet Trump followed the established norms of respect. Such consistency across American history emphasizes the power of such rituals. Even lesser-known presidents, those at the bottom tier of the historical rankings, are recipients of an extended and solemn period of mourning after their deaths.

Presidential memory is a more nebulous concept than presidential mourning. If mourning is consistent, then memory is constantly evolving. Presidential legacies change over time; memory is a developmental, not a static, concept. For example, the legacies of presidents who enslaved people, both at their private homes and at the White House, have transformed considerably within the past decade. Understanding the context of presidential memory is key. Many essays in the volume argue that presidential legacies do not exist in a vacuum impervious to political events and cultural norms.

This collection also substantiates a causal relationship between presidential mourning and memory, affirming John Adams's earlier reflection. The reason why presidential mourning is intensely ritualized, scripted, and planned is because presidents themselves realize that how they are portrayed during the mourning period will directly impact the initial phase of their longer legacy. The narrative shared when the country is captivated by the recent death of a president affects how historians, journalists, political scientists, and other experts analyze a president's legacy and situate it within the larger contours of American history. Of course, interpretations of legacy may change over time, but such initial conceptualizations can prove difficult to dislodge, particularly in the near-term.

At least three recurring variables that affect presidential mourning and memory were identified during the workshop discussion. Each shapes the approach, scope, and focus of mourning and memory. Presidential mourning and memory cannot be fully understood or explained without careful attention to these three factors.

The first critical variable is race. Featured examples in the book, including the chapters on Abraham Lincoln and John F. Kennedy, examine how

African Americans responded to presidential mourning, particularly when such deaths were unanticipated. Even more importantly, race must be considered in evaluations of presidential legacy and memory. This volume posits that the longer-term effects of race on memorialization are uneven. Several examples demonstrate this complicated relationship. Despite owning hundreds of enslaved people, Thomas Jefferson's legacy has not suffered irreparable harm; he remains a Mount Rushmore president with a prominent memorial on the National Mall. Likewise, Andrew Jackson's extermination of Native Americans has tarnished, yet not destroyed, his reputation. A massive statue of Jackson remains directly outside the White House in Lafayette Park, and artistic renderings of Jackson have appeared in prominent Oval Office locations throughout the past century. Andrew Johnson, who weakened Lincoln's plans for Reconstruction, is not typically viewed as an example of presidential greatness. Nonetheless, his statue remains outside the State Capitol in Raleigh, North Carolina, with no current plans to remove it.

Political party also impacts the contours of a president's legacy. As partisan identification is now a salient feature among the American electorate, with individual partisan preferences a stable lifelong characteristic, presidential legacies may be increasingly influenced by the strength of their relationship with their party. Theodore Roosevelt had a complicated relationship with the Republican Party, ultimately resulting in his factional third-party Bull Moose campaign in 1912. Roosevelt's progressive legacy has probably been adversely affected by this uneasy relationship. On the other hand, Ronald Reagan established a robust relationship with his political party, and even though he was incapacitated by Alzheimer's disease for the last ten years of his life, supporters worked diligently to cement Reagan's legacy with the rise of the modern Republican Party.

The third factor is the role that family plays in presidential mourning and memory. Some presidents enjoyed a longer opportunity to shape their legacy because their lives extended well beyond their tenure in office. Other lives were cut short, either tragically or due to unforeseen maladies. In several essays, first ladies and descendants exercised discretion and influenced decisions, thus affecting mourning and memory in substantial ways. In other examples, family members, such as Mary Lincoln, were excluded from mourning and memorialization activities. Presidential descendants can shape their ancestor's legacy, since they often speak for the family and enjoy a degree of autonomy not necessarily available to those who were contemporaries. Lastly, the definition of who qualifies as a presidential descendant is changing, with active participation in nonprofit boards, historical organizations, and other legacy-related groups by descendants of enslaved people who were related to a president or lived on his property.

A final consideration raised by this book, but not directly answered by the essays, is whether the United States, as a republican democracy, places too much emphasis on the rituals of presidential mourning and perhaps not enough on serious reconsiderations of presidential legacies. The weeklong funerals of modern presidents incorrectly situate the executive as the head of the American political system rather than as a leader of a coequal branch of the federal government. This is likely a product of the intense personal connection many Americans feel toward their presidents. Nonetheless, the president is not the only institutional actor that matters in the constitutional system, and ritualistic pageantry may reinforce a major misunderstanding about how American government works.

Given the powerful relationship between mourning and memory, it is valuable to reassess the pomp and spectacle surrounding contemporary presidential funerals. Lasting legacies will change over time, but the process is slow and uneven, leaving layered interpretations and context for future historians to decipher, evaluate, and interpret.

Colleen J. Shogan

MOURNING THE PRESIDENTS

Introduction

→ • ←

Lindsay M. Chervinsky

O N NOVEMBER 30, 2018, former president George H. W. Bush died at age ninety-four. Over the next week, Americans of all colors, creeds, religions, and political affiliations acknowledged the elder statesman. Political foes set aside their differences and came together to celebrate Bush's lifetime of public service. Even President Donald J. Trump, who had frequently bashed members of the Bush family publicly and on social media, curtailed his criticisms. He permitted the Bush family to stay at Blair House—the president's guest house—during the state funeral in Washington, DC.[1]

How the nation responds to the death of a US president reveals much about the political climate, social values, domestic divisions, and international pressures facing the United States at the moment of his passing. In 2018, Democrats and Republicans reacted to President Trump's departure from most political norms by celebrating George H. W. Bush's dedication to the country, ability to work with politicians on both sides of the aisle, and moderate positions on environmental protections and gun reform. In the years ahead, scholars will determine whether these reflections on Bush's legacy were accurate as they reevaluate his presidency. But in 2018, rising racial turmoil and political divisions, escalating international conflict, and deteriorating economic prospects came together to shape politicians' and the public's reverence for a steady, knowledgeable, and experienced version of George H. W. Bush. This version was the one that Americans chose to remember and celebrate—a leader with moral character and steadfast temperament.

Donald Trump's presidency affected more than one presidential legacy. In 2009, President George W. Bush left office with a 33 percent approval rating depressed by an economic recession, a mishandled natural disaster in Hurricane Katrina, and an unpopular war in the Middle East—the second-lowest approval rating since pollsters started calculating public opinion. In contrast, by 2018, 61 percent of Americans held a favorable view of Bush in retrospect. Many Americans recalled the days of Bush's "compassionate conservatism," and forgot his role in instigating the then still ongoing military interventions in Afghanistan and Iraq.[2]

The evolving legacies of the Bush presidents, their shifting positions in historical memory, and their complicated relationship to contemporary events are not unique to these former presidents. Evaluations of each US president's achievements while in office remain malleable as patterns of memory shift. And each new meaning reveals much about the ways in which American culture and society continue to evolve. Americans' reactions to the passing of a president and the immediate discussion of his legacy often says little about that person's tenure in office. Instead, mourning rituals and memory reflect the existing tensions, values, and goals of American society at that moment. Critically, the mourning and memorialization processes have evolved over time, as the nation's needs and values have changed. This volume explores that process for twelve of the forty-five men that have served in the highest office.

Contribution to Scholarship

Presidents take on an almost mythical status in American memory. They are the nation's representative on the world stage, hold a position of immense authority, and are more visible to average American citizens than institutions like the Supreme Court with its lifetime appointees or Congress with hundreds of members and frequent turnover. Many scholars have considered the legacies of individual presidents or compared administrations, but no one has offered a comparative analysis of how mourning and presidential legacy has changed over time, the similarities between presidential deaths, or how different communities' views of presidents have evolved.[3] Similar volumes with multiple contributors have followed two trajectories to make a substantive contribution to the literature. They either examine a theme over an extended chronological timeline, such as presidents at war, or they analyze an event, place, or person from multiple perspectives, like Watergate or the Vietnam War.[4] As of yet, no published work has presented a critical approach on what happens after presidents die.

There are several popular works about presidential death and scandal in the White House and beyond, but they generally don't assess how presidential deaths reflect the moment and how presidential legacies evolve over time.[5] This volume offers a more analytical approach to these pivotal moments in American history and generates greater dialogue among and between presidential historians and scholars of culture, war, and memory.

This volume draws on two bodies of literature, biographies and studies of memory and culture. Several of the presidents covered in this volume have benefitted from extensive biographical attention, which include analyses of their deaths and legacies. By utilizing these works, we hope to identify parallels and transformations in American culture. As for memory studies, most of these books tend to focus on the legacy of one individual, or how the memory and storytelling around one event or period evolved.[6] The authors pulled from a wide variety of works on death and mourning in Civil War studies, slavery, presidential legacy, and military and state funeral customs to offer a nuanced and multifaceted approach to presidential mourning and legacy for the first time.[7]

We hope this volume encourages readers to think critically about the deaths and legacies of American presidents, beyond a single era or administration. By telling these stories over two centuries, these essays contribute to our understanding of the role of the presidency in American culture, how Americans grapple with grief and complex legacies, and the power of the presidency to divide or unite US citizens.

Volume Organization

Offering a chapter on every American president who has passed to date would have been the most thorough approach in examining the rituals and memory practices surrounding their deaths, but practical considerations eliminated that possibility. Accordingly, we sought chapters that met three considerations. First, we designed the volume to have relative balance between nineteenth- and twentieth-century history. Second, we selected chapters that represented both well-known presidents and lesser-studied individuals. The volume would reveal less if it only included George Washington, Thomas Jefferson, Abraham Lincoln, Franklin D. Roosevelt, John F. Kennedy, and Ronald Reagan. While we included these men, we sought to balance their stories with others who have been overlooked, like Zachary Taylor, Andrew Johnson, and Herbert Hoover, to provide new insights. Third, we sought chapters that explored memory and legacy from diverse perspectives. For example, Thomas Jefferson's legacy means something very different to Black Americans who descended from the enslaved community at Monticello—the perspective offered by Andrew M. Davenport.

The chapters generally follow the same outline: an explanation of the death of the specific president, the immediate public reaction, and the mourning rituals at the time. We then encouraged each scholar to explore the ongoing evolution of the president's legacy and what the memory of that president suggests about the shifting values that animate American society and culture. They all approached the source materials and question of memory differently—some focused on presidential libraries, monuments, and memorials, while others analyzed eulogies, changes in historiography, and family participation. We also encouraged the authors to take innovative approaches to avoid repeating past scholarship, especially for the well-known presidents whose deaths have been covered at length, like Washington, Lincoln, and Kennedy. Kennedy's death especially carries unusual weight in American memory—perhaps because of the graphic video footage of the assassination, or the presence of constant television and radio press coverage. In some ways, the nuances of his presidency and legacy have been overshadowed by his assassination and the tragic end of the glamorous "Camelot" era. As a result, the wider public often overlooks Kennedy's relative conservatism and instead credits him for much of the legislation that passed after his death. In the chapter on Kennedy, Dr. Sharron Wilkins Conrad explores the origins of this narrative and examines the ways in which African Americans have elevated Kennedy's presidency and amplified his role in the civil rights narrative. The chapter on George H. W. Bush also takes a slightly different approach. Because his death and the ceremonies took place so recently, we opted to include a contribution from someone who was involved in the planning process. Accordingly, Warren Finch's chapter adopts a more personal tone than the others.

While each of the twelve chapters tells a unique story, some similarities and parallels do emerge that demonstrate continuing themes in American society, including racial inequities and the expansion of the executive branch and its role in daily life. How exactly presidents die—either in or outside of office—affects their memory and legacy. Those who die in office spark national mourning but lack the opportunity to participate in the crafting of their own legacy. For example, the country mourned Franklin D. Roosevelt and Kennedy from coast to coast, but these men did not leave behind the records or thoughtful planning offered by Herbert Hoover or George H. W. Bush.

Other parallels between the presidents cross time and space. The violent nature of Abraham Lincoln's and John F. Kennedy's assassinations produced an outpouring of shock and grief that have rarely accompanied more predictable presidential deaths. These passings also force us to consider the "martyr effect." The tragic nature of a president's death can cause the American public to overlook flaws and failures. For example, despite Kennedy's extramarital affairs, role in the start of the Vietnam War, or foreign policy failures like the Bay of Pigs invasion of Cuba, he still stands in the top ten of presidents in most C-SPAN presidential historian ranking polls.[8]

The martyr effect also has its limitations, as it rarely extends to James A. Garfield or William McKinley. Perhaps length of tenure and Americans' perceptions of their successors determine the extent of martyrdom. Garfield served for only six months, and McKinley was overshadowed by the colorful personality of his successor Theodore Roosevelt. In contrast, memory of Kennedy's term in office benefits from Lyndon B. Johnson's somewhat problematic presidency. Although Johnson shepherded through important civil rights and antipoverty legislation, he never overcame the stain of the Vietnam War, and in presidential polls, Kennedy usually outranks him.

There are also important changes over time. Some eighteenth- and nineteenth-century presidents have presidential libraries and historical sites, but they rarely offer the robust archives for deep scholarly and public engagement provided by the presidential libraries built in the twentieth century and operated by the staff of the National Archives and Records Administration

(NARA). Additionally, twentieth-century presidential libraries have become burial sites for most presidents, including Hoover, Franklin D. Roosevelt, Reagan, and George H. W. Bush, which suggests a closer relationship between legacy, mourning, and memorial.[9] Theodore Roosevelt and Reagan are helpful examples, as they were involved in crafting their legacy and planning their final resting places. Their presidencies and their values continued to dominate politics long after their time in office, often with their encouragement or that of their families, especially former first ladies. They were adored by the American public and their deaths spurred national mourning. They were remembered by their contemporaries as the embodiment of the American experiment and their legacies remained deeply entwined with American identity.[10]

The role of race and civil rights in American society are other themes that weave through the volume. The public responses to Lincoln's and Kennedy's passing, as well as the deaths of Jefferson, Jackson, and Andrew Johnson, revealed divisions within the American populace along racial lines or over issues of civil rights. This process is ongoing. As Americans grapple with their country's complicated racial history, these presidents' continually reassessed relationships to Black Americans, Native Americans, and the intertwined matters of race and citizenship will shape and reshape their evolving legacies.

While issues of race and civil rights challenge presidential legacies, several chapters also reveal the harsh truth that an ineffective presidency limits the potential for legacy and rehabilitation. Taylor and Hoover share similar stories in this regard. Both were celebrated for their careers before their presidencies (and in Hoover's case, after he left office), yet both of their administrations served as a low point in their years of public service. Their inability or inefficacy as presidents proved a stumbling block for mourners and eulogists. Whereas Taylor died too quickly to rehabilitate his image postpresidency, Hoover spent decades emphasizing the parts of his story worth celebrating. Yet both are often relegated to the margins of presidential history for perceived failed or forgettable tenures in the White House.

Finally, as more Americans were counted as citizens and became integrated into the political process, they brought increasingly diverse perspectives to collective mourning rituals that surround a president's death. Mourning was and remains a communal experience that reflects the US president's unique role as the only elected official to represent all Americans. As the body politic has broadened to include more types of people, so too have the mourning rituals expanded to include diverse communities and traditions.

We organized this volume in the fall of 2019, before the national conversation erupted over Black Lives Matter, systemic racism, and police brutality. This social justice movement unfolded alongside the ongoing conversation about Confederate monuments, statues, and how we remember and celebrate the past. These conversations cannot be separated from each other, nor from the history of America's presidents. Take the National Mall, for example. At the east end stands the US Capitol, a symbol of American democracy, and to the north sits the White House, the home of the presidents—both built largely by enslaved labor.[11] In the center of the Mall, the Washington Monument looms over all other buildings in the city, a massive memorial to the nation's first president. Over the course of his lifetime, Washington owned hundreds of enslaved individuals, freed 123 people in his will, and failed to take further action in support of abolition.

At the west end, the Lincoln Memorial celebrates the preservation of the Union and acknowledges the eradication of slavery. Flanking the Tidal Basin are monuments of historic figures that embody the nation's complex history with slavery and race. Thomas Jefferson authored the phrase "all men are created equal," while enslaving hundreds of individuals and carrying on a long-term sexual relationship with an enslaved woman named Sally Hemings. Just across the basin from the Jefferson Memorial, a sculpture of Martin Luther King Jr. looms as a reminder of the unmet promises articulated in the Declaration of Independence.

This volume reflects the nation's centuries-long effort to conceal and come to terms with the president's role in this complicated past. Washington's death forced the nation to consider how it would mourn a president. Like so many aspects of his life, his death set precedent for those that followed. As his family and the nation crafted mourning rituals, white voices were privileged, while the impact of his death on enslaved families was ignored or erased. Mary V. Thompson's essay demonstrates how this practice evolved in real time and established a precedent that official mourning activities privileged the first families and were the purview of white Americans. Of course, Black Americans rejected the idea that presidential deaths did not affect their lives, as Andrew Davenport persuasively notes. Often presidential deaths, from Washington to Taylor, sparked periods of intense disruption, loss, and family separation in Black communities. After the Civil War, Black Americans continued to carve out separate spaces for mourning and commemoration of beloved presidents like Lincoln and Kennedy.

While the monuments that decorate the National Mall have remained unchanged across the decades, how Americans understand the presidents and their legacies rarely remains static. Presidential libraries, foundations, historians, and activists shape our memory and understanding of the presidents and their legacies. Presidential papers projects make this labor possible, revealing valuable details about figures who left little archival record of their own. For example, while most of the enslaved population at Mount Vernon and Monticello was illiterate and left no written documentation, many aspects of their lives were captured in Washington's and Jefferson's papers, including clothing purchases, medical treatment, births and deaths, punishment, occupation and tasks, and family ties. Although these papers projects were funded to document the lives and contributions of prominent white men, scholars have mined the depths of their information to share stories about women, working people, and people of color. The unexpected benefits of presidential archives apply to twentieth-century presidents as well. The archives at the Franklin D. Roosevelt, Kennedy, and Reagan Libraries reveal connections between race, gender, and policy, and missed opportunities in the New Deal, the Civil Rights Movement, and the HIV-AIDS epidemic. These repositories guarantee that future generations of scholars will continue to make important discoveries and offer reassessment of these leaders, and they also demonstrate that the nation's grappling with presidential history and presidential legacies is only just beginning.

We hope that this book will contribute to and continue the conversation.

Notes

1. President Richard Nixon started this tradition in 1973 when he made the Blair House available to the Johnson family during the state funeral.

2. Ryan Struyk, "George Bush's Favorable Rating Has Pulled a Complete 180," *CNN*, January 23, 2018, https://edition.cnn.com/2018/01/22/politics/george-w-bush-favorable -poll/index.html.

3. William Hitchcock, *The Age of Eisenhower: America and the World in the 1950s* (New York: Simon & Schuster, 2018); Annette Gordon-Reed and Peter S. Onuf, *"Most Blessed of the Patriarchs": Thomas Jefferson and the Empire of Imagination* (New York: Liveright, 2016); Martha Hodes, *Mourning Lincoln* (New Haven: Yale University Press, 2015); William E. Leuchtenburg, *In the Shadow of FDR: From Harry Truman to Barack Obama* (Ithaca, NY: Cornell University Press, 2009); Robert Dallek, *Flawed Giant: Lyndon Johnson and His Times, 1961–1975* (New York: Oxford University Press, 1998); Robert Dallek, *An Unfinished Life: John F. Kennedy, 1917–1963* (New York: Little, Brown, 2003).

4. For examples, see Timothy Andrews Sayle, Jeffrey A. Engel, Hal Brands, and William Inboden, eds., *The Last Card: Inside George W. Bush's Decision to Surge in Iraq* (Ithaca, NY: Cornell University Press, 2019); Jeffrey A. Engel and Thomas J. Knock, eds., *When Life Strikes the President: Scandal, Death, and Illness in the White House* (New York: Oxford University Press, 2017); David Anderson, ed., *Shadow on the White House: Presidents and the Vietnam War* (Lawrence: University of Kansas Press, 1993); Elizabeth N. Saunders, *Leaders at War: How Presidents Shape Military Interventions* (Ithaca, NY: Cornell University Press, 2014).

5. Brady Carlson, *Dead Presidents: An American Adventure into the Strange Deaths and Surprising Afterlives of Our Nation's Leaders* (New York: W. W. Norton, 2017). Louis L. Picone, *The President Is Dead!: The Extraordinary Stories of Presidential Deaths, Final Days, Burials, and Beyond* (New York: Skyhorse, 2016).

6. For examples, see Tony Horwitz, *Confederates in the Attic: Dispatches from the Unfinished Civil War* (New York: Pantheon, 1998); Jerry Lembcke, *The Spitting Image* (New York: New York University Press, 1998); Karal Ann Marling, *George Washington Slept Here: Colonial Revivals and American Culture, 1876–1976* (Cambridge, MA: Harvard University Press, 1988). Also see Michael Schudson, *Watergate in American Memory: How We Remember, Forget, and Reconstruct the Past* (New York: Basic Books, 1992); Alice George, *The Assassination of John F. Kennedy: Political Trauma and American Memory* (New York: Routledge, 2013).

7. Drew Gilpin Faust, *This Republic of Suffering: Death and the American Civil War* (New York: Vintage Books, 2008); Mark S. Schantz, *Awaiting the Heavenly Country: The Civil War and America's Culture of Death* (Ithaca, NY: Cornell University Press, 2008); Nancy Isenberg and Andrew Burstein, eds., *Mortal Remains: Death in Early America* (Philadelphia: University of Pennsylvania Press, 2003); Thomas G. Long, *The Good Funeral: Death, Grief, and the Community of Care* (Louisville, KY: Westminster John Knox, 2013); B. C. Mossman and M. W. Stark, *The Last Salute: Civil and Military Funerals, 1921–1969* (Washington, DC: Department of the Army, 1991).

8. "Presidential Historians Survey 2021," C-SPAN, https://www.c-span.org /presidentsurvey2021/?page=overall.

9. Presidents Harry S. Truman, Dwight Eisenhower, and Richard Nixon are buried at their presidential libraries. Gerald Ford is buried at the Ford Museum in Grand Rapids. John F. Kennedy is buried at Arlington Cemetery and Lyndon Johnson is buried at Johnson Ranch in Texas.

10. See the Reagan chapter by Chester Pach. He demonstrates how Reagan's funeral and mourning ceremonies leaned heavily on the concept of Reagan as the embodiment of American values.

11. Felicia Bell, "'The negroes alone work': Enslaved Craftsmen, the Building Trades, and the Construction of the United States Capitol, 1790–1800" (PhD diss., Howard University, 2009); Sarah Fling, "Enslaved Labor and the Construction of the U.S. Capitol," *Slavery in the President's Neighborhood*, White House Historical Association, https://www.whitehousehistory.org/enslaved-labor-and-the-construction-of-the-u -s-capitol/; Lina Mann, "Building the White House," *Slavery in the President's Neighborhood*, White House Historical Association, https://www.whitehousehistory.org /building-the-white-house/.

"In a Private Manner, without Parade or Funeral Oration"

THE FUNERAL GEORGE WASHINGTON WANTED, BUT DIDN'T GET

→ • ←

Mary V. Thompson

O N DECEMBER 18, 1797, Martha Washington wrote a long letter to a Philadelphia friend, Elizabeth Willing Powel. The two women had known one another since the days of the American Revolution and became closer during George Washington's presidency. The letter was chatty, discussing mutual friends, and then turned to "a few words" that George Washington jokingly wanted added "on his behalf." He had made a deal with several "Gentlemen not to quit the theatre of this world before the year 1800." Promising that only "dire necessity" would cause him to break his word, he begged their understanding if he had to leave early, noting that "at present there seems to be no danger of his giving them the slip, as neither his health, nor his spirits were ever in greater flow."[1] Washington was unable to keep that agreement. Two years later to the day, his body was placed in the family vault at Mount Vernon.

Washington's longed-for retirement agreed with the former president. His nephew, Howell Lewis, visited Mount Vernon between November 29 and December 9 of 1799, and later recorded that as he and his wife drove away, "the clear healthy flush on his cheek, and his sprightly manner, brought the remark from both of us that we had never seen the general look so well."[2] Earlier that year, Washington spent considerable time thinking about his death. He had been concerned for years, because, as he often noted, "tho' I was blessed with a good constitution, I was of a short lived family, and might soon expect to be entombed."[3] Being a man of great wealth, with a tendency to abhor loose ends, he felt it was past due to put his affairs in order. He had been retired from the presidency for a little over two years and finally had the time to make plans. Washington drafted a schedule of his property holdings; a detailed description of those enslaved at Mount Vernon, which included 40 people he was renting from a neighbor, as well as the 123 people who belonged to himself and the 153 owned by the estate of Daniel Parke Custis, Martha's late first husband, who were under Washington's control but not his ownership. He then drew up his last will and testament, in which he immediately freed his long-time enslaved valet, William Lee, and left him an annual payment of thirty dollars for his living expenses. The other 122 enslaved people he owned were to be freed upon the death of Martha Washington.[4] The people owned by the Custis estate, by Virginia law, were to be divided among Daniel Custis's remaining heirs, Martha Washington's four grandchildren.[5]

In the 1799 will, Washington requested the construction of a new family tomb and expressed his wishes for his funeral arrangements. He noted that the tomb needed repairs and was also "improperly situated" on a rather steep slope. He requested that a larger tomb of brick be built across from the old one "at the foot of what is commonly called the Vineyard Inclosure," which he had already marked out. Washington then asked that his own body, "with those of my deceased relatives (now in the old Vault) and such others of my family as may chuse to be entombed there, may be deposited." He closed this section of the will with a final thought about his funeral, noting that "it is my express desire that my Corpse may be Interred [sic] in a private manner, without parade or funeral oration."[6]

Descriptions of eighteenth-century funerals provide an idea of how someone of George Washington's status and military background would have been laid to rest in America. Funerals typically included long processions made up of military units associated with the deceased; a band or orchestra; the clergy; physicians; the coffin containing the body of the deceased, surrounded by those carrying the coffin and the honorary pallbearers; officials and members from organizations associated with the deceased; and local citizens. Often artillery units would bring cannons, one of which was fired each minute during the procession to the gravesite or tomb. Following the religious ceremony, infantrymen would fire volleys from their muskets.[7]

This type of ceremony was more elaborate and formal than George Washington had in mind. He was inspired by family examples when he asked that his body be put into the family vault "in a private manner, without parade or funeral oration." When Martha Washington's seventeen-year-old daughter, Patsy Custis, died in 1773 in the throes of an epileptic seizure, she was laid to rest less than twenty-four hours later in the family vault at Mount Vernon. Her body was placed in a newly purchased coffin, covered with a black pall owned by the family (a pall is a large fabric cover, typically adorned with the family coat-of-arms of the deceased). In addition to family, just three other mourners were in attendance: the Reverend Lee Massey, their Anglican parish minister, and long-time neighbors George William and Sally Cary Fairfax from nearby Belvoir Plantation. All came for the service and dinner afterward.[8] About eighteen months before George Washington's own death, the husband of Martha Washington's eldest granddaughter described the funeral of the French governess or nurse who had helped to raise his wife and her sister. The ceremony took place at sunset on a beautiful fall day. An elderly pastor officiated the funeral. He read the prayer for the dead while the assembled family observed a heavy silence. This in-law commented that, "I have never seen . . . a more affecting and more august sight."[9]

George Washington's death was swift and unexpected. On the morning of Thursday, December 12, 1799, he set off on horseback to make his customary circuit of his plantation, checking on work in progress, seeing to the status of his workers—hired and enslaved—and inspecting the livestock. Throughout the day, the weather alternated between rain, hail, and snow, and Washington's secretary, Tobias Lear, noted that when the retired president arrived for dinner about three o'clock, "his neck appeared to be wet . . . the snow was hanging upon his hair." Because he had been slowed by the weather, he did not change clothes, as was his custom, before sitting down to eat. On Friday, heavy snow mostly kept Washington indoors, yet despite the weather and a sore throat, he insisted on marking trees for removal to improve the view of the Potomac River. Although increasingly hoarse during the evening, he "made light of it." Washington went to bed sometime after nine o'clock, after first visiting Martha's granddaughter Nelly Custis Lewis who was recovering from childbirth and giving his blessing to the newborn. It was "the last blessing he ever gave to any one."[10]

Between two and three o'clock on Saturday morning, Washington woke Martha to tell her that he felt worse. He could barely speak and was having difficulty breathing, but he would not permit her to seek help, fearing that she would catch cold (Martha had only recently recovered from a severe illness). When Caroline Branham, one of the enslaved housemaids, appeared to rekindle the fire, Martha Washington was at last able to start rallying people to assist and treat her husband.

As the hours passed and three physicians cared for him, Washington was bled four times, losing about eighty ounces (five pints) of blood; made to gargle with vinegar and sage tea and to inhale vinegar and hot water; had his throat bathed with sal volatile (ammonium carbonate) and his feet with warm water; given various concoctions to drink, including a mixture of molasses, vinegar, and butter; subjected to a blister of Spanish fly on his throat, an enema, and an emetic; and finally had a blister and poultice of wheat bran applied to his legs. All to no avail. He died sometime between ten and eleven o'clock that night, December 14.[11]

According to one family member, Washington "did not take leave of any of the family, as he had frequently disapproved of the afflicting farewells which aggravated sorrow on these melancholy occasions."[12] Martha Washington's response was heartbreaking. Shortly after her husband of forty years took his last breath, she asked from the foot of the bed where she had been sitting, "Is he gone?" Her fears confirmed, she responded, "'Tis well . . . All is now over I shall soon follow him! I have no more trials to pass through!" Two nights later, Thomas Law, the husband of Martha's granddaughter, wrote that Mrs. Washington "displayed a solemn composure that was more distressing than floods of tears." Others also noted her inability to relieve her grief by crying. Hence Tobias Lear observed that she "has preserved the same pious fortitude. It afflicts me to see her. The world now appears to be no longer desirable to her—and yet she yields not to that grief which would be softened by tears." That finally happened a few weeks later when, in First Lady Abigail Adams's words, the widow Washington "had not been able to shed a tear since the Genlls. Death, until she received the Presidents and my Letters when she was two hours getting through them, tho they were not Lengthy."[13]

About midnight (roughly an hour-and-a-half after the death), George Washington's body was taken from the bedchamber to the New Room, where it was "laid out."[14] While Martha Washington largely directed plans for the funeral, Tobias Lear carried them out. Martha had asked Lear to have a coffin made in the nearby town of Alexandria, so he and one of the doctors measured the body. In death, the aging Washington was exactly six feet, three and a half inches from head to foot, while he was twenty-one inches across the shoulders, and two feet, nine inches wide at the elbows.[15]

Letters on mourning paper bordered in black, sealed with black wax, soon went out to family members and important officials, including President John Adams and Alexander Hamilton.[16] To the latter Lear wrote, "With the most sincere grief do I communicate to you the information of the Death of our beloved General Washington . . . ," who bore "his distressed situation with the fortitude of an Hero, he retained his composure and reason to the last moment, and died, as he had lived, a truly great man."[17]

Nearby family members began arriving on Sunday. So did Dr. William Thornton, a family friend, who had trained at the best medical schools in Europe.[18] Not knowing that he had died in the interim, Thornton planned to save Washington's life by performing a tracheotomy. When he arrived at Mount Vernon to find Washington dead, he suggested a means for reviving the corpse, which the family refused to try. Thornton at least got his way on one point, after insisting that the body be enclosed within a lead coffin, so that Washington could eventually be buried at the US Capitol, a move, however, that never happened.[19] Years later Thornton still recalled being "overwhelmed with the loss of the best friend I had on earth."

On Monday, December 16, with full preparations under way, Lear ordered the family vault opened so that workers could "clean away the rubbish from about it, and make everything decent." The estate's carpenters, both hired and enslaved, were set to making a door for the tomb, "instead of closing it again with brick, as had been the custom." Lear also hired two local craftsmen to make a mahogany coffin and, at Dr. Thornton's urging, line the interior with lead.[20] Farm manager James Anderson went into Alexandria to purchase things needed for the funeral and ordered mourning clothing for the family, the enslaved workers in the mansion, and the overseers on the five farms that made up the Mount Vernon estate, in keeping with eighteenth-century mourning customs.[21]

On Monday, too, things began to go wrong, at least in the sense that plans for the small private service George Washington wanted began to go off the rails. His fellow citizens had other plans. Word arrived from

Alexandria that the local militia and the Freemasons, among others, "were determined to show their respect to the General's Memory by attending his body to the Grave." A letter soon announced that a schooner anchored offshore at Mount Vernon would "fire Minute guns" as the body was carried to the tomb. Realizing that the number of attendees was skyrocketing, Lear ordered that food be prepared "for a large number of people, as some refreshment would be expected of them." Then, at Martha Washington's request, Lear sent funeral invitations to thirteen neighboring families.[22] He also wrote to ask the Reverend Thomas Davis, rector of Christ Church in Alexandria, to read the funeral service.[23]

On Tuesday, December 17, preparations for the funeral were in full swing. The adjutant of the Alexandria Regiment arrived to inspect the funeral route and the coffin arrived from Alexandria in a stage, accompanied by the makers. Constructed of mahogany, it was lined with lead soldered at the joints. Once the body was placed in the family vault, a lead cover would then be soldered onto the lead liner. Meantime, the coffin and liner were put into an oak outer coffin, which was lined and covered with black fabric and decorated with silver handles and upholstery tacks.[24]

At some point, the family decided to bury Washington in something other than his military uniform. Perhaps the family wanted it as a keepsake, and certainly Washington's famous relinquishing of military power and resumption of life as a private citizen could have factored into the decision. Fashions in graveclothes had changed in the eighteenth century. In England, for example, between 1700 and 1775, winding sheets went out of style and corpses were being dressed in shrouds, described by one historian as "an open-backed long-sleeved shift with draw-strings at wrist and neck, either with or without an integral hood."[25] George Washington's grave-clothes were made by Mrs. Margaret Gretter, of Alexandria, who charged the estate six dollars for the shroud and a like amount for the pall cloth, which was placed over the coffin.[26] After the body was dressed in the shroud and placed in the coffin, Lear cut off "some of the hair" to be used in mourning jewelry and other mementoes for family, friends, and even total strangers.[27]

By the next morning, Wednesday, December 18, throngs of people started gathering for the funeral. Although scheduled for noon, the late arrival of the military units from Alexandria, along with eleven pieces of artillery, delayed the ceremonies until mid-afternoon.[28] While people waited near the house, they would have noticed signs of a death in the family. According to one source, crape adorning the door told "the sad news" of Washington's passing.[29] Affixed to the exterior of the house, probably on or above the main door, was a hatchment or funeral escutcheon, bearing the joined heraldic arms of Washington's and his wife's families.[30]

Three hours after the scheduled start, the funeral procession for George Washington, a man who hated being late, finally got under way. As Lear described it, "The procession moved out of the Gate at the left Wing of the House; and proceeded round in front of the lawn, & down to the Vault on the right wing of the House."[31] Infantry and mounted units led the cortège, followed by musicians "playing a solemn Dirge" and four clergymen [two Episcopalians and two Presbyterians]. Next came Washington's saddled horse carrying his holsters and pistols and led by two young, enslaved grooms, Cyrus and Wilson. Following them was the coffin, borne by members of the Freemasons and young military officers. Walking immediately behind the coffin were the principal mourners, who included relatives and close friends, followed by Washington's brother Masons from the Alexandria Lodge and members of the Corporation of Alexandria. Finally, Mount Vernon's farm manager, James Anderson, and the overseers of the estate's five farms brought up the rear of the official procession. Once the procession reached the tomb, the Reverend Thomas Davis from Alexandria's Christ Church read the funeral service from the Episcopal Book of Common Prayer and gave "a short extempore speech." Masonic burial rites followed, after which the body was placed in the family vault.[32]

The assemblage then returned to the house for refreshments before retiring "in good order." To warm the mourners who had spent many hours outdoors, the Mount Vernon distillery provided twenty-nine gallons of whiskey to the Mansion House, which were supplemented by ten gallons of "Spirits" from an outside firm. More substantive fare included sixty-one pounds of cheese and a pound cake weighing forty pounds.[33] Afterward, the leftovers "were distributed among the blacks."[34]

A week later, on Christmas Day, the plumber, who made the lead lining for Washington's coffin, soldered on the lead lid to seal the inner coffin. Lear accompanied him to the tomb, where he "took a last look . . .a last farewell of that face, which still appeared unaltered . . . and beheld for the last time that face wh. Shall be seen no more here; but wh. I hope to meet in Heaven."[35]

Two days later, President John Adams sent Martha a copy of the congressional "resolutions . . . occasioned by the decease of your late Consort . . . assuring you of the profound respect Congress will ever bear, to your person and Character, and of their condolence on this afflicting dispensation of Providence." He then asked, "I entreat your assent to the interment of the remains of the General under the marble monument to be erected in the capitol, at the City of Washington to commemorate the great events of his military and political life." Four days later, Martha wrote back, noting that she had received "no inconsiderable consolation" from the "mournful tributes of respect and veneration which are paid to the memory of my dear deceased Husband," whose "best services and most anxious wishes were always devoted to the welfare and happiness of his country." She was especially moved to know that Washington's efforts "were truly appreciated and greatfully remembered." She then went on to say that she had been "Taught by the great example which I have so long had before me never to oppose my private wishes to the public will" and felt that "I must consent to the request made by congress . . . I cannot say what a sacrifice of individual feeling I make to a sense of public duty."[36] Martha agreed to the future removal in principle, but subsequently asked that she not be separated from her husband.[37] News of Washington's death spread from Mount Vernon through conversations, letters, and newspaper stories, beginning with the *Alexandria Times* and *District of Columbia Daily Advertiser,* on December 16. The following day the Georgetown newspaper encouraged local citizens to attend the funeral. The solemn news reached Richmond on December 17, where it was announced in the Virginia Senate and House of Delegates. After passing resolutions that their members wear black crepe mourning badges for the remainder of their legislative sessions, both houses adjourned for the rest of the day. The news reached Augusta, Georgia, on January 4, and Frankfort, Kentucky, on January 9, not quite four weeks after Washington died.[38]

In addition to the funeral at Mount Vernon, Washington probably would have been appreciative but embarrassed by the public mourning that took place after his death.[39] For example, the day after the actual funeral, Congressman John Marshall of Virginia, who later served as chief justice of the United States Supreme Court, presented to Congress a eulogy he had written, and a series of resolutions prepared by "Light-Horse Harry" Lee. The resolutions instructed members of Congress to wear black during the session, pay a condolence call on President Adams, and enshroud the Speaker's chair in black fabric. In addition, special committees from the House and Senate were to determine "the most suitable manner of paying honor to the memory of the MAN, first in war, first in peace, and first in the hearts of his fellow citizens."[40] That phrase, with "countrymen" substituted for "fellow citizens," quickly became the most famous aphorism related to Washington.

Meanwhile, Secretary of War James McHenry forwarded President Adams's announcement of Washington's death to the army. Acknowledging that the officers and men shared their fellow citizens' grief "for so heavy and afflicting a public loss" and noting his own desire to express "the vast debt of Gratitude . . . due to the Virtues, Talents and ever memoriable services of the illustrious deceased," the president ordered that "funeral honors be paid" to him at "all the military Stations" and that all army officers and volunteers wear crape ribbons on their left arms for a period of six months.[41]

There is no way to know how many ceremonies were held in Washington's honor, but the historian Gerald Kahler has discovered that at least 419 mock funerals occurred in sixteen of the seventeen then-existing states, as well as in the District of Columbia, and the districts of Maine and Mississippi.[42] These were extremely popular, public events. The funeral procession in Baltimore, for example, featured nearly 5,000 marchers—civilian and military—and "not less than 20,000 souls in the streets at one time."[43]

In addition to the mock funerals, at least 300 eulogies and funeral orations were delivered across the United States during the winter of 1799–1800, many of which were published and survive in both private collections and historical archives. A wide range of authors prepared tributes, including Dr. Elisha Cullen Dick, a fellow Mason and one of the doctors who cared for Washington during his final illness. Dr. Dick later wrote that "the soul of this great and good man took its final departure to the mansions of eternal rest . . . heaven has reclaimed its treasure."[44] Other speakers, Alexander Macwhorter and Timothy Dwight, knew Washington from the time they served as chaplains in the Continental Army.[45]

In his eulogy, John Carroll, the first Roman Catholic bishop of Baltimore, emphasized the role of God's providence and guiding hand in forming

Washington for the role he played in the great events of the country's formation: "heaven impressed a character on the life of Washington, and a temper on his soul, which eminently qualified him to bear the most conspicuous part, and be its principal instrument in accomplishing this stupendous work." Moreover, "Whilst he lived, we seemed to stand on loftier ground, for breathing the same air, inhabiting the same country, and enjoying the same constitution and laws, as the sublime and magnanimous Washington."[46] In his eulogy at Bruton Parish Church in Williamsburg, Episcopal Bishop James Madison of Virginia, the president of the College of William & Mary, and a relative of the future president of the same name, suggested that "Religion joins in the universal wo[e]; she weeps over the tomb of WASHINGTON! Great in arms, great in peace, great in Piety! And, amidst her sorrow, feels a gleam of consolation in pronouncing his eulogium."[47]

The Reverend Richard Allen of Philadelphia, a Methodist minister, who later founded the African Methodist Episcopal Church, presented one of the most poignant eulogies. Speaking for the African American community, Allen referred to Washington as a "sympathizing friend and tender father," whose "heart was not insensible" to the sufferings of the enslaved. Acknowledging Washington's decision to emancipate his enslaved workers, Allen continued, "He whose wisdom the nations revered thought we [Black people] had a right to liberty. Unbiased by the popular opinion of the state in which is the memorable Mount Vernon—he dared to do his duty, and wipe off the only stain with which man could ever reproach him."[48] Commemorative funerals and church services invited the public to show their respect and love for the late president, as well as to express their grief. Even special music was written in honor of the late president.[49]

Like Washington's own family and friends, the public also donned mourning clothes. First Lady Abigail Adams wrote to her sister, two days before Christmas, that "I shall not have occasion now for any thing but Black, untill Spring. Then I shall put on half mourning. . . . At present the whole Family are in full mourning."[50] A week later, she described a reception she hosted in Philadelphia, at which "Upwards of a hundred Ladies, and near as many Gentlemen attended, all in mourning." Female guests ornamented their white dresses with black fabric fastened on one shoulder, crossing the body at the back and tied at the waist like a military sash, and then again crossing

FIGURE 1. Miniature portrait painted in 1801 by Robert Field of Martha Washington as a widow, seemingly in second mourning. wearing a black lace shawl and a white bonnet trimmed with black ribbon. (Courtesy Mount Vernon Ladies' Association)

the front over the skirt. Other women put fringed black epaulets on the shoulders of their white dresses, which were also ornamented with black fabric. They wore crepe caps, decorated with black plumes or black flowers, and completed the outfit with black gloves and fans. All the men were dressed in black. Afterward Mrs. Adams wrote, "The Ladies many of them wanted me to fix the time for wearing mourning, but I declined, and left them to Govern themselves by the periods prescribed by the Gentlemen."[51]

As people mourned, manufacturers produced memorial items. Washington's portrait appeared on engraved artworks, as well as printed textiles, commemorative medals, porcelain, and pottery. In early 1800, for example, French artist Charles Balthazar Julien Fèvret de Saint-Memin produced two small engravings of Washington in profile, which are believed to have

been based on the artist's final life portrait of his subject, done in Philadelphia in November 1798. One profile depicts Washington in uniform, while
the other, in classical style, shows him in the form of a carved marble bust,
crowned with laurel wreaths. By January and February of 1800, mourning
rings bearing these profiles were being advertised in the Philadelphia and
New York newspapers.[52]

Of the 101 prints of Washington dating from the eighteenth century
through 1802, nearly a third (33) were produced following his death. Many
feature typical portraits, others include motifs—funeral urns, obelisks, weeping willows, and angels—that bespeak death and mourning. For example, a
print entitled *America Lamenting Her Loss at the Tomb of General Washington*,
features an obelisk decorated with a profile of the deceased hero, in front of
which a woman weeps beside a drooping eagle. Two of the best-known prints
depict Washington rising on clouds to heaven. In *The Apotheosis of Washington*, by David Edwin after Rembrandt Peale, the deceased, accompanied by a
cherub holding a laurel wreath over his head, is greeted by Generals Richard
Montgomery and Joseph Warren, who died in the War for Independence.
The other print, by John James Barralet, was described in an advertisement
as "The subject Washington raised from the tomb, by the spiritual and tem-
poral Genius—assisted by Immortality. At his feet America weeping over
his Armour, holding the staff surmounted by the Cap of Liberty, emblemati-
cal of his mild administration, on the opposite side, an Indian crouched in
surly sorrow. In the third ground the mental virtues, Faith, Hope, and Charity." This popular allegorical scene was later reproduced on canvas, English
transfer-printed pottery, and Chinese reverse paintings on glass.[53]

Prints depicting Washington's beloved Mount Vernon were produced
shortly after his death and remained popular throughout the nineteenth
century. While it was unusual at this period to produce prints of American
buildings, Mount Vernon was the exception and inexpensive views of both
the columned East Front of the mansion, and the West Front featuring
the Bowling Green, were available to American consumers. Edward Savage
(1790–91), George Isham Parkyns (1799), and William Birch (1804) were the
first artists to bring Mount Vernon to a wider audience. These views created
a lasting impact, as they were printed on fine Chinese export porcelains,
cheaper English transfer-print ceramics, and American-made banjo clocks,

which "created more opportunities for Americans to encounter Mount Vernon in their everyday lives."[54]

Commemorative medals of events associated with the revolutionary period, including the deaths of its heroes, were also popular at the time. Several styles of funeral medals and badges were struck as souvenirs of two of the mock funerals in Boston. In most of these medals, the obverse features a bust portrait of Washington in uniform, facing left within a laurel wreath, with the words "HE IS IN GLORY, THE WORLD IN TEARS" around. The reverse side of the medals is embellished with either a skull and crossbones or a funeral urn, inscribed with the initials "G.W." Formed of gold, silver, copper, or white metal, they were available to citizens with a range of financial means.[55]

Citizens also named geographical features after Washington in the years after his death to honor his memory. This process had begun during the War for Independence, when local officials in New York City named sites Washington Heights, Mount Washington, and Fort Washington. In the same area, Washington Bridge and the George Washington Bridge were named in 1889 and 1931, which were the centennial of Washington's inauguration as president and the eve of the bicentennial of his birth, respectively. By the 1932 bicentennial, there were at least fifty-three places called Washington in the state of Ohio alone, as well as another thirty-five in Pennsylvania. Altogether, by the 1932 bicentennial, there were at least forty-six geographical sites named after George Washington, including two bridges; a parish; a district; five villages, towns, or plantations; six streets; five forts; four counties; a ferry; eight colleges; a school; a monument; two statues; and nine mountains. Still, as Lawrence Martin noted, "These include only about three percent of the uses of this great American's name in geography."[56]

Some Americans contacted Martha Washington directly for personal remembrances of her late husband, especially his hair. Two months to the day after his death, four young women calling themselves "A Society of Females" wrote from Rhode Island to ask for a lock of Washington's hair. They claimed that their "Fathers fought with Washington! [T]hey taught our Infant lispings to repeat His name and since have shewed to us the vast volume of His worth. . . . [W]hile the memory of Washington shall ever remain in our hearts . . . we wish also for some external remembrance of the Man 'first in War, first in Peace and first in the hearts of his Country.'" Several weeks later, a letter containing a lock of the late president's hair was sent to each of the young ladies.[57] In order to ease the financial burden of responding to the condolence letters and requests for mementoes, two months later, the US Congress ordered that Martha Washington be given the "privilege of franking letters & packages."[58]

Not everyone approved of the intensity with which memorial objects and mock funerals venerated the primary hero of the American Revolution. Hence, even as First Lady Abigail Adams and her family deeply mourned Washington's passing, and even as she believed that he "ought to live in our Memories, and be transmitted to posterity as a Character truly worthy Imitation is Right," she criticized those who "have ascribed to him solely, what was the joint effort & concert of Many. To no one Man in America, belongs the Epithet of Saviour of his Country."[59] Without diminishing the first president's role in creating the new nation, Mrs. Adams yearned for a broader narrative about the war. Washington himself surely would have agreed. While he lived, he was habitually taciturn about his role in winning American independence and establishing the federal government. Still, at the conclusion of the war, and again as he prepared to leave the presidency, he realized the need to document those events, and oversaw the careful removal of his military, government, and personal papers to Mount Vernon. "[They] are voluminous," he wrote in 1796, "and may be interesting."[60]

Countless nineteenth-century Americans sought to perpetuate accurate memories of Washington—via their mementoes; listening to Fourth of July recitations of his Farewell Address, written to announce that he would not seek a third term as president and to leave serious advice for the country's future; and visiting Mount Vernon, the site of both his home and tomb, which was still owned by Washington family heirs. At the same time, others fictionalized his life for teaching purposes, and no one did so to greater effect than Parson Mason Locke Weems. An Episcopal minister, itinerant bookseller, and biographer, Weems was later described by a fellow clergyman who knew him well as someone who would never let truth stand in the way of a good story. In March 1800, he mailed the widow Washington a copy of the first edition of his biography of her late husband, which went through seventy editions between 1800 and 1927 and shaped the public perception of Washington for generations of Americans. Weems was the source of ubiquitous tales about a young

George Washington chopping down a cherry tree and subsequently admit-
ting it because he could not tell a lie; about his father planting cabbage seeds
that, when sprouted, spelled out the name "George Washington"—as a way of
teaching his son that God made everything in the world; and about General
Washington praying in the snow at Valley Forge during the War for Independence. Somewhat less egregiously, Jared Sparks, the first editor of Washington's writings, published in twelve volumes during the 1830s, intentionally
changed some of Washington's phrasing that he (Sparks) deemed improper.[61]

The honoring of George Washington continues to the present day. Americans' interest in keeping Washington in the forefront of their hearts and
minds launched the historic preservation movement in the United States. In
his will, George Washington decreed that, following the death of his widow
Martha, about four thousand acres of the Mount Vernon plantation would
become the property of his nephew, United States Supreme Court Justice
Bushrod Washington, and his heirs.[62] Under the management of the next
three generations of Washingtons, conditions at Mount Vernon deteriorated
from what they had been during George Washington's lifetime. The last private owner of the estate, John Augustine Washington III, agreed to sell 200
acres of land, including the mansion and tomb, to an organization called
the Mount Vernon Ladies' Association of the Union, in 1858. Founded five
years earlier, the Association began with a challenge, "Why was it that the
women of [Washington's] country did not try to keep it in repair, if the men
could not do it?" The Association raised $200,000 to make the purchase and
took over management of the estate in 1860.[63] Known as the oldest national
preservation organization in the country, Mount Vernon is still owned and
preserved by the Mount Vernon Ladies' Association, and served as the model
for later preservation projects, such as President Andrew Jackson's home,
The Hermitage, which was preserved by the Ladies' Hermitage Association,
in the late nineteenth century.[64]

In addition to preserving physical spaces associated with Washington,
later generations of Americans were interested in what Washington had
to say during his lifetime, leading to multiple attempts to publish his writings, either in whole or in part, public and private. Washington himself had
always been interested in the proper care and organization of his papers.
One month after he stepped down from the presidency, he wrote to an old

colleague that he had no more buildings to construct at Mount Vernon "except one, which I must erect for the accom[m]odation & security of my Military, Civil & private Papers, which are voluminous and may be interesting." Although that building had not been started by the time of his death, Washington hired a young male secretary to enter his correspondence into letter books and, on his deathbed, instructed Tobias Lear to "let Mr. Rawlins finish recording my other letters which he has begun."[65]

As part of the major celebration of the 200th anniversary of Washington's birth in 1932, the federal government released a new edition of his papers. The resulting thirty-seven volumes of letters and two-volume-index made even more of Washington's thoughts available to the public, but the facts that incoming mail was not included and the footnoting was scanty were continuing problems for those trying to put Washington's words into context.[66] Then, in the lead-up to the 1976 bicentennial of the American Revolution, the University of Virginia undertook to publish all of Washington's correspondence, both outgoing and incoming. With financial support from the National Endowment for the Humanities, the Mount Vernon Ladies' Association, and the National Historical Publications and Records Commission, this edition of the Washington papers contains copious footnotes, which only increase their value to the user. This project celebrated its fiftieth anniversary in 2018 and is expected to be finished within ten years.[67]

The many efforts to commemorate and celebrate George Washington have continued to the present—but why did the American people gather together throughout the country to honor Washington with mock funerals and reflect on his life in hundreds of eulogies after his death? What led them to place portraits of him in their homes and businesses? Why had the loss of this one sixty-seven-year-old man created such widespread trauma? First, for many Americans, George Washington was someone who had been part of their world for almost five decades. He first came to national attention in late 1753 and early 1754, when he undertook a diplomatic mission to the French forces in the Ohio Valley on behalf of the lieutenant governor of Virginia. The latter was so impressed that he had the young man's journal of this adventure published in both Williamsburg and London, an action that made Washington an international figure at the age of twenty-two.[68] Especially during the 1770s, 1780s, and 1790s, more people came to know of Washington, as he led the

Continental Army against the British in the War for Independence, as he stood at the helm of the Constitutional Convention, and as he served for eight years as the nation's first president. He also gained their trust, as he resigned his military commission at the end of the Revolution, and as he refused to serve more than two terms as president. This was not someone who was searching for unbridled power. And many Americans personally knew, had met, or at least had seen George Washington in person, both during the American Revolution and as he toured every one of the original thirteen states as president. During those years of public service, in actions that called to mind honoring and celebrating the king of England, the American people had started naming their children after Washington and had even begun to celebrate his birthday.[69] The man who had always been there when the country needed him was no longer physically present, but his contemporaries elevated Washington into the national pantheon of heroes, and future generations worked hard to keep him there. They constantly acknowledged and lauded his leadership, quoted his words, and evoked his service to country for a variety of political, social, economic, and religious reasons—all of which demonstrate the gravitas and proliferation of Washington's example, as well as its profound longevity.

While George Washington did not get the type of funeral he wanted, his final wishes regarding his entombment were followed by his Washington family heirs—a process that was not easy. Following the attacks on Washington, DC, and Alexandria during the War of 1812, some Americans were concerned that Washington's remains were no longer safe at Mount Vernon—as the Capitol, now destroyed, had been poised to receive Washington's remains. The eccentric Virginia representative John Randolph went so far as to express fear that the British would "take the body of Washington . . . and transport it to Westminster Abbey." Unlikely as that may seem, both the federal government and the state of Virginia felt compelled to secure possession of Washington's body. When Supreme Court Justice Bushrod Washington, who had inherited Mount Vernon upon the death of Martha Washington in 1802, was approached by the governor of Virginia about selling the estate to Virginia, he responded that "obligations more sacred than anything which concerns myself . . . command me to retain the mortal remains of my venerated Uncle, in the family vault where they are deposited." Additional attempts were made by both the federal and state governments, as well as civic organizations to convince the Washington family to sell, following the death of Judge Washington and his wife in 1829. Thankfully, the next generations of Washington owners of Mount Vernon followed the instructions in George Washington's will and constructed a new tomb where the late president directed it to be built between 1830 and 1831. Both George and Martha Washington's bodies were moved to the new structure, as were roughly another twenty deceased residents.[70] They remain there to this day.

Notes

1. Martha Washington to Elizabeth Willing Powel, December 18, 1797, in *"Worthy Partner": The Papers of Martha Washington,* comp. Joseph E. Fields (Westport, CT: Greenwood, 1994), 309–10.

2. George Washington, diary entries for November 29 and December 9, 1799, Founders Online (hereafter FOL), https://founders.archives.gov/. James K. Paulding, *A Life of Washington,* 2 vols. (New York: Harper & Brothers, 1835), 2:196–97. Thanks to Richard L. Flaig for sharing this description with Mount Vernon, from his unpublished work, "Sketches of George Washington by Those Who Were in His Presence" (2014), 62.

3. George Washington to the Marquis de Lafayette, December 8, 1784, FOL.

4. George Washington, *The Last Will and Testament of George Washington and Schedule of His Property to Which Is Appended the Last Will and Testament of Martha Washington,* 4th ed., ed. John C. Fitzpatrick (Mount Vernon, VA: Mount Vernon Ladies' Association, 1972), 2–4. For the story of Washington's earlier wills, see George Washington to Martha Washington, June 18, 1775, in *"Worthy Partner,"* 159–60; Tobias Lear, *Letters and Recollections of George Washington* (New York: Doubleday, Page & Company, 1906), 132.

5. Mary V. Thompson, *"The Only Unavoidable Subject of Regret": George Washington, Slavery, and the Enslaved Community at Mount Vernon* (Charlottesville: University of Virginia Press, 2019), 313.

6. Eugene E. Prussing, *The Estate of George Washington, Deceased* (Boston: Little, Brown, 1927), 68.

7. For examples of military funerals at this time, see "Notes and Queries," *Pennsylvania Magazine of History and Biography* 24 (1900): 124; Elswyth Thane, *The Fighting Quaker: Nathanael Greene* (New York: Hawthorn Books, 1972), 278–79. For an example of a similar funeral for the Spanish minister to the fledgling United States, see Dr. James Thacher, April 19, 24, and 29, 1780, in *Military Journal of the American Revolution, From the Commencement to the Disbanding of the American Army* (Hartford, CT: Hurlbut, Williams, 1862), 191–93; Mabel Lorenz Ives, *Washington's Headquarters* (Upper Montclair, NJ: Lucy Fortune, 1932), 216–17.

8. George Washington, *The Diaries of George Washington,* ed. Donald Jackson and Dorothy Twohig, 6 vols. (Charlottesville: University Press of Virginia, 1976–79), 3:188. For information on the pall, see Robert Adam to George Washington, September 16, 1773, in

The Papers of George Washington, Colonial Series, ed. W. W. Abbot and Dorothy Twohig, 10 vols. (Charlottesville: University Press of Virginia, 1983–95), 9:325.

9. Julian Ursyn Niemcewicz, *Under Their Vine and Fig Tree: Travels through America in 1797–1799, 1805 with Some Further Account of Life in New Jersey,* trans. and ed. Metchie J. E. Budka (Elizabeth, NJ: Grassman, 1965), 99.

10. Lear, *Letters and Recollections,* 129–30. For Washington's visit, see Mary V. Thompson, *"In the Hands of a Good Providence": Religion in the Life of George Washington* (Charlottesville: University of Virginia Press, 2008), 169–70, 224n3.

11. Lear, *Letters and Recollections,* 130–35. James Craik and Elisha C. Dick to Messrs. T. and F. D. Westcott, Account of their treatment of George Washington, *Farmers' Museum, or Lay Preacher's Gazette,* Walpole, NH, Monday, January 13, 1800, typescript, Fred W. Smith National Library for the Study of George Washington, Mount Vernon, VA (hereafter FWSNL). Estimates describe a first bleeding of twelve to fourteen ounces, followed by "two copious bleedings," and a final one involving thirty-two ounces (two pints) of blood, estimating sixteen ounces each for the second and third bleedings.

12. Thomas Law to a brother, December 15–19, 1799, "Thomas Law's Description of the Last Illness and Death of George Washington," in *The Mount Vernon Ladies' Association of the Union Annual Report 1972* (Mount Vernon, VA: Mount Vernon Ladies' Association of the Union, 1973), 29.

13. Lear, *Letters and Recollections,* 135. Thomas Law to a brother, December 15–19, 1799, in "Thomas Law's Description of the Last Illness and Death of George Washington," 30; Tobias Lear to his mother, December 16, 1799 (typescript, FWSNL). Abigail Adams to Martha Washington, December 24, 1799, and John Adams to Martha Washington, December 27, 1799, in *"Worthy Partner,"* 326, 327–28; Abigail Adams to her sister, January 7, 1800, in *New Letters of Abigail Adams, 1788–1801,* ed. with an introduction by Stewart Mitchell (Boston: Houghton Mifflin, 1947), 227.

14. The New Room is the large reception room, where today's visitors enter the mansion.

15. Lear, *Letters and Recollections,* 136–37.

16. The family members included three nephews (US Supreme Court Justice Bushrod Washington; Colonel William Augustine Washington; and Lawrence Lewis, who was married to Martha Washington's youngest granddaughter, Nelly Custis); step-grandson George Washington Parke Custis; two more nephews (George Steptoe Washington and Samuel Washington); Colonel Burgess Ball and Captain Thomas Hammond, who were married to two of Washington's nieces; and finally to nephew John Lewis, who was asked to pass the word along to his brothers, George, Robert, and Howell. Later, Martha Washington's former daughter-in-law, Eleanor Calvert Custis Stuart, with whom she was still very close, was asked to come as well.

17. Tobias Lear to Alexander Hamilton, December 15, 1799, in *The Papers of Alexander Hamilton,* ed. Harold C. Syrett, 27 vols. (New York: Columbia University Press, 1961–87), 24:100–101.

18. Lear, *Letters and Recollections,* 138.

19. William Thornton, "Sleep," [undated, 1820s] (original in the Thornton Papers at the Library of Congress; typescript, FWSNL).

20. Lear, *Letters and Recollections,* 138, 139.

21. Anne Buck, *Dress in Eighteenth-Century England* (New York: Holmes & Meier, 1979), 23, 60–62, 63, 77, 108, 121, 133, 154–55, 185. For early purchases of mourning clothes for

the family at Mount Vernon, see the following sources: John Parke Custis to Martha Washington, July 5, [1773], in Fields, *"Worthy Partner,"* 152–53. George Washington to Robert Cary & Company, July [10], 1773, "Invoice of Goods to be Shipped by Robert Cary & Co. for the use of George Washington, Potomac River, Virginia." A mourning sword and buckle that belonged to George Washington are now in the Curatorial Collections at Mount Vernon. For mourning clothes after George Washington's death, see Thomas Law to a brother, December 15–19, 1799, in "Thomas Law's Description of the Last Illness and Death of George Washington," 30 and 31; "Estate of Genl George Washington Decd [to] Jnn & Jas Scott," December 23, 1799 (transcript, FWSNL); Tobias Lear to Clement Biddle, March 8, 1800 (manuscript, RM-869/MS-5329, FWSNL); James Anderson, "Account of Hires, and other expences, that will become due on the Estate of Mount Vernon for the Year 1800, Exclusive of funding the Manager, Overseers, & others in Victuals etc, 1800 to Jan 1 1801" (transcript, PS-4, FWSNL); "The Estate of Genl. Geo. Washington Deceased to Smith Keith," December 18, 1799 (manuscript, RM-215/MS-2689, FWSNL); See also, Lear, *Letters and Recollections,* 138; "Estate of Genl George Washington Decd to William Bowie," December 23, 1799 (manuscript, RM-215/MS-2688, FWSNL); Distillery Account Book, 1799–1800 (bound manuscript, FWSNL), 43.

22. Lear, *Letters and Recollections,* 138–39.
23. Lear, *Letters and Recollections* 139.
24. Lear, *Letters and Recollections,* 139.
25. Lear, *Letters and Recollections,* 139; Julian Litten, *The English Way of Death: The Common Funeral Since 1450* (London: Robert Hale, 1991), 76–77, 79, 81.
26. "The estate of General George Washington to Margaret Gretter," February 10, 1800 (manuscript, RM-215/MS-2682, FWSNL).
27. Lear, *Letters and Recollections,* 139.
28. Lear, *Letters and Recollections,* 139–40.
29. The crape was destroyed in a fire at the museum of the Alexandria-Washington Masonic Lodge in 1871. William Moseley Brown, *George Washington, Free Mason* (Richmond, VA: Garrett & Massie, 1952), 381.
30. *The Oxford English Dictionary* (Oxford: Clarendon, 1933), 5:116; *The New Encyclopaedia Britannica* (Chicago: Encyclopaedia Britannica, 1986), 5:7. Fragments of George Washington's funeral hatchment are now in the collections of the Smithsonian Institution.
31. Lear, *Letters and Recollections,* 140.
32. Lear, *Letters and Recollections,* 140–41. Several significant family members were not at the funeral: Martha Washington was too distraught to attend and Lawrence Lewis and George Washington Parke Custis were away on business, while granddaughter Nelly Custis Lewis was still not well enough after giving birth less than a month earlier.
33. Distillery Account Book, 1799–1800 (bound manuscript, FWSNL), 21, 44, and 46; Lear, *Letters and Recollections,* 138–39, 141; "Mr Anderson Bot of George Edick for Genl George Washingtons [*sic*] Estate Decr 20th 1799," March 21, 1800 (manuscript, RM-215/MS-2685, FWSNL).
34. Lear, *Letters and Recollections,* 141.
35. Lear, *Letters and Recollections,* 141.
36. John Adams to Martha Washington, December 27, 1799, and Martha Washington to John Adams, December 31, 1799, in *"Worthy Partner,"* 327–28, 332–33.

37. For more on the politics of disinternment, see Matthew R. Costello, *The Property of the Nation: George Washington's Tomb, Mount Vernon, and the Memory of the First President* (Lawrence: University Press of Kansas, 2019), 17–20.

38. Gerald E. Kahler, *The Long Farewell: Americans Mourn the Death of George Washington* (Charlottesville: University of Virginia Press 2008), 4–6.

39. Margaret Brown Klapthor and Howard Alexander Morrison, *G. Washington: A Figure upon the Stage* (Washington, DC: Smithsonian Institution, 1982), 222–27; John Alexander Carroll and Mary Wells Ashworth, *George Washington: First in Peace* (New York: Charles Scribner's Sons, 1957), 648–53; *New Letters of Abigail Adams, 1788–1801*, 222 and 222–23n, 225–29, 235, 237, 238n; *The Papers of Alexander Hamilton*, 24:108. For a few examples of mock funerals, see "FUNERAL PROCESSION" (Manuscript, H-530, FWSNL); R. W. G. Vail, "A Dinner at Mount Vernon: From the Unpublished Journal of Joshua Brookes (1773–1859)," *New-York Historical Society Quarterly* (April 1947): 83–85; Receipted Bill, Commanders of Fort Washington, Ohio, to the firm of Smith & Findlay for sundry goods purchased for "the purpose of paying Funeral Honors to the memory of the deceased Gen. George Washington," January 28, 1800 (Manuscript, Society of the Cincinnati Headquarters, Library and Museum-Anderson House, Washington, DC).

40. Charles H. Callahan, *Washington: The Man and the Mason* (Washington, DC: Published under the auspices of the Memorial Temple Committee of the George Washington Masonic National Memorial Association by the Press of Gibson Brothers, 1913), 197–98. The final version of Lee's eulogy for Washington would be delivered a week later, with slightly different wording, on December 26, 1799 (John Marshall, *The Life of George Washington*, 5 vols. [New York: William H. Wise & Company, 1925], 5:366n).

41. James McHenry to Alexander Hamilton, December 18, 1799, and Enclosure, December 19, 1799, in *The Papers of Alexander Hamilton*, 24:107–8.

42. Kahler, *The Long Farewell*, 137–49.

43. Kahler, *The Long Farewell*, 14–15.

44. Thompson, *"In the Hands of a Good Providence,"* 178–79.

45. Thompson, *"In the Hands of a Good Providence,"* 180–81.

46. John Carroll, *Eulogy on George Washington: Delivered in St. Peter's Church, Baltimore, February 22, 1800* (New York: P. J. Kenedy & Sons, 1931), 7–13, 24.

47. Thompson, *"In the Hands of a Good Providence,"* 180.

48. Thompson, *"The Only Unavoidable Subject of Regret,"* 293.

49. For examples of special music written in Washington's honor, see the following: Vera Brodsky Lawrence, *Music for Patriots, Politicians, and Presidents: Harmonies and Discords of the First Hundred Years* (New York: Macmillan, 1975), 155–59; Oscar George Theodore Sonneck, *A Bibliography of Early Secular American Music* (New York: De Capo, 1964).

50. Abigail Smith Adams to Mary Smith Cranch, [December] 23, [1799], in *New Letters of Abigail Adams, 1788–1801*, 223.

51. Abigail Adams to her sister, Mrs. Cranch, December 30, 1799, in *New Letters of Abigail Adams, 1788–1801*, 225.

52. Wendy C. Wick, *George Washington, an American Icon: The Eighteenth-Century Graphic Portraits* (Washington, DC: Smithsonian Institution Traveling Exhibition Service and National Portrait Gallery 1982), 142 and 144. "Portraits," in Mount Vernon Ladies' Association, *Annual Report 1993* (Mount Vernon, VA: Mount Vernon Ladies' Association of the Union, 1994), 38 and 39.

53. Wick, *George Washington: An American Icon*, 136–66.

54. Lydia Mattice Brandt, *First in the Homes of His Countrymen: George Washington's Mount Vernon in the American Imagination* (Charlottesville: University of Virginia Press, 2016), 13–20, 13–19.

55. "Funeral Medals," in Russell Rulau and George Fuld, *Medallic Portraits of Washington* (Iola, WI: Krause Publications, 1985), 104–5. Klapthor and Morrison, *G. Washington: A Figure upon the Stage*, 26–95.

56. Lawrence Martin, "The Dates of Naming Places and Things for George Washington," in *History of the George Washington Bicentennial Celebration*, 3 vols. (Washington, DC: United States George Washington Bicentennial Commission, 1932), 3:307–12.

57. A Society of Females to Martha Washington, February 14, 1800, and Martha Washington to Julia Bowen, Mary B. Howell, Abby Chace, and Sally Halsey, March 12, 1800, in *"Worthy Partner,"* 351–52, 352n, 362n, and 363–64n.

58. Tobias Lear to Timothy Pickering, April 20, 1800, in *"Worthy Partner,"* 378–79, 379n1.

59. Abigail Smith Adams to Mary Smith Cranch, January 28, 1800, in *New Letters of Abigail Adams, 1788–1801*, 228–29, 229n1, 229n2.

60. George Washington to James McHenry, April 3, 1797, FOL.

61. The Reverend Mason Locke Weems to Martha Washington, March 8, 1800, in *"Worthy Partner,"* 360, 360n. Thompson, *"In the Hands of a Good Providence,"* 18. Jared Sparks, *The Writings of George Washington: Being His Correspondence, Addresses, Messages, and Other Papers, Official and Private, Selected and Published from the Original Manuscripts, with a Life of the Author, Notes, and Illustrations* (Boston: American Stationers' Company, 1834–37). Harvard Square Library, "Sparks, Jared (1789–1866)," https://www.harvardsquarelibrary.org/biographies/jared-sparks/.

62. Prussing, *The Estate of George Washington, Deceased*, 32–33, 60–61.

63. Elswyth Thane, *Mount Vernon Is Ours: The Story of Its Preservation* (New York: Duell, Sloan and Pearce, 1966); *The Mount Vernon Ladies' Association: 150 Years of Restoring George Washington's Home* (Mount Vernon, VA: Mount Vernon Ladies' Association, 2010); Costello, *The Property of the Nation*, 201–3.

64. The Ladies' Hermitage Association recently changed its name to the Andrew Jackson Association and has added men to its membership (https://thehermitage.com/about/).

65. George Washington to James McHenry, April 3, 1797, FOL.

66. *The Writings of George Washington from the Original Manuscript Sources, 1745–1799*, ed. John C. Fitzpatrick, 39 vols. (Washington, DC: United States Government Printing Office, 1931–44).

67. William M. Ferraro, "Fifty Years of The Washington Papers," *Washington Papers* (Winter 2018): 1 and 11.

68. George Washington, *Diaries*, 1:158; Howard H. Peckham, *The Colonial Wars 1689–1762* (Chicago: University of Chicago Press, 1964), 130–31; Barbara McMillan, "Washington's First Publication," *Mount Vernon Ladies' Association of the Union Annual Report 1988*, 39–40, 49.

69. Mary V. Thompson, "'As if I Had Been a Very Great Somebody': Martha Washington's Revolution," in *Women in the American Revolution: Gender, Politics, and the Domestic World*, ed. Barbara B. Oberg (Charlottesville: University of Virginia Press, 2019), 140–41.

70. Costello, *The Property of the Nation*, 26–36.

Mourning at Monticello

↘ • ↙

Andrew M. Davenport

AS HE LAY DYING in the bedchamber of his Monticello plantation in Charlottesville, Virginia, the eighty-three-year-old Thomas Jefferson likened himself to a fading timepiece. "I am like an old watch," he told a grandson, "with a pinion worn out here, and a wheel there, until it can go no longer."[1] Jefferson lingered before death's threshold, but he willed himself to survive until July 4, 1826. As he moved between fits of delirium and lucidity, he asked, "Is it the Fourth?" hoping to confirm the date.[2] He seemed pleased to die on the fiftieth anniversary of the signing of the Declaration of Independence. Jefferson's last words, whispered to one or two enslaved persons who attended him, have never come to light.[3]

Historians have pored over the written accounts of Jefferson's last days and hours for nearly two centuries. These documents reveal how Jefferson's white relatives mourned the death of their patriarch. Their grief was emblematic of national mourning rituals, which, in the white American popular consciousness, canonized Jefferson as the apostle of freedom. But for Jefferson's nearly 200 enslaved African Americans, his death brought untold suffering and separation. In an attempt to rescue themselves from financial ruin, Jefferson's white relatives sold away nearly all the enslaved people.[4]

Considering how Jefferson's death affected the hundreds of African Americans he enslaved, as well as their descendants, shifts attention away from his achievements and toward a more comprehensive understanding of the profoundly unequal, entangled Monticello community and the "free" nation where they lived, and which Americans have inherited. Although the fates of the vast majority of Jefferson's enslaved community are unknown, historians and researchers continue to search for those who were sold after Jefferson's death to reunite long-ago fractured Black American families and reconstruct an account of what occurred on and beyond Jefferson's Monticello.[5]

When Jefferson left the President's House in March 1809, he resolved to spend as much time at Monticello as he could. "I am full of plans of employment when I get there," he wrote to a friend, and "they chiefly respect the active functions of the body. To the mind I shall administer amusement chiefly. An only daughter and a numerous family of grandchildren will furnish me great resources of happiness."[6] A snowstorm slowed his phaeton's procession from Washington, so Jefferson took off on horseback and arrived at Monticello on March 15.[7]

When he returned from his service as US minister to France in December 1789, Jefferson had been greeted by the enslaved at Monticello joyously. Upon leaving the presidency, he was greeted with more of a muted response.[8] The first occasion had been a show of relief for his survival, as the enslaved had tragic experience of the perilous nature of the transatlantic journey and the importance of Jefferson's continued health for the stability of their Black community. But in 1809, now that Jefferson had returned to Monticello to stay, the clock, as he would liken himself to, had begun to count down.

Jefferson spent the last seventeen years of his life in his native state of Virginia. He beat a path from Monticello to Charlottesville, to friends' homes, and to Poplar Forest, his Bedford County retreat, embarking upon one of the most productive and most well-documented retirements in American history. He loved, he said, the "ineffable luxury of being owner of my own time."[9] During retirement, Jefferson founded the University of Virginia, read widely, maintained a massive correspondence, oversaw his farms, entertained scores of visitors, and looked after his family. For himself, his white family, and guests he spared few, if any, expenses. This largesse, compounded by the debt he had inherited from his father-in-law and several poor financial decisions, led Jefferson into a financial morass. He died with more than $107,000 in debt.[10]

The enslaved had long known that Jefferson's death would mean devastation. The more daringly optimistic of them looked to the examples of Virginian enslavers, most notably Edward Coles, John White, and Jefferson's own kinsman Richard Randolph, who had emancipated considerable numbers of enslaved people.[11] But despite oral promises Jefferson made over the years to certain enslaved people, no one could be confident of their status or future. In November 1824, during Jefferson's emotional reunion with the Marquis de Lafayette, a French visitor interviewed some of Jefferson's enslaved African Americans. The unnamed enslaved people told their interlocutor that they were "perfectly happy, that they were subject to no ill-treatment, that their tasks were very easy, and that they cultivated the lands of Monticello with the greater pleasure, because they were almost sure of not being torn away from them, to be transported elsewhere, so long as Mr. Jefferson lived."[12] The answers provided by the unnamed African Americans demonstrate their deep concern over what would befall them upon their aging enslaver's death.

An experience in October 1825 nearly killed Jefferson. Early that month, he hosted sculptor John H. I. Bowere, who intended to take a plaster cast for a life mask. Bowere applied the wet plaster to Jefferson's face and waited for it to dry. However, the plaster dried much more quickly than Bowere expected and began to smother Jefferson. Although he was unable to talk or breathe, he grasped a nearby chair and shook it to sound the alarm. His enslaved valet Burwell Colbert quickly attended Jefferson and alerted the increasingly frantic Bowere. The two worked in tandem to pry the mask off Jefferson's face. As the former president later related to James Madison, "[Bowere] was obliged to use freely the mallet and chisel to break it into pieces and cut off a piece at a time. These thumps of the mallet would have been sensible almost to a loggerhead [a sea turtle]. The family became alarmed, and he confused, till I was quite exhausted, and there became a real danger that the ears would separate from the head sooner than the plaster. I now bid adieu for ever to busts."[13] Jefferson was lucky to survive the ordeal. Like many of his contemporaries, Jefferson was aware of his own significance to the American story and, as this harrowing episode demonstrates, was more than willing to participate in the mythologizing prior to his death. In this case, "history" had almost killed him.

As he kept James Madison apprised of his activities, Jefferson documented his declining health in letters to other friends and family members. In a January 1826 letter to a friend in Richmond, Jefferson wrote: "[As to] the state of my health . . . it is now 3. weeks since a re-ascerbation of my painful complaint [a severe attack of diarrhea and difficulty urinating] has confined me to the house and indeed to my couch. [R]equired to be constantly recumbent I write slowly and with difficulty. [Y]esterday for the 1st time I was able to leave the house and to resume a posture which enables me to begin to answer the letters which have been accumulating."[14] Despite the physical challenges and the pain of compounding illnesses, Jefferson kept a record of his goings-on and engaged with correspondents. Ever active and willing to experiment, Jefferson discovered he could ride his horse Eagle with a minimum amount of pain if he stationed Eagle on a terrace below and lowered himself into the saddle.[15] He insisted on riding a horse for several hours every day around his property, circumscribing a boundary around his enslaved. A false step, a bucking horse, a low limb, catching a common cold, anything could have ended his life. And the enslaved knew it. They noticed him stooping, slowing down, and using a campstool to sit and talk to them during visits to the fields.[16] He might have been remarkably hale for an old man, but, nevertheless, he was an old man.

In January 1826, his beloved granddaughter Anne Cary Bankhead died just days after giving birth to a son. The tragedy must have reminded Jefferson of the deaths of his wife, Martha Wayles Jefferson, in 1782, and of their daughter, Maria Jefferson Eppes, in 1804. Dr. Robley Dunglison, the attending physician who witnessed Jefferson's shock, recorded that "it was impossible to imagine more poignant distress than was exhibited by him. He shed tears, and abandoned himself to every evidence of grief."[17] The following month, Jefferson learned that his crafty scheme to raise funds to cover his debts through a public lottery must include the house of Monticello itself. The news stunned Jefferson, according to a witness, but he had to agree to the terms if he wished to pay his creditors.[18] He consented, but his plans for a lottery drawing—even with Monticello up for the raffle—would not come to pass. The failure of the lottery foreshadowed the destruction of dozens of enslaved families.

In between illness and personal loss, Jefferson considered his legacy. Writing to the slightly younger Madison in February, Jefferson instructed him to "Take care of me when dead."[19] He prepared his will in mid-March and attended to a task he had long put off: manumitting his enslaved sons by Sally Hemings. Aware of interest in the topic, Jefferson shielded his white family from further notoriety by ensuring that nothing about his relationship with Hemings or their children could be proven by the public paper trail. Despite Jefferson's obfuscations, the descriptions in his will of his sons Eston and Madison, as well as their uncle John Hemings, reveal something of the Black family network as it then existed, and never again would, at Monticello.[20]

Jefferson became bedridden by early July. Dr. Dunglison wrote that "my worst apprehensions must soon be realized."[21] But visitors to Jefferson's bedchamber sensed that he faced death with composure. A week before his death, Jefferson had stated to Henry Lee that death is "an event not to be desired, but not to be feared."[22] The dying patriarch composed a hauntingly beautiful poem and slipped it into a tiny box for his daughter Martha to read upon his death. It read:

> Life's visions are vanished, its dreams are no more;
> Dear friends of my bosom, why bathed in tears?
> I go to my fathers, I welcome the shore
> Which crowns all my hopes or which buries my cares.
> Then farewell, my dear, my lov'd daughter, adieu!
> The last pang of life is in parting from you!
> Two seraphs await me long shrouded in death;
> I will bear them your love on my last parting breath.[23]

Lying in his alcove bed surrounded by his white family and some members of the enslaved Hemings family who attended him, Jefferson's main concern was time. He repeatedly asked those around him to assure him that it was July 4. Slipping in and out of wakefulness, he seemed to be reliving the American Revolution. "Warn the committee to be on the alert," he said, referencing the Revolutionary Committee of Safety. He lifted his right hand and gestured as if he were writing.[24] He may have been writing the Declaration of Independence. "In his last hours he was still struggling to defend the American cause, if only in his flickering imagination," Jon Meacham writes.[25]

Jefferson spoke his last words in the early morning of July 4 to the small retinue of enslaved African Americans who cared for him in his final hours.[26] He was unable to speak the rest of the day. At ten o'clock, he attempted to wordlessly beckon a grandson to comfort him. The grandson was confused, but the enslaved valet Burwell Colbert, who had saved Jefferson from death at least once before, interpreted his directive. Colbert fixed Jefferson's pillow to elevate the patriarch's head.[27] The gesture completed the circle of Jefferson's life. His first memory was of being handed to an enslaved person on a pillow;[28] his last command, to be comforted in the throes of death, was carried out when his enslaved butler plumped a pillow on his deathbed.[29] Thomas Jefferson died at ten minutes to one o'clock on Tuesday, July 4, 1826.[30]

Later that afternoon, church bells tolled in Charlottesville to mark Jefferson's death as the cannons boomed during the celebrations of Independence Day.[31] In fact, due to the holiday, public commemorations of Jefferson's life began even before the vast swath of Americans learned of his passing. On the date of his death the Washington, DC, *National Intelligencer* published a letter, subsequently reprinted in newspapers throughout the country and affixed to mourning ribbons distributed by the public,[32] that Jefferson had written in late June to inspire Americans to remember the Declaration of Independence.[33] Jefferson wrote: "All eyes are opened, or opening, to the rights of man. The general spread of the light of science has already laid open to every view the palpable truth that the mass of mankind has not been born with saddles on their backs, nor a favored few booted and spurred, ready to ride them legitimately, by the grace of God. These are grounds of hope for others. For ourselves, let the annual return of this day forever refresh our recollections of these rights, and an undiminished devotion to them."[34]As Jefferson and John Adams both died on July 4, 1826, Americans remember the deaths of two founders during "the great day of national jubilee," words spoken by Senator Daniel Webster in a eulogy commemorating both men in Boston. "In the very hour of public rejoicing," Webster said, "in the midst of echoing and reechoing voices of thanksgiving, while [Jefferson's and Adams's] own names were on all tongues, they took their flight together to the world of spirits."[35]

More than sixty years later, Peter Fossett, an aged Baptist preacher in Cincinnati, Ohio, reflected on the deaths of Adams and Jefferson. Fossett, who was enslaved as a child at Monticello and sold after his enslaver's death, said that on July 4, 1826, "sorrow came not only to the homes of two great men . . . but to the slaves of Thomas Jefferson."[36] For members of Jefferson's white family, his death was the passing of an era. For his enslaved people, it was the point of no return. Jefferson's death upended the world he had carefully curated at Monticello. If any African American had harbored the distant hope that Jefferson would have a deathbed conversion and free the enslaved, they were disappointed.

Jefferson tried to keep his family close to Monticello.[37] These connections sustained a kind of dreamworld where, regardless of what occurred beyond Monticello plantation, whites and Blacks lived within the enslaver-enslaved paradigm in "orchestrated scenes of domestic tranquility," as Annette Gordon-Reed and Peter Onuf write.[38] At his death, the ordered world came crashing down and the fiction was revealed. Previously, Jefferson's white family could pretend that their patriarch's finances weren't in such dire straits, that they might all emerge from financial disaster unscathed, that their property would remain within their family. Ellen Randolph, writing in 1819 after receiving news of her grandfather's mounting financial difficulties, prayed that after struggles with "with debt & difficulty, we may be reserved as another proof of the capriciousness of fortune."[39] For anyone who had been led to believe in this fiction, the reality was shockingly revealed.

How word of Jefferson's death circulated from his chambers to the ears of the enslaved people across the plantation is unknown. But they learned Jefferson had not had a deathbed conversion from enslaver to liberator. He had not freed them en masse and the enslaved community's worst fears were confirmed. They would forever know him to be one who never lived up to his most famous of declarations.

In the immediate wake of Jefferson's death, the actions of only a handful of Monticello's enslaved people are known. The enslaved carpenter John Hemings made his enslaver's coffin.[40] Unlike Hemings's masterworks, including much of the joinery and some of the furniture in Monticello, the coffin he made for Jefferson was a private work. No one besides himself and those who gathered for Jefferson's funeral would ever see it. Sally Hemings took eyeglasses, an inkwell, and a shoe buckle to remember Jefferson by.[41] These were items that may have carried some meaning. And, in the Jefferson family graveyard, the enslaved gardener Wormley Hughes dug Jefferson's grave between that of his wife Martha and daughter Maria, the "two seraphs" mentioned in his deathbed poem, for the burial on July 5.[42]

As the mourners gathered around the burial ground, their own mortalities were not very far from their minds. Some of the mourners would be buried in the same graveyard years later. Andrew K. Smith's account of the burial, recounted nearly fifty years afterward, puts the number of graveside mourners at thirty or forty.[43] But, given how many enslaved African Americans lived at Monticello, Smith's estimate almost certainly only refers to the number of whites gathered. Most of the white mourners would have been Jefferson's relatives and local friends. If there were enslaved people present, they would have seen approximately thirty or forty whites, some of whom they'd known all their lives, mourning their patriarch during a simple ceremony. The Reverend Frederick Hatch read the burial office from the Episcopal Book of Common Prayer.[44] But as the ceremony concluded, a throng of 1,500 Charlottesville citizens, the single largest crowd to gather at Monticello until after it was turned into a museum nearly one century later, belatedly clambered up the little mountain to attend the ceremony. Jefferson's son-in-law, Thomas Mann Randolph Jr., and his grandson, Thomas Jefferson Randolph, both knew a large procession was on its way for the funeral and had assumed the other one would tell Reverend Hatch to delay the service. The throng was disappointed and reportedly angry to have missed the burial and the opportunity to pay their last respects to their most famous fellow citizen.[45] Among this crowd of 1,500 likely were some whites interested in getting a close look at Jefferson's enslaved people. For the enslaved would soon be sold.

To settle the estate, Jefferson's white descendants organized a public auction of the enslaved families and eventually put Monticello up for sale. On January 15, 1827, the first day of a five-day auction, 130 enslaved African Americans were put up for sale. An advertisement in the Charlottesville *Central Gazette* announced, "the whole of the residue of the estate of Thomas Jefferson, dec., consisting of 130 VALUABLE NEGROES, Stock, Crop, &c. Household and Kitchen Furniture. The attention of the public is earnestly invited to this property. The negroes are believed to be the most valuable for their number ever offered at one time in the State of Virginia."[46]

Among those auctioned was my ancestor, Peter Hemings. He was fifty-six years old. Daniel Farley, his nephew, a free man, purchased him for one dollar in one of several transactions that were anxiously arranged by free relatives and permitted by the Jefferson family. One of the many others sold was eleven-year-old Peter Fossett, one of Hemings's great-nephews. His father, Joseph Fossett, who knew he would be free on July 4, 1827, due to the terms of his manumission by Jefferson's will, asked local whites to purchase his wife and their children until he could repay them.[47] Young Peter Fossett had sometimes worn a special blue suit with a red hat and red shoes, gifts from a free relative, that likely would have made him a colorful presence at Monticello prior to Jefferson's death.[48] His great-uncle Peter Hemings, a tailor, would have been sure to notice him in that fine suit—he may have even tailored it for him. Now, on this blustery January day, the two Peters, and so many others, would be torn from each other. John R. Jones, who purchased Peter Fossett, reneged on the promise he made to Joseph Fossett and refused to sell Peter back.[49]

Two years after the 1827 sale, in the second and last auction of Jefferson's enslaved people, this time conducted in front of the courthouse in downtown Charlottesville, a thirteen-year-old named Edmund Robinson stepped to the auction block. Thomas Jefferson Randolph purchased Robinson and his parents for himself.[50] I often wonder if Peter Hemings witnessed this second sale. After all, he plied his trade as a tailor in downtown Charlottesville. If he witnessed this second auction, he would have seen his future son-in-law on the auction block. Some years later, Edmund Robinson would marry Peter Hemings's daughter Sally.[51] Their child Anderson Jefferson Robinson, born enslaved in 1850, was my grandmother's grandfather.[52]

In the aftermath of Jefferson's death, there were significant deviations in how his enslaved people and their descendants experienced the last two generations of slavery. My ancestors, who were sold at the two auctions of Monticello's enslaved peoples, continued to be enslaved in their home region of central Virginia. They were not freed like some of the Hemingses who eventually relocated to Ohio, but neither were they forcibly transported to plantations in the Deep South. Those who were forced south to Alabama or southwest to Missouri not only experienced the unspeakable loss of family separation but also the profound challenges of large-scale cotton farming. Many of the survivors of the Second Middle Passage, when an estimated one million enslaved people were forcibly transported from the Upper South to the Lower South in the decades before the Civil War, were subjected to the hardships of sharecropping throughout the rest of the nineteenth and into the twentieth centuries.[53] The dispersal sales of 1827 and 1829 had profound intergenerational effects on Monticello's African American families.

"[African Americans'] griefs are transient," Jefferson had written in the *Notes on the States of Virginia* (1785).[54] Jefferson's writings about Black grief may have served to assuage any guilt he felt over separating hundreds of people from one another during his own lifetime, and the great scattering of enslaved families after his death. He could not account for how African Americans would remember him, but he could and did work to create and promulgate a racist body of knowledge that negatively influenced perceptions of people of African descent. *Notes on the State of Virginia* was the most popular nonfiction book in America until the mid-nineteenth century.[55] Jefferson, the architect of American independence, articulated a racist discourse about Black people that thoroughly permeated America's collective consciousness. But whatever Jefferson did to try to convince himself and the innumerable others who took his racist words literally, he could not control how he would be remembered after his death.

For example, in 1847 the seventy-two-year-old blacksmith Isaac Granger Jefferson commented that, "Old master [Jefferson] never dat handsome in dis world," in reaction to the likeness of Thomas Jefferson, his late enslaver, printed in William Linn's *The Life of Thomas Jefferson* (1839). "Dat likeness," the talented blacksmith said as he scrutinized the book's frontispiece, is "right between old master and Ginral Washington."[56] Isaac Granger Jefferson knew both Founding Fathers, and judged Linn's portrait of "old master" Jefferson to be off the mark.

Jefferson obsessed over how he would be received in history. An undated manuscript in his hand that gave the design for an obelisk to mark his grave, eventually erected in 1833, indicated that he wished to be "most remembered" for being the author of the Declaration of American Independence and the Virginia statute for religious freedom, and the father of the University of Virginia.[57] But he could not have imagined that the words of Black Americans would be as carefully analyzed as his own and that their representations of him as a paradoxical patriarch would largely shape the current popular and academic consensus. The opinions expressed by many African Americans from the nineteenth century onward reveal deeply ironic, critical, and consistent interpretations of Jefferson as the quintessential American paradox.

The date of Jefferson's death is strikingly coincidental with the origins of the radical abolitionist movement in the United States, which saw the widespread dissemination of antislavery accounts and was rooted in and expanded upon Jeffersonian natural rights philosophy. Samuel Cornish and John Russwurm's *Freedom's Journal* appeared in the spring of 1827; it was the nation's first Black newspaper, and some of its first articles concerned celebrations of Independence Day.[58] Many other abolitionist publications poured forth as Black and white Americans began to call for slavery's immediate end.[59] Black women were also crucial actors in this movement, as the historian Martha Jones and others have shown. In 1832, Maria Stewart, a free Black woman in Connecticut, proclaimed, "I am a true born American," and stated that "the whites have so long and so loudly proclaimed the theme of equal rights and privileges, that our souls have caught the flame also."[60] Abolitionists embraced the natural rights tenets expressed in Jefferson's Declaration of Independence and worked to ensure equality for all Americans.

Frederick Douglass articulated the most notable attack on Jefferson's legacy with his 1852 speech "The Meaning of July Fourth for the Negro" (commonly known as "What, to the Slave, Is the Fourth of July?"). "This Fourth July is yours, not mine," Douglass told his audience in Rochester, New York. "You may rejoice, I must mourn." Proslavery Americans could not be reasoned with, he said. "At a time like this, scorching irony, not convincing argument, is needed." And then he hit his high note:

> What, to the American slave, is your Fourth of July? I answer: a day that reveals to him, more than all other days in the year, the gross injustice and cruelty to which he is the constant victim. To him, your celebration is a sham; your boasted liberty, an unholy license; your national greatness, swelling vanity; your sounds of rejoicing are empty and heartless; your denunciation of tyrants, brass fronted impudence; your shouts of liberty and equality, hollow mockery; your prayers and hymns, your sermons and thanksgivings, with all your religious parade and solemnity, are, to him, mere bombast, fraud, deception and impiety, and hypocrisy—a thin veil to cover up crimes which would disgrace a nation of savages. There is not a nation on the earth guilty of practices more shocking and bloody than are the people of the United States, at this very hour.[61]

Douglass would often use this framing in his jeremiads before the Civil War. His "scorching irony" directed at Jefferson and the founders was echoed by many fellow abolitionists, including Charlotte Forten who, in Philadelphia in 1857, recorded, "Went to Independence Hall.—The old bell with its famous inscription, the mottoes, the relics, the pictures of the heroes of the Revolution—the *saviours* of their country,—what a *mockery* they all seemed,—here there breathes not a freeman, black or white."[62] Jeffersonian legacies were never far from the minds of abolitionists.

After the election of Abraham Lincoln to the presidency in 1860, southern secessionists—who had long been dismissive of the Jeffersonian ideal that "all men are created equal"—claimed for themselves the right to revolution enshrined in Jefferson's Declaration. The Confederacy abhorred Lincoln, who himself selectively interpreted Jefferson for the preservation of the Union. The Confederate army, which seized Monticello in 1862, included several white Jefferson descendants, including some of the grandchildren and great-grandchildren who had been present for his funeral. Thomas Jefferson Randolph, who had orchestrated the dispersal sales of 1827 and 1829, was named a Confederate colonel.

In 1864, with the Confederacy in its death throes, Frederick Douglass delivered a speech, "The Mission of the War," in which he plainly laid out his vision of the future of the United States. "What we now want is a country— a free country," said Douglass, "a country not saddened by the footprints of a single slave—and nowhere cursed by the presence of a slaveholder. We want a country which shall not brand the Declaration of Independence as a lie."[63] As Henry Louis Gates Jr. writes, "For Douglass, black Americans were the true patriots, because they fully embraced Jeffersonian democracy; they were the most Jeffersonian Americans of all. . . . Here was Jefferson, whom Douglass called 'the sage of the Old Dominion,' cast as the patron saint of the black freedom struggle."[64] Among those serving in the Union, including several grandsons of Jefferson and Sally Hemings (some serving as white, others as Black), were perhaps dozens of men whose parents and grandparents had been enslaved by Jefferson and his relatives. Those soldiers, descendants of people enslaved by Jefferson, were fighting to make the United States live up to Jefferson's words.

Black Americans cast the Emancipation Proclamation and the Declaration of Independence "into the same seamless story." In January 1865, at the AME Bethel Church in New Haven, Connecticut, the Reverend S. D. Berry declared the Emancipation Proclamation to be the Union's Declaration of

Independence. Berry reminded his parishioners that, as Americans, they were the descendants—literally as well as figuratively—of the heroes of the American Revolution. "As our forefathers fought, bled, and conquered for the Declaration of Independence," declared Berry, "just so hard are we now fighting for the Emancipation Proclamation." As David Blight notes, a celebration at another AME church on the same day, but this time in Chester, Illinois, was perhaps even more patriotic: "Similar to New Haven, the Chester celebration ended with a resolution to carry on the war for the 'principles' in the Proclamation and the Declaration, including a recitation of Thomas Jefferson's preamble." Before the war had ended, "blacks were preparing the script and forging the arguments for a long struggle over the memory of the events they were living through."[65] Thomas Jefferson's words had played a key role in their war effort and beyond.

Following the Union's victory in the Civil War, Jefferson's reputation suffered for the remainder of the nineteenth century. Jefferson was viewed as an advocate of secession and slavery, a proto-Confederate, and blamed for the factors that caused the Civil War.[66] Among the Civil War dead was Thomas Eston Hemings, the grandson of Thomas Jefferson and Sally Hemings, who reportedly died at the notorious prison in Andersonville, South Carolina.[67]

Thirty-five years after the war's end, an elderly man made an improbable return to the home of his youth. The eighty-five-year-old Peter Fossett, who had once worn a striking blue suit before being sold away from his family in 1827, visited Monticello in June 1900. Fossett had escaped slavery in 1850 and relocated to Cincinnati where he became a Baptist minister; his church raised funds for him to fulfill his longtime wish of returning to visit Monticello. The Levy family, who had purchased the home in 1834 and had it returned to them following the Civil War, welcomed Fossett to Monticello at the main entrance.[68] He reflected on the dispersal sales that had torn his family and so many others apart. "Then began our troubles," he told a newspaper reporter two years before his visit. "We were scattered all over the country, never to meet each other again until we meet in another world."[69]

At the turn of the twentieth century, Fossett couldn't imagine an earthly reunion of those affected by slavery and the dispersal sales following Jefferson's death. Glorious visions for a country that "shall not brand the Declaration of Independence as a lie," gave way to the powerful and pernicious forces of white supremacy and segregation.[70] Jim Crow laws restricted African Americans' lives throughout the United States. Peter Fossett was living during an epoch between the abandonment of Reconstruction and World War I that Rayford Logan called the "nadir" of race relations in the United States.[71] In Fossett's mind, time would continue to pass, and old associations would be forgotten, ignored, and erased. But pioneering historians in the late twentieth century made Fossett's hoped-for reunion a reality. This work has had profound implications and continues to inspire hope in the deeply divided country Jefferson helped to found nearly 250 years ago.

Modern interpreters of Jefferson do not revise history so much as they seek to restore perspectives that were cast aside during the institutionalization of Jefferson's reputation. In the mid-1910s, a group of well-connected Americans sought to elevate Jefferson into the national pantheon. Their efforts culminated in the purchase of Monticello from the Levy family and the establishment of the Thomas Jefferson Memorial Foundation in 1923 (renamed the Thomas Jefferson Foundation in 2000). On April 13, 1943, the 200th anniversary of Jefferson's birth, President Franklin D. Roosevelt, a great admirer of Jefferson, laid the cornerstone and dedicated the Jefferson Memorial to the founder he coined the "apostle of freedom."[72] He also chose to feature Jefferson's profile and Monticello's West Lawn façade on the nickel.[73] To this day, any time someone looks at the obverse of the nickel, they are looking not only at the seat of the Jefferson family but also a representation of the exact site where, after Jefferson's death, 130 human beings were forcibly sold away from their loved ones.

The canonization of Jefferson as the "apostle of freedom" obscured the civil rights activism of descendants of Monticello's enslaved families who, as Lucia Stanton writes, fought "to make this country live up to the promise of its founding document." Among this extended community, Stanton has identified "a remarkable number of men and women who were crusaders, often on the front lines" in civil rights movements.[74] Frederick Madison Roberts, Coralie Franklin Cook, and William Monroe Trotter are the best-known activist descendants of Elizabeth Hemings, the matriarch of the Hemings family. Roberts, a Californian, became the first African American elected to office in any state west of the Mississippi; Cook, the first identified Monticello-connected descendant to graduate from college, helped found the National Association of Colored Women (NACW); and Trotter, a graduate of Harvard University, and the best-known descendant of the Monticello enslaved community, helped found the Niagara Movement, a forerunner of the National Association of Colored People (NAACP), and was an indefatigable and formidable activist for decades.[75] These individuals, Stanton writes, "believed in the truth of the Declaration's preamble, cherished the hope that it would one day be more than an ideal, and joined with, and often led, countless other African Americans in the cause."[76] These Monticello-connected leaders, who were themselves influenced by radical abolitionists, had successors in the Civil Rights Movement. As Peggy Trotter Dammond Preacely, the activist grandniece of William Monroe Trotter, writes, "it was simply in my blood."[77] Preaceley's and others' work demonstrates a genealogy of activism.

If Jefferson's actions cast hundreds of people deeper into the perils of slavery, his words would still be used to advance the cause of human freedom. As Martin Luther King Jr. addressed the crowd gathered for his "I Have a Dream" speech at the March on Washington on August 28, 1963, he quoted from Jefferson's Declaration of Independence:

> When the architects of our republic wrote the magnificent words of the Constitution and the Declaration of Independence, they were signing a promissory note to which every American was to fall heir. This note was a promise that all men—yes, black men as well as white men—would be guaranteed the unalienable rights of life, liberty, and the pursuit of happiness. It is obvious today that America has defaulted on this promissory note insofar as her citizens of color are concerned. Instead of honoring this sacred obligation, America has given the Negro people a bad check, a check which has come back marked insufficient funds. But we refuse to believe that the bank of justice is bankrupt. We refuse to believe that there are insufficient funds in the great vaults of opportunity of this nation. And so we've come to cash this check, a check that will give us upon demand the riches of freedom and the security of justice.[78]

The crowd at the March on Washington included several descendants of Monticello's enslaved people. The elderly grandchildren of the Robinsons—Edmund, who had been sold at age thirteen, and Sally, whose father Peter Hemings had been sold to his nephew for a dollar in 1827—were among those in attendance.[79] In 2011, nearly a half century after the March on Washington, the Martin Luther King Jr. Memorial was unveiled on the Tidal Basin; it permanently fixes King looking in the direction of the Jefferson Memorial. Long after Jefferson's death, descendants of the enslaved—including many descendants of people Jefferson enslaved himself—have served as sentinels in advancing democracy.

As the nation's Bicentennial approached, American writers and historians sought to publicly reinterpret the hagiographic image of Jefferson and the founders. In 1972, at the College of William & Mary, the very institution Jefferson had graduated from two centuries before, the acclaimed writer Ralph Ellison delivered a stirring commencement speech that highlighted the flaws and ideals of both Jefferson and the United States: "As surely as the values stated in our sacred documents were compelling and all-pervasive and as surely as they were being made a living reality in the social structure, such people as were excluded from the rewards and promises of that social structure would rise up and insist on being included. Such people as were brutalized and designated a role beneath the social hierarchy were sure to rise up, and with the same rhetoric and in the name of the same sacred principles, accuse the nation and insist upon a rectification."[80] Ellison described the crucial appropriation of the founders' words that had led to, and would continue to lead to, an extension of Jefferson's founding ideas despite his refusal or inability to do so himself. Ellison charged his audience to "not bury the past, because it is within us. . . . And because of this we are now able to resuscitate in all its boldness, and with great sophistication, that conscious and conscientious concern for others which is the essence of the American ideal."[81] Two centuries later, Jefferson's words were not only being remembered but were being reinvigorated.

Other writers sought to correct the record about Jefferson's personal life, especially regarding his decades-long relationship with Sally Hemings. Fawn Brodie's *Thomas Jefferson: An Intimate History* (1974) proved the most controversial. Brodie had a deep interest in uncovering Jefferson's relationship with Sally Hemings. Her methods were years ahead of their time. Barbara Chase-Riboud's best-selling novel *Sally Hemings* (1979) was based on Brodie's research. For decades, the Thomas Jefferson Memorial Foundation dismissed the Hemings story and downplayed the contributions of hundreds of enslaved African Americans at Monticello, but the Brodie biography and the Chase-Riboud novel carried word into the last two decades of the twentieth century. Numerous descendants of Monticello's enslaved community would attest to the influence the biography and novel had on all but confirming their families' oral traditions.

Among the most important things to happen since Jefferson's death are the founding of the Getting Word African American Oral History Project and Annette Gordon-Reed's groundbreaking scholarship on Jefferson and the Hemingses. Getting Word was founded by historians Lucia Stanton and Dianne Swann-Wright in 1993, the 250th anniversary of Jefferson's birthday, with the intention to locate the descendants of Monticello's enslaved population, and to record their family stories and histories.[82] The Virginia Foundation for the Humanities (now Virginia Humanities) initially funded Stanton's idea. Stanton hired Swann-Wright, then a doctoral student at the University of Virginia, to be her partner on the as-of-yet unnamed project.

Swann-Wright felt the title of their project embodied how descendants of Jefferson's enslaved families "get word" to one another across generations. After conducting dozens of interviews over the next four years, Stanton and Swann-Wright hosted the Getting Word Gathering, a weekend of events at Monticello in June 1997. The gathering "marked the first coming together of different African American families, all descendants of Thomas Jefferson's enslaved community." More than 100 guests, including participants in Getting Word and their families, traveled from eight states (and the District of Columbia) for the homecoming.[83]

Exactly 170 years after 130 enslaved people were sold on Monticello's West Lawn, dozens of their descendants gathered at the very same spot. Many, meeting for the first time, laughed and hugged one another, and celebrated their homecoming. They also mourned those who had gone before them. Stanton and Swann-Wright had organized a naming ceremony, "to acknowledge those who were unable to leave lasting records of their existence." Small cards, each imprinted with the name of a person enslaved at Monticello, were placed in a handmade white oak basket. Everyone at the gathering took a name from the basket and, "one by one, descendants called out the names of those who had gone before." By chance, "a tow-headed

FIGURE 2. Descendants of Thomas Jefferson's enslaved community gathered at Monticello for the twenty-fifth anniversary of the Getting Word African American Oral History Project in June 2018. (Thomas Jefferson Foundation)

ten-year-old," fifth-great-granddaughter of Sally Hemings, bore in her hand a card with the name of her ancestor. She said the name aloud.[84]

On the very day Getting Word families were gathered at Monticello, the world was getting word from the *New York Times* that Annette Gordon-Reed had ushered in a sea change for reinterpreting Jefferson and American history. Gordon-Reed's *Thomas Jefferson and Sally Hemings: An American Controversy* (1997) had just been published by University of Virginia Press. Gordon-Reed made it clear that generations of historians, wittingly or unwittingly, ignored or overlooked evidence that Thomas Jefferson fathered children with Sally Hemings. "I'm not saying that all these people are racist and that they hate blacks," Gordon-Reed told the *Times*. "No. I think that the response to this story is the legacy of slavery. This is absolutely the way people have been taught to think whether they consciously know it or not, of devaluing black people's words when they are inconvenient."[85] Gordon-Reed reinterpreted historical evidence and persuasively argued that Thomas Jefferson was the father of all of Sally Hemings's children, and would go on to write the National Book Award-winning classic *The Hemingses of Monticello,* which further contextualized the lives of many of Monticello's enslaved families and presented a portion of their lives in the aftermath of Jefferson's death.

By emphasizing and interpreting the perspectives of African Americans from the eighteenth century to the present, Stanton, Swann-Wright, and Gordon-Reed contributed to a revolution in Jeffersonian scholarship. Their work, and the work of other scholars, has had enormous implications not only for understanding Jefferson and the Hemingses, but also, especially in the case of Stanton's research, the wider community of Monticello's enslaved African Americans and their descendants. Stanton and Swann-Wright's Getting Word Project has helped reconstitute dozens of African American families, many of whom can trace their lineage back to the dispersal sales that occurred following Jefferson's death. The research of these scholars, as well as the Charlottesville-born historian Niya Bates and the writer Gayle Jessup White who have followed in their footsteps, honors "the intimacy of the enslaved community" and their descendants, as Christina Sharpe has written, who live in the wake of slavery.[86] Begun as a project to learn more about Black families' oral histories of slavery, Getting Word has since become an important archive of Black freedom, collecting and preserving dozens of families' histories from the era of slavery to the present.

In June 2018, at the twenty-fifth anniversary of the founding of Getting Word, 300 descendants of people enslaved by Jefferson, including myself, my grandmother, and five of her first cousins, gathered at Monticello. Annette Gordon-Reed and Lucia Stanton were present, and Dianne Swann-Wright, who, sadly, had passed away six months before, was honored by the Thomas Jefferson Foundation. When the Getting Word reunion festivities ended on that night in June 2018, our shuttle bus descended from the mountaintop and paused briefly at Jefferson's gravesite. The nightfall obscured the obelisk that marks Jefferson's resting place in the Monticello graveyard. No one on our shuttle—transporting descendants of the many families Jefferson enslaved, including the Herns, Hubbards, Gillettes, Grangers, and others—asked to disembark at the graveyard. Instead, we promised each other that in the morning we would visit the Burial Ground for Enslaved People on the estate, where so many ancestors are buried, to leave flowers and pray.

Notes

1. "Thomas Jefferson Randolph's Account of Thomas Jefferson's Death," in Henry S. Randall, *Life of Thomas Jefferson*, 3 vols. (New York: Derby & Jackson, 1858), 3:543–44.
2. Samuel X. Radbill, ed., *The Autobiographical Ana of Robley Dunglison, M.D.* (Philadelphia: American Philosophical Society, 1963), 32–33.
3. Randall, *Jefferson*, 3:543–44.
4. Annette Gordon-Reed, *The Hemingses of Monticello: An American Family* (New York: W. W. Norton, 2008), 655.
5. Gordon-Reed, *The Hemingses of Monticello*, 655.
6. Thomas Jefferson to Charles Thomson, December 25, 1808, Charles Thomas Papers, Library of Congress. Quoted in Jon Meacham, *Thomas Jefferson: The Art of Power* (New York: Random House, 2012), 439–40.
7. Meacham, *Thomas Jefferson*, 441.
8. For a discussion of Jefferson's 1789 return from France, see Gordon-Reed, *The Hemingses of Monticello*, 397–401, 644; for his 1809 return from the presidency, see Meacham, *Thomas Jefferson*, 440–41.
9. Jefferson to Charles Pinckney, August 29, 1809, Founders Online (hereafter FOL), https://founders.archives.gov/documents/Jefferson/03-01-02-0380.
10. For Jefferson's indebtedness, see Herbert E. Sloan, *Principle and Interest: Thomas Jefferson and the Problem of Debt* (New York: Oxford University Press, 1995); This an estimated $2,815,000 in 2021 dollars. See the CPI Inflation Calculator, officialdata.org.
11. For Coles, see Kurt E. Leichtle and Bruce G. Carveth, *Crusade against Slavery: Edward Coles, Pioneer of Freedom* (Carbondale: Southern Illinois University Press, 2011); for White, see Christina Snyder, *Great Crossings: Indians, Settlers, and Slaves in the Age of Jackson* (New York: Oxford University Press, 2017), 66; for Randolph, see Craig Swain, "Free Blacks of Israel Hill," *Historical Marker Database*, February 28, 2010, revised February 3, 2020, https://www.hmdb.org/m.asp?m=28041.
12. Auguste Levasseur, *Lafayette in America in 1824 and 1825; or, Journal of a Voyage to the United States,* trans. John D. Godman (Philadelphia: Carey and Lea, 1829), 219.
13. Jefferson to James Madison, October 18, 1825, FOL, https://founders.archives.gov/documents/Jefferson/98-01-02-5602. For the event, see Randall, *Jefferson*, 3:540.
14. Jefferson to William Gordon, January 1, 1826, Thomas Jefferson Papers, Library of Congress, https://www.loc.gov/resource/mtj1.055_0795_0795/.
15. Randall, *Jefferson*, 3:539.
16. For Jefferson's horseback riding into his old age and his visits to the enslaved in the fields, see his overseer Edmund Bacon's recollections in Hamilton W. Pierson, *The Private Life of Thomas Jefferson* (New York: Charles Scribner, 1862), 70–84.
17. Dunglison quoted in Sarah N. Randolph, *The Domestic Life of Thomas Jefferson* (1871; rpt. Charlottesville: University of Virginia Press, 1978), 416.
18. John B. Boles, *Jefferson: Architect of American Liberty* (New York: Basic Books, 2017), 511–13.
19. Jefferson to James Madison, February 17, 1826, FOL, https://founders.archives.gov/documents/Jefferson/98-01-02-5912.
20. See Gordon-Reed, *The Hemingses of Monticello*, 647–49.

21. Robley Dunglison to James Madison,July 1, 1826, Library of Congress, https://www
    .loc.gov/item/mjmo19792/.
22. Merrill D. Peterson, ed., *Visitors to Monticello* (Charlottesville: University of Virginia
    Press, 1989), 108–9.
23. Jefferson to Martha Jefferson Randolph, 2 July 2, 1826, FOL, https://founders.archives
    .gov/documents/Jefferson/98-01-02-6184.
24. Randall, *Jefferson,* 3:546.
25. Meacham, *Thomas Jefferson,* 494.
26. Randall, *Jefferson,* 3:543–544.
27. Gordon-Reed, *The Hemingses of Monticello,* 651.
28. Susan Nicholas Randolph, *The Domestic Life of Thomas Jefferson Compiled from Family
    Letters and Reminiseces of His Great-Granddaughter* (New York: Harper and Brothers,
    1871), 238.
29. Meacham, *Thomas Jefferson,* 494.
30. Randall, *Jefferson,* 3:545.
31. Alan Pell Crawford, *Twilight at Monticello: The Final Years of Thomas Jefferson* (New York:
    Random House, 2009), 242.
32. One surviving example of this mourning ribbon with Jefferson's last public letter
    printed on it can be found in the Political History Collections, National Museum of
    American History, Smithsonian Institution, Washington, DC.
33. Crawford, *Twilight at Monticello,* 246.
34. Jefferson to Roger C. Weightman, June 24, 1826, in *Thomas Jefferson: Writings,* ed.
    Merrill Peterson (New York: Library of America, 2011), 1517.
35. Daniel Webster, *The Writings and Speeches of Daniel Webster,* 18 vols. (Boston: Little,
    Brown, 1903), 1:289.
36. "Once the Slave of Thomas Jefferson . . . ," *New York World,* January 30, 1898. For a tran-
    script of the article see "Recollections of Peter Fossett," *Monticello.org,* https://www
    .monticello.org/slavery/slave-memoirs-oral-histories/recollections-of-peter-fossett/.
37. Annette Gordon-Reed and Peter Onuf, *"Most Blessed of the Patriarchs": Thomas Jefferson
    and the Empire of the Imagination* (New York: W. W. Norton, 2016), 35.
38. Gordon-Reed and Onuf, *"Most Blessed of the Patriarchs,"* 265.
39. Ellen Randolph to Martha Jefferson Randolph, August 11, 1819, in *Family Letters.* For
    a transcript, see https://tjrs.monticello.org/letter/826#X3184701.
40. Gordon-Reed, *The Hemingses of Monticello,* 652.
41. Gordon-Reed, *The Hemingses of Monticello,* 374–75.
42. Meacham, *Thomas Jefferson,* 495.
43. *Weekly Chronicle* (Charlottesville, VA), October 15, 1875. For a transcript, see https://
    tjrs.monticello.org/letter/38.
44. Meacham, *Thomas Jefferson,* 495.
45. *Weekly Chronicle,* October 15, 1875.
46. *Central Gazette* (Charlottesville, VA), January 15, 1827. For a reproduction, see https://
    www.monticello.org/slaveauction/.
47. Gordon-Reed, *The Hemingses of Monticello,* 656.
48. *New York World,* January 30, 1898.
49. *New York World,* January 30, 1898.

50. Monticello dispersal sale receipts, University of Virginia, MS 5921. For a reproduction of the 1829 dispersal sale receipt with Edmund Robinson's and his parents' (James and Rachel's) first names' listed among the sold, see https://www.monticello.org /slaveauction/img/Eagle-Hotel-1829sale-1.jpg.

51. 1870 U.S. Census, Charlottesville, VA.

52. Anderson Robinson's gravestone in the Robinson Family Burial Ground, Goochland, VA, lists his birth year as 1850.

53. For details about Monticello-connected families who were forcibly transported to Alabama, see the interviews with families in North Courtland, Alabama, in the Getting Word Archive, Charlottesville, VA; for details about families in Missouri, see Elizabeth Varon, "From Carter's Mountain to Morganza Bend," *Nau Center for Civil War History Blog*, January 11, 2017, http://naucenter.as.virginia.edu/usct_odyssey_part_1.

54. Jefferson, *Writings*, ed. Peterson, 265.

55. Ibram X. Kendi, *Stamped from the Beginning: The Definitive History of Racist Ideas in America* (New York: Nation Books, 2016), 112.

56. Isaac Granger's words were recorded in dialect by a white transcriber in the 1840s. When the memoir was first printed in the 1950s, editor and historian Rayford Logan chose to adhere to the historical record. I have followed Logan's example in the knowledge that the biased representation of Granger's powerful words are a historical artifact of the era of American slavery—and that Granger's piercing insights shine through in spite of how they were represented on the page by a prejudiced mediator. Rayford W. Logan, ed., *Memoirs of a Monticello Slave: As Dictated to Charles Campbell in the 1840's by Isaac, One of Thomas Jefferson's Slaves* (Charlottesville: University of Virginia Press, 1951), 16.

57. Thomas Jefferson, no date, *Epitaph*, Manuscript/Mixed Material, Library of Congress, https://www.loc.gov/item/mtjbib024905/.

58. Leslie M. Harris, *In the Shadow of Slavery: African Americans in New York City, 1626–1863* (Chicago: University of Chicago Press, 2003), 123.

59. Martha S. Jones, *Vanguard: How Black Women Broke Barriers, Won the Vote, and Insisted on Equality for All* (New York: Basic Books, 2020), 44.

60. Maria W. Miller Stewart, "Lecture Delivered at Franklin Hall," September 21, 1832, in *Voices of Democracy: The U.S. Oratory Project,* http://voicesofdemocracy.umd.edu /stewart-lecture-delivered-speech-text/.

61. Frederick Douglass, "What to the Slave Is the Fourth of July?" *Oration Delivered in Corinthian Hall, Rochester* (Rochester: Lee, Man, and Co, 1852), 14–37, https://www .americanyawp.com/reader/democracy-in-america/frederick-douglass-what-to-the -slave-is-the-fourth-of-july-1852/.

62. Erica Armstrong Dunbar, *A Fragile Freedom: African American Women and Emancipation in an Antebellum City* (New Haven: Yale University Press, 2008), 149.

63. Frederick Douglass, "The Mission of the War," January 13, 1864. See the full transcription of the speech at https://www.blackpast.org/african-american-history/1864 -frederick-douglass-mission-war/.

64. Henry Louis Gates Jr., *The Trials of Phillis Wheatley: America's First Black Poet and Her Encounters with the Founding Fathers* (New York: Basic Books, 2003), 26.

65. David Blight, *Race and Reunion: The Civil War in American Memory* (Cambridge, MA: Harvard University Press, 2001), 28.

66. Francis D. Cogliano, *Thomas Jefferson: Reputation and Legacy* (Charlottesville: University of Virginia Press, 2006), 4.

67. *Pike County [OH] Republican*, March 13, 1873.

68. "WAS JEFFERSON'S SLAVE—Rev. P. F. Fossett Visits the Scenes of His Youth," *Charlottesville Daily Progress*, June 13, 1900.

69. *New York World,* 30 January 30, 1898.

70. Many historians point to the Spanish-American War, when Northerners and Southerners, including some veterans of the Civil War, came together to fight a new war. See George C. Herring, *From Colony to Superpower: U.S. Foreign Relations Since 1776* (New York: Oxford University Press, 2008), 334–35; David Blight, *Race and Reunion: The Civil War in American Memory* (Cambridge, MA: Belknap, 2001), 345–52.

71. Rayford Logan, *The Negro in Life and Thought: The Nadir, 1877–1901* (New York: Dial, 1954).

72. Cogliano, *Thomas Jefferson,* 5.

73. Cogliano, *Thomas Jefferson,* 6.

74. Lucia Stanton, *"Those Who Labor for My Happiness": Slavery at Thomas Jefferson's Monticello* (Charlottesville: University of Virginia Press, 2012), 282.

75. Stanton, *"Those Who Labor for My Happiness,"* 286; 290; 297–99.

76. Stanton, *"Those Who Labor for My Happiness,"* 282.

77. Peggy Trotter Dammond Preaceley, "It Was Simply in My Blood," in *Hands on the Freedom Plow: Personal Accounts by Women in SNCC,* ed. Faith S. Holsaert, Martha Prescod Norman Noonan, Judy Richardson, Betty Garman Robinson, Jean Smith Young, and Dorothy M. Zellner (Urbana: University of Illinois Press, 2010), 163–72.

78. Rev. Martin Luther King Jr. "I Have a Dream," August 28, 1963. See full text at https://www.npr.org/2010/01/18/122701268/i-have-a-dream-speech-in-its-entirety/.

79. See Annette Gordon-Reed's interview with Velma Williams in "Monticello Virtual Independence Day Commemoration," July 4, 2020, *Thomas Jefferson's Monticello,* https://www.youtube.com/watch?v=_MRN1HzYlBg.

80. Ralph Ellison, "Commencement Address at the College of William & Mary," in *The Collected Essays of Ralph Ellison,* ed. John F. Callahan (New York: Random House, 1995), 415.

81. Ellison, "Commencement Address," 416.

82. Stanton, "Request for Funding" (grant proposal, International Center for Jefferson Studies, 1993), 1.

83. *Getting Word: The Newsletter* 1, no. 1 (1997): 1.

84. Lucia Stanton and Dianne Swann-Wright, "Bonds of Memory: Identity and the Hemings Family," in Stanton, *"Those Who Labor for My Happiness,"* 249–50.

85. Daryl Royster Alexander, "Looking Beyond Jefferson the Icon to a Man and His Slave Mistress," *New York Times,* June 29, 1997.

86. Christina Sharpe, interview by Siddhartha Mitter, "What Does It Mean to Be Black and Look at This?" *Hyperallergic,* March 24, 2017, https://hyperallergic.com/368012/what-does-it-mean-to-be-black-and-look-at-this-a-scholar-reflects-on-the-dana-schutz-controversy/.

Joining in the "Sacred Sentiment of Public Gratitude" at the Death of Old Hickory

MOURNING, PARTISANSHIP, AND
ANDREW JACKSON'S PROBLEMATIC LEGACY

Todd Estes

W HEN DEATH CAME FOR Andrew Jackson in the spring of 1845, he had spent his final weeks sending and receiving correspondence, summoning clergy, and seeing friends and family. His affairs in order, his final obligations met, Jackson waited for the end, which came peacefully on Sunday evening June 8, 1845, the aged hero breathing gently until the life went out of his body. Two days later, his funeral at The Hermitage drew 3,000 people including friends, neighbors, and former soldiers who paid their respects. The word spread quickly across the nation, and tributes and memorials to the former president were joined over the following weeks by sermons and eulogies as Americans bid farewell to the man who, at seventy-eight years old, was "older even than the nation."[1]

Jackson's death and the mourning rituals it inspired must be understood within the context of American attitudes about death and the meaning of mourning culture in the nineteenth century. In an era when life expectancy could be short, infant mortality high, and the casualties of warfare prevalent even before the carnage of the Civil War, death was a familiar companion. Americans sought "the good death"—at home, surrounded by family and close friends, with comfort being drawn from religious faith and the welcome expectation of being reunited with departed loved ones in heaven. A rich and varied set of customs dictated the funeral services, the burial, the cemeteries, and the mourning clothes and practices Americans utilized to commemorate the lives of loved ones. Death, and the routines it required, were a regular part of life for Americans in the nineteenth century.[2]

Steeped in these cultural traditions—and re-creating the rituals they had used to mourn George Washington, John Adams, Thomas Jefferson, and William Henry Harrison—Americans in the months after Jackson's death honored their fallen leader with eulogies and ceremonies for a beloved general and president. The addresses praised Jackson for his character, his accomplishments, and his significance to the nation. Twenty-four of them were collected and published the following year as *Monument to the Memory of General Andrew Jackson*, a book edited by Benjamin M. Dusenbery, whose title reflected the goal of the publication. The eulogies were drawn from across the country including Washington City and twelve different states: Pennsylvania, New York, New Hampshire, and Massachusetts in the East; Maryland, Virginia, Tennessee, Mississippi, and Georgia in the South; and Ohio, Kentucky, and Indiana in the Midwest. While the addresses in *Monument* are, unsurprisingly, all favorable to Jackson and were generally delivered by local elites, the volume has been widely noted as a definitive and representative collection. Scholars such as Arthur M. Schlesinger and John William Ward have drawn on Dusenbery for their classic works on Jackson; more recently, Andrew Burstein and Matthew Warshauer have done the same for their studies of the way Americans mourned Jackson. Furthermore, several of the eulogies gathered in this book were known to audiences in other locations during the mourning period, presumably through newspaper accounts, meaning that they reached a broader audience after their original delivery. Thus, this collection provides an excellent representation of the sentiments many audiences across the nation heard at these commemorations.[3]

These eulogies were delivered as a keynote event of local memorials and commemorations held that summer. These events, documented in local newspaper accounts that were reprinted in publications in other states, often featured processions of military veterans including some of Jackson's former soldiers, prominent citizens, representatives of different professions and laborers grouped by trades, bands marching and playing solemn music and more. Some of these commemorations—which lasted for hours, included thousands of participants in larger towns and cities, and featured lots of local variations—are profiled in this chapter in conjunction with the eulogy spoken at that town to provide a clearer understanding of the mourning rituals in which these addresses played a prominent role.

The memorials collected in *Monument* exhibit many similarities. Jackson's eulogists reviewed his life and career from a boyhood encounter with British soldiers during the Revolutionary War, to his victory at the Battle of New Orleans, his combat with Native Americans, and finally his political rise in Tennessee and Washington. They connected him to past greats and elevated him into the pantheon of national heroes. They also tried, to varying degrees, to justify or explain away the controversies they inevitably recounted, for the one thread that ran through Jackson's entire life was his penchant for taking actions that were both controversial and polarizing. Personally, Jackson fought many duels and killed a rival, engaged in slave trading, and abused his power as a military commander by executing prisoners and exceeding orders. As president, Jackson pursued Indian removal, attacked the South Carolina nullifiers and the Second Bank of the United States, and was quick to turn to violence in most matters. Some of the eulogists skipped quickly through such episodes; others dug in and defended his record. But nearly all of them seemed aware that eulogizing Andrew Jackson posed challenges not faced by those who eulogized earlier national greats. Despite the efforts to celebrate Jackson as a hero to all—as a mythical figure on par with George Washington—even his most devoted eulogists struggled.[4]

There was another difficulty. As Matthew Warshauer has demonstrated, the "partisan warfare" and "ferocious partisanship" of the second party system in 1845 spoiled any hopes Democrats might have had about the nation setting aside politics to mourn with their erstwhile foes. Warshauer shows that some Whig newspapers and activists did the opposite: they attacked Jackson in death the way they had when he was alive, underscoring the intensity of partisanship. Likewise, Andrew Burstein states bluntly, "As a prophet of national harmony Jackson failed because . . . his partisan identity could never be shed."[5] The chief problem for eulogists then was that Jackson remained a divisive figure just as he had been a polarizing presence in national politics. His life and legacy still divided a nation that itself was steeped in political disputation and awash in decades of fierce party battles and partisanship in which Jackson had taken center stage.[6] At his death, that bitterness could not be wished away. So, the task of the eulogist in 1845 was complicated and frustrated by Jackson's life of personal controversy and party strife.

But with the levels of partisanship so high, the question becomes how did the orators deal with this fact? Did they ignore it in their addresses? Did they try to deny it? Or did they explain its meaning for Jackson's legacy? The eulogies contained in *Monument* reveal significant differences in the ways that orators grappled with the reality of the rampant partisan spirit at the time of Jackson's death. While Warshauer's and Burstein's observations concerning the dominance of partisanship remain valid, the Dusenbery eulogies reveal several fine yet meaningful distinctions that have not been previously examined.

These memorials for Jackson can be divided into three categories. The first type tried to separate Jackson altogether from the partisanship of the period and argued that he had always been greater than any partisan affiliation; these eulogies celebrated him as a figure whose presidency, like his military achievements, was but one of the many duties he undertook for his country. Thus, having been a giant who towered above his fellow citizens, Jackson transcended party labels. Orators praised him as an American hero, not as a creature of party. A second type of eulogy acknowledged that Jackson had been a fierce partisan during his political career, and that his party identity continued to shape how people saw him even after leaving the presidency. But these eulogists now claimed that partisanship ended with his death. In death, they said, Jackson shed his political identity and could now be mourned simply as a national hero. But a third type of eulogy was the most honest. These memorials conceded that because Jackson had long been a full-throated partisan and party feelings still ran at fever pitch in 1845, only the passage of time would enable Jackson to be judged fairly; only when the partisan views of his era had faded would posterity get a true fix on the seventh president and elevate him then beyond politics to the honored status of national hero.[7]

All three categories share an important context: each was shaped by a different reaction to the persistence of partisanship. Each type, in its own manner, sheds light on the intractability of these party passions at the time of Jackson's death and reveals subtle distinctions in the ways their speakers presented the issue for their audience. Collectively, they reveal how Jackson eulogists were divided in the ways they understood—and expressed—the meaning and implications of his controversial life and problematic legacy.

Many of the eulogies in this first category linked Andrew Jackson to the American Revolution, as well as George Washington and other prominent founders.[8] For these speakers, the case for Jackson was clinched. He was already in the pantheon of American greats, a verdict presented as if unanimous from a grateful and grieving nation. Matthew Hall McAllister, a Democrat and former mayor of Savannah, Georgia, exemplified this approach when he mourned the "last great relic of the Revolution is no more." In a review of Jackson's life story, McAllister compared him to Washington in that both men served their country in the military, stepped away, and then were called back into service. The eulogist declined "on an occasion like the present, to discuss parties or their measures," but praised Jackson for his strong record of acting within the Constitution and opposing monopoly. The event marked by his speech, McAllister observed, "is but a single note in the national requiem. The whole country will cherish him . . . and the character of Andrew Jackson, shall be viewed by those who come after us, as land-marks in the waste of the past to connect it with their love, gratitude, and admiration!"[9]

Eulogists in this category either downplayed or omitted Jackson's record of political controversies. Former Ohio congressman William Irvin, a Democrat who also served as Speaker of the state house of representatives, offered his Lancaster, Ohio, audience a lengthy, thoughtful, and somewhat unusual address that presented a nonpolitical assessment of Jackson's presidency. He stressed Jackson's patriotism and made a clear if unstated comparison between Jackson and Washington as men who served the country as generals and then later answered the nation's call to serve in public office. Irvin also linked Jackson to Jefferson, noting that "both had an unwavering and abiding confidence in the people." While Irvin avoided mention of specifics, he praised Jackson as president for his "veneration" of the Union and claimed, "When he retired from the presidential chair . . . it was with a reputation as a statesman, equal, if not superior to that he enjoyed as a warrior." Irvin closed with a recounting of Jackson's deathbed scene, saying, "Thus died the greatest man of his age."[10]

The Reverend D. D. Lore of Pottsville, Pennsylvania, provided a simpler, almost apolitical tribute. First, he discussed the art of the eulogy, noting that eulogies were "intimately connected with republican institutions . . . tributes paid by a brave and free people, to worth, to wisdom, and to virtue.

They are," Lore intoned, "in a word, republican monuments," thus providing a basis for the title of Dusenbery's eulogy collection. Lore traced Jackson's life and presented a factual overview of his political accomplishments. His address assumed that Jackson would ascend to that highest level of hero status and made no mention of any conflicts that arose during his military and political careers. He linked Jackson to Washington and hailed him as a fit model to be cherished and emulated.[11]

Pennsylvania's Democratic governor Francis Shunk took a similar tack in his eulogy at Harrisburg, giving a detailed review of Jackson's presidency and its key issues. He also linked Jackson to the country's founders, stating that "the man whose death we have assembled to commemorate [had] . . . a career of usefulness, of heroism, and of devotion to his country, which give him a rank with the great men who founded the nation." Shunk defended Jackson, telling listeners to disregard "the voice of accusation" coming alongside the "plaudits of his countrymen." Shunk even reframed Jackson's well-known stubbornness as a political virtue. When Jackson believed he was right, as in the Bank War, "he advanced in the course he had prescribed for himself with unfaltering and uncompromising decision, until his object was accomplished." Ultimately, Shunk suggested, Jackson's true greatness would be revealed by his influence on "the future destiny of the country. The American government and the American people are invested with the glory of his triumphs."[12]

Some orators made the Jackson-Washington connection by focusing more on military exploits. Wilson McCandless, a Pennsylvania Democrat and judge, spun a highly romanticized comparison of the two men for his Pittsburgh audience that dwelt at length on Jackson's great battlefield exploits, primarily at New Orleans. He did not elide Jackson's controversial contests with the Creek Indians in Florida but rather defended his actions and motives. That Jackson's military glory led to political honors was natural, McCandless observed. "To the victor was awarded a nation's blessing. . . . Idolized by the people whose city he had saved; cheered by the huzzas of the multitude wherever he went." His soldiers were devoted to him and defended him against critics. So, too, were the many around the country who sought to reward him with political office. "The Union never had a warmer or more attached friend," McCandless noted, presenting Jackson's values exactly as he himself would have wanted them stated.[13]

John Van Buren, the attorney general of New York and son of Jackson's vice president and successor, delivered an address in Albany on June 30 following a lengthy procession.[14] Known as a dynamic speaker, Van Buren told his audience that the country was undergoing "*a national mourning for a nation's loss,*" which was only fitting since Jackson has, he said, "in an unsurpassed degree, engrossed the public attention for the last thirty years." Van Buren stated that Jackson's most distinguished characteristic was his "irresistible energy," and then made an unusual comparison linking the late president to Napoleon. Both men had some of the same ambition and energy, although Jackson put his talents and actions to work only for his nation whereas Napoleon aimed at conquest and failed. In contrast, "Jackson drew his sword only at his country's call; it was never wielded but in defence of her soil, her rights, and liberties." Van Buren closed with a prediction: in fifty years' time much will have changed but "the fame of him we now honour will be perpetuated in song and in story."[15]

The New York City commemoration of Jackson on June 24 may have been the largest in the nation. Church bells rang all day, an artillery corps fired seventy-eight times at noon to mark Jackson's age, and a procession of numerous military, civic, professional, voluntary, and tradesmen's organizations was so vast that it took three hours to pass by a given point. The entirety of the day's events lasted six hours.[16]

Capping the day was a eulogy by Benjamin F. Butler, a New Yorker who served as US attorney general for both Jackson and Martin Van Buren. His eulogy was pointed and partisan, defending Jackson's record and reviewing his life in a manner that was detailed and forceful, more like a campaign speech than a eulogy. His enunciation of Jackson's Seminole War record read like a brief for the defense. Butler did not shy away from the political controversies of Jackson's career—as some eulogists in this category did—but he added a bit of spin as he recounted the tales. In Butler's telling, Jackson was drawn into "violent collisions with the interests, passions, and prejudices of men in different quarters of the union." Jackson reacted to such provocations forcefully, because he was driven by "the love of democratic liberty, and filled with the zeal for the constitution." Yet Butler's eulogy was also animated by a persistent linkage of Jackson to Washington. Butler connected not only the two men but also their homes at Mount Vernon and The

Hermitage: "embosomed in a sacred solitude, stands the tomb of the Hermitage,—henceforth to divide with Mount Vernon the respect, the admiration, and the reverence of mankind."[17]

Perhaps the most eloquent of the eulogies in this first category was delivered in Charlotte, Tennessee, by J. G. Harris, a newspaperman, Navy Department official, and strong backer of Jackson and James K. Polk. "He is gone.
He sleeps with his fathers. . . . The American people knew him, and without his solicitation they repeatedly heaped upon him their highest honors,"
said Harris, recounting a series of responsibilities and honors afforded him.
"His entire life is a striking example of the rich rewards which sooner or later
unfailingly crown patriotic deeds," Harris noted. Jackson was to the American nation and people "as the sun to the mariner," and Harris suggested
why. "Instead of compelling the masses of the people to coincide with him,
he foresaw their inclination, and coincided with them as their champion,"
he observed, yet Jackson admittedly took such stands forcefully: "Andrew
Jackson never occupied a doubtful position upon any question. . . . In his
vocabulary, the words 'temporize' and 'expediency,' were not to be found."
Harris cast Jackson's decisive leadership as in line with American national
destiny: "Born in the East, he sleeps in the West—the defender of the South,
the champion of the North." Harris cemented the connection between Jackson and Washington, immediately putting the seventh president on a pedestal with the first. "Like the Father of his country, he descended to the grave
loaded, with all the civil and military honours of his countrymen. . . . An
admiring posterity shall make frequent pilgrimages to Mount Vernon in the
East, and the Hermitage in the West . . . to commune with the spirits of the
immortal Washington and Jackson."[18]

In short, the speakers in this first category delivered eulogies that suggested that Jackson already belonged in the pantheon of American heroes.
Their addresses focused on Jackson's life, his heroic exploits and virtues, and
the mutual love between him and the American people. The party passions
of his day, the contentious business of his life, were passed over quickly and
the deification of Jackson, reinforced by linking him with Washington, was
presented as undisputed and indisputable.

A second category of eulogies in the *Monument* volume were more transparent about the tensions of the day yet nonetheless argued that while

Jackson had been at the mercy of political disputes that affected his reputation while living, he had now, in death, moved beyond the voices of contentious partisanship and party passions. In some ways, this was the reason for publishing the volume. The compiler, Benjamin M. Dusenbery, attached a preface to the collection that articulated its goal of creating "a permanent literary MONUMENT TO THE MEMORY OF JACKSON," whose life, Dusenbery stated, "is full of instruction for the people," and it was the people who had elevated Jackson to his public offices. "No public man ever appealed so frequently and boldly to the people for support in his public acts," he wrote. But politics often interfered. "Party spirit, of course, misrepresented his character and actions, while he was at the head of affairs; but the moment he resigned the reins of government, his merit and ability were almost universally acknowledged; and when death had set the seal of immortality upon his name, it was unhesitatingly enrolled among the great and good of all ages." Dusenbery announced with approval that the addresses in the volume "speak one language—that of unqualified eulogy."[19]

These were stirring sentiments and no doubt the way Dusenbery and other Jacksonians understood their project. So, this second type of eulogy argued that if Jackson had been a deeply divisive figure during his lifetime, his death ended that partisan strife and all Americans now saw him as a national hero, alongside George Washington, Benjamin Franklin, and Thomas Jefferson, who were also beyond partisanship and political passions. His death had made Jackson an immortal hero for all, not the captive of any political party.

Ellis Lewis in Lancaster, Pennsylvania, exemplified this approach. He began by noting that "The voice of party . . . is again stilled to give place, in the hour of death, to the tolling bell—the funeral gun, and the wailing voice of a sorrowing nation." He reviewed Jackson's life and career, approving of his partisan stance in the war on the Bank of the United States. Lewis claimed that his presidency continued his "contest[s] for his country." Lewis cast Jackson's political battles in exactly these terms. "His death," Lewis concluded, "has opened the way to a just decision upon his life. The scythe of time is removing obstructions, and his hour-glass is rapidly measuring out the period when history shall do justice to the life and character of ANDREW JACKSON."[20]

One of Jackson's most prominent eulogists was Levi Woodbury of New Hampshire, who served him as both secretary of the navy and secretary of the treasury and was appointed to the Supreme Court by President James K. Polk in 1845. Speaking at the Universalist Church in Portsmouth, New Hampshire, two days before the Fourth of July and two months before becoming an associate justice, Woodbury cast the late president's life as a coming-of-age story that revealed Jackson's growth over time. In fact, "his whole life may be considered as spent in a practical school of politics; the intervals devoted to arms being brief and rare, and often mingled somewhat with the political agitations of the day." He called the seventh president almost a providential gift to the nation, joined with "the Washingtons and Jacksons, the Jeffersons and Franklins, that crowd the bright galaxy of our history." But Woodbury knew that partisan passions still ran high. Now, however, "the curtain of life has fallen . . . it is time that the prejudices of party should soften. The death of so much greatness and glory . . . should induce human charity to revise any harsh opinions formed under circumstances less auspicious." Death should quell party passions and end the practice of seeing Jackson through the lens of party politics.[21]

Pride of place in *Monument* belonged to George Bancroft—historian, statesman, Navy secretary in 1845 and soon to be minister to the United Kingdom. President Polk invited him to give the primary eulogy at the US Capitol to pay tribute to Jackson, a man Bancroft deeply admired. His oration was a soaring work, "sparse in detail and broad in conception," as a Bancroft biographer noted.[22] Bancroft portrayed Jackson as a brave young prodigy who conquered the wilderness and furthered the push to the frontiers, evoking the spirit later captured so well by the scholar John William Ward in his iconic work on Jackson.[23]

Bancroft's eulogy touched the litany of themes and tropes covered by other speakers: He linked Jackson to Washington and the Revolution; invoked the coming-of-age metaphor; stated how offices and honors sought Jackson, not the reverse; stressed his strong and mutually felt connection to the nation's working people; reiterated his devotion to the Union; and reassured listeners that Jackson experienced "a good death," peacefully, among friends and family at his home. In an account of his political views and accomplishments, Bancroft airbrushed the bitter partisan divisions that those views created or exacerbated. Central to his story of Jackson's presidency was his fierce battle with the Bank. In fact, he noted that Jackson "came to the presidency . . . resolved to deliver the government from the Bank of the United States, and to restore the regulation of exchanges to the rightful depository of that power—the commerce of the country." While the Bank War was a bitterly partisan contest, in Bancroft's skilled hands Jackson's struggles were clear, straightforward, and pursued as a matter of course.[24]

Bancroft struck the theme of a life well lived and a death met with honor and courage. "Behold the warrior and statesman, his work well done, retired to the Hermitage, to hold converse with his forests, to cultivate his farm, to gather around him hospitably his friends! Who was like HIM? He was still the loadstar of the American people." At the end of his life, "while his affections were still for his friends and his country, his thoughts were already in a better world." Americans should know, too, Bancroft said, "that Andrew Jackson had faith in the eternity of truth, in the imperishable power of popular freedom." By the time he was finished, Bancroft had elevated Jackson into immortality. Jackson had "conquered everywhere in statesmanship; and when death came to get the master over him, he . . . escaped from earth in the triumphant consciousness of immortality." Jackson's spirit "rests upon our whole territory." Now, in death, "The fires of party spirit are quenched at his grave." Bancroft—both a participant in, and a chronicler of, the politics of the Jacksonian era—could not deny that party passions had affected the views of Americans toward their former president. But now those passions had finally been stamped out: "Whatever of good he has done, lives, and will live for ever."[25]

If Bancroft's powerful message exemplified the thesis of the second type of eulogies, the third category of eulogists were the most realistic about the effects of partisanship. While no less effusive in praising Jackson and upholding his accomplishments, the orators in this group denied that the intensity of party passions had vanished at Jackson's death and that the whole nation now embraced him as a great hero. The speakers in this third category shared the plain truth: Much as they and their audiences might admire him, Jackson had been a fierce partisan himself and still stirred up party intensity. Political passions remained so high following his death that it would require the passage of time before Jackson could be fairly judged by posterity.

Virginia's Andrew Stevenson, former Democratic Speaker of the US House of Representatives during the Jackson presidency, presented a thoughtful eulogy to a Richmond audience that reviewed the late president's career. While "not a man of great learning and genius," Jackson nonetheless possessed "a common sense, a discretion and prudence . . . without which, knowledge was useless, and genius contemptible." Stevenson noted the fierce political opposition he drew but said "this hostility was to be expected, and must therefore be regarded as the result of party feeling . . . rather than the evidence of deliberate and candid judgment." The ultimate judgment of Jackson's decisions and actions would be left to "time and experience," suggesting that at present—"even when uninfluenced by party feelings"—some partisans might lack the capacity to take Jackson's measure. Ultimately, "With respect to his administration, it is, perhaps, impossible, at the present moment, to make up an impartial opinion. . . . It is not the time for calm and deliberate judgment in relation to those troubled scenes." But, Stevenson ventured, "when the angry passions shall have been allayed; the judgment unwarped by prejudice; the heart no longer embittered with disappointment or revenge," only then would Jackson get his just due.[26]

Pennsylvania's Hendrick B. Wright, a former state legislator and future member of the US House, praised Jackson and the bold, sure-footedness of his decision-making. "With him there was no temporizing policy," just "that peculiar firmness which ever characterized the man on the field amidst the din of arms and the deadly embrace of foes, or in the council hall of his country." Wright further suggested that Jackson was a proper role model for "the young man who is ambitions for durable fame," that his career showed that "true merit" always received its just reward, and that republics honored "men who have served their country faithfully." But Wright's most telling comment came in reference to Jackson's presidency. He could not deny that "some of his measures, while president of the United States, have been and will continue to be subjects of political difference among party men." In other words, the persistent passions of these "party men" kept Jackson from receiving the universal acclaim that Wright believed he deserved upon his death. These partisan divisions would continue, despite what he claimed was the "hearty approval and concurrence of the *whole* American people" of some of his executive measures and actions.[27]

Vice President George M. Dallas offered a variation on the theme of partial or qualified approval for Jackson despite the lingering partisan animosity he still occasioned. Speaking in Philadelphia's Washington Square in late June, Dallas was the honored eulogist at a massive tribute that featured civic and military parades organized by trades, professions, and organizations processing through the city's streets. The heat was fierce that day, leading some members of the various companies of marchers to drop out. But thousands waited and watched from early in the day throughout the tribute, which culminated in Dallas's speech.[28]

Dallas presented a compact oration that touched on many of the standard themes of the Jackson eulogy: the heroic career of "the stripling orphan" dating to his boyhood in the revolutionary struggle, his unceasing devotion to the Union as the core of his political convictions, and his piety even amid his warrior temperament and experience. He would emphasize, Dallas told his audience, "the martial merits of the deceased . . . because these merits are incontestable." He wished he could extend his review of Jackson's merits even further, but since he entertained "a real deference for the sentiments of others," he could not honestly do so. For "[t]he time has not come, and among a free, fearless, and frank people, such as you are, it may possibly never come, when the civic characteristics of Jackson during his chief magistracy of eight years, can be other than topics of sincere differences of opinion." Dallas lamented this fact, but he could not deny it, and his oration revealed the depths of the party passions and the political storms that still raged, engulfing Jackson even after his death.[29]

Thomas L. Smith of Kentucky, publisher of the *Louisville Weekly Democrat*, also told his audience that party spirit affected Jackson's legacy. Smith began by linking Jackson to an older conception of disinterested service to the nation. He stated directly that "General Jackson certainly possessed all the elements of greatness. . . . Yet he never courted offices or honours." He denied that Jackson sought his political positions because "Andrew Jackson was not ambitious, in the ordinary sense of the term." Instead, Smith noted that he "preferred peaceful tranquility, and domestic felicity, in the bosom of his own family, to all the allurements of ambition. Nothing had power to call him forth but necessity," and Jackson always answered these calls of duty. But while he observed that "[m]en of all parties, and of all grades, pursuits and occupations, are united on this occasion" to pay tribute, and that "[a] united people attend as mourners at his funeral," there was not an undivided consensus about the late president. Jackson had unquestionably exercised enormous influence over his countrymen, but "[h]ow much of that influence was beneficial, and how much evil, in its results, has been the subject of violent party contests, and it is, therefore, perhaps, not for the present generation to determine." Rather, he told his audience, "The time has not yet arrived when the country can form a united judgment" regarding Jackson's public life and his presidency. Not until "some future time, when the remembrance of the fierce contests and the interest and passions, which came in collision during the party conflicts of the day shall have passed," will it be possible to reckon fairly. At such time, Smith concluded, "posterity will do him impartial justice and pronounce a proper verdict upon his political course."[30]

Another newspaperman, Indiana's A. F. Morrison, editor of the *State Democrat*, delivered a similar sentiment in his June 26 eulogy given in Indianapolis. This eulogy was given at a major event that had been planned weeks in advance. It involved a procession of townspeople gathered by occupation and organizations including officers and soldiers, Masons, local officials past and present, members of the bar, the city's clergy, the male youth of the city, and a band to perform "appropriate" music throughout. Businesses were closed, church bells rung, and guns fired in salute.[31] The "nation mourns the loss of a cherished and favourite son," Morrison began, and called Jackson "a great, a good, and a wonderful man." As president, when Jackson was "convinced of the correctness of his premises, he faithfully pursued his conclusions. In this consisted the main secret of his overshadowing greatness." But Morrison recognized that the nation's political fractures would continue to color the way Americans viewed Jackson. "The agitating questions which marked his administration, are in some measure, still before the eyes of the nation, and the decisions of some of them are still viewed with different optics. Time and impartial history," he predicted, "will do justice to the prophetic wisdom, the mature, and patriotic labours of his government." At the moment of Jackson's passing, however, "the greatest excitement existed throughout the community, and their influences have scarcely ceased to operate in the minds of the public."[32]

Similarly, Washington McCartney, a mathematics professor at Lafayette College and later a judge, delivered a tightly argued eulogy for Jackson in Easton, Pennsylvania, in late June that contemplated Jackson as a military man, a political leader, and a citizen. But as president, "His administration is too recent to be correctly appreciated" and his record "can be more properly valued when time shall have healed the wounds of party. . . . When time mellows the passions of men, and pure reason sits in judgment upon the illustrious dead, then is pronounced the historical sentence of posterity." McCartney assured his audience that the verdict would be positive because Jackson's life "was animated by the pure spirit of republicanism." But he could not attain this level until the "wounds of party" and the "passions of men" were healed and soothed.[33]

Two additional orations elegantly exemplify this third category of Jacksonian eulogy. Pliny Merrick, a Worcester, Massachusetts, attorney and judge, delivered an address in Boston on July 9 at a large event that featured a band, muffled drums, the ringing of church bells, a procession that took an hour and a half to complete, including twenty-one companies of infantry, "all classes" of men, civic societies, Masons and Odd Fellows, with banners and streamers carried in the throng and displayed on houses and buildings. Stores and businesses suspended their activities and all present demonstrated "solemnity and decorum." The procession ended at historic Faneuil Hall where Merrick delivered what one paper called "one of the most eloquent and beautiful compositions, which the great national bereavement has called out."[34]

Merrick's review of Jackson's presidency was laudatory; he particularly praised his sense of constitutionalism as executive. But he also acknowledged that not all would agree. "It is not to be disguised that his administration was illustrated by a severe and intense opposition," although Merrick acquitted the president against the charges of his critics. Nonetheless, he recognized that even at Jackson's death, eight years out of office, political passions had not yet cooled. "And leaving the heated controversies of the past to the consideration of other times more remote from the ardour of that excitement which may not yet have all been soothed into rest," Merrick assured his large audience that "when the passion that disturbs, the interest that warps, and the prejudice that confounds the judgment, shall no longer interpose their misguiding influences, a grateful people may unite in a common homage of veneration." In short, Merrick believed that Americans would reach a clear, positive outlook on Jackson. But he was shrewd enough, even while delivering a eulogy, not to suggest that such a thing would come to pass any time soon.[35]

One of the longest eulogies in the volume belonged to Hugh Garland and was delivered to a Petersburg, Virginia, audience in mid-July. Garland was a lawyer, a member of the Virginia House of Delegates, and clerk of the US House of Representatives during the Van Buren presidency. The Petersburg commemoration, like so many others, featured a procession of civil and military entities, voluntary associations, and ordinary citizens in carriages and on horseback. Despite the day being "oppressively hot," a large throng participated in the march as the city's businesses suspended operation. The local paper took pride in the good decorum of all, noting "that our Whig friends committed no public act . . . by which it might be known whether they were Whigs or Democrats." Evidently, at least some inhabitants of the city were familiar with some of the prominent eulogies given elsewhere that summer by George Bancroft, Benjamin Butler, Andrew Stevenson, Levi Woodbury, and Benjamin Howard since the paper contended that Garland's speech that day was as impressive of any of those, not only because Garland delivered it without notes, but also because he managed to find new things to say. Garland spoke for an hour and forty-five minutes and the *Petersburg Republican* exclaimed that he commanded "the unbroken attention" of his large audience. "We have yet to meet with the first man who was not gratified at the effort."[36]

Garland's oration resonated with Merrick's and presented Jackson's complicated legacy in the same manner. He profiled Jackson's life as a coming-of-age story for the "poor prisoner boy of Camden." He established a comparison to Washington midway through the address to which he would return at the end. And Garland reviewed Jackson's political career, lingering on what he considered his heroic and courageous assault on the Bank of the United States. Because the memory of the Bank War persisted, "Too much of the prejudice and selfish interests of the times still linger about our feelings, and obscure our judgments. Posterity alone can judge of its importance," he stated.

Next, Garland made a brief aside to ask, "What made him great?" a question answered in part by suggesting that Jackson was "an instrument, in the

hands of God, to work out his purposes among the children of men." After
a bit more of that trope, he closed this section of his eulogy summarily:
"Thus lived, thus died Andrew Jackson; great in war, great in peace, triumphant in death." And in his conclusion, Garland picked up the Washington
comparison again: "Washington was the father of his country. Jackson its
defender and saviour. . . . What Washington began, Jackson finished." However, "he was not allowed to wear in peace, the laurels he had so nobly won.
He, too, was called to administer the affairs of government; and to mingle
in the strife and conflicting interests of party. He, too . . . did many things
to excite opposition—many to awaken the bitterest hostility; and he left the
government with a large portion of his countrymen opposed to the measures of his administration."

But Jackson's fortunes might yet change, Garland believed. "All the men
of his generation, with their passions, their prejudices, and their conflicting
interests, will soon pass away, perish, and be forgotten; then will the character of Jackson stand forth in its just proportions; and posterity, without
reservation or condition will pronounce him second only to Washington in
the hearts of his countrymen. And they two," Garland announced in his final
sentence, "like twin stars in the firmament, undistinguished, undivided, will
shine on from age to age, shedding a glorious lustre on their country." For
Garland, for Merrick, and for the other eulogists in this category, party spirit,
political passions, and partisan tensions were still too high and Jackson's
tumultuous time in office was too recent for a considered verdict on his life
and career.[37]

It is fitting—and perhaps unintentionally revealing—that the *Monument*
volume of eulogies closed with the sermons of two ministers, both preached
on July 5 in Philadelphia but at different churches. George Bethune and
Thomas Brainerd each called for cooling the political passions and toning
down the partisanship. Their appeals were directed to the citizens of the
nation in 1845, urging them to be calm and to "sooth" the passions. Both
sermons said less about Jackson himself, abjuring the standard biographical
review and instead concentrating, appropriately, on Jackson's spiritual life
and his death.

George Bethune, pastor of the Dutch Reformed Church in New York, was
an outspoken Democrat. But his address was a meditation on the character

of a happy nation and the duties of a nation and its citizens to God. After recounting various characteristics, Bethune assured his listeners that "Andrew Jackson is with God" and then offered a context for understanding Jackson's controversial actions. He asked, "Could a character be subjected to censure more merciless, than he provoked by a policy original and unhesitating, at open war with long-established usages, and dogmas that had grown into questioned axioms." It was Jackson's lot, he claimed, while "Compelled to resolve stupendous, unprecedented questions of government and political economy, he roused the hostility of opposite schools in those difficult sciences." Jackson acted boldly; "If he were wrong, public opinion has since adopted the chief of his heresies."

He suggested that present political disputes might resolve in the same way: "Let us . . . while we mourn the conflicts of evil passion, not forget the actual good, which, by the Divine favour, is working out health from the mysterious fermentation." And there was cause for hope, Bethune noted. Despite "occasional agitation, a calm good sense among our people, sufficient to recover and maintain the equilibrium" was appearing. However, he cautioned, "It is not to be seen blustering around the polls; it is not heard vociferating and applauding in party meetings; nor, unhappily, does it often appear on the arena, where misnomered statesmen struggle rather for personal advancement than their country's good." And he closed by recasting the term "party" and moving away from partisanship. He hoped that a "party of the honest and intelligent" might be in the offing. It might be smaller in size, he said, but "it has still the controlling voice from the divisions of the rest."[38]

Thomas Brainerd's sermon echoed many of those themes. Brainerd, who served churches in Cincinnati before spending over thirty years at Philadelphia's Old Pine Street Church, delineated for his audience five elements of "national happiness and prosperity" and then turned to Jackson and the present moment. He admitted that the American Revolution had "demanded the cultivation of the stronger passions—the nourishing of a sense of wrong." But the present time was different. "Now we need the passions to be soothed, lest they break out in violence on ourselves. Now we need to cultivate the intellect, the conscience, and the heart." The "patriot now is fulfilled, by the exhibition of an example of industry, temperance, self-control, of warm domestic affections, and love of public order in subjection to the laws of God and man." He granted that Jackson had not always mastered his own passions, for "his defects were as open as his virtues," and he mixed the capacity and energy for doing great good with an occasional tendency to give in to "precipitation, violence, and obstinacy." However, Brainerd lamented, "We cannot have the strength of the wind to swell our sails without a liability to tempests—nor the warmth of fire without danger of conflagration. So, neither can we find in man great abilities and energy for good, without corresponding infelicities. To this our great Washington alone seems to have been an exception. It is enough to excite our best feelings in view of the death of Jackson," Brainerd reflected, "if we can *all* say—as I believe we can—that in spite of the defects, moral or political, imputed to him, he had a lofty patriotism—a large, honest, and brave heart, and the ends 'he aimed at were his country's.'"[39]

Bethune and Brainerd had every reason to be troubled by the intensity of partisanship, sparked anew rather than being subdued by Jackson's death and mourning rituals. These ministers were merely responding to unfolding tensions and rising anger in the nation at the time. A year after Jackson's death, his protégé James K. Polk launched a war against Mexico fought largely to advance the interests of the South and the spread of slavery. This act exploded simmering sectional tensions and animosities, added those to the already corrosive partisan feelings of the day, and further inflamed a divided nation. Historians Joanne Freeman, Stephen Maizlish, and Heather Cox Richardson and others have documented the acceleration of political violence in the newspapers, the streets, and the floor of the House and Senate and the war that came soon after.[40]

It was upon Jackson's indelible connection to this coming violence—along with his fierce partisanship—that his deification ran aground. After all, his career, actions, and policies did much to contribute to the rising animosity and violence in the nation. Andrew Burstein has argued persuasively that this element complicated Jackson's linkage to his predecessors "in the great cosmology that the eulogists of the founders had constructed." George Washington, he suggests, "received a singular kind of adoration, for he had singularly bequeathed a future to his nation in his farewell address." Thomas Jefferson and John Adams, forever linked by their mutual deaths on July 4th, "gave America its voice[;] . . . their definition of liberty was the catechism of the national creed." Jackson was upheld as the chronological successor, "the first apostle of those who preceded him, especially Washington; but here the cosmology crumbled. As a prophet of national harmony," Burstein writes, "Jackson failed because, unlike Adams and Jefferson, his partisan identity could never be shed." Jackson's patriotism "was consumed by other, less ethereal attributes in the historic memory. He was too bloodthirsty to be remembered as the eulogists wished."[41]

Some of the Americans who gathered in 1845 to commemorate and mourn Andrew Jackson seemed to know even then that his legacy would be problematic. Was the third set of eulogists like Morrison, Merrick, and Garland correct that the passage of time would cool the passions and result in an unbiased evaluation of their hero? In the short run, the answer was yes. In the years following the Civil War, Jackson was celebrated for his strong defense of the Union in the Nullification Crisis. By the first half of the twentieth century, Jackson had reached an apotheosis. The Democratic Party's annual dinners commemorated "Jefferson-Jackson Day"; his visage adorned the twenty-dollar-bill starting in 1928, one century after his election as president. Historians grouped his presidency as an indispensable link between Thomas Jefferson and Franklin D. Roosevelt, a crucial part of a long populist and popular Democratic tradition. Arthur Schlesinger's *The Age of Jackson* won the Pulitzer Prize for 1945 and a decade later John William Ward's *Andrew Jackson—Symbol for an Age* became a canonical work in American Studies. Both books cemented Jackson firmly in the pantheon of national greats as a champion of liberty, democracy, and union.[42]

But the past half century has seen Jackson's reputation take a precipitous tumble, mirroring in many ways (and for many of the same reasons) Thomas Jefferson's declining reputation. First, many post-Schlesinger historians demolished the premise that Jacksonian America had been a great age of the common man or an era of robust democracy. Increasingly, and accelerating in the twenty-first century, scholars and others have emphasized the decidedly dark side of the man and his policies: Indian removal; the spread of slavery, racism, white nationalism, settler colonialism; and a relentless western expansionism that intensified all these developments. Recent historical treatments have been harsh. Jackson's own personal history as a violent, racist, southern slaveowner has become the defining interpretation of his life and presidency, supplanting the previous view of him as a champion for ordinary Americans doing battle on their behalf against powerful economic and political elites. Even his political party has distanced itself. The Jefferson-Jackson Day dinners have been renamed by many state and local Democratic party organizations since both the honorees have become embarrassing to modern-day party leaders and rank-and-file members. Public pressure has built recently to replace Jackson with Harriet Tubman on the twenty-dollar bill and to remove the Jackson statue in Lafayette Park in Washington, DC. And the symbolic embrace of Jackson by the forty-fifth president has only seemed to hasten the expressions of disapproval of the seventh president.[43]

Andrew Jackson's reputation and legacy have already undergone several swings of the pendulum. If his image could not have been higher in the 1950s, today it seems to be at its nadir. Like so many historical figures, Jackson's complicated legacy has produced peaks and valleys in the years since his death. His most realistic eulogists—those who grasped something of this mixed record and its effect on reactions to him in 1845—have been only half right. He did escape the narrow bounds of Democratic-Whig partisanship but not forever. Jackson's profound blemishes in personality and policy have proved just as controversial in our time as in his. Virulent partisanship and cascading violence defined and roiled the nation in the middle of the nineteenth century just as they still shape it into the twenty-first century. Jackson remains lastingly identified with the nation's record of violence and partisanship. Those traits were not, and are not, how most Americans like to see themselves nor think about the country they have created. But Jackson's legacy has suffered from offering a distressing and accurate mirror of his nation and his era with the troubling reflections visible still down to the present.

Notes

1. Jon Meacham, *American Lion: Andrew Jackson in the White House* (New York: Random House, 2008), 343–47; Robert V. Remini, *Andrew Jackson and the Course of American Democracy, 1833–1845* (New York: Harper & Row, 1984), 520–26; Mark R. Cheathem, *Andrew Jackson, Southerner* (Baton Rouge: Louisiana State University Press, 2013), 200–205.

2. Drew Gilpin Faust, *This Republic of Suffering: Death and the American Civil War* (New York: Vintage Books, 2008); Mark S. Schantz, *Awaiting the Heavenly Country: The Civil War and America's Culture of Death* (Ithaca, NY: Cornell University Press, 2008). See also the essays in Nancy Isenberg and Andrew Burstein, eds., *Mortal Remains: Death in Early America* (Philadelphia: University of Pennsylvania Press, 2003). See also Thomas Lynch, *The Undertaking: Life Studies from the Dismal Trade* (New York: W. W. Norton, 1997); and Thomas Lynch, *Bodies in Motion and At Rest: On Metaphor and Mortality* (New York: W. W. Norton, 2000).

3. I am indebted to David C. Hendrickson of Colorado College for alerting me to this collection. The Dusenbery collection is available at https://ia600200.us.archive.org/14 /items/monumenttomemor02dusegoog/monumenttomemor02dusegoog.pdf.

4. Gerald E. Kahler, *The Long Farewell: Americans Mourn the Death of George Washington* (Charlottesville: University of Virginia Press, 2008); Matthew Costello, *The Property of the Nation: George Washington's Tomb, Mount Vernon, and the Memory of the First President* (Lawrence: University Press of Kansas, 2019).

5. Matthew Warshauer, "Ridiculing the Dead: Andrew Jackson and Connecticut Newspapers," *Connecticut History* 40 (Spring 2001): 13–31; Matthew Warshauer, "Contested Mourning: The New York Battle over Andrew Jackson's Death," *New York History* 87 (Winter 2006): 28–65. Andrew Burstein, "Immortalizing the Founding Fathers: The Excesses of Public Eulogy," in *Mortal Remains: Death in Early America*, ed. Isenberg and Burstein, 91–107.

6. For examples of key treatments since the 1950s see Charles Grier Sellers Jr., "Andrew Jackson versus the Historians," *Mississippi Valley Historical Review* 44 (1958): 615–34; Ronald P. Formisano, "Toward a Reorientation of Jacksonian Politics: A Review of the Literature, 1959–1975," *Journal of American History* 63 (1976): 42–65; Edward Pessen, "We Are All Jeffersonians, We Are All Jacksonians: Or a Pox on Stultifying Periodizations," *Journal of the Early Republic* 1 (1981): 1–26; Sean Wilentz, "On Class and Politics in Jacksonian America," *Reviews in American History* 10 (1982): 45–63; Daniel Feller, "Politics and Society: Toward a Jacksonian Synthesis," *Journal of the Early Republic* 10 (1990): 135–61; Jonathan Atkins, "The Jacksonian Era, 1825–1844," in *A Companion to 19th-Century America*, ed. William L. Barney (Malden, MA: Blackwell, 2001), 19–32; and, most recently, Todd Estes, "Beyond Whigs and Democrats: Historians, Historiography, and the Paths toward a New Synthesis for the Jacksonian Era," *American Nineteenth-Century History* 21, no. 3 (2020): 255–81.

7. Burstein, "Immortalizing the Founding Fathers," 91–107.

8. Stephanie Kaye Lawton, "Substance or Window-Dressing? Classical Conceptions of Patriotic Citizenship in the Eulogies of George Washington and Andrew Jackson" (M.A. thesis, University of Virginia, 2016), 30–48.

9. *Monument*, 118–132. "The Political Graveyard: A Database of American History," https://politicalgraveyard.com/index.html.

10. *Monument*, 306–15.

11. *Monument*, 333–42.

12. *Monument*, 144–54.

13. *Monument*, 108–17.

14. For some details, see the *Albany [NY] Evening Atlas*, July 1, 1845; Warshauer, "Contested Mourning," 53.

15. *Monument*, 96–107. See also Jonathan Earle, *Jacksonian Antislavery and the Politics of Free Soil, 1824–1854* (Chapel Hill: University of North Carolina Press, 2004), 167.

16. For details on the New York events see "The Grand Funeral Obsequies of General Jackson," *New York Herald*, June 25, 1845; Warshauer, "Contested Mourning," 54–59; Remini, *Andrew Jackson and the Course of American Democracy*, 527–29.

17. *Monument*, 59–69.

18. *Monument*, 316–32.

19. *Monument*, iii–v.

20. *Monument*, 155–66. Lewis was an attorney and judge, served as state attorney general in 1833, and later, from 1854 to 1857, as chief justice of the Pennsylvania State Supreme Court.

21. *Monument*, 70–86. Woodbury was one of only three Americans to serve in all three branches of government and also as governor of a state (Salmon P. Chase and James F. Byrnes being the others).

22. See Lilian Handlin, *George Bancroft: The Intellectual as Democrat* (New York: Harper & Row, 1984), 210.

23. See John William Ward, *Andrew Jackson: Symbol for an Age* (New York: Oxford University Press, 1953).

24. *Monument*, 33–51.

25. *Monument*, 48–51. Handlin, *George Bancroft*, 210–11, 382n33. Russel B. Nye, *George Bancroft, Brahmin Rebel* (New York: Alfred A. Knopf, 1945), 149–50.

26. *Monument*, 249–271. Stevenson also served as Speaker of the Virginia State House of Delegates and then served in the US House from 1821 to 1834, the last seven as Speaker. He later became US minister to Great Britain under Martin Van Buren.

27. *Monument*, 235–248.

28. *United States Gazette* [Philadelphia], June 23, 24, 26, 1845.

29. *Monument*, 52–58. Dallas's eulogy also provides, in its closing line, part of the title for my chapter: "To all of us it will be some relief to join in the simple and sacred sentiment of public gratitude" (58).

30. *Monument*, 272–79.

31. *Indiana State Sentinel* [Indianapolis], June 19, July 2, 1845. My thanks to Matthew Costello for alerting me to the existence this citation.

32. *Monument*, 133–43.

33. *Monument*, 280–91.

34. *Pittsfield [MA] Sun*, July 17, 1845.

35. *Monument*, 167–82.

36. The Petersburg memorial was reported in the *Richmond [VA] Enquirer*, July 18, 1845.

37. *Monument*, 183–211. The *Albany [NY] Argus* wrote that "Soon, history, divested of the passions and interest with which he came in conflict, will do him justice, and all honor" (June 18, 1845). The same day's *New York Herald* commented, "After the partisan passions and prejudices of the present generation shall have ceased to operate, posterity will pronounce a just and united judgment" (June 18, 1845). Both quoted in Matthew Warshauer, "Andrew Jackson and the Legacy of the Battle of New Orleans,"

in *A Companion to the Era of Andrew Jackson,* ed. Sean Patrick Adams (Malden, MA: Wiley-Blackwell, 2013), 81.

38. *Monument,* 343–55.

39. *Monument,* 356–69.

40. Joanne B. Freeman, *The Field of Blood: Violence in Congress and the Road to Civil War* (New York: Farrar, Straus and Giroux, 2018); Stephen E. Maizlish, *A Strife of Tongues: The Compromise of 1850 and the Ideological Foundations of the American Civil War* (Charlottesville: University of Virginia, 2018); Heather Cox Richardson, *How the South Won the Civil War: Oligarchy, Democracy, and the Continuing Fight for the Soul of America* (New York: Oxford University Press, 2020).

41. Burstein, "Immortalizing the Founding Fathers," 105–6. Andrew Burstein, *The Passions of Andrew Jackson* (New York: Vintage Books, 2003). See also J. M. Opal, *Avenging the People: Andrew Jackson, The Rule of Law, and the American Nation* (New York: Oxford University Press, 2017). Nathaniel C. Green, *The Man of the People: Political Dissent and the Making of the American Presidency* (Lawrence: University Press of Kansas, 2020), 249–82.

42. Arthur M. Schlesinger Jr., *The Age of Jackson* (Boston: Little, Brown, 1945); Ward, *Andrew Jackson: Symbol for an Age.* Multiple essays in Adams, ed., *A Companion to the Era of Andrew Jackson.*

43. See the essays cited in note 6 above and Green, *Man of the People.* R. B. Bernstein, *Thomas Jefferson* (New York: Oxford University Press, 2003); Francis D. Cogliano, *Thomas Jefferson: Reputation and Legacy* (Charlottesville: University of Virginia Press, 2006); Peter S. Onuf, ed., *Jeffersonian Legacies* (Charlottesville: University of Virginia Press, 1993). Mark R. Cheathem, "Donald Trump Is Not a Twenty-First-Century Andrew Jackson," *American Historian* 11 (2017): 17–21; Daniel Walker Howe, "The Nineteenth-Century Trump," *New York Review Daily* (June 27, 2017), http://www.nybooks.com/daily/2017/06/27/the-nineteenth-century-trump/.

The Mixed Legacy of Zachary Taylor

MOURNING A SOLDIER, LOSING A PRESIDENT

Camille Davis

O N THE NIGHT OF July 9, 1850, Zachary Taylor, president of the United States and hero of the Mexican-American War, died at the White House from a stomach illness that started only five days earlier. When the *Baltimore Sun* reported the president's death the next day, one columnist mused: "Among the numerous lessons read to us by 'the great destroyer' [death], this [Taylor's death] is one of the most impressive, one which proclaims with a most emphatic voice what all know, but few appear to realize, the uncertainty of life and the empty and the transient, and fugitive character of all earthly honors; of fame, of renown, of everything we are in the habit of making 'the desire of the heart,' or which the heart desires to look upon."[1] This commentary assessed the irony of the president's passing. Until then, Taylor, a victorious general who ascended to the country's highest elected office, had shown no indications of failing health.

Taylor's illness began on July 4 after an Independence Day celebration near the unfinished Washington Monument, where he sipped ice water and nibbled on fresh fruit.[2] Though his initial discomfort did not reveal the seriousness of his condition, he soon received a diagnosis of "cholera morbus," a disease that caused infection of the bowels, and his condition quickly became acute.[3] Though he received treatment for several days, by the evening of July 9, the president's doctors offered a grim prognosis. Taylor's family gathered near his bedside as he prepared for the inevitable. He reportedly told his wife, "I have always done my duty. I am ready to die. My only regret is for the friends I leave behind me."[4] Sometime between 10:30 and 10:35 p.m., he succumbed.[5]

The news that the president, who was healthy five days prior, had died, jolted the populace. Newspapers recounted details of the president's death to the American citizenry and encouraged collective mourning. Washington DC's *Daily Intelligencer*'s coverage of the tragedy articulated the pervasive feeling of shock: "No longer ago than Thursday last, he [the president] was apparently in the full enjoyment of health and strength, participating in the patriotic ceremonies of our nation's birthday, and now is he numbered with the dead!"[6] Most, if not all the news reports of the time, eulogized the president in glowing terms, commending his patriotism and virtuous character. However, one newspaper went beyond praising the president's life and recounting his death. Although it spoke warmly of President Taylor, it provided a more nuanced perspective of his legacy and foreshadowed that the president would be remembered for his exemplary military service instead of his short-lived political career. On July 10, the *Boston Evening Transcript* provided this summary of the late president: "Whatever may have been the opinion of politicians as to the qualifications of General Taylor for the presidential chair, or as to the wisdom of his policy, and the character of his cabinet, no man, whose opinion has a feather's weight with the public, will rise to question the old soldier's stern integrity of purpose, his perfect patriotism, his honesty and purity of heart."[7]

No statement more accurately predicted the immediate, subsequent, and continuing public memory of the twelfth president of the United States.

The Politics of the Moment

At the time of Taylor's death, the United States was engulfed in another sectional crisis that eventually led to civil war. Congress was squabbling over the 525,000 square miles of western territory gained from the Mexican-American War, and there was no clear consensus regarding whether future states would be admitted to the Union as either slave or free states. New states had been previously assessed by the Missouri Compromise in 1820, which prohibited slavery in the Louisiana Territory north of the 36° 30′ latitude line, with Missouri the exception to the rule. To balance the admission of Missouri as a slave state, Maine was admitted as a free state. Eight years after the Missouri

Compromise, tensions erupted when South Carolinians attempted to nullify federal tariff laws that they believed favored northern manufacturing interests. South Carolina's flagrant dismissal of federal law sparked conflict between northerners and southerners, between members of Congress, and between those in the White House. President Andrew Jackson and Vice President John C. Calhoun were on opposite sides of the issue. The vice president was a native South Carolinian and proponent of the nullification movement. President Jackson vehemently opposed nullification and issued a proclamation expressing his disapproval.[8] In response, Congress authorized the use of military force. A detente came only after Senator Henry Clay of Kentucky facilitated a bill that lowered tariffs.[9] Both the Nullification Crisis and the Missouri Compromise were shaped by the politics of regional identity and intertwined with a larger debate over the powers and authority of the federal government. Since no long-term solution to the problem was found, these tensions lingered for decades and continued into Taylor's presidency.

As president, Taylor chose a different approach than the more proactive Jackson. President Taylor refused to offer any guidance on the newly acquired western territories from the Mexican-American War, leaving Congress to resolve whether to admit the territories as slave or free states. The debate between national sovereignty and states' rights reflected a conspicuous conflict within Taylor's own psyche. On the one hand, as a career solider, Taylor believed in the sovereignty of the national government and rejected the South's demand for unequivocal expansion of slavery into the western territories. On the other hand, Taylor was born in Virginia and grew up in Kentucky, two states that permitted slavery. Over the course of his lifetime, he enslaved more than one hundred people. When Taylor was elected to the presidency, he owned 118 enslaved people and purchased 64 more individuals only a few weeks before he passed.[10] Only after President Taylor's death did lawmakers resolve the question of the western territories by passing the infamous pieces of legislation that became known as the Compromise of 1850.

However, this legislation proved a political pacifier rather than a real solution. The Compromise of 1850 made small concessions toward abolition, while propagating the interests of slaveowners. On one hand, the legislation abolished the slave trade within the nation's capital, an abolitionist demand. On the other, the law amended the Fugitive Slave Law to the benefit of slaveowners in the South.

The Fugitive Slave Law of 1850 enhanced the powers contained in the previous Fugitive Slave Law, which was passed in 1793 and that originated from article 4 of the Constitution. The amended version exhibited greater hostility toward enslaved persons and those who aided their pursuit of freedom. The original Fugitive Slave Act allowed slaveholders to recapture *their* enslaved persons who attempted to self-emancipate.[11] The more strident 1850 version of the law made running away a federal offense and tasked federal commissioners with the responsibility of returning runaways. Furthermore, the law required white civilian bystanders to assist with the capture of enslaved people, and it prohibited enslaved individuals from defending themselves in federal court.[12] The Compromise of 1850 also allowed New Mexico and Utah to choose whether they would enter the Union as slave or free states, which appealed to both northern and southern interests. This provision laid the groundwork for what would become known as popular sovereignty—a practice that determined the status of other new states as they entered the Union.

Despite these legislative attempts to solve the sectional crisis in 1850, the division within the United States remained. The Compromise of 1850 was a conglomeration of laws that were in moral and philosophical opposition and could not preserve an already fragile nation. As President Abraham Lincoln later professed, a house divided against itself could not stand. The United States could either uphold or disband slavery. While Congress attempted to compromise through policies that advocated and privileged division, the nation would ultimately be forced to choose between slavery and abolition.

Taylor the President

Zachary Taylor had little practical knowledge to guide his actions in office, as he had no prior elected experience. Taylor was a career soldier, and until the presidency, he had never held a position in the civil service. During his military career, he distinguished himself in the War of 1812 and the Black Hawk War, and in 1845 he received the commission that poised him for fame as the hero of the Mexican-American War.[13] In May 1846, Taylor led American forces to victories in the battles of Palo Alto and Resaca de la Palma. Subsequently, he burnished his legacy when he captured the city of Monterrey. In 1847, he delivered a decisive victory in the Battle of Buena Vista. For

Americans, these battles became the most well known of the war, and they catapulted Taylor to national and international acclaim.[14]

Taylor's popularity generated considerable demand for images and likenesses of the country's most famous general. While a market existed for memorial images and objects of Taylor immediately after his passing, that demand was nowhere near what it was during the zenith of his military career. The visage of "Old Rough and Ready" could be placed on the surface of nearly anything and sold for profit, including flasks, tapestries, medals, and even mirrors.[15] On May 9, 1848, Congress commissioned a bronze medal with Taylor's profile embedded upon it to celebrate both the victor and victory of the Mexican-American War.[16] Additionally, Taylor proved a popular subject for prints. The printer Nathaniel Currier made only one new image of Taylor when he died, but during the years of the Mexican-American War, Currier printed scenes from each of the battles that brought Taylor acclaim. In 1846, he published *Gen'l Ampudia Treating for the Capitulation of Monterey* [sic] *with Gen. Taylor, 24th Sept. 1846*. The following year, he printed *Flight of the Mexican Army at the Battle of Buena Vista, Feb. 23, 1847*.[17] Other prints included *General Taylor at the Battle of Palo Alto*[18] and *General Taylor at the Battle of Resaca de la Palma*.[19] Currier printed at least fifteen scenes from the war and unashamedly incorporated the words "General Taylor" in their titles when he felt as though it were necessary.[20] The hero of the battles drew as much attention as the battles themselves.

In 1848, both the Whig and Democratic parties courted Zachary Taylor for the presidency. Since 1789, political parties had occasionally nominated a military hero for president. Successful examples included George Washington, Andrew Jackson, and William Henry Harrison.[21] Unlike some previous candidates, Taylor did not fit ideologically with either party, but both Whigs and Democrats knew that his military record made him an attractive candidate. On January 1, 1848, the *Boston Semi-Weekly Atlas* reported a political meeting in which General Taylor was mentioned as a potential candidate who transcended party lines: "The people had taken up Gen. Taylor by their own spontaneous movement."[22] Historian Brainerd Dyer argued that "the Taylor-for-President movement began to appear irresistible. . . . Taylor fought no more battles and won no further military laurels, but those already won were sufficient to carry him to the White House."[23]

Usually politicians who "transcend" party politics found success once in office by aligning themselves with one political party, even if they plan to operate with more independence. Forgoing this trend, Taylor obtained the Whig nomination and the presidency while being transparent about his unwillingness to commit himself to a party agenda. On January 30, 1848, Taylor described his approach to the presidential nomination. Although the letter was private, it was published on February 26 in the *Daily Union*. Since Taylor was never known for his subtlety, one wonders if he encouraged the letter's disclosure:

> [I]f they [the people] think fit to bring me before them for this office, through their legislatures, mass meetings or conventions, I cannot object their designating these bodies as whig, democratic, or native. But in being thus nominated, I must insist on the condition—and my position on this point is immutable—that I shall not be brought forward by them as the candidate of their party, or considered as the exponent of their party doctrines. In conclusion, I have to repeat, that if I were nominated for the presidency, by any body of my fellow citizens, designated by any name they choose to adopt, I should esteem it an honor, and would accept such nomination provided it had been made entirely independent of party considerations.[24]

Taylor's presidency reflected this promise. After winning the 1848 election as the Whig candidate, he resolutely avoided the legislation put forth by Whigs that was intended to save the Union and rejected counsel from party leaders. Even the most powerful Whig senators of the day, Henry Clay and Daniel Webster of Massachusetts, could not secure the president's cooperation. Clay, the great legislative compromiser, described his relationship with the president as "cold."[25] Webster agreed, but he kept an open mind and provided an objective, balanced assessment of the Taylor presidency. Nevertheless, the political ostracization remained at the forefront of his mind: "I feel neither indifferent, or distant towards our good President. He is an honest man and a good whig, and I wish well to his administration, for his sake and the country's. But what can I do? He never consults me, nor asks my advice; nor does anyone of his cabinet, except Mr. Meredith. His whole cabinet was formed, originally, without asking any opinion of mine, and some are friendly and others are cross gained towards me and excessively jealous. I shall support, cordially, the President's measures whenever I can."[26] Senator William Seward of New York enjoyed more success forging an amiable relationship with the president than others, but the rapport between Seward and Taylor did not translate into Taylor accepting Seward's council on matters of state, or Seward having any more confidence in the president. In a personal letter to his friend and newspaper publisher Thurlow Weed, Seward provided his initial impressions of Taylor just before the inauguration: "He is a sensitive and sagacious man, but uninformed about men, and will fail to secure a cabinet practically strong. It remains to be seen how far honesty and the purest and most exalted patriotism will cover the defect of political sagacity."[27] Seward reiterated his doubts that same day, March 1, 1849, when he wrote to his wife that the president-elect wanted nothing from him except "acquiescence."[28]

In the early national period, the litmus test for political office was the ability to make decisions for the public good. In theory, Taylor's capacity to maintain order, enforce discipline among those in his command, and lead those forces through the tactical nuances of battle meant he was well equipped to administer civil government. However, Seward knew that ability and knowledge in one sphere did not translate to skills in another. He could appreciate the president's accomplishments and recognize the president's good intentions, but he knew that those qualities were not necessarily a formula for good governance. They could not replace the ability to make sound political calculations and decisions.

Seward's concerns proved prophetic. The gravitas that characterized Taylor's time as general never emerged during his presidency. He provided no legislative solutions for the sectional divide, and he intensified political tensions by encouraging two of the western territories in dispute—California and New Mexico—to apply for statehood without adhering to the legislative process for becoming a state.[29] Additionally, Taylor never formed a cabinet of individuals who could balance his weaknesses or advise him on matters beyond his expertise.[30] After all, the first president (a former general himself) and standard-bearer of American governance had established the institution of the cabinet to alleviate the burden of leadership. George Washington learned quickly that a successful presidency was only possible with strong executive department heads who could provide knowledge, expertise, and counsel to the commander-in-chief.[31] However, Taylor had a different approach. He avoided robust decisions as president and did not seek advice from those who could help him with decision making.

Taylor did not have much time to grow into his role. He was president less than eighteen months. Perhaps with more time and more opportunity, he would have adjusted his approach and grown into the office. Instead, President Taylor failed to provide leadership over what was then the largest political crisis in the country's history.

How the Nation's Leaders Handled News of Taylor's Death

Although the severity of the president's condition was initially unclear, members of Congress began preparing for the worst-case scenario on July 9. They adjourned their proceedings early after receiving word that the president was steadily declining. The *Congressional Record* indicates that the House of Representatives announced the president's condition around one p.m. and that they adjourned before the Senate. The Senate records indicate that "Mr. Webster," presumably Senator Daniel Webster, recommended that the Senate follow the House's example by adjourning its meetings: "The intelligence, which within the last few moments, has been received, indicates that a great misfortune is now immediately impending over the country. It is supposed by medical advisors and others that the President of the United States cannot live many hours. This intimation comes in a shape so authentic, and through so many varieties of communication, and all tending to the same result, that I have thought it my duty to move the Senate to follow the example which has already been set in the other branch of the National Legislature."[32]

When the prediction of the doctors proved correct, Congress met the next day to oversee the transition of power and deliver orations to honor the deceased president. In less than ten years' time, two sitting American presidents had died while in office. John Tyler's decision to take the oath of office without involving Congress created controversy that lasted his entire administration, as opponents frequently questioned his presidential authority. While there were many unanswered questions regarding the constitutional process of presidential succession, Millard Fillmore avoided controversy by pursuing a different course. In his July 10 address to the joint legislative body, Vice

President Fillmore formally resigned his position as head of the Senate and requested to take the oath of office before Congress at noon. Additionally, he explained that the president's death "penetrated no heart with deeper grief" than his own.[33] The nature of Fillmore and Taylor's relationship is unclear, but once Fillmore became president, he quickly supported the legislative compromise that Taylor ignored. On the day he took office, Fillmore spoke well of the president, but he also exhibited a readiness to accept his constitutional responsibility of assuming the presidency.

Additionally, the Senate records indicated that later that day a "Mr. Downs," probably Senator Solomon W. Downs of Louisiana, addressed Congress about the transition of presidential power. Downs expressed relief that the brief vacancy of the presidency did not produce unrest or violence. Though his sentiments were cheerful, they revealed an underlying anxiety about America's survival and the viability of republican governments more broadly. For Downs, America's ability to move forward proved that the nation could abruptly lose a president without imploding: *"Within little more than twelve hours after the event, the new President has taken the oath of office, without any military parade, and been installed in command of the ship of state, which moves on over the billows of time, more bright and buoyant than ever,* bearing at her masthead the proud emblems of national glory and greatness, and presenting to the world a sublime spectacle of the beauty and perfection of self-government."[34]

Most of July 10 was awash in approbations of the late Zachary Taylor. His colleagues agreed that the country had lost a good man and an exceptional general. However, there was not much else to say about his presidency because his tenure in office was short and his political achievements minimal. Taylor's life before the presidency provided most of the content for the day's speeches. Daniel Webster delivered one of the most magnanimous addresses, even though he and Taylor had disagreed on how to save the Union from collapsing. Webster described the deceased president's strengths while graciously glossing over his political ineffectiveness with a rhetorical salve that could have been reserved for a president who had performed more adeptly while in office:

> The late President of the United States, originally a soldier by profession, having gone through a long and splendid career of military service, had at the

close of the late war with Mexico, become so much endeared to the people of the United States, and had inspired them with so high a degree of regard and confidence, that without solicitation or application, without pursing any devious paths of policy, or turning a hair's breadth to the right or left to the path of duty, a great, and powerful, and generous people saw fit, by popular vote and voice, to confer upon him the highest civil authority in the nation.[35]

Webster also engaged in a bit of revisionist history by claiming the deceased president possessed a docile temperament that further ingratiated him with the American citizenry: "He was especially regarded as a both a firm and mild man in the exercise of authority . . . the prevalent motive with the masses of mankind for conferring high power on individuals, is often a confidence in their mildness, their paternal, protecting, and safe character."[36]

The sentiments were kind, but the statement was false. Taylor had not ascended to the presidency because of a reputation for restraint. His nickname was "Old Rough and Ready," and a large portion of his appeal came from his proverbial rough edges. Despite this rhetorical deviation, Webster was correct when he asserted that military might alone did not account for the public esteem that lifted Taylor to the presidency. Taylor was also regarded for his admirable character. People knew that he made decisions based on conviction. Webster was also correct when he stated that Taylor had not grasped for the mantle of the presidency; rather, it was placed upon him by citizens. Ambition was not the impetus for Taylor's presidency; rather, it was a desire to serve the country that requested his service.

American citizens contributed to the public mourning of Taylor's death. On July 12, the day before the funeral, the streets of Washington filled with people from all over the country who came to honor the president.[37] The large number of crowds did not create a disturbance that ruined the solemnity of the occasion. On the contrary, the sadness within the city was compared to "a great and appalling stroke [that] had fallen upon the community."[38] That day, a public viewing occurred within the East Room of the White House, and visitors observed the president's casket covered in black velvet with "draperies of silver" and lined with velvet of "the purest white."[39] Flowers and other flora rested upon the bier. Many people took pieces of the arrangements as memorial souvenirs.

On Saturday, the president's funeral was held at the Executive Mansion. The presiding minister and rector of St. John's Church, the Reverend Smith Pyne, delivered the eulogy. He attributed Taylor's success as a general to his virtue as a man; he stated that the convictions of Taylor's soul provided him with the direction to lead effectively in battle. Pyne addressed the delicate subject of the presidency by contending that Taylor followed his conscience, and that he would have conducted his presidency the same way, even if he had known of his untimely death.[40]

Citizens waited in the streets for hours to see the funeral procession.[41] Congress had arranged for full military honors and presidential regalia to be used, as well as for the president's famous horse from the Mexican-American War, "Old Whitey," to be a part of the day's ceremonies. The "mourning train" was two miles long, beginning at the White House and winding all the way to the Congressional Cemetery. The *New Republic* reported that along the way "every spot was availed of . . . as well as every window, roof, or tree, that would command a view of the procession; numbers sat or stood in the burning sun, so great was the desire to witness the solemn spectacle."[42] The public demonstrations suggested a regard for the office of the presidency that overshadowed any legislative concern of the moment.

On Monday, July 15, members of Congress agreed to print all the orations from the House and Senate, and sent the pamphlet to Taylor's widow, Margaret. They delivered the pamphlet with a message to "assure her of the profound respect of the two Houses for her person and her character, and of their sincere condolence of the late afflicting dispensation of Providence."[43] The record of the orations, the funeral, and the subsequent plan to honor Mrs. Taylor are testaments to the collective effort of President Taylor's colleagues to exhibit esteem for the office of the presidency that transcended political preferences.

On Wednesday July 17, 1850, the Senate initiated a bill to erect a "neat and appropriate monument to the memory of Zachary Taylor."[44] The monument was to be placed in the nation's capital and include the late president's "name, station, age, and time of death."[45] The House and Senate unanimously agreed to the tribute, and they entrusted their wishes to the commissioner of the Public Buildings.[46] Congress also created a budget for the project, agreeing to pay no more than two thousand dollars from the US

Treasury. What is most interesting about this theoretical monument is that it is unclear whether it was ever constructed, as no monument exists today. Taylor was temporarily entombed at Congressional Cemetery in Washington and later buried at the Taylor property in Louisville, Kentucky. In 1883, the state of Kentucky erected a statue and a fifty-foot granite monument of Taylor, and the US government erected a limestone, neoclassical-style building with a marble interior in 1926 to house Taylor's remains at the Zachary Taylor National Cemetery.[47]

Although there is not an extensive record of how the country mourned Taylor, there are some local newspapers of the period that discussed commemorations of the late president. The *Daily Picayune* of New Orleans reported that the city held a day of mourning to honor the deceased.[48] The *Alexandria Gazette* described how the city provided transportation for citizens to attend the president's funeral in Washington, DC.[49] The *Portsmouth Journal* explained that the city of New Hampshire ordered the tolling of bells and the firing of guns for one hour on July 13 in honor of the late president. Additionally, the city council asked that shipowners display their flags at half-mast.[50]

Cultural artifacts of the time also reflected the public's sentiments about the president's demise. Nathaniel Currier, one of the most prolific lithograph publishers of the nineteenth century, created a colored print that depicted Taylor's death.[51] Prints were the poor man's art of the time, and the creation of a print was intended for a mass audience of consumers instead of connoisseurs of fine art. Currier intentionally named his lithograph *The Death of General Z. Taylor, 12th President of the United States* and placed "General Z. Taylor" in large, bold, clear letters and placed "12th President of the United States" in small, faint, almost illegible letters. Arguably, highlighting Taylor's military success appealed to the common people whose admiration for Taylor brought him political ascendancy.

A glass snuffbox with Taylor's portrait painted on one side of the exterior and the words "Forget Me Not" on the other side of the exterior is another relic from the period. The item appears to be mass produced. First, dipping snuff tobacco was a regular practice of the day. Secondly, the most expensive material used in the creation of the object was glass, which was a relatively easy material to obtain. Lastly, the words "forget me not" would have not

FIGURE 3. Glass-covered snuffbox manufactured in the shape of a book, approximately 7 x 4 cm. The left exterior displays a hand-colored portrait of Taylor, while the right exterior exhibits printed text that states, "FORGET ME NOT." The box is identified as a memorial item created after Taylor's death in 1850. (Susan H. Douglas Political Americana Collection, #2214. Division of Rare and Manuscript Collections, Cornell University Library, Ithaca, NY)

been necessary if the object was commissioned by someone in Taylor's family or inner circle. They would have not needed a "Forget Me Not" snuffbox to remember their loved one. Taylor's passing had created a market for mourning memorabilia. Like the flora on Taylor's bier, these objects provided the public with keepsakes associated with individual and collective grief.

A lyricist of the time, Alfred Street, composed a song in honor of the somber occasion. The song's words reflect the citizenry's shared sense of sadness:

> A star hath vanished from our sky
> That there so great a glory shone
> A pillar in our temple high
> Late reared so firm is now o'erthrown
> With dropping plume, among her spear
> Our nation stands, in sorrow bent,
> Above her vanished hero's bier
> Her hero and her president.[52]

In addition to the market for Taylor memorabilia in 1850, that year also saw a surge in commissions for paintings that depicted America's first president. The country's loss of Taylor during an impending national crisis likely inspired nostalgia among the citizenry. Americans craved a nostalgic past that they believed represented national unity. As the country transitioned from Taylor's presidency, two of the most iconic images of Washington emerged: Rembrandt Peale's eightieth copy of the *Patriae Pater,* a Roman appellation that means "Father of the Country" and German expatriate Emmanuel Leutze's *Washington Crossing the Delaware.*[53]

This sentimentality about the founding reflected the public's uncertainty about the political turmoil that accompanied Taylor's death. Three months after the president's death, Congress passed the Compromise of 1850 with the support of President Millard Fillmore. However, the compromise did not ease political tensions. Instead, it made them worse. American citizens felt the strain. They read about the feuds between legislators in newspapers; they saw the advertisements for runaway slaves; they witnessed the recapture of those who escaped from slavery; and they knew of the heightened rhetoric and efforts of the abolition movement. They took sides in the sectional debate, but they also recalled a time when American politics appeared more serene. Their weariness fostered a desire for the past. Neither the present nor the future seemed to evoke the same optimism or security. Since Zachary Taylor's death, his legacy has been inextricably intertwined with the political quagmire of the 1850s. Taylor admirably served as a general yet struggled to master the political questions that dominated his time in office.

Those questions revealed his own personal shortcomings. He was a slaveowner who believed that the interest of the Union superseded regional interests. However, the sovereignty of the Union could not be maintained if slavery existed within the nation. For slavery to remain intact, the entire country had to participate by owning slaves or upholding laws that privileged slaveowners. Taylor could live with that contradiction as a private citizen and as a general, but his presidency could not bear the weight of supporting the diametrically opposed concepts of slavery and union. This incongruity created a paralysis of leadership from which Taylor never recovered.

If Taylor's presidency had been longer, he may have chosen a different path. There is no reason to believe that he would have become a great emancipator or an ardent secessionist, but perhaps a longer tenure in the presidency would have given Taylor the motivation to engage with the great and burdensome questions that challenged the office. Taylor's decision to ignore the sectional crisis compared to Abraham Lincoln's choice to conquer it, highlights the importance of tenure in office. Lincoln slowly developed into a great president. His famous sentiment in his Second Inaugural Address that a drop of blood from the whip would be repaid with another from the sword was not his initial response to the problem of slavery. Lincoln's willingness to grapple with complex issues, evolve his thinking, and shift his opinions or positions made his leadership in times of crisis extraordinary. This evolution took time. Since Taylor held the presidency for such a short moment, one cannot know if he would have ever learned to shoulder its mantle well.

Despite the tenuousness of Taylor's legacy, interest in his presidency temporarily resurfaced during the late twentieth century. In 1991, author Clara Rising theorized that Taylor had been assassinated by poisoning. She convinced the Kentucky medical examiner, Dr. George Nichols, Louisville County Coroner Richard Greathouse, and Taylor's descendants that his body should be exhumed and tested. Presumably, Rising believed that this experiment was necessary to prove that Abraham Lincoln was actually the first president to be assassinated.[54] On June 26, Nichols publicized his findings. He stated that arsenic was found in the remains of the deceased, but there was not enough of it to suggest poisoning. According to Nichols, a person who was poisoned would have 200 to 1,000 times more of the arsenic than the late Taylor had in his system. Nichols admitted that he could not determine a definitive cause of death, but he did say that Zachary Taylor's symptoms were consistent with "a myriad of natural diseases that would have produced the symptoms."[55] If Taylor had been poisoned, historians and scholars would have seriously reconsidered his legacy. Perhaps he would have been recast as a martyr who died for his unwillingness to engage in an ideological conflict that nearly destroyed the country.

Today, Taylor is acknowledged in a few perfunctory ways. Each year on his birthday, November 24, military personnel from Fort Knox lay a wreath near his gravesite in Kentucky.[56] Americans have remembered and celebrated him more as a general instead of a president, as there is no Zachary Taylor presidential library, historic site, or museum in existence today.

Even the former Taylor family home, Springfield, remains in private hands; a basic state historical marker notes that the house was his boyhood home. There are no national celebrations of Taylor, and he is rarely critically evaluated by historians. Most assuredly, his legacy would be remembered differently had Taylor ended his public service after the Mexican-American War and avoided the presidency. Taylor's ascension to the presidency resulted in a blot from which his legacy never recovered.

Notes

1. "Death of President Taylor," *Baltimore Sun,* July 10, 1850.
2. "Death of the President of the United States. Earth to Earth—Dust to Dust," *Boston Evening Transcript,* July 10, 1850; "Timeline, 1848–1850: An illustrated chronology of key events in the life of Zachary Taylor (1784–1850), twelfth president of the United States, from his presidential nomination in 1848 through his presidency (1849–50) until his death and funeral in July 1850," Library of Congress.
3. "Illness of the President," *American Commercial Daily Advertiser* [Baltimore, MD], July 9, 1850.
4. Michael Holt, "Zachary Taylor: Death of the President," University of Virginia, Miller Center, https://millercenter.org/president/taylor/death-of-the-president/. According to Vice President Millard Fillmore, the president's final words were: "I am not afraid to die; I have done my duty; my only regret is leaving those who are dear to me." *Daily National Intelligencer* [Washington DC], July 10, 1850.
5. "Illness of the President"; *Daily National Intelligencer,* July 10, 1850.
6. *Daily National Intelligencer,* July 10, 1850.
7. "Death of the President of the United States. Earth to Earth—Dust to Dust," *Boston Evening Transcript,* July 10, 1850.
8. "Nullification Proclamation: Primary Documents in American History," *Library of Congress Research Guides,* https://guides.loc.gov/nullification-proclamation/.
9. "Nullification Proclamation."
10. Holman Hamilton, *The Three Kentucky Presidents: Lincoln, Taylor, Davis* (Lexington: University Press of Kentucky, 2003), 23.
11. US Congress, *An Act Respecting Fugitives of Justice, and Persons Escaping from the Service of Their Masters,* 1793, Library of Congress.
12. "Northern Opposition to the Fugitive Slave Law of 1850," *Negro History Bulletin* 14, no. 1 (October 1950): 13–15. "Effects of the Fugitive-Slave-Law," Library of Congress.
13. Hon. Solomon W. Downs, "Address to the US Congress on July 10, 1850," from the US Congress, *Obituary Addresses Delivered on the Occasion of the Death of the Zachary Taylor, President of the United States,* {which number Congress?} 31st Cong., 1st sess., 1849–50. The *Congressional Record* simply lists him as "Mr. Downs," but it is likely Solomon W. Downs, a senator from Louisiana at the time.

14. Downs, "Address."

15. The Winterthur Museum, Garden, and Library has the flask and tapestry. The Metropolitan Museum of Art holds at least three bronze medals of Taylor, two created by Charles Cushing Wright named "Medal of Major General Z. Taylor," which was created in 1848; the second one is called "Louisiana to General Zachary Taylor," which was probably created between 1846 and 1848. Franklin Peale created the third medal in 1849. Cornell University possesses a portrait mirror of Taylor.

16. *United States Senate Catalogue of Fine Art* (Washington, DC: GPO, 2002), https://www.govinfo.gov/content/pkg/GPO-CDOC-107sdoc11/pdf/GPO-CDOC-107sdoc11-2-116.pdf.

17. Library of Congress, Photo, Print, Drawing Collection. Yale University Art Gallery, Mabel Brady Garvan Collection.

18. In the collections at the Home of William P. Murchison, descendant of President James K. Polk.

19. Home of William P. Murchison. The National Archives has a different print by Currier of this battle that is similarly named, but the full title of that print is *General Taylor at the Battle of Resaca de la Palma. Captain May Receiving His Orders to Charge the Mexican Batteries, May 9, 1846.*

20. "Nathaniel Currier Mexican War Lithographs, 1846–1847," Dolph Briscoe Center for American History, University of Texas at Austin.

21. "William Henry Harrison, the 9th President of the United States," www.whitehouse.gov.

22. *Boston Semi-Weekly Atlas*, January 1, 1848.

23. Brainerd Dyer, "Zachary Taylor and the Election of 1848," *Pacific Historical Review* 9, no. 2 (June 1940): 173–74.

24. Z. Taylor to Peter Sken Smith, January 30, 1848, *Daily Union*, February 26, 1848.

25. Henry Clay to James Harlen, March 16, 1850, from William O. Lynch's "Zachary Taylor as President," *Journal of Southern History* 4, no. 3 (August 1938): 284.

26. Daniel Webster to J. Prescott Hall, May 18, 1850, from Lynch's "Zachary Taylor as President," 284.

27. William Seward to Thurlow Weed, March 1, 1849, from Lynch's "Zachary Taylor as President," 285.

28. William Seward to wife, March 1, 1849, from Lynch's "Zachary Taylor as President," 285.

29. Lynch, "Zachary Taylor as President," 291.

30. "Zachary Taylor, 1849–1850," whitehousehistory.org.

31. Lindsay M. Chervinsky, *George Washington and the Creation of an American Institution* (Cambridge, MA: Harvard University Press, 2020).

32. *Records of U.S. Senate*, Tuesday, July 9, 1850.

33. *Records of U.S. House and Senate*, July 10, 1850.

34. Downs, "Address." Emphasis in original.

35. Daniel Webster, "Oration of Zachary Taylor before Congress, July 10, 1850," in *Obituary Addresses Delivered on the Occasion of the Death of Zachary Taylor, President of the United States, in the Senate and House of Representatives, July 10, 1850; with the Funeral Sermon by the Rev. Smith Pyne, D.D.* (Washington, DC: William M. Belt, 1850), 13–16.

36. Webster, "Oration."

37. *National Influencer*, July 1850.

38. *National Influencer,* July 1850.

39. *National Influencer,* July 1850.

40. Rev. Pyne, funeral eulogy for President Zachary Taylor, July 13, 1850, cited in *Obituary Addresses Delivered on the Occasion of the Death of Zachary Taylor, President of the United States, in the Senate and House of Representatives, July 10, 1850, with the Funeral Sermon by the Rev. Smith Pyne, D.D., Rector of St. John's Church Washington, Preached in the Presidential Mansion, July 13, 1850. Printed by the Order of the Senate and House of Representatives* (Washington, DC: Printed by William M. Belt, 1850).

41. *New Republic,* July 1850.

42. *New Republic,* July 1850.

43. Joint Meeting of the United States House and Senate, Monday, July 15, 1850.

44. *US Senate Records,* July 17, 1850.

45. *US Senate Records,* July 17, 1850.

46. The record does not provide the name of the commissioner.

47. "Zachary Taylor National Cemetery," National Cemetery Administration, US Department of Veterans Affairs, https://www.cem.va.gov/cems/nchp/zacharytaylor.asp.

48. *New Orleans Daily Picayune,* July 13, 1850. This newspaper was also listed as the *Times-Picayune.*

49. *Alexandria [VA] Gazette,* July 12, 1850.

50. *Portsmouth [NH] Journal,* July 13, 1850.

51. Nathaniel Currier, *Death of General Z. Taylor,* 1850, Print (Hand Colored Lithograph), Smithsonian National Portrait Gallery, Washington, DC.

52. Alfred B. Street, "Lines on the Death of General Zachary Taylor, President of the United States," Library of Congress.

53. According to the Metropolitan Museum of Art, Leutze painted an earlier version of this piece in 1849. In 1850, he began a subsequent, and more famous, version that he finished the following year.

54. "Verdict In: 12th President Was Not Assassinated," *New York Times,* June 27, 1991. The Zachary Taylor file of the Amon Carter Museum of American Art.

55. "Verdict In: 12th President Was Not Assassinated."

56. The US Senate Collection and the National Cemetery Administration.

Unimaginable Catastrophe

THE NATION'S FIRST PRESIDENTIAL ASSASSINATION

Martha Hodes

THE MURDER OF GREAT leaders is at least as old as Julius Caesar, but the assassination of an American president seemed nearly unimaginable. When it happened, Washington residents were still celebrating the end of the Civil War. The surrender of Confederate general Robert E. Lee's Army of Northern Virginia had come on April 9, 1865, and for days the capital city remained "alive with enthusiasm," observers noted, streets jammed, every house and public building "blazing with candles from top to bottom," everyone "wild with excitement" and "crazy with joy." On April 11, President Abraham Lincoln delivered a speech from the window above the north entrance of the White House, outlining his vision for reconstructing the nation. Among his listeners was John Wilkes Booth, roused to fury as the president spoke of voting rights for Black men. "Now by God," Booth uttered, according to a companion, "I'll put him through." Whatever he said aloud that night, Booth had already written down his conviction that "this country was formed for the *white* not for the black man."[1]

Inside Ford's Theatre three days later, the crack of the pistol came just as the audience was roaring with laughter at a line in the play. Booth, standing directly behind the president, in a box hovering above stage left, had fired a single shot into the back of Lincoln's head, then leapt to the stage to make his escape. While authorities searched for the vanished assassin, doctors and soldiers transported the unconscious president to a bed in a boardinghouse across the street. News traveled swiftly, and soon thousands of the city's Black residents congregated in front of the White House. Some asked

FIGURE 4. This 1865 Currier & Ives lithograph shows John Wilkes Booth firing the fatal shot that killed President Abraham Lincoln at Ford's Theatre in Washington, DC. (Courtesy of Prints and Photographs Division, Library of Congress, Washington, DC, LC-USZ62–2073)

soldiers if the president was gone. Others wondered aloud if Lincoln's passing would mean a return to enslavement. Death came the next morning, not long after seven o'clock. When Secretary of War Edwin Stanton spoke, some heard the words, "Now he belongs to the ages," others heard "Now he belongs to the angels." Ages or angels, history or heaven, Lincoln belonged to both. Abraham Lincoln's was the nation's first presidential assassination.[2]

People ran straight to the telegraph office, reporters wrote headlines from the dispatches, and newsboys scooped up the sheaves of "extras," setting out on their rounds and calling out the tidings. Across the country, laborers and servants were among the first to know. Night watchmen, coal shovelers, and lamplighters passed the news along to one another, as cooks preparing breakfast at dawn and valets building fires to warm bedrooms stepped outside to investigate the ruckus of shouting and hurried footsteps, then apprised their employers.[3]

Imparting the news became an early act of mourning. Knocking on neighbors' doors and calling into windows, saying the words aloud, was one way to try to comprehend what had happened. Everywhere, people gathered, and everywhere they searched one another's faces for verification, reading the meaning in eyes, brows, lips, and complexions, telling of genuine consternation, alarm, and woe. In Boston, a well-to-do woman ordered her driver to take her through the streets in her horse and buggy.

"Is it true what they say, that our president—" called out a man in a passing wagon.

"Yes—murdered!" the woman called back.

"Oh dear, oh dear!" the man moaned, driving on.[4]

By telegraph, news of the crime quickly reached small towns in northern New England and the Mid-Atlantic, as well as Chicago, Kansas, and Salt Lake City. In Sacramento, the first mentions arrived at nine in the morning, local time. By the next day, smaller cities in Ohio, Wisconsin, and Minnesota knew. Where no telegraph lines ran, people would not know until newspapers arrived by mail; Union soldiers in Alabama got word at the end of April, right around the same time telegrams arrived in London and Jamaica—in fact in Jamaica, news of Union victory and the assassination arrived together. Parts of New Mexico and Utah Territory would not hear until May, and the news would not reach Sierra Leone, China, and Australia until mid-June.[5]

Astonished. Astounded. Startled. Stupefied. Thunderstruck. A calamity. A catastrophe. A dagger to the heart. A thunderbolt. A thunderclap from a clear blue sky. It was "too horrible to be true" and "too terrible to believe." It was simply impossible to "realize"—that was a favored nineteenth-century locution, meaning *to make real*, and over and over again people invoked that word: "I can scarcely realize it." "I cannot realize it." "But how can we realize it?" People could not and would not believe it. "I cannot have it so," one woman wrote; "it must not be so."[6]

Disbelief was most intense for African Americans, whose stake in the Civil War's outcome and promise was so tangible. For the Black soldiers of the Fifty-fourth Massachusetts, the news was "too overwhelming, too lamentable, too distressing" to apprehend. In Louisville, Kentucky, "distress was visible in every colored person's face." A joke, a sham, a deception: the words people invoked conveyed all manner of the unreal.[7]

If passing on the news was one way to make sense of the senseless, another was to record the event. Michael Shiner, a formerly enslaved man who worked in the Washington Navy Yard, noted in his journal a set of details that a great many others would write down as well: the day, date, and place of the shooting, and the date of Lincoln's death (connecting himself personally to the event, Shiner added that the president had visited the Navy Yard on the very day of the assassination). When Sarah Putnam, fourteen years old, heard the news at the breakfast table, she drew a picture of her feelings—a face with two wide, round eyes and a wider circle for a mouth—thereby preserving visible expressions of incredulity (Putnam later became a portrait painter).[8]

People preserved their reactions on paper in all kinds of ways. They drew heavy black lines to signal the separation of everything that came before the assassination from everything that would come after. They recorded the deed, then drew a box around the words to make them stand out on the page. People drew pictures of graves or penned the facts in beautiful calligraphy. They wrote down everything. How the president's bodyguard had gone ahead to the theater but was nowhere to be found when the assassin approached. How the president's personal valet unwittingly let the assassin by. How Booth entered the anteroom and looked through a peephole in one of the doors that led directly to the presidential box. How he had earlier carved that peephole himself, since he was permitted access to Ford's as a well-known Shakespearean actor. How he opened the door and wedged it shut from the inside. How First Lady Mary Lincoln screamed. How Booth broke his leg on his clumsy vault to the stage. How he cried out, "Sic semper tyrannis!"—*Thus always to tyrants!*—or maybe "The South is avenged!" How another conspirator attacked Secretary of State William Seward with a knife. That the president expired on Saturday, April 15, 1865, at twenty-two minutes past seven o'clock in the morning.[9]

Every detail recorded and absorbed made it less a hallucinated nightmare or a theatrical drama, less a lie or a hoax. If recording the facts helped people cope with their shock, so too did observing and preserving the public scenes of reaction. Many noted not only the desolation etched onto every face, but also the pervasive mood of despondency, thereby fitting their own despair into something larger: a whole village, an entire city. Mourners everywhere imagined—and newspapers confirmed—that their own feelings were multiplied across the nation and around the world.

Magnifying the shock was the crime's timing. The "frantic joy" of Union victory, a woman observed, turned instantly to "frantic grief." Union soldiers in Nashville, Tennessee, were strutting in a parade when the news came "like a crash," prompting the musicians to switch from quicksteps to death marches. All in the same day, another woman recorded in her diary, "the sun rose upon a nation jubilant with victory" and set "upon one plunged in deepest sorrow." Over and over, people tried to articulate the nature of the change. Unitarian minister Edward Everett Hale could not believe he was "in the same world, and in the same week."[10]

Excitement and *gloom*. Those were the two words people wrote down again and again, the first emanating from within, the second seeming to descend from the atmosphere. In the nineteenth century, to *excite* meant to elicit strong emotions of any sort. Cities everywhere were in "a state of great excitement," indeed the whole Union was in a state of the "most intense excitement ever known." *Gloom*, in counterpoint, implied melancholy, shadows, and darkness, all of which endured after the excitement died down. John Nicolay, President Lincoln's private secretary, described the gloom in Washington as "heavy and ominous," as if "some greater calamity still hung in the air, and was about to crush and overwhelm every one." Among the freedpeople of Wilmington, North Carolina, wrote a white teacher, the news caused "a dreadful gloom to settle in our midst."[11]

In communities of freedpeople across the South, from Norfolk and Portsmouth, Beaufort and Charleston, arose the most "heartfelt sorrow." One woman described herself as "nearly deranged" with grief, and a man compared the circumstances to a horrific scene he had witnessed when enslaved: a mother whipped forty lashes for weeping when white people took away her children. The violence had traumatized him, "but not half so much as the death of President Lincoln," he confessed. In Petersburg, Virginia, the Black journalist Thomas Morris Chester saw both "unfeigned grief" and an "undisguised feeling of horror," for the question had not gone away: Would they "have to be slaves again"? Indeed, African Americans claimed for themselves a special place in the outpouring of anguish. Black clergymen in the North allowed that their people felt the loss "more keenly" and "more than all others," journalists singled out the "dusky-skinned men of our own race" as the "chief—the truest mourners," and Black soldiers maintained that "as a people none could deplore his loss more than we." Even the most stricken white mourners conceded the point. In the words of one minister, "intense as is our grief," no white person could "fathom the sorrow" of African Americans.[12]

Mourners found confirmation of the catastrophic event as they immersed themselves in public rituals. Cities, towns, and villages seemed instantaneously drenched in black drapery, complemented by white, the two traditional colors of nineteenth-century mourning. Businesses that had opened early on Saturday soon began to close—stores, theaters, bars—with the exception of shops that carried anything that could be fashioned into a mourning decoration. By the end of the day on Saturday, A. T. Stewart's department store in New York City had sold a hundred thousand dollars' worth of black goods. Sundown brought the rituals of illumination—now as bereavement instead of celebration—combining burning candles in residential windows, kerosene and gas lamps all aglow, and bonfires lighting up the streets. The death of an eminent statesman also warranted the donning of mourning emblems, some with likenesses or mottoes, others fashioned more plainly from the ubiquitous crinkly fabric called *crape*, pinned to bonnets, collars, or sleeves. Shopkeepers began selling the badges on the morning of April 15 and would keep up a steady business through the spring.[13]

The near-immediate shrouding of public buildings, which to privileged observers seemed to have been accomplished by magic, in fact fell to workingmen, just as the draping of private homes fell to wives and servants. Washington was the first to be transformed, as workers followed orders to cloak the White House, the Capitol, the War Department, Treasury Building, Post Office, and Patent Office. African Americans, many of them poor, along with the city's poorer whites, displayed their sentiments with as much black cloth as they could scare up, and soon the city was shrouded in "miles upon miles of material," as a federal clerk put it, or as one resident described the scene, the drapery went "on and on," the daytime streets presenting "only the blackness of darkness."[14]

Across the country the labor continued for more than a week, "hammers & stepladders everywhere," black and white bunting concealing the façades, columns, window frames, and door frames of city halls, churches, banks, department stores, shops, hotels, libraries, schools, and houses from tenement to mansion. Up went black-bordered flags, swags and streamers, bows and ribbons, banners pronouncing the nation in mourning, and photographs of the slain president, their frames fringed in black. In the defeated Confederacy, freedpeople and Yankee occupiers got to work too. On Saint Helena Island in South Carolina, one little girl cut her black bonnet into pieces small enough that she "supplied the whole school."[15]

People loved Abraham Lincoln. That was the word they used. "I never felt before how deep a hold he had on the hearts of the people," wrote a Union soldier, and women tended to describe such feelings with even greater effusion. "O that good, great man, whom we so loved & revered!" one fretted. Lincoln had crossed the boundary between leader and loved one, and at his death the categories blurred yet more, with many, as one put it, "personally afflicted" by his demise. Some invoked similes, mourning "as if for a dear friend." For others, no simile or metaphor was necessary; to the readers of the *San Francisco Elevator,* the city's Black newspaper, the president had been a "beloved friend." Union soldiers, a white man wrote, "could not of felt any worse if evry one of them had lost their nearest reletave." In Chicago, mused one mourner, "almost every family circle seems to be broken."[16]

In particular, people thought of Lincoln as a father, a symbol that held religious as well as familial meaning. An elderly freedwoman called the slain president "a mighty good father to us," and a white soldier said that the men "all claimed him as a father" (Union soldiers had long spoken of Lincoln as "Father Abraham"). Lincoln's mourners, one woman mused, were like orphans, a term defined in the nineteenth century as fatherless children. Symbolic as this paternal imagery may have been, Lincoln's mourners also felt moved to compare their feelings to personal losses. An American in Paris mourned for Lincoln "as sorrowfully and far more bitterly than I mourned for my dear father." Even more, when a freedwoman in North Carolina got word, she felt as if both her father and mother had died at the same time.[17]

Shot on Good Friday and dead on Saturday: the assassination made Easter Sunday a particularly important occasion, if also a confusing one, as distraught mourners came to church for what should have been a day of rejoicing over both the resurrection of Christ and military victory. The reversal of fortunes was manifested materially, as churchwomen searched for black fabric and placed portraits of the late president amid the arrangements of springtime flowers. The crowds were phenomenal. Pews always filled to capacity on Easter, but no one had ever seen anything like April 16, 1865. Wherever the news had arrived, from the East Coast to the Midwest to the Pacific, the aisles and galleries of Black churches and white churches were packed. Many who spilled out the doors strained to hear the services, and those at the back of the outdoor crowds could hear nothing at all.[18]

Mourners came to church longing to make sense of what felt incomprehensible. Lincoln's death had to be the design of God, but how could that be? The line between acceptance of God's will and the effort to understand God's will was a fine one. Where mourners recorded a struggle, they also asserted faith; where they asserted faith, they hinted at inner conflict. For a Quaker woman, Lincoln's death was such an "incredible atrocity" that she could not tell "whether love & mercy still reign in Heaven." A white captain in a Black regiment wondered if God had forsaken them all and the nation was "drifting into Anarchy."[19]

Clergymen were forced to dispense with their prepared sermons, attempting, on a day's notice, to address the palpable despair without entirely jettisoning Easter-season exultation. They had to think about the problem of calamitous evil in the world God created, and they had to make sense of Union victory and the end of slavery, followed by the president's murder. From the pulpit, the men spoke candidly about both their disheartened congregants and God's unerring will. With the victorious Union's claim of divine favor now complicated by Lincoln's death, preachers strove to convey that this very complication added even greater meaning to the war's outcome. Implicit, if unspoken directly, was the idea that a puzzling and mysterious message from God (taking Lincoln away at such a crucial moment) was more powerful and significant than the mere fulfillment of what the faithful had always expected (Union victory by God's decree).[20]

The loss, Jacob Thomas told his Black congregation in upstate New York, was "more than we can bear"—strong words indeed, but Thomas reminded his flock that "in God is our consolation" and asked them to "hope for the best." Chauncey Leonard, one of the few Black chaplains in the Union Army, knew that Lincoln had piloted the soldiers through the war to achieve "Liberty, and Equal Political right," and yet he knew too that God, "in his wise Providence," had taken Lincoln away. On Easter Sunday, ministers strove to make their congregants understand that the assassination should intensify faith in God's ultimate plan precisely because it was so mysterious. Stead-fastness of faith required resignation to God's incomprehensible ways.[21]

But Lincoln's assassination as the will of God did not necessarily con-stitute a complete answer—after all, vindictive Confederates explained the assassination the same way. Putting one's faith in divine intention, then, prompted a further question, one that even some of the most devoted could not stop themselves from asking: *Why?* Slavery was the people's sin, and a possible compelling answer could be found there. Though this explanation echoed the idea of a judgmental Calvinist God, it also came wrapped in the optimism of liberal Protestantism, for if God had taken Lincoln as punish-ment for the national sin of slavery, then Lincoln was also a martyr to slav-ery. A letter-writer to the *San Francisco Elevator* told his fellow Black readers that Lincoln's life had been sanctified by the *"Freedom of the Bondmen,"* that every drop of Lincoln's blood "redeemed a bondman" and foretold a time when "the whole earth shall be free." In a spontaneous sermon in Rochester, New York, the fiery abolitionist and fugitive slave Frederick Douglass told his listeners that although the president had been murdered, "the nation is saved and liberty established forever." White abolitionists offered similar messages. Wendell Phillips asserted that because God took Lincoln for the sake of antislavery, his death would "seal the sure triumph of the cause."[22]

The murder of Lincoln on Good Friday made parallels with Jesus ines-capable, not to mention a Christian understanding that saw the president's recent entry into the enemy capital as parallel to Jesus's entry into Jerusa-lem before crucifixion. "Lincoln died for we, Christ died for we," said a freed-man in South Carolina, and the two were the same man. "Mankind has lost its best friend since the crusifiction of Christ," wrote a white army officer. Just as they had done all through the war, mourners continued to search for consolation in faith, and with President Lincoln gone, they both deified him and tried to reckon with the fact that the godlike Lincoln was also a mortal.[23]

Over the days, weeks, and months following the assassination, from Europe and the Mediterranean, Central and South America, Liberia, Russia, China, and Japan, official tributes poured into Washington. The testimonials came from lords and princes, prime ministers and presidents; temperance societies, ladies' societies, and secular societies; cotton brokers, railroad companies, and workers' associations. From groups as disparate as Creoles of African descent in Guadeloupe and Polish refugees in Switzerland, nearly all the messages invoked a vision of universal grief.[24]

Within the nation, too, Lincoln's mourners insisted on describing to themselves and one another just such a singular vision, imagining the so recently divided nation now united by grief at the assassination of its leader—even as they saw evidence to the contrary all around them. The fact was, not everyone mourned the assassination of President Abraham Lincoln. "Pity it hadn't been done years ago," one Confederate soldier wrote in his diary. When a seventeen-year-old girl in South Carolina heard the news, she was ecstatic. "Hurrah!" she wrote. "Old Abe Lincoln has been assassinated!" while around her the grown-ups shouted, "Isn't it splendid?" It was not simply that Confederates wished to avenge the destruction of their attempted nation and its precious institution of slavery, it was also that they wished to return the humiliating glee that Yankees expressed at conquering their land. One woman called the news the "first gleam of light in this midnight darkness"; another, who had lost two brothers in the war, felt gratified that Lincoln could no longer "rejoice in our humiliation." Still, Confederates understood that their joy was fleeting. Slaveowner Mary Chesnut listened to the men around her talk about "a nation in mourning," with no reference to Lincoln or the Union, aware that the Confederacy's downfall was her people's abiding tragedy; "glorious young blood poured out like rain on the battle fields," Chesnut wrote. "For what?"[25]

Although Confederates contradicted comforting visions of universal grief, Lincoln's mourners could at least wave them away as the stubborn enemy and bitter losers. Northerners who declined to mourn the assassination, on the other hand—or, worse, openly celebrated it—proved more irksome to the loyal bereaved, turning the Union home front into a battleground. It was these subversives who most uncomfortably disrupted the idea of a unified victorious and grieving nation at war's end, for these antagonists dwelled within the Union states, among the mourners, in their own towns and cities, some even right next door. Named by their opponents after a poisonous snake, these were the *Copperheads*, members of the northern Democratic Party who disagreed with the whole premise of a war over slavery. In Chicago, a woman seen tearing down mourning drapery was quickly surrounded by an angry crowd, while in Boston a group of Irish servants made clear that they were "*so glad* Lincoln was dead!" As their employer explained it to herself, "They hate him for emancipating the negroes, fearing we shall employ them, & reduce the wages."[26]

Traitorous and seditious conduct within the Union Army and Navy included laughter, cheering, waving one's cap, and general joviality in response to news of the assassination, and Copperhead soldiers and sailors let loose all kinds of inflammatory remarks that resulted in assault by mourning comrades and arrest by authorities. They damned Lincoln and said he had gone to hell. They called him a cur, a son of a bitch, a damned son of a bitch, "a long slab-sided Yankee son of a bitch," and a "damned old whoremaster." A Union mate on the Mississippi River said he would find Lincoln's grave and "shit on it."[27]

Together, Confederates and Copperheads disrupted the illusion of a country convulsed by sorrow. Neither the majority of white southerners nor the vocal minority of white northerners belonged to the conjured nation-in-shock. Both groups earned the wrath of Lincoln's mourners, not only because the mourners loved Lincoln, but also because the words and actions of the renegades played havoc with visions of the nation at the exact moment in which the Union had triumphed, at least on the battlefield. Lincoln's mourners contradicted themselves all the time when they wrote about the grief of "the nation," sometimes conjuring the entire population ("North & South are weeping together," one woman wrote), other times clearly excluding Confederates or largely ignoring the Copperheads in their midst, and much of the time writing in sweeping phrases too vague to interpret one way or the other.[28]

If anything was intended to affirm worldwide grief, it was the funeral held in Washington, DC, on Wednesday, April 19, a beautiful spring day in the capital. Mourners came by the thousands, arriving on foot, on horseback, in carriages, and on special trains that the railroad companies added to their timetables. They filled every hotel and boardinghouse, slept in spare rooms, on floors, in their own conveyances, and out of doors. They came looking to participate in rituals that would help them understand God's purpose and the meaning of Lincoln's death. They came to take part in the making of history.[29]

Early the day before, people had begun lining up outside the heavily draped White House for the privilege of viewing the president's body, lying in state in the East Room. The catafalque stood so high that workmen had to remove an entire chandelier to accommodate it. The coffin revealed the top third of the president's body, clad in the same black suit he had donned for his second inauguration. Some who filed past found it majestic and imposing, but others found the experience disconcerting. One mourner found herself "jammed almost to death" before she even got in, and once inside, spectators were hurried along, each one given little more than a second to glance at the president, instructed not to linger, and prodded by guards whose job it was to see that only as many people entered as exited.[30]

The service held in the East Room was for dignitaries only: the new president, Andrew Johnson, along with cabinet members, generals, governors, senators and representatives, Supreme Court justices, ambassadors, and other eminent men. Missing, though, was Secretary of State William Seward, still recovering from the wounds inflicted by one of Booth's co-conspirators. Elder son Captain Robert Lincoln was there, struggling to retain his composure, but Mary Lincoln stayed away, unable to bear the rites surrounding her late husband.

Men from the Veteran Reserve Corps soon transferred Lincoln's coffin to the hearse that would carry it the mile and a half from the White House to the Capitol, where it would rest on a second custom-built catafalque in the Rotunda, also heavily draped. A carriage drawn by six horses and followed by one riderless mount, empty boots turned backward in the stirrups, conveyed the body. Many from the indoor service marched in the procession, joined by all manner of contingents: fraternal orders, workingmen, college students, hospital convalescents. First in the procession of infantry and cavalry were Black soldiers, though not by design. The Twenty-second US Colored Troops, who had welcomed President Lincoln to Richmond, Virginia, after the Confederate capital fell, were called to Washington "to represent the Colored Soldiers." Arriving by boat in the nick of time, they had met the procession head-on. Some sixty thousand spectators watched approximately forty thousand marchers, from curbs and pavement, windows and balconies, rooftops and treetops. Even as many "roasted in the sun" for hours (and those who stood too far back could follow along only by the gun salutes and clip-clop of horses' hooves), the gravity was palpable. One witness found it "a splendid sight and a mournful one," and a soldier listening from his hospital bed described an otherwise "solemn hush" over the whole city.[31]

For mourners at home in their own cities, towns, and villages that day, there were funeral services too. Bells, guns, and cannon began the formalities, complete with processions honoring flag-draped and empty horse-drawn coffins. Union soldiers everywhere, still in camp, polished their guns and boots for dress parades. In occupied southern cities, Yankees and Black residents marched together. In a Florida town, Sergeant Thomas Darling, once enslaved, offered an oration that included "the claims of our race to all legal rights."[32]

Planning and executing the funeral train—the homeward journey of Lincoln's body, from Washington, DC, to Springfield, Illinois—proved a herculean effort. Roughly three hundred passengers would ride in the nine-car train during any given segment, including all manner of federal and state officials, who traded places from city to city. In the eighth car lay two coffins: that of the president and that of Willie Lincoln, who had died in 1862, at the age of eleven, disinterred in Washington to be reburied with his father at home. At each major stop, guards kept watch over the boy while Lincoln's body was removed for local ceremonies. Robert Lincoln rode to Baltimore, then returned to Washington to stay with his mother. He would join the mourning rituals again only in Springfield. Mary Lincoln, her anguish and torment undiminished, stayed in the White House for the duration of the journey.

Wherever the train puffed into view, people gathered to watch. Once again, mourners walked, rode their horses, drove their buggies, and boarded other, specially scheduled trains to arrive at the closest venue at just the right moment. When that moment came, the mourners knelt, wept, prayed, doffed hats, removed bonnets, and held children aloft for a sight they would remember for the rest of their lives. Where springtime rains fell, spectators got wet and stayed damp, shoes and hemlines caked with mud, flags and white handkerchiefs soggy. Where the train traveled in darkness, mourners built bonfires or lit lanterns and torches. Even when the train chugged through a village at three o'clock in the morning in a heavy downpour, throngs paid tribute, often by the thousands.[33]

Mourners also crowded into the eleven cities chosen for the funeral train's stops along the way. In Philadelphia, a "living tide" gushed through the streets as the ceremonies ran late, and as dusk turned to darkness no one could see much of anything. Male spectators were "fumbling the women," and frustrated viewers became so unruly that policemen "beat the people back with their clubs." In New York, one mourner estimated a crowd of a hundred thousand lined up at two o'clock in the morning to view the body; another observer detected entirely too much gaiety the following day (women smiling in their spring dresses!). In the Midwest, a critic scoffed that the supposedly somber events amounted to "more of a show than respect for Lincoln." The weather was at its springtime best in New York, Albany, and Chicago, but heavy rains fell in Baltimore, Harrisburg, Cleveland, and Indianapolis, soaking the train's black drapery and causing the dye of mourning fabric to bleed onto building façades.[34]

Banners proclaimed emotion, in words both plain and poetic: "The Nation Mourns" or "The great heart of the nation throbs heavily at the Portals of his Grave." Everywhere, mourners pushed, shoved, and fainted, while pickpockets collected wallets and watches, and thieves worked the empty houses. Where a week or two earlier mourners had searched one another's faces for the meaning of the tragedy, now they read the placards. Nearly everywhere the words from Lincoln's Second Inaugural were visible: *With malice toward none.*[35]

No matter how satisfying or unsatisfying the rituals were, many of Lincoln's mourners had come for a single objective: to view the president's body up close, and for many that turned out to be a reverent experience. In Philadelphia, African American student and servant Emilie Davis eagerly anticipated the arrival of the funeral train. "The President comes in town this afternoon," she wrote in her diary, as if Lincoln were still alive. Davis's first two attempts to view the body failed because the crowds were so great, and the next day she waited hours for her turn; yet even that briefest glimpse was, for her, "a sight worth seeing." By the time the train got to New York, though, the decay of the president's face was evident. In Albany, mourners noticed the putrefying skin, and by Chicago the face had darkened nearly beyond repair. People there expressed surprise, disillusioned that Lincoln did not look "as they fancied great men did." Even before full deterioration set in, the face seemed more a mask: eyes shut and mouth artificially set, unable to impart either emotion or meaning to those shuffling past.[36]

Thursday, May 4, was an unusually hot day in Springfield. Mourners toured Lincoln's home, law offices, church pew, even his barbershop. Some had slept outside or just walked the streets all night, waiting for the train's arrival. Once off the train, Lincoln's body traveled in a lavish hearse drawn by six black horses, preceded by an Illinois regiment, and accompanied by a choir, gun salutes, and drumbeats. Robert Lincoln followed, and African Americans brought up the rear, as the procession moved toward Oak Ridge Cemetery. After two weeks and nearly seventeen hundred miles, the president would rest in a vault alongside a stream, with the much smaller coffin of Willie Lincoln beside him. Services at the cemetery opened with a prayer that invoked grief for the slain chief and acknowledged that millions had "come out of bondage." In his funeral oration, Bishop Matthew Simpson, from Washington, spoke of "sadness inexpressible" and "anguish unutterable," of God's will and of mercy, "with malice toward none." Already those four words had become the scripture of civil religion. Across the nation, mourners read about the burial and recorded their emotions. "Oh! how our hearts *ache* when we think of the cruel deed which ended his noble life," one woman wrote. Some were willing to think of Lincoln, finally, as a replaceable leader. His influence would be mighty, one man acknowledged, yet "the world will move on," he believed, "with other men" to "guide our national affairs."[37]

For the widow Mary Lincoln, there was no moving forward. *Poor Mrs. Lincoln.* How often the president's mourners invoked that phrase!

"Poor Mrs. Lincoln," wrote an eyewitness at Ford's Theatre. "How I pity her."

"Poor Mrs. Lincoln, her utter desolation," wrote a Boston mourner, "and how many years she has got to struggle on."

Even a Copperhead who had once referred to Mr. Lincoln as "Uncle Ape" could not help exclaiming to her diary, "Poor Mrs. Lincoln!"

Strangers to the president thought about the Lincolns' younger son too. "Poor little Tad," one woman wrote, recording (from the newspapers) how the twelve-year-old boy was "overcome with grief." Some included Robert in their thoughts as well. "The tears of sympathy flow for the widow & orphans of our martyred chief," another mourner told her diary. From around the world, letters of condolence flooded the family.[38]

For Mary Lincoln, there was little comfort to be taken in having been near her husband when he died. The president had passed his final hours in a too-small bed, in a cramped room at a random boardinghouse, with a steady stream of visitors coming and going, an investigation into his murder taking place in the very next room, even before he breathed his last. The men in charge had soon barred Mrs. Lincoln from the bedroom where her husband lay dying, finding her state of extreme distress overly irritating. Mary had already endured the deaths of two children (before Willie, son Eddie had died at the age of three, in 1850), and now she shut herself up in the private quarters of the White House. (One man in Washington recorded that when carpenters were setting up for the funeral services, the shattered first lady cried that each hammer blow sounded to her like a pistol shot.) After the burial in Springfield, a close friend wrote, "Mrs. Lincoln still sick and miserable." The widow would long remain troubled by emotional instability, never recovering from the trauma of her husband shot in the head before her eyes.[39]

If the funeral ceremonies appeared to imply a vision of universal mourning in a reunited nation, they also offered evidence of strife, both present and future. On Market Street in San Francisco, Irish soldiers broke through the April 19 procession, cutting off Black mourners from the rest of the parade. In New York, city officials wanted to bar Black people from the procession, but African Americans protested so adamantly that Secretary of War Stanton reversed the decree. Despite the yearned-for universality, mourners could find signs all through the grand funeral ceremonies that reconstruction would come hard to the post–Civil War nation.[40]

Lincoln's assassination compounded the uncertainty of what would happen next for the triumphant Union, with that uncertainty especially acute for African Americans. Although Black leaders had criticized the president's hesitancy regarding emancipation early in the war, Lincoln had over time been deeply influenced by the convictions of Black and white abolitionists. While Black southerners articulated the terrible question, *Would they be slaves again?*, free African Americans up north felt the loss of hope they had built on the escape of enslaved people to Union lines, on the Emancipation Proclamation affirming those actions, and on Confederate surrender affirming it decisively. Writing to the Black-owned *Christian Recorder*, correspondents relayed the mood around them: in Indiana, "The hope of our people is again stricken down"; in Chicago, "We felt as if all our hopes were lost."[41]

With the Confederacy and President Lincoln both gone, the future of the nation lay with President Andrew Johnson. African Americans and their allies were the first to voice concerns, worrying that the new executive "might not be as friendly toward the colored race" as his predecessor. Would disloyal white men be permitted to vote in the states of the former Confederacy while loyal Black men would not? In petitions to the new president, African Americans invoked Lincoln, in hopes, they told Johnson, that "the mantle of our murdered friend and father may have fallen upon your shoulders." Johnson's answers proved far from satisfying, including such dismissals as "It is not necessary for me to give you any assurance of what my future course will be."[42]

Most bereaved whites at first envisioned Johnson as "a sterner man," a "more radical man," a man of "*less yielding* nature" than Lincoln. It was Johnson's roots as a poor white southerner that led Black and white mourners to their divergent conclusions. Black mourners knew that impoverished Confederates (just the same as their better-off compatriots) believed that Black people were "made to be slaves," as one writer put it, and could not, wrote another, be "emancipated from negro-hate." White mourners, by contrast, took heart that, as one minister thought, Johnson despised the southern aristocracy as could only "a poor white, from the ranks." (Karl Marx himself agreed, writing to Friedrich Engels that the murder of Lincoln was the "greatest piece of folly" for Confederates, since Johnson "as a former poor white has a deadly hatred of the oligarchy.") Yet Johnson very soon revealed that his dislike for the southern aristocracy would be overruled by his virulent racism. As Black mourners cast Lincoln as a champion of freedom, his successor was rapidly turning out to be just the opposite.[43]

White abolitionists now followed the lead of African Americans, marshaling the words in Lincoln's April 11 speech suggesting voting rights for Black men as a forceful counterpoint to Johnson's favorable attitude toward former slaveowners. That spring evening in Washington, Lincoln had said that if some form of Black suffrage were not permitted, the "cup of liberty" held to the lips of those once enslaved would be dashed to the ground. Precisely because Lincoln was murdered and martyred, his Black mourners and their white allies felt free to extend those ideas however they saw fit in order to accomplish their goals.[44]

A little over three weeks after Lincoln's burial, President Johnson issued his first pardon proclamation, in effect granting voting rights to the white men who had fought against the United States while leaving the Black men who had, in the words of one petitioner, "poured out their blood lavishly," without political rights. As one freedman wrote ominously, "We see that the Rebels are being pardon'd verry fast." For his part, Johnson continued to brush off African Americans, telling them impatiently not to "expect progress to be too rapid" or asserting that there were "a great many things we would all prefer to have different." When Johnson unveiled his lenient plans for readmitting former rebellious states into the Union, former Confederates found their hopes rising, like the Tennessean who wrote to tell the new president that he wanted to see "a *white* Mans Government in America." As a discouraged white commander of Black troops wrote home from New Orleans in early summer, "If Andy doesn't put his foot on slavery hard, they will try to start it again somehow."[45]

God had taken Lincoln away, his more radical mourners now came to believe, to alert the victors to the enduring intransigence of their vanquished enemies. The assassination had opened the eyes of these radicals, both Black and white, to the necessity for revolutionary policies following Confederate defeat on the battlefield, because defeated Confederates who held political power could still win the war off the battlefield. Here again was God's providence. As the white Unitarian minister James Freeman Clarke had told his congregants on Easter Sunday, "As Abraham Lincoln saved us, while living, from the open hostility and deadly blows of the slaveholders and secessionists, so, in dying, he may have saved us from their audacious craft, and their poisonous policy." Clarke's language could not have been clearer. Without the assassination, the Union "might not have insisted on these conditions": he meant Black suffrage and the disfranchisement of slaveholders. Thus, had it been "necessary for Lincoln to die," Clarke explained, "to bring the nation to the point of mandating them." Here was the meaning of God's mysterious design, and political activists put forward the same message. On the Sunday after Easter, Wendell Phillips told his listeners that land and ballots for loyal Black men formed the "lesson God teaches us in the blood of Lincoln"—not, he made clear, as payback for the assassination, but rather "to teach the nation in unmistakable terms, the terrible foe with which it has to deal." In that light, the nation would best be served by the political impotence of slaveholders, coupled with the political power of formerly enslaved men.[46]

It would take two more years for moderate and radical Republicans in Congress to join forces to override Andrew Johnson, exchanging the president's policies for a much more far-reaching program that would establish voting rights for Black men, overseen by the occupying Union Army and the federal government. Here—if at times faltering from northern racism—was realized much of the vision of African Americans, as formulated in their petitions to President Johnson in the wake of Lincoln's assassination. These mourners were not avenging Lincoln's death; instead, as they made clear in the aftermath of the assassination, they wanted to avenge secession and war, and the cause of the war: slavery, which they understood as well to be the root cause of the assassination.[47]

That stunning moment of democracy and racial equality known as radical Reconstruction was accompanied by the horrific violence of the Ku Klux Klan, and with the end of Reconstruction in 1877 came the era of Jim Crow segregation and lynching, when once-radical white northerners abandoned their ideals for the sake of reconciliation with the white South. For those who mourned for the nation that they imagined President Lincoln would have created in the war's aftermath, the meaning of the assassination became more complicated in the post-Reconstruction world, the question *Why?* once again unanswerable. If slavery had indeed been the root cause of the assassination, had God truly intended Lincoln's death as a means to ensure equality by showing the victors that they must remain vigilant over their vindictive enemies? Or was the assassination nothing more than a catastrophe that disastrously slowed the long journey toward justice?[48]

With malice toward none, with charity for all. Many at the time thought they knew what President Lincoln meant by those oft-quoted words from his Second Inaugural Address, delivered a little more than a month before he died, and many today understand these words in the same way: as the Union Army approached triumph, it seemed Lincoln wanted the conquerors to treat their vanquished Confederate enemies with mercy. But African Americans, both North and South, interpreted Lincoln's imperative differently: to apply not to former Confederates, but just the opposite—to apply to themselves in their quest for equality. Accordingly, a Black woman had written a letter to a newspaper a few weeks after Lincoln's death, saying, "We all remember well the late President's last Inaugural Address, and what he said about paying back the blood drawn by the lash"—she was referring to Lincoln's pronouncement that the Civil War would continue "until every drop of blood drawn with the lash, shall be paid by another drawn with the sword." Accordingly, too, Lincoln's Black mourners had inscribed the two phrases, *with malice toward none* and *with charity for all,* on the banner they carried through the nation's capital on the Fourth of July 1865.[49]

That is what Lincoln meant as well, apparent in his call for the first steps toward granting voting rights to Black men, offered in the White House speech on April 11 that the bullet of John Wilkes Booth transformed into his last public address. Or at least that was the case made by African American victors-turned-mourners when they looked to the spirit of the martyred president to realize their visions of freedom and equality. That is why Frederick Douglass concluded that "to the colored people," Lincoln's death was "an unspeakable calamity."[50]

On the same July Fourth, Frederick Douglass reached for more of the words in Lincoln's Second Inaugural: to "strive on to finish the work we are in" as a means to achieve "a just, and a lasting peace." With that imperative in mind, Douglass believed that justice demanded voting rights for Black men, and that Black suffrage was the only road toward "permanent peace." In the twenty-first century, protestors against racial injustice echo these words in the phrase, "No justice, no peace."[51]

President Lincoln apparently thought little about his legacy—not only because he met an unexpected death, but also because, despite threats to his life during the Civil War, he remained indifferent to the possibility of his own demise. Across more than a century and a half, Lincoln's legacy has in fact been considerably dynamic, encompassing not only images of the Great Emancipator, but also more surprising depictions—as the best friend of the defeated Confederates (during Reconstruction and into the Jim Crow era) or the enemy of African Americans (during the Civil Rights Movement). When, in the early twenty-first century, protestors in the Black Lives Matter movement advocated tearing down the Freedman's Memorial in Washington—a monument that shows President Lincoln standing tall, with a mostly unclothed Black man kneeling at his feet, shackles broken, gazing into the distance—counterprotestors included Black historians and their white allies. That monument, designed by a white sculptor and funded by African Americans, had been unveiled in 1876, on the eleventh anniversary of the assassination, and the words of Frederick Douglass perhaps best capture the nuances of Lincoln's legacy.[52]

That day, Douglass had insisted on the complexity of the Civil War's history. Abraham Lincoln, he told the enormous crowd of mostly African American celebrants, was "preeminently the white man's President, entirely devoted to the welfare of white men." Douglass's fellow African Americans were, in turn, "at best only his stepchildren." But Douglass then asked his listeners to "take a comprehensive view" and to "make allowance for the circumstances," for if President Lincoln had not acted to retain the support of white Americans, the war would not have resulted in Black freedom. Toward the end of his oration came Douglass's most astute words: "Viewed from the genuine abolition ground, Mr. Lincoln seemed tardy, cold, dull, and indifferent," he intoned, "but measuring him by the sentiment of his country, a sentiment he was bound as a statesman to consult, he was swift, zealous, radical, and determined."[53]

If Abraham Lincoln created his own legacy, he did so unwittingly in his Second Inaugural, and before that, in the Gettysburg Address. The full texts of both are carved into another monument in the nation's capital, the Lincoln Memorial. Built in the era of Jim Crow, the memorial would later stand as a backdrop to civil rights activism. In 1939, contralto Marian Anderson performed on its steps, after the Daughters of the American Revolution denied her entry to the whites-only Constitution Hall, and in 1963, Martin Luther King Jr. delivered his "I Have a Dream" speech on those same steps, at the March on Washington for Jobs and Freedom.[54]

We cannot know what would have come to pass had Lincoln lived. We do know that the slain president's martyrdom permitted Black Americans and their white allies to invoke his name in the quest for equality. In the twenty-first century, we know also that this quest is not yet resolved, the meaning of the Civil War not yet resolved, and in this way the words of President Abraham Lincoln spoken on the battlefield at Gettysburg, in 1863, remain enduring too: "It is for us the living," he said that day, "to be dedicated" to "the unfinished work" that "government of the people, by the people, for the people shall not perish from the earth."[55]

Notes

This essay is drawn in part from Martha Hodes, Mourning Lincoln *(New Haven: Yale University Press, 2015).*

1. Alive: R. B. Milliken to "Friend Byron," Washington, DC, April 16, 1865, #54, Lincoln Room Miscellaneous Papers, Houghton Library, Harvard University, Cambridge, MA (hereafter HLH). Blazing, wild, crazy: John B. Stonehouse to John B. Stonehouse Jr., Washington, DC, April 16, 1865, #00368, Gilder Lehrman Collection, New-York Historical Society, New York (hereafter GLC-NYHS). Speech: Abraham Lincoln, "Last Public Address," April 11, 1865, in *The Collected Works of Abraham Lincoln,* ed. Roy P. Basler, 9 vols. (New Brunswick, NJ: Rutgers University Press, 1953–55) (hereafter *CWL*), 8:399–405. Booth: William H. Herndon and Jesse W. Weik, *Abraham Lincoln: The True Story of a Great Life,* 2 vols. (New York: D. Appleton, 1900), 2:289; John Wilkes Booth, "To Whom It May Concern," Philadelphia, November 1864, in *"Right or Wrong, God Judge Me": The Writings of John Wilkes Booth,* ed. John Rhodehamel and Louise Taper (Urbana: University of Illinois Press, 1997), 125.

2. Examples of accounts: Charles A. Sanford to Edward Payson Goodrich, Washington, DC, April 15, 1865, in "Two Letters on the Event of April 14, 1865," *Bulletin of the William L. Clements Library* 47 (February 12, 1946); George B. Todd to Henry P. Todd, Washington, DC, April 15, 1865, McClellan Lincoln Collection, John Hay Library, Brown University, Providence, RI (hereafter Brown); Gideon Welles diary, April 15, 1865, Welles Papers, Library of Congress (hereafter LC); W. R. Batchelder to mother, Washington, DC, April 16, 1865, Patricia D. Klingenstein Library, New-York Historical Society, New York (hereafter NYHS); Clara Harris to "Mary," Washington, DC, April 25, 1865, NYHS. Stanton: Adam Gopnik, "Angels and Ages: Lincoln's Language and Its Legacy," *New Yorker,* May 28, 2007.

3. Telegraph: George B. Todd to Henry P. Todd, Washington, DC, April 15, 1865, McClellan Lincoln Collection, Brown; Caroline Dunstan diary, April 15, 1865, New York Public Library (hereafter NYPL). Laborers and servants: William Warland Clapp diary, April 15, 1865, Clapp Diaries and Correspondence, HLH; Anna Cabot Lowell diary, April 15, 1865, Massachusetts Historical Society (hereafter MHS).

4. Doors: Mrs. Bardwell diary, April 15, 1865, Helen Temple Cooke Papers, Schlesinger Library, Harvard University, Cambridge, MA (hereafter SL); Emily Watkins to Abiathar Watkins, Jersey City, NJ, April 16, 1865, Watkins Papers, NYPL. Windows: Martha Fisher Anderson diary, April 15, 1865, MHS. Faces: Sarah Browne diary, April 15, 16, 1865, Browne Family Papers, SL. True: Anna Cabot Lowell diary, April 15, 1865, MHS.

5. Telegraph: John Wolcott Phelps commonplace book, April 15, 1865, Phelps Papers, NYPL; Henry Wirt Shriver diary, April 15, 1865, Shriver Family Papers, H. Furlong

Baldwin Library, Maryland Historical Society, Baltimore; "H.H." to cousin, Freeport, IL, April 15, 1865, Jefferson Hartman Correspondence, David M. Rubenstein Rare Book and Manuscript Library, Duke University, Durham, NC (hereafter Duke); Susan B. Anthony diary, April 15, 1865, Anthony Papers, LC; Patty Bartlett Sessions diary, April 15, 1865, ts., reel 15, Utah State Historical Society, American Women's Diaries: Western Women, Readex Newsbank, microform; Frederick G. Niles diary, April 15, 1865, Huntington Library, San Marino, CA (hereafter HL); Henry W. Pearce to "Lena," Marietta, OH, April 16, 1865, #00066.150, GLC-NYHS; C. R. Tolles to uncle, Kenosha, WI, April 16, 1865, Myron Tolles Papers, Duke; Eugene Marshall diary, April 16, 1865, Marshall Papers, Duke. Newspapers: Julius Ramsdell diary, April 19, 1865, Ramsdell Papers, Southern Historical Collection, University of North Carolina, Chapel Hill (hereafter SHC); Thomas J. Kessler diary, April 16, 19, 1865, #04562, GLC-NYHS; Charles Oscar Torrey diary, April 29, 1865, Torrey Papers, LC; Benjamin Moran diary, April 19, 24, 1865, Moran Papers, LC; T. B. Penfield to George Whipple, Brainerd, Jamaica, April 28, 1865, #F1–3841, reel 231, American Missionary Association Archives, Amistad Research Center, Tulane University, New Orleans, microform (hereafter AMA); "President Lincoln's Assassination," Santa Fe, NM, May 8, 1865, *New York Anglo-African* (published June 17, 1865); Charles Lowell Walker diary, May 8, 1865, HL; H. H. Himman to George Whipple, Sierra Leone, West Africa, June 16, 1865 (part of June 3 letter), #F1–9664, reel 242, AMA; Martha Green journal, July 13, 1865, MHS; Lowell H. Harrison, "An Australian Reaction to Lincoln's Death," *Lincoln Herald* 78 (1976): 12–17.

6. Astonished: Bruno Trombley diary, April 19, 1865, Civil War Miscellaneous Letters and Papers, Manuscripts, Archives and Rare Books Division, Schomburg Center for Research in Black Culture, NYPL. Astounded, calamity: George Comfort to Samuel Comfort, Morrisville, PA, April 16, 1865, Comfort Papers, Rare Books and Special Collections, Princeton University, Princeton, NJ (hereafter Princeton). Startled: Martha Fisher Anderson diary, April 15, 1865, MHS. Stupefied: George Bedson to Ichabod Washburn, Manchester, Eng., April 29, 1865, Washburn Family Papers, American Antiquarian Society, Worcester, MA (hereafter AAS). Thunderstruck: Charles Edward French diary, April 15, 1865, French Diaries and Papers, MHS. Catastrophe: John G. Nicolay to Therena Bates, "Chesapeake Bay," April 17, 1865, Nicolay Papers, LC. Dagger: Charles Oscar Torrey to Mira Torrey, Montgomery, AL, May 1, 1865, Torrey Papers, LC. Thunderbolt: Julia Anna Hartness Lay diary, April 15, 1865, NYPL. Thunderclap: Carl Schurz to wife, Raleigh, NC, April 18, 1865, in *Speeches, Correspondence, and Political Papers of Carl Schurz*, ed. Frederic Bancroft, 6 vols. (New York: G. P. Putnam's Sons, 1913), 1:253. Sky: Henry W. Pearce to "Lena," Marietta, OH, April 16, 1865, #00066.150, GLC-NYHS. Horrible: Lydia Stark to Franklin W. Fuller, Baldwinsville, NY, April 23, 1865, #03523.42.56, GLC-NYHS. Terrible: Sophia E. Perry diary, April 15, 1865, College of Physicians, Philadelphia. Scarcely: Edwin Greble Sr. to Susan Greble, Baltimore, April 16, 1865, Greble Papers, LC. Cannot: "Em" to Lewis J. Nettleton, Milford, CT, April 19, 1865, Nettleton-Baldwin Family Papers, Duke. How: Ruth Anne Hillborn journal, April 15, 1865, Hillborn Papers, Friends Historical Library, Swarthmore College, Swarthmore, PA (hereafter FHL).

7. Overwhelming: John Ritchie journal, April 23, 1865, Records of the Fifty-fourth Massachusetts, MHS. Distress: B. L. D. to editor, Louisville, KY, April 24, 1865, *Christian*

Recorder (published May 6, 1865). Untrue: Mary S. Pond to George Whipple, Portsmouth, VA, May 13, 1865, #H1–7147, reel 210, AMA; Edwin Greble Sr. to Susan Greble, Baltimore, April 16, 1865, Greble Papers, LC; Charles Edward French diary, April 15, 1865, French Diaries and Papers, MHS.

8. Michael Shiner diary, April 15, 1865, LC. Sarah G. Putnam diary, April 15, 1865, MHS.

9. Lines: Samuel Canby diary, April 15, 1865, Delaware Historical Society, Wilmington. Box: Caroline Barrett White diary, April 14–15, 1865, White Papers, AAS. Calligraphy: Ruth Anne Hillborn journal, April 15, 1865, Hillborn Papers, FHL. Details: John Williams diary, April 16, 1865, Duke; Washington H. Penrose diary, April 15, 1865, Penrose Papers, Historical Society of Pennsylvania (hereafter HSP).

10. Frantic: Sarah Browne to Albert Browne, Salem, MA, April 20, 1865, Browne Family Papers, SL. Crash: Richard M. Williams to Robert H. Williams, Nashville, TN, April 19, 1865, Goff-Williams Papers, HL. Sun: Caroline Barrett White diary, April 15, 1865, White Papers, AAS. Same: Edward Everett Hale to Charles Hale, Boston, April 15, 1865, box 6, Hale Papers, Manuscripts and Special Collections, New York State Library, Albany (hereafter NYSL).

11. State: Alfred Goldsborough Jones journal, April 15, 1865, NYPL. Intense: Simon Newcomb diary, April 15, 1865, Newcomb Papers, LC. Heavy: John G. Nicolay to Therena Bates, Washington, DC, April 18, 1865, Nicolay Papers, LC. Dreadful: S. L. Daffin to George Whipple, Wilmington, NC, April 30, 1865, #100009, reel 169, AMA.

12. Heartfelt: Hope R. Daggett to George Whipple, Norfolk, VA, April [n.d.], 1865, #H1–7058, reel 210, AMA. Deranged: P. B. S. Nichuston to George Whipple, Roanoke Island, NC, April 22, 1865, #100001, reel 169, AMA. Half: "From the Regiments," Charles Davis, Rock Island Barracks, IL, April 23, 1865, *New York Anglo-African* (published May 13, 1865). Unfeigned: Chester dispatches, Petersburg, VA, April 19, 1865, in *Thomas Morris Chester: Black Civil War Correspondent—His Dispatches from the Virginia Front,* ed. R. J. M. Blackett (Baton Rouge: Louisiana State University Press, 1989), 312, 318. Slaves: Mary S. Pond to George Whipple, Portsmouth, VA, May 13, 1865, #H1–7147, reel 210, AMA. Keenly: Joseph A. Prime, "Sermon Preached in the Liberty Street Presbyterian Church (Colored)," in *A Tribute of Respect by the Citizens of Troy* (Troy, NY: Young and Benson, 1865), 155. More: Jacob Thomas, "Sermon Preached in the African Methodist Episcopal Zion Church," in *Tribute of Respect,* 44. Dusky: "From Baltimore," *New York Anglo-African,* May 6, 1865. People: "From the Regiments," Richard H. Black, Fernandina, FL, *New York Anglo-African,* May 27, 1865. Intense: Theodore L. Cuyler, "Sermon IX," in *Our Martyr President* (New York: Tibbals and Whiting, 1865), 170.

13. Businesses: John Worthington to Mary Worthington, Cooperstown, NY, April 15, 1865, Autograph File, HLH. $100,000: Anne Baldwin to Charlotte Nettleton, New York, April 17, 1865 (part of April 16 letter), Nettleton-Baldwin Family Papers, Duke. Badges: Abigail Williams May to Eleanor Goddard May, Washington, DC, April 22, 1865, May and Goddard Family Papers, SL. See Lou Taylor, *Mourning Dress: A Costume and Social History* (London: Allen and Unwin, 1983); *crape* is the nineteenth-century spelling. Illumination: L. S. Currier to H. C. Rowley, Cincinnati, April 15, 1865, L. S. Currier and Co. Papers, AAS.

14. Wives, servants: Edwin Greble Sr. to Susan Greble, Baltimore, April 16, 1865, Greble Papers, LC. Buildings, miles: Charles A. Sanford to Edward Payson Goodrich,

Washington, DC, April 18, 1865, in "Two Letters." African Americans: Jane Swisshelm to *St. Cloud Democrat,* Washington, DC, April 17, 1865 (published April 27, 1865), in *Crusader and Feminist: Letters of Jane Grey Swisshelm, 1858–1865,* ed. Arthur J. Larsen (Saint Paul: Minnesota Historical Society, 1934), 288. On and on: Julia Adelaide Shepard to father, near Washington, DC, April 16, 1865, in "Lincoln's Assassination Told by an Eye-Witness," *Century Magazine* 77 (1909): 918.

15. Hammers: "Cornelia" to parent(s), New York, April 17–19, 1865, Lincoln Miscellaneous Manuscripts, NYHS. Bunting: Sarah Browne to Albert Browne, Salem, MA, April 20, 1865, Browne Family Papers, SL. Flags: Otis Norcross diary, April 15, 1865, MHS. Photographs: Emmeline Yelland to Albert Yelland, Galena, IL, May 1, 1865, Yelland Family Correspondence, Duke. Supplied: Laura Towne to unknown, Saint Helena Island, SC, April 29, 1865, in *Letters and Diary of Laura M. Towne,* ed. Rupert Sargent Holland (1912; rpt., New York: Negro Universities Press, 1969), 162.

16. Never: Henry J. Peck to Mary Peck, Burkeville Junction, VA, April 20, 1865, Peck Correspondence, NYSL. Good: Anna Cabot Lowell diary, April 15, 1865, MHS. Personally: Anne Baldwin to Charlotte Nettleton, New York, April 16, 1865, Nettleton-Baldwin Family Papers, Duke. Dear: Annie P. Chadwick diary, April 15, 1865, Chadwick Family Papers, NYSL. Beloved: "New York," *San Francisco Elevator,* April 28, 1865, #4917, Black Abolitionist Papers, ProQuest (hereafter BAP). Worse: J. Harry Keyes to Sarah Ogden, City Point, VA, April 30, 1865, #06559.060, GLC-NYHS. Almost: Mattie Smith diary, April 16, 1865, Chicago History Museum Research Center.

17. Mighty: Charles Barnard Fox, *Record of the Service of the Fifty-Fifth Regiment of Massachusetts* (Cambridge, MA: John Wilson, 1868), 75 (April 19, 1865, diary entry). Claimed: Franklin Boyts to Hiram Boyts, Washington, DC, April 17, 1865, in Boyts diary, HSP. Father Abraham: W. C. Cooper to Mercy Schenck, Nottaway Courthouse, VA, April 27, 1865, Schenck Family Papers, NYSL. Orphans: Caroline Barrett White diary, May 14, 1865, White Papers, AAS. Sorrowfully: Mary Ingham Emerson diary, May 28, 1865, Emerson Family Papers, NYPL. Father, mother: P. B. S. Nichuston to George Whipple, Roanoke Island, NC, April 22, 1865, #100001, reel 169, AMA.

18. Decorations: Mrs. Samuel Batchelder to Mary (Batchelder) James, Cambridge, MA, April 17, 1865, James Family Papers, SL. Crowds: Anna Cabot Lowell diary, April 16, 1865, MHS.

19. Atrocity: Anna M. Ferris diary, April 16, 1865, Ferris Family Papers, FHL. Drifting: Levi S. Graybill diary, April 17, 1865, Graybill Papers, HL.

20. Ministers: Edward Everett Hale to Charles Hale, Boston, April 15, 1865, box 6, Hale Papers, NYSL; James Thomas Ward diary, April 16, 1865, Ward Papers, LC.

21. Jacob Thomas, "Sermon Preached," in *Tribute of Respect,* 46. Chauncey Leonard to Lorenzo Thomas, Alexandria, VA, April 30, 1865, Letters Received, #287L, M619, roll 374, Adjutant General's Office, RG94, National Archives and Records Administration, Washington, DC (hereafter NARA).

22. Why: Mary Elizabeth Moore to James Otis Moore, Saco, ME, April 15, 1865, Moore Papers, Duke. Freedom: "Cosmorama," *San Francisco Elevator,* May 12, 1865, #4999, BAP. Frederick Douglass, "Our Martyred President," in *The Frederick Douglass Papers,* ed. John W. Blassingame and John R. McKivigan (New Haven: Yale University Press, 1979–92; hereafter *FDP*), ser. 1, 4:76. Wendell Phillips, "The Lesson of President

Lincoln's Death," in *Universal Suffrage, and Complete Equality in Citizenship* (Boston: Rand and Avery, 1865), 14.

23. Died: Laura Towne to unknown, Saint Helena Island, SC, April 29, 1865, in *Letters and Diary*, 162. Mankind: [illegible] to mother, "Potomac River," April 23, 1865, Nathaniel H. Harris Papers, SHC.

24. Tributes: *The Assassination of Abraham Lincoln . . . Expressions of Condolence and Sympathy* (Washington, DC: Government Printing Office, 1867); B. F. Morris, *Memorial Record of the Nation's Tribute to Abraham Lincoln* (Washington, DC: W. H. and O. H. Morrison, 1865).

25. Pity: William Calder diary, April 24, 1865, Calder Family Papers, SHC. Hurrah: Emma F. LeConte diary, April 20 and "Friday" [April 21], 1865, reel 22, Southern Historical Collection, University of North Carolina, Chapel Hill, American Women's Diaries: Southern Women, Readex Newsbank, microform. Gleam: Clara Dargan MacLean diary, April 20, 1865, MacLean Papers, Duke. Rejoice: John Q. Anderson, ed., *Brokenburn: The Journal of Kate Stone, 1861–1868* (1955; rpt., Baton Rouge: Louisiana State University Press, 1995), 341 (May 15, 1865, entry). Nation: C. Vann Woodward, ed., *Mary Chesnut's Civil War* (1981; rpt., New Haven: Yale University Press, 1993), 805 (May 7, 1865, entry).

26. Crowd: Elon N. Lee to family, Chicago, April 19, 1865, ts., Lee and Bastin Papers, Special Collections Research Center, University of Chicago (hereafter Chicago). Glad: Mrs. Samuel Batchelder to Mary (Batchelder) James, Cambridge, MA, April 17, 1865, James Family Papers, SL. Jennifer L. Weber, *Copperheads: The Rise and Fall of Lincoln's Opponents in the North* (New York: Oxford University Press, 2006).

27. Insults: John W. Nash, MM2531; John H. Casey, OO908; Henry Lopshire, MM2145; John McCarty, MM2226; Eli Smith, OO1173; James Walker, MM2771; John Ryman, OO1129, all in Court-Martial Case Files, entry 15, Office of the Judge Advocate General (Army), RG153, NARA; Thomas Smith, #4082, vol. 146, M273, roll 155, General Courts-Martial and Courts of Inquiry of the Navy Department, Office of the Judge Advocate General (Navy), RG125, NARA.

28. Weeping: Mary Peck to Henry J. Peck, Jonesville, NY, April 16, 1865, Peck Correspondence, NYSL.

29. Scott D. Trostel, *The Lincoln Funeral Train* (Fletcher, OH: Cam-Tech, 2002); Dorothy Meserve Kunhardt and Philip B. Kunhardt Jr., *Twenty Days: A Narrative . . . of the Assassination of Abraham Lincoln* (North Hollywood, CA: Newcastle, 1985).

30. Viewing: David Homer Bates diary, April 18, 1865, Bates Papers, LC. Imposing: James Williams to sister, New York, May 6, 1865, Simon Gratz Autograph Collection, HSP. Jammed: Rose Pickard to Angeline Flagg, Alexandria, VA, April 24, 1865, Pickard Papers, LC. Hurried: Charles A. Sanford to Edward Payson Goodrich, Washington, DC, April 18, 1865, in "Two Letters"; Helen Varnum Hill McCalla diary, April 18, 1865, LC.

31. Represent: James Otis Moore to Mary Elizabeth Moore, "Potomac River," April 19, 1865, Moore Papers, Duke. Roasted: Simon Newcomb diary, April 19, 1865, Newcomb Papers, LC. Splendid: Gertrude Dunn diary, April 19, 1865, Diaries Box, NYPL. Solemn: Selden Connor to sister, Washington, DC, April 19, 1865, Connor Papers, Brown.

32. Services: Doug Phillips to Aaron S. Crosby, Fallen Timber, PA, April 23, 1865, box 1, Miscellaneous Documents Relating to Abraham Lincoln, HLH; "Day of the Obsequies,"

San Francisco Elevator, April 21, 1865, #4812, BAP. Camp: William H. Richards to "Anna," Camp Lowell, VA, April 20, 1865, Brown Family Papers, NYSL. Claims: "From the Regiments," Richard H. Black, Fernandina, FL., *New York Anglo-African,* May 27, 1865.

33. See for example Jennie M. Smith to Mercy Schenck, Syracuse, NY, May 7, 1865, Schenck Family Papers, NYSL.

34. Tide: Anna M. Ferris diary, April 22, 1865, Ferris Family Papers, FHL. Fumbling: anonymous diary, April 23, 1865, John L. Smith Papers, HSP. Beat: Alexander M. Thackara to Benjamin Thackara, Philadelphia, April 24, 1865, Sherman Thackara Collection, digital .library.villanova.edu. 100,000: Samuel S. Halsey to Joseph J. Halsey, Morristown, NJ, May 1, 1865, Morton-Halsey Papers, ser. E, part 1, reel 37, University of Virginia Library, Records of Ante-Bellum Southern Plantations, microform. Gaiety: Ellen Kean to "Miss Sherritt," Baltimore, May 13ff., 1865, in *Death and Funeral of Abraham Lincoln . . . in Two Long Descriptive Letters . . .1865* (London: Privately printed, 1921), 22. Show: William M. Myers to William H. Henshaw, Danville, IL, May 12, 1865, Ann Henshaw Gardiner Papers, Duke.

35. Banners: "Funeral Honors on the Route from Washington to Springfield," in Morris, *Memorial Record,* 195, 200, 183. Malice: "Notebook containing drawings and transcriptions of memorial tributes to Abraham Lincoln," McLellan Lincoln Collection and Center for Digital Scholarship, Brown.

36. President: Emilie Davis diary, April 22, 23, 24, 1865, HSP. Face: Asa Fitch diary, April 25, 1865, Fitch Papers, Manuscripts and Archives, Sterling Memorial Library, Yale University, New Haven. Fancied: Elon N. Lee to family, May 3, 1865, ts., Lee and Bastin Papers, Chicago.

37. Springfield: Robert Steele to "Mrs. Wood," Cairo, IL, May 9, 1865, box 2, Miscellaneous Documents Relating to Abraham Lincoln, HLH. Bondage: "Prayer," in Morris, *Memorial Record,* 226. Simpson: "Funeral Oration by Bishop Simpson," in Morris, *Memorial Record,* 230, 236. Hearts: Caroline Barrett White diary, May 4, 1865, White Papers, AAS. World: Elon N. Lee to family, Chicago, May 3, 1865, ts., Lee and Bastin Papers, Chicago.

38. Mrs. Lincoln: John Downing Jr. to "My Dear Friend," [no place], April 26, 1865, in Timothy S. Good, *We Saw Lincoln Shot* (Jackson: University Press of Mississippi, 1995), 68; Sarah Hale to children, Brookline, MA, April 18, 1865, box 10, Hale Family Papers, Sophia Smith Collection, Smith College, Northampton, MA; Maria Lydig Daly, *Diary of a Union Lady, 1861–1865,* ed. Harold Earl Hammond (New York: Funk and Wagnalls, 1962), 357 (April 25, 1865, entry), xli (Uncle Ape). Tad: Anna Cabot Lowell diary, April 20, 1865, MHS. Tears: Caroline Barrett White diary, May 4, 1865, White Papers, AAS. Letters: Justin G. Turner and Linda Levitt Turner, *Mary Todd Lincoln: Her Life and Letters* (New York: Alfred A. Knopf, 1972), 225.

39. Pistol: Edgar Welles to George Harrington, Washington, DC, April [20?], 1865, Harrington Papers, HL. Sick: Elizabeth Blair Lee to Samuel Phillips Lee, Washington, DC, May 12, 1865, Blair and Lee Family Papers, Princeton. Catherine Clinton, *Mrs. Lincoln: A Life* (New York: HarperCollins, 2009), 248–291.

40. "Day of the Obsequies," *San Francisco Elevator,* April 21, 1865, #4812, BAP; J. Sella Martin, "Colored People Excluded from the Funeral Procession," *Liberator,* May 5, 1865, #2863, BAP.

41. Slaves: Alonzo A. Carr to brother and sister, Beaufort, SC, April 21, 1865, Cynthia Anthonsen Foster Papers, SL. Hope: "From Our Indiana Corresponding Editor," New Albany, IN, April 17, 1865, *Christian Recorder* (published April 29, 1865). Felt: "Ruth," "Chicago Correspondence," May 3, 1865, *Christian Recorder* (published May 20, 1865). Eric Foner, *The Fiery Trial: Abraham Lincoln and American Slavery* (New York: W. W. Norton, 2010).

42. Friendly: Hope R. Daggett to George Whipple, Norfolk, VA, April [n.d.], 1865, #H1–7058, reel 210, AMA. Mantle: "From North Carolina Blacks," New Bern, NC, May 10, 1865, in *The Papers of Andrew Johnson*, ed. Paul H. Bergeron, 16 vols. (Knoxville: University of Tennessee Press, 1967–) (hereafter *PAJ*), 8:58. Assurance: "Reply to Delegation of Black Ministers," May 11, 1865, *PAJ*, 8:63.

43. Sterner: Samuel Comfort to Susan Comfort, Petersburg, VA, April 21, 1865, Comfort Papers, Princeton. Radical: Hallock Armstrong to Mary Armstrong, near Petersburg, VA, April 16, 1865, in *Letters from a Pennsylvania Chaplain . . . 1865* (n.p.: Privately published, 1961), 28. Less: Caroline Butler Laing to Mary Butler Reeves, Brooklyn, NY, April 21, 1865, Butler-Laing Family Papers, NYHS. Made: "The Blacks and the Ballot," *Christian Recorder*, May 27, 1865. Emancipated: "Emancipation of the White Man," *New York Anglo-African*, July 23, 1865. Poor: Edward Everett Hale to Charles Hale, Boston, April 25, 26, 1865, box 6, Hale Papers, NYSL. Folly: Karl Marx to Friedrich Engels, May 1, 1855, in Karl Marx and Friedrich Engels, *The Civil War in the United States* (New York: International Publishers, 1937), 275. Annette Gordon-Reed, *Andrew Johnson* (New York: Henry Holt, 2011).

44. Cup: Abraham Lincoln, "Last Public Address," April 11, 1865, *CWL*, 8:404.

45. Pardons: Andrew Johnson, "Amnesty Proclamation," May 29, 1865, *PAJ*, 8:128–131. Poured: "From Delegation Representing the Black People of Kentucky," Washington, DC, June 9, 1865, *PAJ*, 8:203–5. Pardon'd: William Benjamin Gould diary, July 11, 1865, MHS. Expect: *Chicago Tribune*, June 15, 1865, cited in *PAJ*, 8:205n8. White: John W. Gorham to Andrew Johnson, Clarksville, TN, June 3, 1865, *PAJ*, 8:173. Andy: Samuel Miller Quincy to mother, New Orleans, June 28, 1865, Quincy, Wendell, Holmes, Upham Family Papers, MHS.

46. James Freeman Clarke, "Who Hath Abolished Death," in *Sermons Preached in Boston on the Death of Abraham Lincoln* (Boston: J. E. Tilton, 1865), 101–2. Wendell Phillips, "The Lesson of President Lincoln's Death," in *Universal Suffrage*, 16, 14.

47. See Eric Foner, *Reconstruction: America's Unfinished Revolution, 1863–1877* (1988; updated ed.: New York: Harper Perennial, 2014).

48. See Henry Louis Gates Jr., *Stony the Road: Reconstruction, White Supremacy, and the Rise of Jim Crow* (New York: Penguin Books, 2019).

49. Remember: "Ruth," "Chicago Correspondence," May 3, 1865, *Christian Recorder* (published May 20, 1865). July Fourth: "Washington Correspondence," *Christian Recorder*, July 15, 1865. See Abraham Lincoln, "Second Inaugural Address," March 4, 1865, *CWL*, 8:333.

50. Frederick Douglass, "Abraham Lincoln, a Speech," late December 1865, 16, Frederick Douglass Papers, LC.

51. Strive: Abraham Lincoln, "Second Inaugural Address," March 4, 1865, *CWL*, 8:333. Permanent: "Letter from Frederick Douglass," Rochester, NY, July 1, 1865, in *Celebration*

by the Colored People's Educational Monument Association (Washington, DC: McGill and Withernow, 1865), 5.

52. Indifferent: Michael Burlingame, *Abraham Lincoln: A Life* (Baltimore: Johns Hopkins University Press, 2008), 2:807–9. Legacy: Richard Wightman Fox, *Lincoln's Body: A Cultural History* (New York: W. W. Norton, 2015), 127–327; John McKee Barr, *Loathing Lincoln: An American Tradition from the Civil War to the Present* (Baton Rouge: Louisiana State University Press, 2014); Barry Schwartz, *Abraham Lincoln and the Forge of National Memory* (Chicago: University of Chicago Press, 2000). David W. Blight, "Yes, the Freedmen's Memorial Uses Racist Imagery. But Don't Tear It Down" and Clarence Williams and Hannah Natanson, "Lincoln Statue Sparks Arguments," *Washington Post,* June 25, 27, 2020. Kirk Savage, *Standing Soldiers, Kneeling Slaves: Race, War, and Monument in Nineteenth-Century America* (1997; rev. ed.: Princeton, NJ: Princeton University Press, 2018), 89–128.

53. Frederick Douglass, "The Freedmen's Monument to Abraham Lincoln," *FDP,* ser. 1, 4:431, 432, 433, 436.

54. Scott A. Sandage, "A Marble House Divided: The Lincoln Memorial, the Civil Rights Movement, and the Politics of Memory, 1939–1963," *Journal of American History* 80, no. 1 (June 1993): 135–167.

55. Abraham Lincoln, "Address Delivered at the Dedication of the Cemetery at Gettysburg," November 19, 1863, *CWL,* 7:23.

Andrew Johnson's North Carolina Legacy

HOW A SOUTHERN CAPITAL REMEMBERS ITS NATIVE SON

Brandon A. Robinson

I N RALEIGH, NORTH CAROLINA, tourists visit the historic 1840 State Capitol on Union Square, unaware of the lingering historical and spatial tensions between Andrew Johnson's legacy and North Carolina's efforts to fulfill the promises of the Reconstruction Era that began under his watch. One hundred yards to the south on Fayetteville Street stands the spot where the seventeenth president was born.[1] An imposing bronze memorial to three presidents with ties to North Carolina also stands on the Capitol grounds: Andrew Jackson, born near the border between North and South Carolina, and who studied law in the piedmont town of Salisbury; James K. Polk, born near present-day Charlotte and an 1818 honors graduate of the University of North Carolina; and Andrew Johnson, born in Raleigh, who with no formal education or father to guide him, rose to the highest office in the United States. Whereas the monument credits Jackson for revitalizing democracy and Polk for expanding America's boundaries, Johnson's tribute is "He defended the Constitution."

Johnson's epitaph comes into sharp relief against another backdrop in downtown Raleigh. Just a ten-minute walk to the west of Johnson's statue is St. Paul African Methodist Episcopal (AME) Church, one of Raleigh's oldest African American churches. The contrast between these two sites highlights North Carolina's painful reckoning with the legacies of slavery, the failures of Reconstruction, and the entrenchment of Jim Crow. At the church site, participants at the 1865 Freedmen's Convention demanded full citizenship and equal treatment of formerly enslaved people in a new state constitution required for North Carolina's readmission into the Union.[2] Until 1877, federal troops occupied the old Governor's Mansion (today the site of the Duke Energy Center for the Performing Arts) at the south end of Fayetteville Street.[3] Finally, just a couple of blocks north of the Capitol there is a developing square between the Executive Mansion and the North Carolina General Assembly. Recently dedicated as Freedom Park, this green space commemorates the struggles of African Americans to achieve freedom in North Carolina, and was designed by Phil Freelon, the same architect who designed the Smithsonian Museum of African American History and Culture in Washington, DC. These landmarks coexist in Raleigh's center—and within a mile or two of each other—yet they also represent the complicated legacies of North Carolina and Andrew Johnson as they relate to the Constitution, Reconstruction, race, and southern politics.

Those tensions among slavery, freedom, and equality have reemerged in recent years because of racial injustice and police brutality, which has generated new interest in racism in America, both historically and at present. For example, a Confederate statue known as "Silent Sam" was removed from the University of North Carolina–Chapel Hill campus after multiple protests in the wake of the violence at the 2017 "Unite the Right Rally" in Charlottesville, Virginia. Other Confederate monuments across the state met the same fate, including one on the grounds of Durham County's former courthouse, and two at the State Capitol itself, which had been there since 1895 and 1914.[4] Yet, as of this writing, not only does Andrew Johnson's statue sit beside those of his presidential peers; but there have also been no prominent calls for its removal from the Capitol grounds, where it has been since President Harry S. Truman dedicated it in 1948 with much fanfare. Recent history raises the question why the statue of Andrew Johnson—consistently ranked as one of the worst presidents in American history—continues to command such staying power in North Carolina.

Despite his lackluster rankings among presidential historians—he ranked twenty-third of thirty-one presidents in Arthur M. Schlesinger Jr.'s famous 1962 poll, and has sunk to and remained in the bottom five ever since—Johnson continues to be an enduring, even revered figure with many North Carolinians, including those who acknowledge his flaws and mishandling of Reconstruction.[5] This goodwill stems from three sources: first, Johnson's deep Scotch-Irish roots, shared widely among white North Carolinians from the mountain and piedmont regions, and his dogged determination to overcome poverty to achieve high station; second, his leniency toward the South in executing Reconstruction policies; and third, the inspiration that Johnson provided for a populist, Democratic Party tradition in North Carolina, right through the 2008 presidential candidacy of former US senator John Edwards.[6] Johnson was neither saint nor sinner in the annals of North Carolina, but rather a human link to its imperfect past—an inspiration to a formerly impoverished state that spent the entire twentieth century modernizing its economy, society, and institutions.

The first seventeen years of Andrew Johnson's life were spent principally in Raleigh, where he was born in 1808 in a detached kitchen at Casso's Inn. Located near today's Fayetteville and Morgan Streets (where the Supreme Court of North Carolina's Justice Building presently sits), the inn was a popular attraction since its 1759 founding by Peter Casso, a French immigrant to the United States.[7] The Johnson family had English and Scotch-Irish roots, and barely subsisted from the earnings Jacob Johnson made as a porter at Casso's, as well as from other odd jobs. By age three, Johnson was fatherless, and at age fourteen, he and his brother William were forced by their mother, Mary "Polly" McDonough Johnson, to become apprentices to James J. Selby, a tailor. Johnson labored for Selby in return for board, clothing, and training. After just two years, however, the Johnson brothers broke their contract by fleeing, prompting Selby to post an ad in the *Raleigh Gazette:* "Ran away from the Subscriber, on the night of the 15th instant, two apprentice boys, legally bound, named William and Andrew Johnson. . . . I will pay the above Reward [ten dollars] to any person who will deliver said apprentices to me in Raleigh, or I will give the above Reward for Andrew Johnson alone."[8] After briefly returning to Raleigh while hiding from Selby, Johnson ventured westward into Tennessee with his mother and stepfather in a one-horse cart carrying everything they owned.[9] The seventeen-year-old settled in what would be his home base for the rest of his life—Greeneville, Tennessee. Here he opened his own tailor shop, and, without ever attending formal schooling in North Carolina, pored over printed speeches of the English politicians William Pitt the Younger and Charles James Fox to teach himself how to read.[10]

Johnson's temperament and character were forged by the state that was considered a backwater by early nineteenth-century cultural standards, especially compared to its genteel neighbors Virginia and South Carolina. Despite selecting Tennessee as his adopted home, Johnson's North Carolina roots shaped the adult and politician he became. From its colonial beginnings, North Carolina was a hardscrabble, unstratified society for its white inhabitants, who were financially unable to purchase enough enslaved people to support a true slaveocracy like their counterparts in other southern states. As a result, North Carolina did not become a slave-centered society in the manner that allowed figures such as George Washington, Thomas Jefferson, James Madison, William Byrd II, or Henry Laurens to exercise outsized authority over society in Virginia and South Carolina.[11] In addition, North Carolina's economy was highly diversified for a southern state, and Germans and Scotch-Irish settlers in the mountains and piedmont regions relied upon manufacturing, the trades, mining, and eventually railroads for economic sustenance. As the historian Victoria Bynum noted, "The religious, class, and ethnic diversity of North Carolina's white population encouraged leaders to cultivate an egalitarian rather than aristocratic ideal of republicanism."[12]

This kind of society foreshadowed both Johnson's and North Carolina's ambivalence about secession in 1861. Although not objecting to white supremacy as an organizing principle, North Carolina's poorest whites (most of whom were Scotch-Irish) were reluctant to leave the Union, seeing no direct benefit to fighting a civil war to protect a way of life in which they were not considered much better than enslaved people or free Blacks. North Carolina legislators had authorized the nation's first public university and had guaranteed public higher education for the common people in the state constitution. But a lingering resentment had remained of the English planter class from the east who dominated state politics.[13] This tension was exacerbated by both the American Revolution and the Civil War. In 1860, 85 percent of North Carolina's General Assembly members were slaveholders, despite comprising only 27.7 percent of the state's population.[14] While the North Carolina population generally did not own slaves, the majority of its policymakers in Raleigh did, and thereby possessed an economic stake in the outcome of secession and the Civil War.

Because Johnson was neither English in heritage, nor Anglican or Episcopalian in religious persuasion, his kin's distaste for centralized authority in the hands of easterners would have been a powerful cultural force during his childhood and informed his populist politics as he climbed the political ladder in Tennessee. The farther west one traveled in North Carolina toward Tennessee—perhaps even along the route Johnson took at age seventeen with his family—the more one would have encountered white communities where the inhabitants were German or Scotch-Irish rather than English, and where the dominant religious persuasions would have been Moravian, Presbyterian, Methodist, or Baptist, rather than Anglican or Episcopalian.[15] And while Johnson would have felt comfortable with the racism in the towns where he lodged on his journey, he would have seen, almost with every dozen or so miles, an increasingly attenuated bond with slavery as a way of life.

Accordingly, Johnson's power base during his tenures as governor of Tennessee, US senator from Tennessee, and military governor of Tennessee were the regions in Tennessee most hostile to slavery and secession. Given the similarity in ethnicity, geography, cultural norms, and economic systems between western North Carolina and eastern Tennessee, it is understandable that the future Confederacy struggled to suppress dissent in those areas, but also why Johnson would have appealed to Lincoln as a running mate in 1864, as a southerner loyal to the Union. Lincoln never envisioned a weighty portfolio for Johnson, not unlike his predecessors up to that time, and many successors afterward.

All the same, Johnson did own slaves once he became an established tailor in Greeneville because he viewed African Americans as naturally inferior and sought to fit in with the elite community. A prosperous tailor, small businessman, and state legislator by the 1830s, Johnson purchased his first enslaved person—a teenage woman named Dolly—for a hefty sum of $500. Johnson later owned up to at least half a dozen enslaved workers, three of whom included Dolly's children, whom some historians have speculated were either the offspring of Johnson himself or another member of the Johnson family. Given the relatively small number of enslaved individuals he owned—relative to his financial means at the time—Johnson likely owned them more for domestic convenience and as a status symbol rather than as a deep-seated commitment to a slavocracy. In 1858, Johnson boasted, "I have not got many slaves; I have got a few; but I made them by the industry of these hands. . . . What I own cost me more labor and toil than some who own thousands, and got them because they were the sons of moneyed people."[16]

Despite this claim and Johnson's pride in showcasing his newfound social status, this social benefit never clouded his views on union and secession. Johnson "at times exhibited a morbid distress and feeling against negroes" according to his private secretary—mainly because he feared both race wars and widespread miscegenation—but he remained a Union man at heart, even as a proud southerner. As the author Milton Lomask noted, Johnson "dreaded the effects on the South of the destruction of slavery, he was certain that slavery could not survive a civil war."[17] When faced with the choice of loyalty to slavery and loyalty to the Union, the latter was Johnson's choice without hesitation. But even as Johnson took public stands against slavery, at the same time he clung to the predicate of Black inferiority that made slavery justifiable to himself and his neighbors.[18]

Having made his life and political career in Tennessee, Johnson did not meaningfully register in the public mind of North Carolina until he ascended to the presidency after Abraham Lincoln's assassination just over a month into his vice presidency.[19] Upon becoming president in April 1865, Johnson's primary challenge was to oversee Reconstruction and readmission of the former Confederate states into the Union. How he managed this task, and how Congress reacted to him, dominates the historical discussion of Johnson, whether one is a critic of, or apologist for, his actions.

Some North Carolinians, who were less likely to share the politics of the Republican Congress that impeached Johnson, warmly embraced the state's native son in the White House. After Johnson's acquittal in the US Senate by one vote in late May 1868, Fred G. Roberts of Edenton, North Carolina, wrote a congratulatory note to Johnson: "I feel proud that you was [sic] born in the old North State—that you are not ashamed of it, that you do not shrink from proclaiming to the world that you were a working man—I again congratulate you on your signal victory over your enemies—God bless you & family."[20] William T. Dortch, a prominent lawyer and state legislator during the Confederate era, complained about North Carolina governor William Holden's Reconstruction reforms. Dortch feared social unrest and pleaded with Johnson, "[a]t the request of the white people of this section of the State," to "have the 40th Reg. colored troops, removed from this place & that they may be replaced by white troops if deemed necessary."[21] Johnson also received many supportive letters from North Carolinians of all walks of life when the Tennessee state legislature voted to return the former president to the US Senate in 1875.[22]

Tennessee was the natural backdrop for Johnson's postpresidential retirement and death, as well as public mourning of him. His Greeneville home had survived the Civil War years, although he lamented that "Rebel troops" had stolen his books during wartime occupation.[23] Recalling his childhood efforts at literacy, Johnson was particularly pained at losing the volume of speeches by English statesmen, noting, "When I was learning my trade at Raleigh, North Carolina, a gentleman used to come into the shop and read aloud, and seeing that we tailors enjoyed it so much, he used frequently to come, and finally gave me the book which was the first property I ever owned."[24] Johnson credited this book with "caus[ing] my thoughts to take a channel which they might not and probably would not have otherwise taken."[25] For this self-taught man, his private library was so valuable that Johnson tried unsuccessfully to find the stolen books and papers by contacting former Confederate general James Longstreet, whose troops had raided Johnson's house during the Confederate occupation of Greeneville in 1864.[26]

Although Johnson was comfortable in Greeneville, he desired to return to politics in some capacity. The seeds of his brief return to Washington began in 1869, when a split between radical and conservative Republicans allowed Democrats to recapture the Tennessee legislature.[27] US senators were still elected by state legislatures rather than by direct popular vote, and Johnson came within three votes of returning to the Senate.[28] According to neighbors, Johnson became depressed and resumed his heavy drinking habits, and assumed that now in his early sixties, his political career was over.[29]

A surprise political revival occurred in January 1875—Johnson's last year alive—when, on the fifty-fourth ballot, Johnson won election to the US Senate by one vote. Once chosen, the senator-elect received a letter from the senator who saved him from conviction for impeachment in 1868, Edmund G. Ross of Kansas, who observed: "Your vindication from the slanders born of the hatred & malice of the impeachers of 1868 is now well nigh complete."[30] To this day, Johnson remains the only US president to serve in the Senate following a White House tenure.

Johnson did not live long enough to engage in any extensive policymaking upon returning to the Senate. He did manage to attend a February 1875 special session to consider the ratification of a treaty with Hawaii. When Johnson returned to the Senate, just one of the nineteen members who had voted for his acquittal remained in office, and only thirteen of the thirty-five who voted guilty. On March 5, Johnson was formally seated, and was sworn into office by Vice President Henry Wilson, who as a senator had voted to convict Johnson during his impeachment trial.[31]

Senator Johnson's death came as a surprise to both his kin and the nation, although tell-tale signs had subtly alerted Johnson's family in the weeks before his death, mainly in the form of headaches and heart problems.[32] In July of 1875, Johnson planned a trip to visit his daughter, Mary Stover Brown of Carter County, Tennessee. During his journey, he penned his last writing—a brief note requesting a carriage meet him at Carter's Station, several miles from his daughter's house. As a postscript, Johnson writes, "Excuse my letter paper as I happen to be out at the moment, A.J."[33] Already suffering headaches, Johnson arrived at Carter's Station but did not see the carriage, so he set out for his daughter's home on a borrowed horse. About halfway on the final leg, he was intercepted by the carriage, and comfortably rode to his daughter's front door. After relaxing and enjoying a large family dinner and postprandial banter, the former president retired to his room upstairs. Shortly thereafter, his granddaughter heard a loud thud, and the family discovered that Johnson had fallen to the floor after suffering a massive stroke.[34]

When Johnson's relatives found him on the floor, he could barely speak, but managed to tell them that he could not move anything on the left side of his body. After he was placed in his bed, Johnson forbade any calls for a doctor, insisting he would recover naturally. His instructions were followed, and Johnson seemed to be rallying. The next day, local Masons from the Elizabethton lodge—just two miles away—showed up and offered their services when reports of the former president's illness began to circulate. At this point, it became increasingly clear to all but Johnson that he was dying. Less than thirty-six hours later, a second stroke occurred, this time prompting the family to call two local doctors for assistance. Immediately recognizing that Johnson's condition was grim, the doctors nonetheless made repeated efforts to revive the former president, who was numb and unconscious for his final hours. Between two-thirty and three in the morning on July 31, 1875, the seventeenth president of the United States died.[35]

The public mourning began almost immediately. President Ulysses S. Grant issued a proclamation to the country, praising Johnson as a "distinguished public servant," and ordering that all federal government buildings in Washington, DC, be draped in black until the funeral, with all public business suspended on July 31.[36] In Greeneville, local churches tolled their bells, and all businesses closed their doors. The Elizabethton Masons returned to Mary Stover Brown's house, this time with a pine box filled with ice, to hold Johnson's body until it could be relocated to his home in Greeneville for funeral preparations. Johnson's remains were wrapped in blankets and deposited in the box, then escorted back to Carter's Station.[37]

Once the six-mile trip was complete, the Masons opened the pine box to inspect Johnson's body, and, not noticing any obvious signs of decomposition, promptly closed it again. From Carter's, a train was boarded to Greeneville, where Johnson's body was received by Greeneville Masonic Lodge No. 119—the same order to which Johnson was officially inducted into Freemasonry as an adopted Tennessean—and performed Masonic rites over the body. The pine box was placed upon a wagon and driven to Johnson's home, where his body was washed, prepared, and dressed for burial. By this time, the body had begun to decompose, necessitating a closed-casket funeral.[38] The former president was placed in a new casket that featured silver emblems of the Masonic order, and a plate that read, "ANDREW JOHNSON, AGED 67 YEARS." The casket was displayed in the parlor of Johnson's house, where hundreds of Greeneville residents visited until Monday at noon.[39]

According to a lengthy obituary from the Greeneville Intelligencer, "every store, office and public building" in Greeneville "was put in dressings of sorrow," including Johnson's retirement office and old tailor shop. A committee of the town's civic leaders convened to organize the public ceremonies for Johnson's funeral; it was chaired by the prominent lawyer, Joseph R. Brown, and included the mayor and county sheriff. After visitation at the Johnson home concluded, the Masons returned to transport the casket to the Greeneville courthouse, where Johnson laid in state until his final procession. An estimated 5,000 mourners congregated in downtown Greeneville, witnessing Johnson's final march to his place of interment.[40]

Just before the procession, two local groups—a cadre of young men who called themselves the "Johnson Guards" and a separate contingent called the "Dickinson Light Guard," with its own band—merged at the Greeneville train station and marched in step to the courthouse to retrieve the former president. Local marshals, bands, civic figures, and the Masons accompanied a hearse drawn by four dark-colored horses; next came Johnson's family, Governor James Porter of Tennessee, and other public dignitaries, and finally, the public. Counting all participants, the funeral procession was a mile long, and several funeral marches were played as Greeneville's residents ululated their adopted son from North Carolina.[41]

On a prominent hill on family-owned land, not far from Johnson's house, a grave of five to six feet in depth had been dug—in the bottom of which was placed a zinc-lined vault, to better safeguard the casket and its contents. At Johnson's request, his body was wrapped in the American flag, with either his head or his hand (depending on which account one reads) resting on his 1835 copy of the US Constitution, which Johnson believed he had defended against congressional overreach in a partisan impeachment seven years before. In one final act of homage, members of the Knight Temple Masons ascended the hill with commanding views of eastern Tennessee and western North Carolina and formed a 200-foot circle around Johnson's casket. After final rites were performed, a prayer was uttered, and several stanzas of mourning were sung, Andrew Johnson was laid to rest.[42]

Johnson's reputation in his native and adopted states has closely paralleled the direction that southern historiography has taken in the century and a half since his presidency. Johnson's character in the public eye reflects the way historians viewed him before and after the 1960s. His legacy rose with Jim Crow and racial segregation, but since the advancement of the Civil Rights Movement, he has declined in the public's mind. Johnson historiography falls into two distinct schools: first there is the "Dunning School" that dominated Reconstruction scholarship for roughly the first half of the twentieth century, followed by the "New Left School" that emerged during the 1960s. This bottom-up approach to the past—examining the lives and experiences of peoples who were either marginalized or excluded from the larger historical narrative—continues to influence and shape scholarship today.

The Dunning School of Reconstruction was named for its founder, William A. Dunning, a prominent Columbia University history professor. Dunning and his acolytes assumed outsized influence over the public's view of Andrew Johnson and Reconstruction due to their tenured positions at America's leading colleges and universities and their standing as the first professional historians to emerge as the modern academy was born in the late nineteenth century.[43] In the nineteenth century, upper-class gentlemen like Henry Adams, George Bancroft, and Francis Parkman dominated scholarship up to the age of the modern academy. Starting in the twentieth century, professional scholars with doctorates influenced the field of history, under the auspices of the modern academic department.[44] Dunning and those who followed him used this power to depict Reconstruction as one of the nadirs of American history.

By Dunning's interpretation, Reconstruction was destined to fail from the beginning because it was predicated on the idea that racial equality was achievable or desirable. The Dunning School's central thesis was that Black Americans, naturally uncivilized, could never be trusted to participate in self-government alongside whites, and that allowing this created a self-fulfilling prophecy of political incompetence and corruption, thereby necessitating the return of the South to "home rule" by whites, even if doing so required violence and discrimination.[45]

This view of Reconstruction coincided with several larger social, political, economic, and demographic shifts at the turn of the twentieth century. As racial discrimination and violence grew, and Jim Crow laws were strengthened by the Supreme Court's ruling in *Plessy v. Ferguson*, some six million African Americans began leaving the South for other parts of the country. The Dunning School interpretation was also widely disseminated through D. W. Griffith's popular film, *The Birth of a Nation* (1915), later spurring the revival of the Ku Klux Klan in the 1920s across the United States. Dunning's thesis proved highly useful to southern politicians after World War II when Black Americans, along with their liberal white and Jewish allies, attempted a Second Reconstruction through racial integration.[46] Dunning School supporters, including President Woodrow Wilson who supported racial segregation of the federal workforce in 1913, believed that the same perceived failures of Reconstruction would upend society in the mid-twentieth century and do injustice to whites who rightly deserved to govern the South alone.[47] W. E. B. Du Bois, the prolific Black academic, writer, and activist, was the Dunning School's greatest critic and foil, but it would be almost two generations before his groundbreaking work, *Black Reconstruction* (1935), shifted Reconstruction perspectives in history graduate programs across the country. In his stand that Reconstruction anticipated a truly representative American democracy, Du Bois sowed the seeds of a historiographical paradigm shift.[48] He conceded that some Reconstruction Era Black officials had faltered in their political and public administration roles but explained that this failure was due to a lack of training and the recent lived experience of enslavement, as opposed to innate incompetence.[49]

Despite Du Bois's efforts as scholar and public intellectual, Andrew Johnson greatly benefitted from the Dunning School narrative.[50] He was portrayed as a hero—mainly because of his strong resistance to federal civil rights legislation, his support for white supremacy, and his willingness to allow the former Confederate states to govern their own institutions and customs, including race relations. Whereas President Lincoln, acting on his Second Inaugural Address pledge to govern "[w]ith malice toward none; with charity for all," desired to treat the South with grace as it gradually reentered the Union,[51] Johnson took it a step further in his desire to end federal oversight of Reconstruction altogether. As historian C. Vann Woodward later observed, "Andrew Johnson aligned himself politically with opponents of equal rights of black freedmen in the North and with white resistance in the South, and by liberal use of pardon and veto and appointive power did all he could to block or frustrate the enforcement of civil liberties, voting rights, and equal protection of the law for the newly created black citizens."[52] Along with the creation and proliferation of "Lost Cause" ideology, Johnson's actions as president laid the groundwork for Dunning and his followers, and their interpretation and distortion of the Reconstruction Era continued for decades.

Given the power of the Dunning School, it is no surprise that Johnson biographies would mostly reflect vanguard thinking. To this day, the most authoritative treatments of Johnson's life are from the Dunning period, although some full-length biographies have since been published. The cornerstone of all Johnson secondary literature is Lloyd Paul Stryker's 881-page *Andrew Johnson: A Study in Courage* (1929), a highly sympathetic, cradle-to-grave biography that bolstered Johnson's reputation as a defender of the Constitution, a victim of an unfair impeachment, and as a standard-bearer of the Old South. Although generally well received, it was harshly criticized

in a 1930 issue of the *North Carolina Historical Review*. R. W. Winston, a
noted North Carolina lawyer, state legislator, and man of historical letters,
faulted Stryker's work for its uncritical treatment of Johnson's administrative skills in overseeing Reconstruction, and the absence of close com-
parisons between Johnson's political style and Lincoln's, despite the book's
voluminous length.[53] Winston pointed to Johnson's lack of any meaningful
legislative accomplishments while serving in Congress, and his poor relationships with his legislative peers, which foreshadowed his troubles with
Congress when he later became president. Rather than serving his poorer
constituents, Johnson was a populist demagogue who stirred social passions without constructively channeling or allaying them through policy.[54]

Whether Winston's views reflected popular consensus on Johnson—or
Stryker's benign view of him—North Carolina's political elite wholeheartedly
embraced Raleigh's native son. Nowhere is this demonstrated better than
at the 1948 dedication of the bronze presidential monument at the North
Carolina State Capitol, where the life-scale depictions of Andrew Jackson,
James K. Polk, and Andrew Johnson sit to this day. North Carolina governor R. Gregg Cherry and other leading civic officials spoke at the dedication,
and the keynote speaker was Johnson's greatest champion among his modern presidential successors: President Harry S. Truman.

President Truman was in the middle of a bitter election campaign when
he arrived in Raleigh in October to dedicate the new memorial. He came
to the event with a deep interest in Andrew Johnson. Besides their obvious similarities as southern Democrats from humble beginnings, Truman
likely also identified with the burden of following a larger-than-life predecessor who died in office. As Truman biographer David McCullough noted,
"But with the exception of Andrew Johnson, no vice president had ever suc-
ceeded so towering a figure as Franklin D. Roosevelt, and though Lincoln
loomed larger than any President in history, Lincoln had not been a world
leader, nor the Civil War a titanic, global conflict."[55]

Truman had approvingly read Stryker's life of Johnson and wrote a glowing review of both biographer and subject for the *North Carolina Historical
Review*. Praising Stryker's biography as "the best biography I have seen," the
thirty-third president recounted Johnson's rise from poverty and the various positions that carried him to the presidency, giving generous credit to

FIGURE 5. Charles Keck's statue honoring three North Carolina–born US presidents—James K. Polk, Andrew Jackson, and Andrew Johnson—outside the state capitol in Raleigh, North Carolina. (Photo by Carol M. Highsmith, between 1980 and 2006. Carol M. Highsmith Collection, Prints and Photographs Division, Library of Congress, Washington, DC, LC-HS503–4171, https://www.loc.gov/item/2011632478/)

Johnson's wife, Eliza, for assisting in her husband's self-education efforts while raising his five children.[56] Of Johnson's stature among presidents, Truman elaborated: "He became a real Constitutional President and knew more about the Constitution than any President before or since has known. He became great because of that document. It has taken ninety years for the facts to come out, but they have. The facts will always come out if we have the right sort of historians. Few historians, so-called, are objective. The truth will usually come to the view of the people if enough historians write about the truth."[57] Without commenting on Johnson's racial views or slaveholding prior to the Civil War, Truman distinguished Johnson from other presidents for his willingness to withstand congressional overreach in defense of his perspective on a chief executive's constitutional prerogatives.[58]

In this spirit, Truman and the North Carolina political elite celebrated Johnson at the steps of the 1840 State Capitol in Raleigh. Between 1945 and 1948, a commission of political notables oversaw the purchase of a bronze monument to Presidents Jackson, Polk, and Johnson. Attendees included R. W. Winston, state legislator and future US senator Willis Smith, and Josephus Daniels, longtime publisher of the Raleigh *News & Observer*, secretary of the navy under Woodrow Wilson, and US ambassador to Mexico under Franklin D. Roosevelt. Governor Melville Broughton made all initial appointments, and his successor, Governor R. Gregg Cherry, accepted the monument on behalf of the State of North Carolina.[59]

Looking down historic Fayetteville Street to the block where Johnson was born 140 years prior, the crowed enjoyed lively music—the National Anthem at the beginning, and "Stars and Stripes Forever" at the end—by the 82nd Airborne Division Band from Fort Bragg, North Carolina. After an invocation by Pastor Broadus E. Jones of Raleigh's First Baptist Church, the bronze memorial was unveiled with the help of C. Lawrence Winn, President Jackson's great-great-grandson by adoption; James Knox Polk, President Polk's great-nephew; and Margaret Johnson Patterson, President Johnson's great-granddaughter.[60] After Willis Smith recognized the sculptor, Charles Keck, by asking him to stand in front of the crowd, Governor Cherry and President Truman delivered their impressions of the three North Carolina–reared presidents.

Governor Cherry, mindful of the tenable argument that Tennessee also deserves credit for the North Carolina-native presidents' successes, carefully mediated between the two states by observing that although Jackson, Polk, and Johnson all came to maturity and political notoriety in Tennessee, their roots, and egalitarian spirit, came from the great state of North Carolina. Noting that North Carolina, unlike its neighbors Virginia and

South Carolina, never embraced an established, statewide culture centered on large plantations, Governor Cherry added that North Carolina also never had a consolidated, dominant culture that lorded its power over white yeoman farmers. "The result was, I believe, that [North Carolina] maintained an informal and refreshing spirit of democracy which was ingrained in the men she sent to the White House," the governor deduced.[61]

Governor Cherry expressed pride that the seventeenth president "belongs not only to North Carolina; he belongs especially to the City of Raleigh."[62] The governor analogized Johnson with Jackson and Polk in the sense that they—all Democrats from the South—fought for the common (white) man, remarking, "Southerners have a special reason to admire this man who defended them in time of tragedy against the extremists who would make the South a conquered province."[63] Before concluding his remarks, Governor Cherry pointed 100 yards down from Fayetteville Street to the site of Johnson's birth, noting also that the president's father, Jacob Johnson, remained interred at Raleigh's old City Cemetery.[64]

At this point, President Truman, accompanied on the platform stand by First Lady Elizabeth "Bess" Truman and their daughter Margaret, stood up to deliver the keynote address. After praising his "old friend" Josephus Daniels as "that great North Carolinian who contributed so much to the creation of this monument," the president thanked Charles Keck (with whom he had had worked in the past on other projects), and mused that through its three native presidential sons, "the State of North Carolina has much to teach the country."[65] Truman believed that Jackson, Polk, and Johnson had been "almost completely discarded by later generations," and "because they were misunderstood they were libeled beyond the lot of most Presidents."[66] These presidents' subpar reputations were due to their service during existential crises for democracy and peace. Because of their willingness to make tough decisions, each was in some way a scapegoat at which popular frustrations were misguidedly aimed. Truman saw in his three predecessors a lesson that he hoped would prevail for himself, whatever the outcome of his candidacy in the 1948 presidential election two weeks later: "Do your duty, and history will do you justice," adding, "Each of these men did his duty as President of the whole nation against the forces of pressure and persuasion which sought to make him act as a representative of a part of the nation only."[67]

Since Truman's dedication, history has attempted to do "justice" to Andrew Johnson, though probably not in a form Truman would find desirable, accurate, or fair. Johnson's reputation began to shift from commendable to blameworthy after the 1960s, when liberals achieved cultural and political ascendancy following the Dwight Eisenhower years, and the Civil Rights Movement inspired a "New Left" school of American historiography.[68] Subsequent waves of scholarship have explored history through the lenses of race, gender, ethnicity, class, and sexuality. Historians also began to place more emphasis on social and cultural history, microhistories, and mass movements, rather than just presidential administrations, wars, and geopolitical developments. The Dunning School, which had held sway for most of the twentieth century up to that time, gave way to a redefining of Reconstruction as a second American Revolution and acknowledgment of the centrality of race in American democracy. As the historian Eric Foner put it, the "Second Reconstruction"—that is, the post–World War II Civil Rights Movement—inspired historians to rethink the first Reconstruction, and as result, "in rapid succession virtually every assumption of the old viewpoint was dismantled."[69]

This historiographical shift has defined Reconstruction ever since and continues to influence new studies and scholarship across disciplines. The voices of enslaved people, working-class whites, grassroots activists, and other underrepresented or excluded groups such as women, Native Americans, and immigrants that were virtually invisible in the Dunning narrative are now examined in vivid detail.[70] This evolution has undermined the legacy and others, not by diminishing their historical importance, but by reducing their space in the overall narrative and judging their actions based on the social and racial mores that gained ascendancy after the social movements of the 1960s. Whereas the Dunning consensus held that "radical" Republicans had imposed Black supremacy on innocent white southerners only wishing to defend their honor after the Civil War, the new interpretation viewed fusion politics as America's first genuine attempt at racial equality (echoing what Du Bois had espoused in the 1920s and 1930s). Congressional Republicans like Charles Sumner and Thaddeus Stevens, no longer depicted as vindictive partisans out to get Johnson, emerged as noble reformers and statesmen.[71] Johnson was revealed as a racist politician "too stubborn to compromise with his critics."[72] The congressional Republicans did not destroy Johnson by enacting the Tenure of Office Act and impeaching Johnson for its violation. Instead, Johnson destroyed his own presidency by the dint of his stubbornness, racism, and lack of the political sensitivities that characterized Lincoln's leadership.[73] While book-length treatments of Johnson's life are few since the 1960s, in the overall, broader narrative of Reconstruction, there is little to no resemblance to his stature per Dunning, Stryker, Truman, or Cherry.[74]

Today, however, the populist spirit that Johnson embodied nurtures the ambitions of aspiring North Carolina politicians. Perhaps no one illustrates this better in modern times than former US senator and presidential candidate John Edwards. Campaigning for president in 2008 on the idea of "two Americans"—one for haves, and one for have-nots—Edwards drew from his roots as a boy who grew up in a small North Carolina mill town, where class resentments seemed to resonate more strongly than racial ones.[75] As longtime Raleigh *News & Observer* political columnist Rob Christensen observed, "Edwards' populism—delivered with a smile and the pleasant personality of a suburban evangelist or a midmarket TV news anchor—tapped into the growing insecurities of Joe Lunch Bucket."[76] Edwards's populism echoed the insecurities of Andrew Johnson—a variation on an old nineteenth-century theme. Edwards became the first native North Carolinian to become the vice presidential nominee of a major political party since Andrew Johnson in 1864, but also the most viable presidential candidate from North Carolina (with the possible exception of former governor and US senator Terry Sanford, in the 1970s) since Jackson, Polk, and Johnson.[77] Although the hegemony of the southern Democratic Party dissipated after the 1960s, the democratic populism that helped shape Johnson will not only power future political careers in North Carolina, but will also continue to be part of Johnson's enduring appeal to many southerners and North Carolinians of working class and Scotch-Irish roots, whatever Johnson's less palatable qualities may be.

If Johnson were standing near his bronze statute today at the State Capitol, he would notice under way the newest addition to Raleigh's official state mall: North Carolina Freedom Park, the only monument in the capital's center dedicated to African Americans, and the most prominent testament to their story in Raleigh, other than the Martin Luther King Jr. Memorial on the nearby boulevard bearing his name. Supported by both public and private funds, the park was conceived in 2002 and included as supporters some of North Carolina's most notable figures—the late historian John Hope Franklin; the late former president of the UNC system, William C. Friday; the late civil rights lawyer and North Carolina Central University chancellor, Julius Chambers; and the late philanthropist Mary Duke Biddle Trent Semans. As it nears completion on a one-acre site between the Executive Mansion and the General Assembly, the park will eventually be gifted to the state in perpetuity as a tribute not only to the millions of enslaved African Americans who helped build North Carolina's economy in the eighteenth and nineteenth centuries, but also to those who took an active role in shaping and influencing its modern institutions through its forward-looking 1868 Constitution, and making the promise of that historical document real in the spirit of the state's Latin motto, *Esse Quam Videri* ("to be, rather than to seem"), during and after the Jim Crow era.[78] By depicting the agency of Black men and women during the Reconstruction period that Johnson's apologists omitted from their accounts of the period, the architect, founders, and supporters of Freedom Park do not seek to erase Johnson from that chapter of North Carolina's history, but to bring into proper balance the forces and aspirations that shaped events from that formative period. So far, none of these efforts have been accompanied by calls for Johnson's removal from the downtown he once walked as an adolescent North Carolinian. The seventeenth president's statute overlooks a fuller, more comprehensive picture of the state's past, with his role and attribution preserved.

Andrew Johnson, though not generally well regarded by historians, scholars, and the public today, will continue to matter in the state and city where he was born. To North Carolinians, Johnson is a source of pride as well as contempt, and it is impossible to tell its full story without him. The president's Scotch-Irish roots, populist tendencies, rags-to-prosperity life trajectory, and paradoxical views of the Union and African Americans are as relevant today as they were in the nineteenth century. As both North Carolina and America grapple with questions of race and Reconstruction's yet-unfulfilled promise on that front, it is likely that a more nuanced

146 BRANDON A. ROBINSON

appreciation of Johnson as a full, multidimensional human being—like most of us—will emerge.

Notes

1. A stone marker commemorates that event. The structure where Johnson was born has been relocated to Historic Mordecai Park, just a mile northeast of the Capitol: https://raleighnc.gov/places/mordecai-historic-park/.
2. Jeffrey Crow, Paul D. Escott, and Flora J. Hatley, eds., *A History of African Americans in North Carolina* (Raleigh: North Carolina Office of Archives and History, 1992, 2002), 79, 85.
3. The white supremacist campaign of 1898–1900 engineered a coup d'état against an elected government, in Wilmington in 1898, which disenfranchised Black men in 1900. Glenda Elizabeth Gilmore, *Gender and Jim Crow: Women and the Politics of White Supremacy in North Carolina, 1896–1920* (Chapel Hill: University of North Carolina Press, 1996); David Zucchino, *Wilmington's Lie: The Murderous Coup of 1898 and the Rise of White Supremacy* (New York: Atlantic Monthly Press, 2020).
4. "Protesters Topple Silent Sam Confederate Statue at UNC," *News & Observer,* August 21, 2018, https://www.newsobserver.com/news/local/education/article217035815.html. "NC Governor Orders Confederate Monuments Removed at Capitol after Statues Toppled," *News& Observer,* June 21, 2020, https://www.newsobserver.com/news/local/article243682477.html.
5. William A. DeGregorio, *The Complete Book of U.S. Presidents* (Fort Lee, NJ: Barricade Books, 2005), 255; C-SPAN Presidential Historians Survey 2017, available at https://www.c-span.org/presidentsurvey2017/?page=overall.
6. H. Tyler Blethen and Curtis W. Wood Jr., *From Ulster to Carolina: The Migration of the Scotch-Irish to Southwestern North Carolina* (Raleigh: North Carolina Division of Archives and History, 1998).
7. Jennifer A. Kulikowski and Kenneth E. Peters, *Images of America: Historic Raleigh* (Charleston, SC: Arcadia, 2002), 12.
8. DeGregorio, *Complete Book of U.S. Presidents,* 247–48.
9. DeGregorio, *Complete Book of U.S. Presidents,* 248.
10. DeGregorio, *Complete Book of U.S. Presidents,* 249.
11. Gordon S. Wood, *The Radicalism of the American Revolution* (New York: Vintage Books, 1991), 117–18.
12. Victoria E. Bynum, *Unruly Women: The Politics of Social and Sexual Control in the Old South* (Chapel Hill: University of North Carolina Press, 1992), 18–23.
13. Bynum, *Unruly Women,* 19.
14. Bynum, *Unruly Women,* 19. *Encyclopedia of North Carolina,* s.v. slavery, https://www.ncpedia.org/slavery/.
15. Bynum, *Unruly Women,* 21–23.
16. Sarah Fling, "The Formerly Enslaved Households of President Andrew Johnson," White House Historical Association, https://www.whitehousehistory.org/the-formerly

-enslaved-households-of-president-andrew-johnson/. Annette Gordon-Reed's *Andrew Johnson* (New York: Times Books, 2011) details how Johnson began to purchase slaves as his stature in Greeneville society grew.

17. Milton Lomask, *Andrew Johnson: President on Trial* (New York: Farrar, Straus, 1960), 17.

18. Gordon-Reed, *Andrew Johnson*, 12.

19. David Herbert Donald, *Lincoln* (New York: Simon and Schuster, 1995), 505–7.

20. "Impeachment Trial of President Andrew Johnson, 1868," US Senate, https://www .senate.gov/about/powers-procedures/impeachment/impeachment-johnson.htm. Fred G. Roberts to President Andrew Johnson, June 12, 1868, in "Letters to Andrew Johnson," *North Carolina Historical Review*29, nos. 1–4 (January–October 1952): 572.

21. William T. Dortch to President Andrew Johnson in "Letters to Andrew Johnson," 573.

22. "Letters to Andrew Johnson," 576–77.

23. Albert Castel, *The Presidency of Andrew Johnson* (Lawrence: Regents Press of Kansas, 1979), 213.

24. Castel, *Presidency of Andrew Johnson*, 214.

25. Castel, *Presidency of Andrew Johnson*, 213.

26. Castel, *Presidency of Andrew Johnson*, 214.

27. Castel, *Presidency of Andrew Johnson*, 214.

28. Castel, *Presidency of Andrew Johnson*, 214.

29. Castel, *Presidency of Andrew Johnson*, 214–15.

30. Castell, *Presidency of Andrew Johnson*, 216.

31. Castel, *Presidency of Andrew Johnson*, 216–17.

32. *The Papers of Andrew Johnson*, vol. 16, *May 1869–July 1875*, ed. Paul H. Bergeron (Knoxville: University of Tennessee Press, 2000), 769.

33. *Papers of Andrew Johnson*, 760.

34. *Papers of Andrew Johnson*, 770.

35. *Papers of Andrew Johnson*, 770–71.

36. *Papers of Andrew Johnson*, 764.

37. *Papers of Andrew Johnson*, 771.

38. *Papers of Andrew Johnson*, 772; DeGregorio, *Complete Book of U.S. Presidents*, 255.

39. *Papers of Andrew Johnson*,772.

40. *Papers of Andrew Johnson*, 773–74; 775.

41. *Papers of Andrew Johnson*, 775–77.

42. *Papers of Andrew Johnson*, 775, 777; Castell, *Presidency of Andrew Johnson*, 230. For the Johnson family burial site, see: https://www.nps.gov/anjo/cemeteryhist.htm.

43. Eric Foner, *The Second Founding: How the Civil War and Reconstruction Remade the Constitution* (New York: W. W. Norton, 2019), xxi–xxiii.

44. Louis Menand, *The Metaphysical Club: A Story of Ideas in America* (New York: Farrar, Straus and Giroux, 2001), 215, 230, 414–417.

45. Menand, *The Metaphysical Club*, 215, 230, 414–17.

46. Menand, *The Metaphysical Club*, xxii–xxiii.

47. Patricia O'Toole, *The Moralist: Woodrow Wilson and the World He Made* (New York: Simon & Schuster, 2018), 77–81; Kendrick A. Clements, *Woodrow Wilson: World Statesman* (Chicago: Ivan R. Dee, 1999), 97–101; A. Scott Berg, *Wilson* (New York, G. P. Putnam's Sons, 2013), 409.

48. David Levering Lewis, *W.E.B. Du Bois: Biography of a Race, 1868–1919* (New York: Henry Holt, 1993), 462.

49. Lewis, *W.E.B. Du Bois*, 384.

50. Lewis, *W.E.B. Du Bois*, 15.

51. Mark E. Neely Jr., *The Last Best Hope of Earth: Abraham Lincoln and the Promise of America* (Cambridge, MA: Harvard University Press, 1993, 1995), 177–81.

52. C. Vann Woodward, *The Burden of Southern History* (Baton Rouge: Louisiana State University Press, 1960), 238–39.

53. R. W. Winston, review of *Andrew Johnson: A Study in Courage,* by Lloyd Paul Stryker, *North Carolina Historical Review* 7, nos. 1–4 (January-October 1930): 155–56.

54. Winston, review, 156.

55. David McCullough, *Truman* (New York: Simon & Schuster, 1992), 356.

56. Harry S. Truman, "The Most Mistreated of Presidents," in the *North Carolina Historical Review* 36, no. 1 (January 1959): 197.

57. Truman, "Most Mistreated of Presidents," 204.

58. Truman's view of overreach exemplified in Youngstown Sheet & Tube Co. v. Sawyer, 343 U.S. 579 (1952).

59. *Addresses and Papers in Connection with the Unveiling of a Monument to the Three Presidents North Carolina Gave the Nation* (Raleigh: Graphic Press, 1949), 1–10.

60. *Unveiling of a Monument,* 9.

61. *Unveiling of a Monument,* 23.

62. *Unveiling of a Monument,* 25.

63. *Unveiling of a Monument,* 25–26.

64. *Unveiling of a Monument,* 26.

65. *Unveiling of a Monument,* 32.

66. *Unveiling of a Monument,* 33.

67. *Unveiling of a Monument,* 34.

68. Eric Foner, ed., *The New American History* (Philadelphia: Temple University Press, 1997), 96.

69. Foner, ed., *New American History,* 97.

70. Examples include Edward L. Ayers, *The Promise of the New South: Life after Reconstruction* (New York: Oxford University Press, 1992, 2007); Eugene D. Genovese, *Roll, Jordan, Roll: The World the Slaves Made* (New York: Vintage Books, 1972, 1974); Charles Wilkinson, *Blood Struggle: The Rise of Modern Indian Nations* (New York: W. W. Norton, 2005). While the "New Left" and many subsequent historiographical fields draw upon the bottom-up approach to history, it should be noted that these are all distinct and compelling ways of studying the past.

71. See Fergus M. Bordewich, "Back in the American Pantheon," review of *Thaddeus Stevens,* by Bruce Levine, *Wall Street Journal,* March 6–7, 2021, C7–C8.

72. Foner, ed., *The American History,* 97.

73. Foner, ed., *The American History,* 97.

74. One of the more recent Johnson biographies is a brief, 192-page work by Annette Gordon-Reed, *Andrew Johnson* (2011), published through the Times Books series on American presidents, inspired by Arthur M. Schlesinger Jr., who edited the series and recruited scholars to write brief sketches of all past American chief executives.

75. Rob Christensen, *The Paradox of Tar Heel Politics: The Personalities, Elections, and Events That Shaped Modern North Carolina* (Chapel Hill: University of North Carolina Press, 2008), 300–301.

76. Christensen, *Paradox,* 301.

77. Christensen, *Paradox,* 301–2.

78. Information and background on North Carolina Freedom Park can be found at https://ncfmp.nationbuilder.com/.

"The Old Lion Is Dead"

THEODORE ROOSEVELT AND THE CREATION
OF AN AMERICAN ICON

Matthew R. Costello

D URING THE SUMMER OF 2020, countless demonstrations against systemic racism and police brutality unfolded across the United States and around the world. In addition to protesting the killings of unarmed Black men and women, many activists took their frustrations out on physical representations of the American past. For years, citizens and organizations had been petitioning state and city governments to remove statues of Confederate leaders from public places. They argued that these statues celebrated traitors who had rebelled against the United States and fought to preserve racial slavery. When that effort was defeated, they and others created a Lost Cause mythology that elevated the nobility of their fight while reinforcing wider societal beliefs in white supremacy. This debate was not a new one; however, the nation's reckoning with racism expanded this dialogue, as demonstrators targeted all kinds of historical figures. Statues of Christopher Columbus, George Washington, and Abraham Lincoln were vandalized, and some were even toppled. As Americans grappled with the violent deaths of Ahmaud Arbery, Breonna Taylor, and George Floyd, some sought justice by deliberately destroying statues of individuals who had espoused racist views during their lifetimes or enacted prejudicial policies. Others pursued change by challenging organizations, institutions, universities, and museums to make their sites more equitable, accessible, and inclusive for all Americans.

One of the statues that faced a new wave of criticism was the equestrian statue of Theodore Roosevelt outside the American Museum of Natural History in New York City. The statue features the twenty-sixth president on horseback, accompanied by one Native American man and one African man on foot. Commissioned by the Roosevelt Memorial Association (RMA), it was designed by sculptor James Earle Fraser in collaboration with architect John Russell Pope, who was tasked with creating the Theodore Roosevelt Memorial within the museum. The statue listed the years of Roosevelt's life, as well as his terms as governor and president, and was created to celebrate his support of the museum. According to Fraser, "The two figures at [Roosevelt's] side are guides symbolizing the continents of Africa and America, and if you choose may stand for Roosevelt's friendliness to all races."[1] The Roosevelt family approved the design, and seventy-nine-year-old Edith Roosevelt unveiled the statue on October 27, 1940—what would have been her husband's eighty-second birthday. President Franklin Delano Roosevelt did not attend the festivities that day—but he did send Major General Karl Truesdell, commander of the First Division, to Youngs Memorial Cemetery with a special White House wreath and instructed him to call on Mrs. Roosevelt at Sagamore Hill afterward to pay his respects.[2]

For decades, historians, academics, community organizers, advocacy rights groups, and museum professionals have criticized the Roosevelt statue and its symbolism, arguing that it represented a legacy of colonialism, violence, and racial hierarchy in US history—and should not be the first thing that visitors encounter. In 2019, the museum opened a new exhibition, *Addressing the Statue*, which provided more historical context for the monument, its design, and how interpretations of the statue changed over time. The following summer, the museum requested the city remove the statue. Theodore Roosevelt IV, great-grandson of the president and museum trustee, approved of the decision and released the following statement: "The world does not need statues, relics of another age, that reflect neither the values of the person they intend to honor nor the values of equality and justice. . . . The composition of the Equestrian Statue does not reflect Theodore Roosevelt's legacy. It is time to move the statue and move forward."[3]

Few presidents were elevated into the national pantheon of American heroes as quickly as Theodore Roosevelt. After his death on January 6, 1919, politicians, memorial associations, and civic organizations spent the next several decades constructing new, physical sites and spaces to commemorate his legacy. In fact, very few surviving historic sites were directly connected to Roosevelt at the time of his death. His birthplace, 28 East 20th Street in New York City, had been demolished in 1916. In Buffalo, New York, the Wilcox Mansion, where Roosevelt took the oath of office after the assassination of William McKinley, remained in private hands and later fell into disrepair. Sagamore Hill, his residence on Long Island, remained the home of his widow, Edith, for almost thirty more years until her death in 1948. Thus, at the time of Roosevelt's death, there were few places that citizens, admirers, and tourists could visit to contemplate the life and legacy of Theodore Roosevelt.

As a result, individuals and private organizations stepped forward to invent sites of memory. The Woman's Roosevelt Memorial Association replicated the Roosevelt birthplace in New York City by purchasing the brownstone next door and rebuilding Roosevelt's childhood home. This effort was funded in part by the Roosevelt Memorial Association, an organization of affluent gentlemen who also supported the equestrian statue outside the American Museum of Natural History, the establishment of Theodore Roosevelt Memorial Park in Oyster Bay, and the creation of a Roosevelt memorial in Washington, DC. Out west in South Dakota, Gutzon Borglum envisioned a massive sculpture featuring four of America's most acclaimed heroes— George Washington, Thomas Jefferson, Abraham Lincoln, and Theodore Roosevelt. Borglum worked with state and national politicians, business leaders, and private supporters to acquire the necessary funds to build his colossus; his son, Lincoln, completed the monument in 1941. Many of these sites were later given over to the National Park Service (NPS). Additionally, NPS and several other federal agencies continue to steward the millions of acres of land Roosevelt set aside for the American public during his presidency.

Today, the Theodore Roosevelt Presidential Library Foundation plots a similar course as it raises private funds with some state assistance to build a presidential library near Medora, North Dakota, adjacent to Theodore Roosevelt National Park. While some have criticized this placement, as presidential libraries are typically near a family home or in the president's home state, Roosevelt's legacy has never been restricted by geography. It has been shaped by family members, friends, Roosevelt enthusiasts, and citizens who created sites, spaces, and memorials across the American landscape to honor him. After his death, likenesses of Roosevelt grew steadily across the United States from Portland, Oregon, to Benton Harbor, Michigan, to San Antonio,

Texas.[4] These commemorative markers also suggest that Roosevelt's passing was felt by far more people than just his family, friends, and allies.

While Theodore Roosevelt did not run for office again after the presidential election of 1912, he was never far from the political arena. He opposed President Woodrow Wilson's policy of neutrality during World War I and became increasingly vocal after the sinking of the RMS *Lusitania*. Roosevelt even attempted to volunteer for the war but was denied permission to serve. After the United States declared war on Germany in 1917, Theodore Jr., Archibald, Quentin, and Kermit joined the fight with their father's support. While Roosevelt's sons served the military in different capacities, his daughter Ethel and her husband, Dick Derby, worked with the Red Cross to aid soldiers and civilians. With nearly all the Roosevelt children involved in the Great War, it was only a matter of time before tragedy struck. Twenty-year-old Quentin was killed in action on July 14, 1918, and buried in France by German airmen with full military honors. Theodore and Edith were devastated by the news, but the former president released this statement to the press: "Quentin's mother and I are very glad that he got to the front and had a chance to render some service to his country and to show the stuff there was in him before his fate befell him."[5] While Roosevelt's testimonial suggests that he had accepted Quentin's death, the loss of his youngest child deeply wounded him.[6]

Over the course of the next six months, Roosevelt's health steadily declined at Sagamore Hill. He suffered from bouts of inflammatory rheumatism and nearly died from a pulmonary embolism in early December 1918.[7] After Christmas, Roosevelt's health appeared to be improving, and the former president was hard at work dictating letters, articles, and editorials. On the evening of January 5, he began to have difficulty breathing and told his doctor, George W. Faller, that he had considerable pain in his legs. He was treated and retired to bed in good spirits. Edith checked on him at 2:00 a.m., and all seemed well. At around 4:00 a.m., James Amos, an African American man and longtime employee of the family who had returned to assist his former boss, thought that Roosevelt's breathing sounded strange. Amos sent for the nurse Evelyn Thomas but by the time she arrived the president had already stopped breathing—it was about 4:15 a.m. Amos later recalled Roosevelt's last spoken words: "James, will you please put out the light?"[8] His doctor and two consulting physicians attributed his death to an embolism caused by a blood clot, but they were unsure if it had entered his lungs or his brain. While he was only sixty years old, he had lived a full life by many measures.[9]

Both Houses of Congress adjourned out of respect for Roosevelt and flags at the US Capitol were lowered to half-staff. Condolences poured into Oyster Bay, New York, from across the country and around the world. King George V of Great Britain, Premier Georges Clemenceau of France, King Victor Emmanuel III of Italy, King Christian X of Denmark, Prime Minister Robert Borden of Canada, along with dozens of senators, representatives, governors, foreign ministers, and ambassadors, sent their sympathies to widow Edith Roosevelt. One of the more touching messages came from former president William Howard Taft, her husband's one-time protégé and Republican opponent in the 1912 election: "My heart goes out to you and yours in your great sorrow . . . we have lost a great patriotic American, a great world figure, the most commanding personality in our public life since Lincoln. I mourn his going as a personal loss."[10] President Woodrow Wilson, who was traveling back to France for the Paris Peace Conference, wired his condolences: "Please accept my heartfelt sympathy in the death of your distinguished husband, the news of which has shocked me very much." President Wilson issued a proclamation announcing Roosevelt's death on January 7, 1919. He acknowledged Roosevelt's extensive career of public service and that the United States had "lost one of its most distinguished and patriotic citizens." He directed that the "flags of the White House and the several Departmental Buildings be displayed at half-staff for a period of thirty days, and that suitable military and naval honors under orders of the Secretaries of War and of the Navy may be rendered on the day of the funeral."[11] It was rather convenient that President Wilson was abroad when Roosevelt died, as the two men were not on good terms and Wilson's presence, invited or otherwise, would have been awkward.

On January 8, sculptor James Earle Fraser created a death mask and plaster molds of Roosevelt's fingers and hands for future artistic works. Roosevelt's funeral began shortly after 1:00 p.m. at Christ Church in Oyster Bay. It was a simple affair, with family members, intimate friends, government

FIGURE 6. A group gathered outside of church in Oyster Bay, New York, during the funeral of Col. Theodore Roosevelt, 1919. (New York World-Telegram and the Sun Newspaper Photograph Collection, Prints and Photographs Division, Library of Congress, Washington, DC, LC-DIG-ppmsca-37618, https://www.loc.gov/item/2013651370/)

officials, party politicians, and veterans present; as was customary, Edith did not attend the service. The Department of War had offered a full military funeral for Colonel Roosevelt, but the family declined the offer. Captain Archibald Roosevelt acknowledged "the efforts to do honor to the ex-President and to show sympathy for his family," but reasoned that it was his father's wish to "be buried with as simple ceremony as possible in Oyster Bay, the place where he had so long and happily lived."[12] Since President Wilson was in France, Vice President Thomas R. Marshall served as the administration's representative at the funeral. Wilson also sent Chief of Staff of the United States Army General Peyton C. March and Rear Admiral Cameron McRae Winslow. Joining them were former president William Howard Taft, Massachusetts Senator Henry Cabot Lodge, and Major General Leonard Wood. The Reverend George Edwin Talmage officiated the funeral service, which lasted

only twenty minutes. Roosevelt's flag-draped oak coffin was loaded into a
waiting hearse and transported a mile-and-a-half down the road to Youngs
Memorial Cemetery, escorted by an honorary guard of New York City policemen on horseback. Roosevelt had selected the burial site after leaving the
presidency, as the elevated knoll provided a scenic view of Oyster Bay harbor
and the adjacent cove near his beloved Sagamore Hill estate.[13]

The former president's death influenced Americans across racial and religious lines. Emmett J. Scott, special assistant to Secretary of War Newton
Baker and secretary of the Tuskegee Institute, sent condolences to Edith
Roosevelt: "Twelve million Negroes of America learn with sincere regret
of the death of your distinguished husband. . . . I beg to assure you of the
deepest sympathy of the Negro people and of Tuskegee Institute, of which
he was an honored trustee."[14] The following month, the institute hosted
a memorial service for Roosevelt on the national day of mourning.[15] Eva
Bowles, a teacher and organizer for the Young Women's Christian Association, sent her sympathies "on behalf of the Colored women of the United
States, and especially the women under the National Board of the YWCA."[16]
In St. Paul, Minnesota, parishioners of Pilgrim Baptist Church, the city's
first Black Baptist congregation, gathered to honor the late president with a
rendition of "The Star-Spangled Banner," prayer, and a eulogy.[17] Pastor Daniel Arthur Holmes of Metropolitan Baptist Church in Kansas City, Kansas,
lauded Roosevelt as a "great Christian, [a] fearless leader with a strenuous
life." The service closed with "The Star-Spangled Banner," "Gloria Patria,"
and a benediction.[18]

While many Black Americans acknowledged Roosevelt's significance and
participated in various mourning events and remembrances, some used the
occasion to criticize his views on race, specifically his handling of the 1906
Brownsville riots. After several bouts of violence and the death of one white
man in Brownsville, Texas, local citizens accused Black soldiers of the 25th
Infantry at nearby Fort Brown. Roosevelt infamously discharged more than
160 African Americans from the military without trial and against testimo-
nies by their officers who vouched for the soldiers. Despite considerable criticism and contradictory investigative findings, Roosevelt refused to change
his mind on the matter. One columnist retorted that Roosevelt was a great
figure in American life, but not a great man. "He proved this when he failed

to return to the army that 'discharged without honor Black Battalion,' after it was proven innocent of the crime charged against it."[19]

Spiritual leaders of different faiths and denominations commemorated Roosevelt by highlighting his character, as well as ideas or beliefs that resonated with their congregations. "No great man was more worthy of being loved by the Jewish people than Colonel Roosevelt," said Dr. Samuel Schulman at Temple Beth-El, Fifth Avenue and 76th Street in Manhattan. Schulman recounted several instances where Roosevelt rejected anti-Semitism, remarking "he was always a conspicuous friend of Americans of [the] Jewish faith."[20] Indeed, Roosevelt had made history when he nominated Oscar Straus to serve as secretary of commerce and labor in 1906—the first Jewish person to serve in a presidential cabinet. In Cambridge, Massachusetts, the Reverend E. A. Elliott of the Harvard Street Methodist Church called Roosevelt the "idol of the American people . . . a man whose first thought was that of a lover and helper of humanity. He had no use for the worshiper who praised God in the abstract and neglected his fellow man in the concrete."[21] The Reverend Stefano L. Testa of the Franklin Avenue Church in Brooklyn preached a message in both English and Italian on Roosevelt's "Religion and Americanism, a pattern for all Americans."[22] At Broad Avenue Presbyterian Church in Altoona, Pennsylvania, the Reverend A. F. Heltman praised Roosevelt as the "apostle of the square deal" and the embodiment of "rugged Americanism." He also credited the president for "unifying the nation for the great conflict with the German machine and its evils."[23]

A national day of mourning took place on February 9, 1919, and millions across the country and around the world gathered in cities, churches, auditoriums, and other public spaces to pay tribute to Roosevelt. In Kansas City, a crowd of fifteen thousand attended a memorial service featuring keynote speaker Major General Wood.[24] In Salt Lake City, some ten thousand people gathered in and around the Mormon Tabernacle to pay tribute to Roosevelt in a memorial service.[25] There were two memorial services yet "several thousand people were unable to gain admittance to the afternoon services" in Cleveland, Ohio.[26] In Louisville, "hundreds of persons found it impossible to gain admission to the crowded auditorium," and at nearby Camp Zachary Taylor, former governor of Michigan Chase S. Osborn spoke to several thousand soldiers.[27] In San Diego, California, another ten thousand people congregated in Balboa Park.[28] In Washington, DC, a joint session of Congress was held in honor of the former president, and Roosevelt's life-long friend, Senator Lodge, gave the oration in his memory.[29] That afternoon, a group of seventy-five suffragists attempted to burn an effigy of President Wilson outside the White House for his opposition to women's suffrage.[30] While not an official tribute to Roosevelt, he likely would have enjoyed the spectacle at Wilson's expense.

As the country mourned Roosevelt, private citizens began forming memorial associations to honor his legacy. Three days after the funeral, the Roosevelt Memorial Association of Oyster Bay was organized by local enthusiasts, and William Loeb Jr., Roosevelt's former personal secretary, was elected president.[31] The following month, a group of affluent men organized the Roosevelt Permanent Memorial Committee (also known as the Roosevelt Memorial Committee), then later changed its name to the Roosevelt Memorial Association (RMA). At the same time, another organization—the Woman's Roosevelt Memorial Association (WRMA)—was already putting together a memorial committee to honor Theodore Roosevelt in New York City.[32] The WRMA decided that it would raise the necessary funds to reconstruct Theodore Roosevelt's birthplace at 28 East 20th Street in the Flatiron District of Manhattan. The actual brownstone where Roosevelt grew up no longer existed—it had been converted for commercial use before it was razed in 1916. The WRMA purchased both 28 and 26 East 20th Street—the latter had belonged to Robert Roosevelt, Theodore's uncle. They hired female architect Theodate Pope Riddle to reconstruct Roosevelt's home as it appeared during his childhood. The WRMA relied on Roosevelt's autobiography, as well as the Roosevelt family, to provide heirlooms, artwork, furniture, and any other recollections of the home that would improve its authenticity. Between the two buildings, there was space set aside for a museum and library, as well as multipurpose rooms for schoolchildren, as the WRMA aspired for the memorial to serve as a place for patriotic or "Americanization" education. On January 6, 1921, Major General Wood, former commander of Roosevelt's Rough Riders, laid the cornerstone of the house as Edith Roosevelt and Theodore Roosevelt Jr. looked on.[33]

Edith, along with her husband's sisters Anna and Corinne, assisted with locating furnishings and objects within the Roosevelt family. Family members also drew diagrams of the rooms as they existed during Theodore's childhood, and the WRMA acquired many significant artifacts such as Roosevelt's original bedroom set and the portrait of his mother Martha that once hung over the fireplace. Unfortunately, construction costs soared, and the organization struggled to keep pace with its growing expenses. On February 13, 1922, representatives of the RMA met with several members of the WRMA to discuss a possible collaboration. The women of WRMA needed funds, and the men of RMA required additional space for their growing collection of Roosevelt books, pamphlets, photographs, and letters. While there was a mutual suspicion, both groups realized that their counterparts had something very desirable for their respective organizations. After months of back-and-forth negotiations, both sides agreed to the following arrangement: in exchange for a donation of $150,000, the WRMA leased the second and third floors of 26 East 20th Street to the RMA, where the men created a research library and an administrative headquarters.[34]

The funds provided by the RMA invigorated the reconstruction, and on October 27, 1923, the WRMA opened the Roosevelt birthplace and museum to the public. One newspaper columnist proclaimed that the site was dedicated as "a shrine of American patriotism."[35] While only three hundred attendees could squeeze inside the building's auditorium, thousands more gathered outside for the occasion, which coincided with Roosevelt's birthday and "Navy Day" (also set to Roosevelt's birthday). President Calvin Coolidge did not attend the ceremonies but instead sent a message that was read to the crowd: "All eyes may well turn reverently today to the birthplace of Theodore Roosevelt, given back to the world by the women and children of the nation.... Reaching beyond our shores, he is the possession of all men, whatever their race, whatever their color, whatever their creed, who are willing to live by his principles and follow his example." Coolidge commended the efforts of the WRMA to make Roosevelt's memorial a center "for the promulgation of his ideals." On behalf of the American people, Coolidge thanked the organization for rendering a great service to the country.[36] George Murray Hulbert, the acting mayor of New York City, commended the women of the WRMA in his remarks, noting that "the people of the city would always be thankful for a place where not only aliens coming to New York, but the children of all who live in the city, might visit and learn the lessons taught by the life of so great an American."[37] Other speakers included former secretary of the interior James R. Garfield and Governor Gifford Pinchot of Pennsylvania, formerly chief of the United States Forest Service.

The Roosevelt Memorial Association was well funded and politically connected—so much so that it received an act of incorporation from the United States Congress on May 31, 1920. This legislation tasked the RMA with erecting a "monumental memorial in the city of Washington, District of Columbia, to the memory of Theodore Roosevelt"; acquiring and developing a public park in Roosevelt's memory in the town of Oyster Bay; and establishing an endowment fund "to promote the development and application of the policies and ideals of Theodore Roosevelt for the benefit of the American people."[38] Over the next several decades, the RMA made significant strides to achieve its goals. In 1923, the same year that the WRMA opened the Roosevelt birthplace, the RMA opened a new research library in New York City for those wishing to study Roosevelt. Five years later, it and the Roosevelt Memorial Association of Oyster Bay opened more than thirty acres of land along the southern shore of Oyster Bay as Theodore Roosevelt Memorial Park. Theodore Roosevelt Jr.'s son, Quentin, "unfurled the flag which officially opened the park to the public."[39] Also present for the festivities were Edith Roosevelt, Theodore Jr. and his wife Eleanor, Kermit Roosevelt and his wife Belle, and several other relatives. William Loeb, the president's former secretary and president of the RMA Oyster Bay, managed the event and introduced the principal speaker, President James R. Garfield of the RMA. The invocation was delivered by the Reverend George E. Talmage of Christ Church, the same pastor who had presided over Roosevelt's funeral in 1919.[40] The RMA retained ownership of the park for nearly fifteen years before it was gifted to the city of Oyster Bay in a public ceremony on January 1, 1943.[41] That same year, the RMA donated its library's holdings of ten thousand photographs, twelve thousand books and pamphlets, and thousands of manuscripts to Harvard University, the president's alma mater.[42] Within the next decade, the organization also spearheaded and funded the publication of *The Letters of Theodore Roosevelt*, which consisted of eight volumes and more than six thousand pieces of Roosevelt's correspondence.

While the RMA successfully created a memorial park in Oyster Bay, things were much more difficult in Washington, DC. The primary goal of the RMA in its congressional charter was to build and dedicate a monument to Roosevelt in the nation's capital—but placing a very recent president in a highly visible space near or on the National Mall was extremely political and contentious. The RMA selected John Russell Pope to create a design proposal for a Roosevelt monument with the intent of building it along the Tidal Basin, the last prominent space within the four points on the National Mall. Pope's memorial featured a fountain on a marble island that could propel a column of water 200 feet into the sky, flanked by two white marble colonnades. The estimated cost was more than $10 million, a number that would make any politician groan.[43] The timing was also not in the RMA's favor, as the Thomas Jefferson Memorial Foundation had recently purchased Jefferson's Monticello plantation and 1926 marked the 100th anniversary of Jefferson's death. He was considered by many to be one of the country's most significant founders, and the Democratic Party claimed him as its champion. The architect of the Declaration of Independence ultimately won the right to be commemorated at the Tidal Basin with the support of President Franklin Delano Roosevelt, who approved of the creation of the Thomas Jefferson Memorial Commission and their choice of architect—John Russell Pope. Roosevelt laid the cornerstone on November 15, 1939, and later dedicated the Jefferson Memorial on April 13, 1943, the 200th anniversary of Jefferson's birth.[44]

It became clear that despite the RMA's significant assets, connections, and support, there was simply too much resistance in Washington, DC, to the idea of immortalizing Theodore Roosevelt on or near the National Mall. While Roosevelt certainly had his accomplishments as president, was it appropriate to build something for him so close to the Washington Monument and the recently completed Lincoln Memorial? This was a difficult question to answer, especially since Roosevelt had only been gone less than a decade and was still very much associated with the modern Republican Party. The Tidal Basin was the last key spot on the mall, but without wider congressional support, the RMA begrudgingly set out to construct a memorial elsewhere in the nation's capital. On October 13, 1931, RMA president James R. Garfield announced that the organization would purchase Analostan Island on the Potomac River from the Washington Gas Light Company for $364,000.[45] The sale was finalized the following year, and Congress later passed legislation to accept the island as a gift, changing its name from

Analostan to Roosevelt Island. On December 12, 1932, President Herbert Hoover accepted the deed for the island in a ceremony in the East Room of the White House, declaring that "Analostan Island shall hereafter be known as Theodore Roosevelt Island and dedicated to the Nation."[46] While Edith Roosevelt did not attend the event, Alice Roosevelt Longworth and members of the Roosevelt Memorial Association, along with RMA president Garfield, made up the "small but distinguished group."[47]

During the 1930s and 1940s, the Civilian Conservation Corps, the National Park Service, and several other agencies worked to improve the island under the direction of Frederick Law Olmsted Jr. The goal was to create a "living memorial" by restoring the island's forests, trees, plants, and wildlife. Olmsted's plan was mostly carried out but later ran into problems as some members of the RMA advocated for a physical statue or memorial honoring Roosevelt. The park was first opened to the public in 1938, and the debate over a monument continued for decades. Between World War II, the postwar recession, and a feud with city planners who wanted to build a multilane bridge above the island to reduce traffic congestion, Roosevelt Island languished as invasive plants and vegetation reclaimed portions of the island and its walkways.[48]

In 1953, the RMA changed its name to the Theodore Roosevelt Association (TRA) to clarify which Roosevelt they honored. The TRA set out to build a memorial on the land in anticipation of the coming Roosevelt centennial celebration in 1958. The organization hired renowned architect Eric Gugler, who proposed a giant bronze armillary sphere and twelve granite panels with quotations representing Roosevelt's civic ideology. The plan received little congressional support and considerable ridicule from members of the press.[49] Conservationists argued that disturbing the island with such idolatry betrayed the original intent of the memorial; when members of the Roosevelt family began to voice disapproval, appropriations for the project stalled.[50] Admiral Neill Phillips, chairman of the Committee of One Hundred on the Federal City, suggested that the TRA build a national cultural center as an alternative. Alice Roosevelt Longworth responded, "The hell with the cultural center as a memorial. I flee from thinking about things like that. It has nothing to do with a memorial to my father."[51]

Gugler revamped his design to include a moat, two large fountains, and four twenty-foot-high tablets inscribed with Roosevelt quotes revolving around nature, youth, manhood, and the state.[52] Gradually, members of the Roosevelt family approved the redesign and its accompanying seventeen-foot-tall bronze statue, completed by Paul Manship and unveiled during a public ceremony on October 27, 1967. Some 1,500 spectators attended the event, which was presided over by President Lyndon B. Johnson, Supreme Court Chief Justice Earl Warren, Secretary of the Interior Stewart L. Udall, and Alice Roosevelt Longworth on what was her father's 109th birthday. "Mrs. Longworth, in one of the broad-brimmed hats that she wears in all colors, fabrics and seasons, pulled the ropes, with Mr. Johnson, that unshrouded the . . . bronze statue of her father," wrote *New York Times* reporter Nan Robertson. Joining Alice that day were four grandchildren and four great-grandchildren of Theodore Roosevelt.[53]

In his remarks President Johnson noted, "Roosevelt spoke with force to the problems of his day. He fought the trusts, he fought the selfish interests, he fought those who plundered this land. The Nation changed because of what he said, and because he put his words into action. . . . If Theodore Roosevelt had wanted any memorial at all, he would have wanted it here—in this wild little island in the center of a historic river—where his statue is sheltered in the trees. May our people always remember the generous, passionate spirit that is memorialized here. May it inform and strengthen all of us in our hours and our time of our greatest trials."[54] Perhaps Johnson hoped to channel some of Roosevelt's resiliency. A week earlier, 75,000 to 100,000 demonstrators had gathered at the Lincoln Memorial to pressure the president into ending the war in Vietnam. After the rally, tens of thousands marched to the Pentagon for a two-day sit-in. "I do not know what his response would be to the specific problems of our decade," remarked Johnson, "but we do know that it would not be the easy answer—if he believed the hard answer was the right one."[55] While she didn't give formal remarks at the ceremony, Alice Roosevelt Longworth did provide a brief comment: "I have a rather mean disposition, but I have nothing critical [to say] about it—I think it's excellent."[56]

The final invented site of memory dedicated to Roosevelt's legacy was not only the largest but also the most controversial. While Roosevelt supporters struggled to memorialize him in the nation's capital, there were fewer restrictions and obstacles out west. Gutzon Borglum, who had begun working on a massive sculpture of General Robert E. Lee, General Thomas "Stonewall" Jackson, and President Jefferson Davis of the Confederacy at Stone Mountain, Georgia, was ultimately dismissed from that project and looked elsewhere to make his mark. As word spread about Borglum's ambitious Lost Cause memorial, he was contacted by Doane Robinson, the state historian of South Dakota, who suggested a similar sculpture near the vicinity of Harney Peak (now Black Elk Peak). Beginning with congressional authorization in 1925, Mount Rushmore National Memorial took more than fifteen years and the labor of thousands of workers and engineers to finish—in fact, Borglum did not live to see its completion, dying on March 6, 1941. While Mount Rushmore is often credited to Borglum, there were also countless lawmakers, lobbyists, out-of-state patrons, business owners, and hospitality entrepreneurs who supported the memorial in hopes for an economic boom sustained through tourism.[57]

President Calvin Coolidge delivered remarks to about three thousand people on August 10, 1927, to commence the "official" start of the mountain carving. The president was given a startling "21-dynamite salute" upon his arrival. After a short speech, the president handed "a lot of drills to Borglum," who began the first ceremonial drilling.[58] The first figure completed was George Washington, dedicated on July 4, 1930, in front of a crowd of about twenty-five hundred people. Borglum credited Washington with the birth of the country and explained that the monument "would include the heads of Jefferson, Lincoln, and Roosevelt, with a brief history of the nation's founding and expansion."[59] Jefferson's Louisiana Purchase had added another 828,000 square miles of territory, effectively doubling the size of the country. Borglum chose Lincoln for his efforts to preserve the Union and steer the country through a civil war. Theodore Roosevelt remained the odd member of the bunch, as he had only been dead for about a decade and seemed much too recent to be compared with the likes of Washington, Jefferson, and Lincoln. Nonetheless, Senator Peter Norbeck of South Dakota championed Roosevelt as the fourth figure for the memorial, maintaining that his policies were key to the development of the modern United States. Another rationalization was that Roosevelt had historical and personal connections with the Dakotas and the American West—certainly more than Washington, Jefferson, or Lincoln. During the 1880s, about 250 miles north of Mount Rushmore, Roosevelt

had spent time (and a considerable amount of money) hunting bison, ranch-
ing cattle, and building two cabins—the Maltese Cross and Elkhorn Ranch.[60]

While President Franklin Roosevelt was in office during the completion
of Thomas Jefferson, Abraham Lincoln, and Theodore Roosevelt, he only
attended one dedication ceremony. On August 30, 1936, President Roosevelt
gave a very short speech to commemorate the completion of the Jefferson
figure to some five thousand citizens. He admitted that he "had seen photographs" and drawings of the mountain, yet he "had no conception until about
ten minutes ago, not only of its magnitude, but of its permanent beauty and
of its permanent importance." The president concluded, "I am happy to congratulate all of you not only on what we see today but on what is going to
happen in the future at Mount Rushmore."[61] Another five thousand spectators turned out for the dedication of Abraham Lincoln on September 17, 1937.
Borglum gave the order to "unveil a great flag from the face of the Civil War
President," and the crowd erupted with cheers.[62] The likeness of Roosevelt
was dedicated on July 2, 1939—coinciding with the fiftieth anniversary of
South Dakota's statehood. Some twelve thousand people attended the festivities, where they heard from Governor Harlan Bushfield, western movie
star William S. Hart, and Judge A. R. Denu, who lauded Borglum's "shrine of
democracy." According to several accounts, Governor Bushfield was inducted
into the Sioux tribe as "Washee Ac-te," which means "Kills One" because of
the governor's marksmanship in killing two bison the day before. Newspaper
accounts suggest that this was the first time that Native Americans participated in ceremonies for a Mount Rushmore dedication, mentioning Sioux
ceremonial dances and pageantry, and that "prominent roles were played by
Chiefs Oscar One Bull and Red Bear."[63]

While some interpreted Native American participation in the ceremony
as approval of the memorial, the mountain (known as the Six Grandfathers)
and the Black Hills were historically and culturally meaningful to the Sioux
Nation and the memorial was a desecration of sacred territory. In 1868,
representatives of the federal government agreed to terms with the Sioux
at Fort Laramie and acknowledged the Sioux Nation's exclusive claim to
the Black Hills by incorporating them into the Great Sioux Reservation.
This peace was temporary, as by 1874 a military expedition led by General
George Armstrong Custer in search of gold brought miners, speculators,

and investors to the Black Hills. As white settlers began encroaching more and more on Sioux hunting lands, violence broke out and the United States Army was ordered to quell these disputes. By 1877, the federal government had confiscated land from the Sioux Nation and rebuffed any physical resistance or legal challenges to its ownership.[64]

Decades later, Borglum set out to carve the massive faces of four white men who had all believed in American expansionism, often at the expense of Native peoples and cultures. While Roosevelt was somewhat removed from nineteenth-century approaches to Indian-US government relations than his monumental peers, his *The Winning of the West* series reflected his beliefs in American exceptionalism and imperialism, and racialized views of American Indians that fit within the unsettling history of the memorial—a monument built to honor the white men who made and preserved America. In 1980, the Supreme Court ruled in *United States v. Sioux Nation of Indians* that the federal government had illegally seized the Black Hills and ordered compensation for their loss of lands. The Sioux Nation has refused to accept anything less than the return of the Black Hills. The government appropriated compensation continues to accrue interest and is now worth more than $1.3 billion dollars.[65]

After his death in 1919, Theodore Roosevelt was mourned and celebrated across the country and abroad. During the mourning period and for several decades afterward, individuals and private groups raised funds and built memorials, monuments, and statues in his honor. The Roosevelt Memorial Association, the Woman's Roosevelt Memorial Association, and the Theodore Roosevelt Association all made vigorous efforts to commemorate Roosevelt with projects, campaigns, and civic celebrations. Strategic fundraising, extensive political networking, and the backing of the Roosevelt family all played a role in these early manifestations of Roosevelt's legacy. Except for Mount Rushmore, all these monuments had strong support from the Roosevelt memorial associations, Edith Roosevelt, Theodore Roosevelt Jr., Alice Roosevelt Longworth, and others, demonstrating that approval from the family was critical for any type of public memorial or historic site in Oyster Bay, New York City, or Washington, DC.[66]

This evolution continues today with both digital and physical efforts in North Dakota. At Dickinson State University, the Theodore Roosevelt Center seeks to create a comprehensive digital library for more than one million TR-related items. About forty miles west of the university, the Theodore Roosevelt Presidential Library Foundation is building a presidential library near Theodore Roosevelt National Park. Theodore Roosevelt V, great-great-grandson of the president, offered this assessment: "This will be the only presidential library alongside a national park . . . it will invite visitors to see and experience the very cradle of conservation. That is why this location in North Dakota is perfect for the Theodore Roosevelt Presidential Library."[67] These two endeavors are making Roosevelt more accessible and readily available, rooted in the physical landscape that transformed him during the 1880s.

In June 2021, the New York City Public Design Commission voted unanimously to remove Roosevelt's equestrian statue from the American Museum of Natural History. Five months later, New York City agreed to a long-term loan of the statue to the Theodore Roosevelt Presidential Library. The library also announced plans to establish an advisory council with representatives from Indigenous and Black communities, as well as members with different areas of expertise such as historians, scholars, and artists, all of whom will guide the library's interpretation of the statue. Roosevelt commented, "It is fitting that the statue is being relocated to a place where its composition can be recontextualized to facilitate difficult, complex, and inclusive discussions."[68] The library is another invented site of memory that exemplifies Roosevelt's love of the outdoors, conservationism, and his efforts as president to protect millions of acres of public land. It can also serve as a middle ground between Native peoples who were displaced or removed from those lands, and the man who used his presidential powers to preserve them.

Notes

1. The title of the article is drawn from a telegram sent by Archie Roosevelt to his siblings after their father's death. See https://www.trgravesite.org/gravesite.html; Sculptor James Earle Fraser, https://www.amnh.org/exhibitions/addressing-the-theodore-roosevelt-statue/making-the-statue/; "Roosevelt Statue by J. E. Fraser," *New York Times*, October 29, 1940.

2. "Unveils Statue of 'Rough Rider': Widow of Theodore Roosevelt Shares in Ceremony on His 82d Birth Anniversary," *New York Times*, October 28, 1940; "Memorial to Teddy," *Daily News*, October 28, 1940; Jennifer Dawn Heth, "Imagining TR: Commemorations and Representations of Theodore Roosevelt in Twentieth-Century America" (PhD diss., Texas A&M University, 2014), 182–236.

3. "Roosevelt Statue to Be Removed from Museum of Natural History," *New York Times*, June 21, 2020; *Mayoral Advisory Commission on City Art, Monuments, and Markers, Report to the City of New York*, January 2018, 25–27, https://www.amnh.org/exhibitions/addressing-the-theodore-roosevelt-statue/mayoral-advisory-commission-report/.

4. The Roosevelt statue in Portland was toppled on October 11, 2020, during the "Indigenous Day of Rage." For more on the placement of monuments, see National Monument Audit, Monument Lab, https://monumentlab.com/audit/.

5. "Roosevelts Meet the Blow Bravely," *New York Times*, July 18, 1918.

6. Edmund Morris, *Colonel Roosevelt* (New York: Random House, 2010), 432–39, 537–39, 543–44; Lewis L. Gould, *Edith Kermit Roosevelt: Creating the Modern First Lady* (Lawrence: University Press of Kansas, 2013), 127–29; Brady Carlson, *Dead Presidents: An American Adventure into the Strange Deaths and Surprising Afterlives of Our Nation's Leaders* (New York: W. W. & Norton, 2016), 237; Stacy A. Cordery, *Alice: Alice Roosevelt Longworth, from White House Princess to Washington Power Broker* (New York: Viking, 2007), 270–72.

7. "Roosevelt Had Previous Attack: Colonel Nearly Died Early in December, Says His Physician in Describing Cause of Death," *Atlanta Constitution*, January 7, 1919; "Embolism Caused Death: Blood Clot, Physicians Announce, Killed Col. Roosevelt In His Sleep," *New York Times*, January 7, 1919; "Col. Roosevelt's Condition Serious," *New York Times*, February 8, 1918; "Roosevelt in Hospital," *New York Times*, November 12, 1918; "Col. Roosevelt Now Able to Walk," *New York Times*, December 7, 1918; "Col. Roosevelt to Leave Hospital," *New York Times*, December 9, 1918.

8. "Roosevelt's 'Please Put Out the Light' His Last Words, Says Witness of His End," *New York Times*, August 3, 1926. See also James E. Amos, *Theodore Roosevelt: Hero to His Valet* (New York: John Day, 1927), 156.

9. "Embolism Caused Death: Blood Clot, Physicians Announce, Killed Col. Roosevelt In His Sleep," *New York Times*, January 7, 1919; "Ex-President Roosevelt Dies in Sleep at Sagamore Hill; Family Plans Private Burial on Wednesday Afternoon," *Evening Sun*, January 6, 1919; Michael Patrick Cullinane, *Theodore Roosevelt's Ghost: The History and Memory of an American Icon* (Baton Rouge: Louisiana State University Press, 2017), 1; Morris, *Colonel Roosevelt*, 550–552; Gould, *Edith Kermit Roosevelt*, 129.

10. "Wilson's Sympathy for Mrs. Roosevelt," *New York Times*, January 8, 1919; "Congress Mourns Colonel's Death," *New York Times*, January 7, 1919; "Theodore Roosevelt's Last Resting Place: Where Former President Was Buried Yesterday in Small Long Island Cemetery," *Chicago Daily Tribune*, January 9, 1919.

11. Woodrow Wilson, Proclamation [Announcing the Death of Ex-President Theodore Roosevelt,] January 7, 1919, https://www.presidency.ucsb.edu/documents/proclamation-1506-b-announcing-the-death-ex-president-theodore-roosevelt/.

12. "Nation to Mourn at the Bier of Roosevelt Today," *New York Times*, January 8, 1919.

13. "Nation to Mourn at the Bier of Roosevelt Today"; "Omit Funeral Pomp for Col. Roosevelt: Simple Services Planned at Sagamore Hill and at Oyster Bay Church," *New York Times*, January 7, 1919; "Bury Roosevelt with Simple Rites As Nation Grieves:

Government's Representatives and Old Friends Pay Last Tribute at His Bier," *New York Times*, January 9, 1919; Cullinane, *Theodore Roosevelt's Ghost*, 1–2; Morris, *Colonel Roosevelt*, 553–60; http://www.trgravesite.org/gravesite.html.

14. "Emmett J. Scott Wires Sympathy of Negro Race to Widow of Colonel Roosevelt," *Savannah Tribune*, January 11, 1919.

15. "Services in the South," *Indianapolis News*, February 10, 1919.

16. "A Y.W.C.A. Tribute to Colonel Roosevelt," *Broad Ax*, February 1, 1919.

17. "St. Paul. Record of Happenings in Minnesota's Capitol," *The Appeal*, February 15, 1919.

18. "Metropolitan Temple Notes," *Kansas City Advocate*, February 14, 1919.

19. "Cleveland Social and Personal," *Cleveland Gazette*, February 1, 1919; "Negro Troops Must Go, the President Declines to Modify His Order," *Baltimore Sun*, November 22, 1906; Thomas G. Dyer, *Theodore Roosevelt and the Idea of Race* (Baton Rouge: Louisiana State University Press, 1980), 114–15.

20. "Roosevelt Is Eulogized in City Pulpits," *New York Tribune*, January 13, 1919.

21. "Memory Services for Col. Roosevelt," *Boston Globe*, February 10, 1919.

22. "To Pay Tribute to Roosevelt," *Brooklyn Daily Times*, February 8, 1919.

23. "City Churches Give Tribute to Roosevelt," *Altoona Tribune*, February 10, 1919.

24. "Roosevelt the Friend Is Eulogized by Wood," *Topeka Daily Capital*, February 10, 1919.

25. "Audience of 10,000 Hears T.R. Extolled," *Salt Lake Herald Republican*, February 10, 1919.

26. "McCormack Sings; Lauder Speaks," *Indianapolis News*, February 10, 1919.

27. "At Louisville and Camp Taylor," *Indianapolis News*, February 10, 1919.

28. "Services at San Diego," *Sacramento Bee*, February 10, 1919.

29. "Honor Roosevelt Here and Abroad," *Washington Times*, February 10, 1919.

30. "Save Wilson Effigy," *Washington Post*, February 10, 1919.

31. "For Oyster Bay Memorial Villagers Organize Association," *New York Times*, January 12, 1919.

32. "T.R. Memorial Association Is Organized Here," *Chicago Daily Tribune*, February 7, 1919; "Plan to Honor Roosevelt: Women Organize Memorial Committee and Elect Officers," *New York Times*, January 28, 1919; Cullinane, *Theodore Roosevelt's Ghost*, 18–24.

33. "Roosevelt Birthplace Sold," *New York Times*, January 16, 1919; "Tearing Down Birthplace of Colonel Roosevelt," *New York Times*, November 16, 1916; "To Mark Roosevelt Home: Gen. Wood Will Lay Cornerstone at Birthplace Next Tuesday," *New York Times*, January 3, 1921; "Thousands Honor Roosevelt Memory," *New York Times*, January 7, 1921; Theodore Roosevelt, *The Autobiography of Theodore Roosevelt* (Digireads.com Publishing, 2019), 9. The first edition of this autobiography was published in 1913 by the Macmillan Company.

34. Cullinane, *Theodore Roosevelt's Ghost*, 63–64.

35. "Roosevelt House Becomes a Shrine of Patriotism," *New York Times*, October 28, 1923.

36. "Roosevelt House Becomes a Shrine of Patriotism."

37. "Roosevelt House Becomes a Shrine of Patriotism."

38. An Act to Incorporate the Roosevelt Memorial Association, 66th Congress, 2nd sess., May 31, 1920, 691–94, https://www.loc.gov/law/help/statutes-at-large/66th-congress.php.

39. "Roosevelt Park Formally Opened: Oyster Bay Tract Dedicated to Ex-President, Who First Proposed Project," *New York Times*, May 31, 1928.

40. "Roosevelt Park Formally Opened."

41. "Roosevelt Memorial Offered as a Park: National Group Would Present Site to Oyster Bay," *New York Times*, October 7, 1942; "Park Memorializes Theodore Roosevelt: National Group Presents Site to Oyster Bay Township," *New York Times*, January 2, 1943; "Roosevelt Park Cost $858,503, Says Report," *New York Times*, March 24, 1930.

42. "Noted Collection Goes to Harvard: Theodore Roosevelt House to Transfer Its Material to College Library," *New York Times*, July 7, 1943; "History of the TRA," https://www .theodoreroosevelt.org/content.aspx?page_id=22&club_id=991271&module_id=333067.

43. "200-Foot Fountain Plan of Memorial Here to Roosevelt: More Than $10,000,000 Estimate on Project Sent to Congress," *Washington Post*, December 13, 1925.

44. "First $100,000 Is Paid on Jefferson's Home," *Washington Post*, December 10, 1923; "President Urges Fitting Jefferson Memorial Tribute," *Washington Post*, February 13, 1937; "Roosevelt Requests $500,000 to Start Jefferson Memorial," *Washington Post*, April 5, 1938; "Roosevelt Hits Dictatorship in Jefferson Talk: Lauds Democracy as He Lays Cornerstone of Memorial Here," *Washington Post*, November 16, 1939; "Roosevelt to Honor Jefferson," *Washington Post*, April 11, 1943; "Jefferson Shrine Rites Set for Noon: President to Speak Briefly," *Washington Post*, April 13, 1943.

45. "Island in Potomac to Honor Roosevelt: Analostan, Near Washington, Is Bought by Association as Site for Memorial," *New York Times*, October 14, 1931; "Analostan Island Sale Is Completed," *Washington Post*, January 9, 1932; Jon Daly, "The New Island: The Purchase of Analostan Island," *Washington Post*, November 1, 1931.

46. "Senate Approves Island Memorial: Bill for Project to Honor President Roosevelt Is Sent to House," *Washington Post*, March 3, 1932; "Analostan Island Deed to be Given President Today," *Washington Post*, December 12, 1932; "Analostan Island, Named Roosevelt, Accepted by U.S.," *Washington Post*, December 13, 1932.

47. "Analostan Island, Named Roosevelt, Accepted by U.S.," *Washington Post*, December 13, 1932; Cullinane, *Theodore Roosevelt's Ghost*, 151–56; National Park Service, "Developing the Memorial," https://www.nps.gov/media/photo/gallery.htm?pg=2944999&id= 972AE277-1DD8-B71C-076DD4615675854D.

48. "Roosevelt Island," *Washington Post*, December 14, 1932; "Theodore Roosevelt Park," *Washington Post*, July 15, 1934; "Roosevelt Island Plans," *Washington Post*, August 2, 1937.

49. "T. Roosevelt Memorial Is Backed Amid Gibes," *New York Times*, July 2, 1960.

50. Cullinane, *Theodore Roosevelt's Ghost*, 160–61.

51. "T.R. Daughter Dissents: Mrs. Longworth Denounces Cultural Center Plan," *New York Times*, January 17, 1961; Heth, "Imagining TR," 237–92.

52. Theodore Roosevelt Memorial Quotations, Theodore Roosevelt Island National Memorial, https://www.theodorerooseveltcenter.org/Research/Digital-Library/Record ?libID=0273899, Theodore Roosevelt Digital Library, Dickinson State University, Dickinson, ND.

53. Nan Robertson, "Memorial to Theodore Roosevelt Unveiled: 1,500 at Ceremony in the Capital Johnson, Udall, and Warren Speak," *New York Times*, October 28, 1967; Cullinane, *Theodore Roosevelt's Ghost*, 151–63.

54. Lyndon B. Johnson, "Remarks at the Dedication of the Theodore Roosevelt Memorial in Washington," October 27, 1967, https://www.presidency.ucsb.edu/documents /remarks-the-dedication-the-theodore-roosevelt-memorial-washington/; Willard

Clopton, "Rough Rider 'Rides' Again: Excellent Likeness Perfect Setting," *Washington Post*, October 28, 1967.

55. Johnson, "Remarks at the Dedication of the Theodore Roosevelt Memorial in Washington."

56. "Theodore Roosevelt Memorial Unveiled," *Chicago Tribune*, October 28, 1967.

57. Heth, "Imagining TR," 138–81; Cullinane, *Theodore Roosevelt's Ghost*, 72–79.

58. Carlisle Bargeron, "Coolidge Travels Four Miles in Saddle to Laud Presidents," *Washington Post*, August 11, 1927.

59. "Washington's Face Unveiled on Mt. Rushmore; Borglum's 60-Foot Carving Visible for Miles," *New York Times*, July 5, 1930; "Crowd Views Washington of Mt. Rushmore; Carved Head 60 Ft. High Unveiled Amid Rites," *Chicago Daily Tribune*, July 5, 1930.

60. "Theodore Roosevelt the Rancher," National Park Service, https://www.nps.gov/thro /learn/historyculture/theodore-roosevelt-the-rancher.htm.

61. Franklin D. Roosevelt, "Informal Extemporaneous Remarks by the President, Mount Rushmore National Memorial," August 30, 1936, http://www.fdrlibrary.marist.edu /daybyday/resource/august-1936-3/; "President Praises Sculpture in Hills: Dakota Memorial Symbolizes Efforts for Better Living, He Says in Dedicating Image," *New York Times*, August 31, 1936; "Roosevelt Dedicates Huge Memorial to Jefferson," *Los Angeles Times*, August 31, 1936.

62. "Lincoln Head Unveiled: 5,000 See Dedication at Dakota 'Shrine of Democracy,'" *New York Times*, September 18, 1937.

63. Harold S. Milner, "Four Stone Portraits Visible on Mountainside in Black Hills," *Argus-Leader*, July 3, 1939; "S.D. Jubilee Is Colorful, Gay Event," *Rapid City Journal*, July 3, 1939.

64. Jeffrey Ostler, *The Lakotas and the Black Hills: The Struggle for Sacred Ground* (New York: Viking, 2010); John Taliaferro, *Great White Fathers: The Story of the Obsessive Quest to Create Mount Rushmore* (New York: PublicAffairs, 2002); Pekka Hämäläinen, *Lakota America: A New History of Indigenous Power* (New Haven: Yale University Press, 2019), 337–82.

65. Dyer, *Theodore Roosevelt and the Idea of Race*, 54–55; The Treaty of Fort Laramie (1868), National Archives, https://www.archives.gov/education/lessons/sioux-treaty/.

66. "Ask Roosevelt Approval," *New York Times*, March 2, 1920.

67. "Theodore Roosevelt Presidential Library Foundation Selects Snøhetta for Design Architect Commission of the Theodore Roosevelt Presidential Library in Medora, North Dakota," September 18, 2020, https://8d05842xs2ewhrr625bejk1b-wpengine .netdna-ssl.com/wp-content/uploads/2020/09/EMBARGOED_Design_Architect _TR_Library-3.pdf; Jack Dura, "Theodore Roosevelt Presidential Library Organizers Raise $100M, Can Tap into $50M in State Money," *Bismarck Tribune*, October 27, 2020, https://bismarcktribune.com/news/local/govt-and-politics/theodore-roosevelt -presidential-library-organizers-raise-100m-can-tap-into-50m-in-state-money/article _c5498a0f-646c-5ed8-9f44-62bbed26f67a.html.

68. "Roosevelt Statue to Head to Presidential Library in North Dakota," *New York Times*, November 19, 2021.

Farewell to the Chief

MOURNING AND MEMORIALIZING HERBERT HOOVER

➔ • ←

Dean J. Kotlowski

ERBERT HOOVER (1874–1964) EMERGED from modest beginnings to win national and international fame during his lifetime and widespread acclaim in the decade following his death. Engineer, entrepreneur, humanitarian, US Food Administrator (1917–18), secretary of commerce (1921–28), president of the United States (1929–33), and Republican Party elder statesman (1933–64), the person known to confidants as "Chief" served America and the world for more than fifty years.[1] His death prompted condolences from heads of state, effusive obituaries, and the attendance of President Lyndon B. Johnson and presidential candidate Barry Goldwater at his state funeral. Retrospectives appeared in the press across Latin America, the Anglophone world, and Europe, where his relief efforts had saved lives during and after both world wars. In the United States, newspapers largely lionized him. "Today all of us are saluting Herbert Hoover," the baseball broadcaster Joe Garagiola declared.[2] Hard work, diligent networking, and skilled self-promotion had enabled Hoover to recapture much of his early image as a nonpartisan public servant and self-made man. Yet the Great Depression-era president rejected by the electorate had not entirely vanished. The University of Kansas's newspaper characterized Hoover as "Maligned, but Great."[3]

The mourning of Hoover proved uncomplicated, for it had been long in the making. Hoover, his family, and his allies had worked to secure his legacy. The future president in 1919 founded what became the Hoover Institution on War, Revolution, and Peace at Stanford University. In 1962, he dedicated the Herbert Hoover Presidential Library-Museum in West Branch, Iowa, where he chose to be buried. As ex-president, Hoover made campaign speeches, lectured, wrote several books, and most importantly, befriended Democratic president Harry S. Truman. Starting under Truman, he chaired two presidential commissions on executive-branch organization (1947–49 and 1953–55). Longevity enabled Hoover to outlast critics and project a gravitas lightened by wit and warmth. Yet the judgment of Americans, and of posterity, preoccupied him. In 1958, Hoover approved plans for his state funeral. Blending martial, majestic, and modest motifs, the funeral, according the *New York Herald Tribune*, achieved "an Historic Tribute."[4]

Memorializing Hoover was more problematic. To be sure, assorted honors were bestowed upon Hoover in the decade following his funeral, including a commemorative postage stamp and the designation of his birthplace environs as a national historical site—acts initiated under Lyndon B. Johnson who, along with Richard Nixon and Robert F. Kennedy, praised him.[5] Yet not unlike Johnson and Vietnam or Nixon and Watergate, Hoover's response to the Great Depression was the stain that refused to come out. Many Americans regarded him as heartless, hapless, or both for failing to provide relief from and a solution to the country's worst economic crisis. Such failings galvanized Democrats, who perfected the election-year tactic of "running against Herbert Hoover" in order to portray Republicans as incapable of managing the economy.[6] Although Franklin D. Roosevelt's New Deal failed to achieve a complete recovery during the 1930s, it promoted economic security for Americans and made Roosevelt a popular president. Hoover's attacks on the New Deal did little to boost his reputation or to tarnish FDR's. He has surfaced infrequently in popular culture, usually as a foil to his upbeat successor. Since the mid-1960s, memorials to Hoover have proven scattered or localized, attached to causes or places associated with him. Many observers have struggled to assess a leader who defies facile labels.

Aided by his funeral, Hoover won qualified rehabilitation: praise for his nonpresidential achievements and acknowledgment of his troubled presidency. He strove, like other White House occupants, to sculpt his legacy, doing so in a chronologically backwards fashion: Hoover first told his side of the story about the Depression, the catalyst for his electoral defeat, and later on, he highlighted his public service and humanitarianism. As his life drew to a close, he pointed to his Horatio Alger–style ascent as emblematic of the American Dream. His reputation rebounded, as his resilience, compassion, and administrative skill shone through. Yet his lack of charisma, ill-starred presidency, and harsh critique of the New Deal, World War II, and Cold War state discouraged many people from embracing him wholeheartedly. Beginning in 1964, Americans mourned and memorialized Hoover the person more than Hoover the president.

Shaping a Legacy, Planning a Funeral

Hoover's story begins with his remarkable rise, captured in a headline at the time of his death: "Herbert Hoover, Orphan Who Became President."[7] Born in West Branch, Iowa, to a Quaker family of modest means, Hoover lost both parents before he turned ten. After living with an uncle in Oregon, he entered Stanford in 1891, when the university first opened, and graduated in 1895 with an AB in geology. Hoover brokered his expertise into a lucrative career as a global mining engineer and entrepreneur. He worked in, among other places, Australia, China, and England, where he was when World War I began. The war propelled Hoover into leadership of the Commission for Relief in Belgium, which dispensed food and supplies in a land occupied by Germany. Hoover's efficiency became further apparent when he ran the US Food Administration during the Great War. Following the armistice, he oversaw the American Relief Administration, which provided food, medicine, and technical assistance to some 300 million Europeans, and he later led food relief efforts in the famine-plagued Soviet Union. Leaders in both parties, including FDR, touted him as a presidential possibility.[8] He instead settled for, and made the most out of, his appointment as secretary of commerce, serving under Presidents Warren G. Harding and Calvin Coolidge. Hoover became a symbol of the prosperity of the 1920s. He championed voluntary cooperation among businesses, oversaw the regulation of radio and civil aviation, and organized assistance to victims of the Mississippi flood of 1927, which helped him to secure the Grand Old Party's (GOP) nomination for president a year later.[9] He overwhelmed Democratic candidate Al Smith in the election of 1928.

Hoover's presidency shattered his standing with the public. Before entering the White House, he had been a Progressive of sorts: a backer of Theodore Roosevelt's Bull Moose campaign in 1912 and an advocate of solving problems via scientific reasoning and impartial administration. Expectations for his presidency soared, but Hoover's responses to the Great Depression—reliance on private charity to help poor people, confidence-boosting sessions with industrial leaders, loans to banks, and acceleration of public works projects— failed to curb unemployment and allay discontent. Americans blamed him for hard times by labeling impoverished areas "Hoovervilles" and bemoaning "Hoover's depression."[10] The administration's heavy-handed expulsion of indigent veterans in the Bonus Army from Washington, DC, in 1932 sealed Hoover's fate: He lost to FDR in a landslide.

Following the defeat, Hoover stayed politically engaged, albeit with few positive results. He angled without success for the Republican nominations in 1936 and 1940, and he assailed the New Deal as "collectivism" and at odds with "the American system of liberty."[11] Such verbal salvos positioned Hoover closer to conservatives, who earlier had distrusted him, while making him a "forgotten Progressive and remembered reactionary" to the general public.[12] Hoover's opposition to US involvement in World War II earned praise from isolationists, but the attack on Pearl Harbor in 1941 left him sidelined: Roosevelt declined to give his former foe a wartime assignment and "raise him from the dead."[13] Many Republicans, including presidential nominee Thomas E. Dewey, wanted no association with the former president or the Depression, which remained Hoover's albatross.[14] In his *Memoirs* (1952), Hoover blamed the downturn on events overseas and on FDR's New Deal, which he claimed had delayed recovery.[15] Yet a stale writing style hindered his argument. Reviewing Hoover's *The Ordeal of Woodrow Wilson* (1958), the historian John Morton Blum jibed: "This is the prose that launched a thousand Democrats."[16]

Understanding Hoover's funeral, and the mourning and memorialization of him, requires a deep dive into his bid for rehabilitation. This effort underscored his talent for self-promotion, first evident during the 1910s and 1920s when he relied on "the press and public relations" and made "unprecedented use of radio."[17] Following Roosevelt's death in 1945, Hoover's attacks on the New Deal lessened, at least in public, and he managed to burnish his reputation. Consistent with his earlier self-promotion, he seized opportunities, reached out (and listened) to others, kept—and put—his name on institutions, and told his version of his life story, about the farm boy who became a renowned humanitarian and public servant. The campaign culminated in Hoover's decisions to build his presidential library in the town where he was born and to be buried there.

Nonpartisan service, a hallmark of his early career, enabled Hoover to regain some measure of appeal by the 1950s. His cordial bond with President Truman did much to boost his reputation. The association endured rough patches, such as during the election of 1948, when Truman linked Dewey to Hoover and the Great Depression. Overall, the Iowa native respected his Missouri counterpart, who flattered Hoover's ego and made use of his experience. Truman, unlike FDR, invited Hoover to the White House, and then sent him abroad to survey the postwar food situation. Between 1947 and 1949, Hoover chaired a presidential panel that explored ways of reorganizing the Executive Branch. In 1953, Dwight D. Eisenhower appointed him to head a second "Hoover Commission." Although Hoover's influence on food policy proved limited and some of the second commission's proposals reflected Hoover's antipathy to the New Deal, these activities reminded people of his humanitarianism and devotion to efficient government. Hoover helped himself by forgiving past rivals, such as Dewey; by curtailing his campaign speaking; and by expressing fondness for fishing and baseball during an hour-long televised interview on the National Broadcasting Company (NBC)—a continuation of his earlier use of emerging technologies.[18] A new generation discovered his "modesty and humor" and his compassion.[19] Concerned about underprivileged youth, he served as a "super-uncle" to the Boys Clubs of America, which named its national headquarters building in New York after him.[20] His rehabilitation received an official boost in 1947, when Congress voted to rename Boulder Dam "Hoover Dam," reversing a tendency by the Roosevelt administration to avoid using Hoover's name even for a structure that he had helped to establish.[21] Yet mass adulation eluded the stiff, dour man forever tied to the Depression. Hoover never earned a spot on the Gallup Poll's annual list of most-admired men.[22]

At ease courting elite figures, Hoover won applause across the political aisle during, and even beyond, his lifetime. Praise came from the family of

Joseph P. Kennedy Sr., a conservative Democrat who "worshipped Hoover" and served under him on both Hoover Commissions.[23] Joe's son, Robert, worked on the staff of the second Hoover Commission, enjoyed visiting with Hoover, and displayed in his front hall a letter of appreciation from the former president.[24] An aging Hoover later received, but declined, an invitation from John F. Kennedy to chair an advisory committee on the Peace Corps.[25] His relationship with Richard Nixon proved mutually beneficial. Hoover contributed to Nixon's earliest campaigns and backed him for president in 1960.[26] The vice president, in turn, helped Hoover secure a speaking engagement at the 1958 World's Fair in Brussels.[27] After making the address, Hoover sent it to Senate Majority Leader Lyndon B. Johnson. LBJ thanked him and praised the former president's ties to, and past relief work in, Belgium.[28] Save for Joe Kennedy, stricken by a stroke in 1961, and Jack Kennedy, who predeceased Hoover, all these leaders later played a part in mourning or memorializing Hoover.

Hoover built a pair of eponymous institutions that showcased his life story and service—and later became sites for people to learn about him and even to mourn him. The first was the Hoover Institution on War, Revolution, and Peace, an archive and conservative think-tank that originated from the Hoover War Library, a collection of records gathered by Hoover during the Great War. Situated in the 285-foot-high Hoover Tower at Stanford University, where Hoover was a trustee, the War Library documented twentieth-century international history.[29] It also served as a monument to Hoover's experiences as a global figure who promoted peace, liberty, and free enterprise in the face of war, revolution, and communism. Hoover kept his name on the library, whose resources he touted to national leaders.[30] The mere existence of the Hoover Institution on War, Revolution, and Peace (its name starting in 1957) garnered respect for the former president, whose visage appeared on its brochures.[31] In 1958, Leopold III, former king of the Belgians, visited the institution to express his esteem for Hoover.[32] The press lauded the archive, which FDR claimed as inspiration for his presidential library at Hyde Park.[33]

The second institution bearing Hoover's name, his presidential library at West Branch, developed as he took renewed interest in his early life and ascent to the White House—themes increasingly important to his rehabilitation and, ultimately, his funeral. Hoover had left Iowa long ago, and starting in 1934, he resided at New York's Waldorf Astoria Hotel. Nevertheless, in 1935, the Hoover family purchased the former president's birth cottage in West Branch, had it restored to the era of Hoover's youth, and encouraged the formation of a society to manage the site. Adjacent to the cottage, Hoover acquired tracts of land, which became a public park named in his honor. Period buildings went up nearby, including a replica of the blacksmith shop where Hoover's father had worked. The environs blended Hoover's humble beginnings and faith with his lofty achievements. While Allan Hoover, his younger son, opposed making the birth house a "show place," Hoover reminded visitors of its significance: "This cottage where I was born is physical proof of the unbounded opportunity of American life."[34] The grounds featured a statue of Isis, the Egyptian goddess of life, given to Hoover—and initially stored at Stanford—by the people of Belgium in gratitude for his relief work.[35]

The transfer of Isis from California to Iowa foreshadowed Hoover's decision to move his personal papers from Stanford to a presidential library in West Branch, which he opened with great fanfare. Hoover grew frustrated with a "left of center" perspective among the staff at the Hoover Institution Archives and around his alma mater generally.[36] At the same time, he felt renewed connection to West Branch, where residents feted him on his birthday (August 10) in 1948 and 1954.[37] In 1958, Hoover resolved that his presidential materials would be "of more interest to the people who visit the Hoover Birthplace" than to researchers at the Hoover Institution. While the war archive would remain at Stanford, he wanted his papers housed in a federally run library similar to "the Truman and Roosevelt collections." He proposed building a single-story facility in the park at West Branch, situating it so "as not to overshadow" the birth house.[38] Hoover dedicated the library in 1962, on his eighty-eighth birthday. Truman came to applaud the feats of his "good friend," and JFK sent a message trumpeting Hoover's "selfless devotion to public service."[39] The library's displays also flattered him. Those devoted to "World War I Relief" and "Secretary of Commerce" eclipsed the section on "The Presidency."[40] Neil MacNeil, a journalist and family friend, labeled the library "a worthy tribute to a great man."[41]

By the time of the library's dedication, Hoover had decided to be buried in West Branch, in a manner that acknowledged his modest beginnings and grandest achievements. Hoover's thoughts about his burial site had shifted: He doubtless intended to be interred in Palo Alto alongside his wife, Lou, an alumna of Stanford who had died in 1944. But William B. Anderson, head of the Hoover Birthplace Foundation and a former funeral home director, persuaded him to be buried near the presidential library. Anderson wanted the "expanse" at the edge of West Branch to narrate Hoover's "great life" through "physical evidence": birth cottage, Isis statue, library, and grave. Allan Hoover agreed to the proposal, as did the former president.[42] Discretion, humility, and gravity marked subsequent discussions. Allan and his brother, Herbert Hoover Jr., favored "simplicity at its utmost" in designing the gravesite.[43] They insisted that two marble slabs cover the resting places of their father and mother, to be reinterred at West Branch, and that these markers should "not be raised as to become too prominent."[44] And they rejected a suggestion by the architect William J. Wagner to represent Hoover's life story on a stone wall. Wagner, Anderson, and Allan Hoover referred to the gravesite as the "Overlook," for it would be set amid grass and shrubbery atop an incline peering down at the library and cottage.[45] As time passed, Wagner waxed reflective. "All of a sudden I feel mighty small," he admitted in 1963. "Not more than 30 other people in the history of our country have had this responsibility."[46]

Not unlike the gravesite, plans for Hoover's funeral blended pageantry, solemnity, and modesty. Approved by the former president in 1958, events spanned six days in three locales: New York, Washington, and West Branch. He and his family decided on a state funeral, which gathered representatives of the federal government's three branches, state leaders, and the US military.[47] As of 1958, the last president to receive a state funeral was William Howard Taft in 1930, while Hoover occupied the White House, and the most recent to die was FDR, who did not have a formal state funeral due to wartime austerity. The extent to which Hoover sought to emulate Taft or surpass Roosevelt is unclear.[48] This much was certain: Hoover's "demise" ("D-Day") would initiate the first phase of his funeral, in New York, where he had lived. The succeeding two days ("D + 1" and "D + 2") called for observances at Universal Funeral Chapel, followed by a public viewing and memorial service at St. Bartholomew's Episcopal Church in Manhattan. Over the next three days ("D + 3," "D + 4," and "D + 5,"), Hoover would lie in state at the US Capitol Rotunda. On the sixth and final day ("D + 5"), his remains would be flown to

Iowa for interment. The World War II–inspired "D-Day" designations signified a meticulous roadmap: US Army commands in New York, Washington,
and the Midwest would oversee phases of the ceremonies; scheduling displayed military-style timing and precision; and diagrams marked the movement of the casket, caisson, cars, and escort formations as well as placement
of bands, flags, and honor guards. Offsetting the pomp was the president's
burial in rural Iowa.[49] Hoover was one of many chief executives to be interred
where his life began and the second to be buried near his presidential library:
Roosevelt had been laid to rest at Hyde Park in 1945.

From Mourning to Memorializing

Hoover's death on October 20, 1964, prompted mourning and memorialization. Beginning in 1962, the former president had suffered gastrointestinal
ailments. Internal bleeding ended his life. For many days afterward, the
United States and parts of the world went into mourning, as people expressed
sorrow at news of Hoover's passing. Expressions of grief or praise—for a life
well-lived—became evident at the state funeral; via bipartisan tributes; and
in largely favorable commentary about Hoover in the press. Efforts to memorialize him—to honor him in a formal, lasting manner—ensued, with the US
government leading the way, especially during the year or so following the
funeral.

The mourning of Hoover began with the funeral, a bipartisan affair that
unfolded with few glitches. In New York, luminaries gathered for the service
at St. Bartholomew's Church. Republican attendees included Thomas Dewey,
Richard and Patricia Nixon, and Barry Goldwater. Among the Democrats
were Senator Hubert H. Humphrey of Minnesota; Robert Kennedy, accompanied by his wife, Ethel, and mother, Rose; and President Lyndon Johnson
and First Lady Claudia "Lady Bird" Johnson.[50] The next day in Washington,
LBJ walked with Hoover's cortège from Union Station to the Capitol, where
he laid a wreath at the same catafalque used for Abraham Lincoln and JFK.
Twenty-one-rounds saluted the fallen former head-of-state.[51] In Iowa, there
was no presidential participation, horse-drawn caisson, or gunfire salutes.
Yet people lined Interstate 80 as the motorcade advanced from Cedar Rapids Airport to West Branch, where 75,000 mourners gathered, including US

Army and Iowa National Guard troops. Dr. Elton Trueblood, a Quaker theologian and family friend, offered the only remarks. Such simplicity did not erase all officialdom: there was a bugler playing "Taps," and floral arrangements in the shapes of an eagle, shield, and American flag.[52] An Iowa newspaper noted the tethering of "a simple burial" with "visible marks of respect" given to departed presidents.[53]

The funeral signified the apex of Hoover's campaign to restore his reputation. He had formed ties with all the major participants: LBJ, Nixon, RFK, and Goldwater, whom Hoover had pushed for the vice-presidential nomination in 1960.[54] These leaders, along with Truman and Eisenhower (both hospitalized and unable to attend the ceremonies), lauded his public service and humanitarianism.[55] The rites in New York, Washington, and West Branch underscored that Hoover had ascended the political mountaintop, and then returned to his roots. The family reaffirmed this man-of-the-people messaging: "He wished to be buried near his birthplace. In Iowa, he always felt a warmth of understanding."[56] His wife's earlier burial in Palo Alto and his recent embrace of West Branch elicited little notice as the Iowa press stressed the "quiet tribute" paid to Hoover's "fulfillment of the American dream."[57] A Pathé newsreel about the funeral featured images of the birth cottage, Old Glory at half-staff, and mourners paying respect to "the farm-boy who was to become the first president born west of the Mississippi River and a man who dedicated his long life largely to the good of others."[58]

Following the funeral, newspapers across the United States praised Hoover while wrestling with his record. The *New York Times* averred that he died "rich in years and honors and far beyond the reach of partisan criticism."[59] Retrospectives extolled his energy, perseverance, honesty, devotion to principle, and "compassionate concern for his fellow man."[60] During a time of Cold War rivalry with the Soviet Union, Hoover's life appeared to validate his country's highest ideals: the *Dallas Morning News* saluted "a success story in the finest tradition, symbolic of American individualism."[61] Editorial writers addressed Hoover's presidency in varied ways. A common response was to absolve him of blame for Depression and to lament his "misfortune" in being president when it began.[62] Others defended him. The *Arizona Republic* hailed Hoover's respect for state and local authority and devotion to the Constitution as "the soul of true conservatism."[63] Conservative opinion-writers Russell Kirk, William F. Buckley Jr., and Richard Wilson exalted Hoover's small-government instincts and noted the New Deal's deficiencies.[64] Commending Hoover and condemning Big Government enabled the budding conservative movement to flex its muscles. Not to be outdone, editorialists of liberal persuasion either accepted Hoover into their tradition or chided his faults. Walter Lippmann labeled Hoover "a radical innovator" for organizing a federal response to the Depression.[65] Yet the *St. Louis Post-Dispatch* and *New York Post* adjudged his policies insufficient.[66] Greatness in relief work or public service generally could not erase great failings as president. "Herbert Hoover," the *Wall Street Journal* conceded, "was not a giant of history."[67]

Such wide-ranging analyses showed how Americans used Hoover—or, more precisely, aspects of Hoover's ideas, life, or legacy—to advance specific aims or to affirm widely shared values. By applauding Hoover's "totally incorruptible" character and inability "to theatricalize" his public service, Buckley drew a contrast with, and took swipes at, liberalism's patron saint: FDR.[68] Although the wounds of 1932 endured, several newspapers took the opportunity to sound nonpartisan by trumpeting Hoover's positive attributes, even if doing so entailed polite exaggeration. Undeterred by evidence to the contrary, the *Atlanta Constitution* stated that Hoover "was not embittered by his name's being synonymous with the depression."[69] The praise of Hoover's achievements reflected Americans' desire to see the best, and the best of themselves, in Hoover. His ascent from modest circumstances to the presidency resonated with Americans' reverence for social mobility, which Harry Truman also exemplified.[70]

Many Americans mourned Hoover the person rather than Hoover the president. The trustees at American University passed a resolution that absolved Hoover of responsibility for the Depression and proclaimed him a "symbol of integrity."[71] Others stressed his beneficence. "We learned that he was a great humanitarian," a class of fifth-graders wrote the Hoover family. "We are grateful for his many services."[72] Upon hearing of Hoover's death, one man recalled his impoverished childhood in Russia, when his stepfather "came home with a sack of white flour" and declared, "Mr. Hoover is responsible for this."[73] Affection for Hoover proved especially heartfelt in the Midwest, where one woman ended a poem about him with the lines: "He who befriended nations near and far;/ Befriends us still. He is our morning star."[74] A resident of St. Louis found Hoover's "humble home" in West Branch, and the library's exhibit on food relief, testament to "what can be done when a person has ambition and lives a good life."[75] The *Hartford Courant* insisted that Hoover's "whole life as a dedicated American humanitarian" outweighed "the trying times of his presidency."[76]

Overseas reactions to Hoover's death included expressions of sympathy, acclaim for his relief efforts, and recognition of his shortcomings. Condolences arrived from Queen Elizabeth II, the Duke and Duchess of Windsor, Generalissimo and Madame Chiang Kai-shek, and West Germany's former chancellor Konrad Adenauer, who credited "this generous statesman" with pushing for US assistance to Germany in 1947.[77] Messages of sympathy came from leaders of countries helped by Hoover during the Great War: President Urho Kekkonen of Finland, former prime minister Stanislaw Mikolajczyk of Poland, and Baudouin, king of the Belgians.[78] The heads of both houses of Belgium's parliament eulogized Hoover, whom the country's press heralded as the "great benefactor."[79] West Germans echoed Adenauer: one newspaper called Hoover "the great friend of the German people" and another gushed that he had "sated the hunger of millions."[80] Yet the memory of the Great Depression, and Hoover's response to it, lingered in the minds of many. A Swedish newspaper labeled Hoover the "crisis president," as did a French headline.[81] The *Cork Examiner* maintained that "he never really rid himself of the stigma" of the downturn, his response to which the *Irish Independent* termed "pitifully inadequate."[82] Such criticism was commonplace in Anglophone countries that had both endured the slump and admired FDR's leadership. The *Times* of London dubbed Hoover "overwhelmed by economic storms," and the *Nottingham Guardian-Journal* agreed: "To sorely-beset Americans his successor's famous 'New Deal' came as a blessing from Heaven."[83] Similar themes surfaced in Australia and Canada, alongside paeans to Hoover's virtues. The *Canberra Times* proclaimed: "Nation mourns its former scapegoat." The *Vancouver Sun* opined that "Hoover's only failure was in the greatest task he undertook—the presidency."[84]

Hoover's death drew less attention from African Americans and countries of the Global South. Black-owned newspapers, many of them weeklies, gave little coverage to a president who wooed white southerners, stayed silent on civil rights, and remained "ignorant about racism and its workings."[85] A columnist for *Chicago Defender* highlighted the political consequences of the fallen president's misguided policies: "The man who is considered responsible for thousands of Negroes deserting the Republican party, has finally left it himself."[86] Since decolonization unfolded after Hoover exited the White House, he never became an important figure to the peoples of Africa as did Kennedy, who had criticized France's war in Algeria. Condolences for Hoover arrived from a handful of governments, such as those of Liberia, a US client state, and South Africa, run by a white minority.[87] Hoover's death elicited notice across Latin America, where his administration had acted to end US military interventions. Memories of Hoover's 1928 tour of the region surfaced in the press, and the Organization of American States expressed "deep sorrow" at his demise.[88] A Canadian newspaper noted that Hoover, rather than FDR, had coined the phrase "good neighbor policy."[89] Hoover's death invariably received greater attention from America's friends than from its adversaries. Although Hoover had few ties to Japan or South Korea, the leaders of those countries conveyed condolences, doubtless to pay homage to the United States, their chief ally, as much as to its former president.[90] Gratitude for Hoover's relief efforts in Eastern Europe and the Soviet Union came from émigrés or exiled leaders more than from the governments in power.[91]

The Hoover family's imprint, so vivid at the funeral, faded as mourning turned to memorialization. The Hoover commemorative postage stamp proved a case in point. The Post Office had issued stamps for FDR and Kennedy within a year of their deaths, and one for Hoover was in the offing. Hoover's sons stepped forward to push a design by William Wagner, architect of the gravesite, which perpetuated the funeral's West Branch–to–Washington motif.[92] Shaded principally in blue (Hoover's favorite color), the stamp had the birth cottage in the foreground, the White House at the top-right, and Hoover's signature in the opposite corner. Wagner's "keep it simple" sensibility pleased Hoover's family, but not the Citizens' Stamp Advisory Committee, a sounding board for the postmaster general.[93] Preferring a more traditional look, the committee approved a stamp featuring Hoover's likeness, partially framed by the words: "Humanitarian • Engineer • President."[94] By highlighting Hoover's varied career, it boosted him in a manner the original design had not. Stanford-red in color, the stamp pleased collectors, who flocked to West Branch on its first day of issuance: August 10, 1965—Hoover's ninety-first birthday. The launch and the birthday festivities spawned further tributes. Eisenhower came to West Branch, as did Nixon, who spoke on foreign policy.[95] Assistant Postmaster General Richard Murphy welcomed the opportunity "to memorialize in philatelic fashion one of the great Americans of our time."[96]

To memorialize Hoover further, the US government in 1965 designated his birthplace a national historic site. The project "delighted" Hoover's family and the birthplace foundation.[97] Boosted by the tributes given to Hoover, it won bipartisan support, beginning with members of Iowa's congressional delegation. "I do not anticipate any difficulty," Representative John Kyl, a Republican, wrote of the bill's prospects.[98] LBJ backed the measure, which advanced several of his aims, including showing respect for former presidents, as he later would be. At a ceremony in the Rose Garden, Johnson signed the legislation, which empowered the secretary of the interior to acquire land in West Branch to establish the Herbert Hoover National Historic Site, to be managed by the National Park Service. Infused with federal funds, the site eventually encompassed sixty-seven acres, including the birthplace, period buildings, and gravesite.[99] The Herbert Hoover Presidential Library and Museum, which remained under the jurisdiction of the National Archives and Records Administration, did not escape the notice of LBJ, who visited West Branch with his wife in February 1969. Crowds thronged the former president as he toured the grounds and laid a wreath on his predecessor's grave.[100]

Over time, applause for Hoover grew softer, even at places linked to him. To be certain, he remained a hero to the Belgian American Educational Foundation, heir to his Commission for Relief in Belgium, and to the Boys Clubs of America, which raised funds in his name.[101] In 1965, the Hoover Institution dedicated a gallery named for its founder. Family and friends attended the ceremony, but such invitees as Truman, Eisenhower, Nixon, and Goldwater did not, a hint that interest in honoring Hoover may have begun to wane.[102] In 1969, Iowa's legislature designated Hoover's birthday an annual day of "recognition" rather than a state holiday; the gesture merely endorsed observances organized by the presidential library and national historic site.[103] Reactions to Hoover shifted over time, and for predictable reasons. While he lay in state at the Capitol in 1964, the Department of Commerce held a memorial service at its main office building, opened by former secretary Hoover in 1929. In 1981, Congress voted to name the edifice after Hoover, but not before a few House Democrats likened Ronald Reagan's economic program to Hoover's "failed" policies during the early 1930s.[104] The library in West Branch acknowledged his millstone. Brochures from the 1970s discussed Hoover's life, accomplishments, and White House initiatives without using the phrase "Great Depression." They instead euphemistically depicted the president fighting "for a stable economy" after "the stock market collapse and succeeding crises."[105]

As memories of the Depression persisted and those of Hoover's funeral ebbed, cheering for him became less bipartisan. To be sure, Robert Kennedy professed to admire "a lot in Herbert Hoover's career."[106] And a pair of Senate resolutions to mark the centenary of Hoover's birth, introduced by Republicans Barry Goldwater and Mark O. Hatfield, garnered co-sponsorship from Democrats Ted Kennedy, Hubert Humphrey, Walter F. Mondale, and Mike Mansfield, among others.[107] No one contested Goldwater's tribute to Hoover's "distinguished service."[108] Yet he remained a Democratic bogeyman. In 1972, Sargent Shriver, the Democratic nominee for vice president, assailed President Richard Nixon as a Hoover-style reactionary, sentiments echoed by Senator Henry M. Jackson a year later.[109] During the election of 1976, Jimmy Carter portrayed President Gerald R. Ford as another Hoover for failing to take "bold action" to assist an ailing economy.[110] In 1984, Mondale linked Reagan to Hoover by repeating Will Rogers's quip about the Great Depression president: "It's not what he doesn't know that bothers me. It's what he knows for sure that just ain't so."[111] Eight years later, a recession inspired Democratic Senator Tom Harkin of Iowa to denounce "George Herbert Hoover Bush."[112]

Republican presidents and White House hopefuls stopped short of fully embracing Hoover. Nixon went the furthest, sending his daughter Julie to tour the Hoover Library during the 1972 campaign.[113] But Ford and Bush crossed the aisle to find kinship with Truman, who beat the odds and held onto the presidency (as they failed to do). And Ronald Reagan revered Calvin Coolidge, a conservative untainted by the Depression.[114] Hoover backers could take solace from editorial sighing at the Democrats' hackneyed attacks.[115] More worrisome was Republican disavowal of Hoover. Secretary of Housing and Urban Development Jack Kemp preferred his GOP to be "the party of Abraham Lincoln, not the party of Herbert Hoover."[116]

Kemp's comment highlighted the persistence of Hoover's image as a downbeat president, either out of touch with or crushed by (or both) an historic calamity. "He was sincere, honorable, but believed only business could grow us out of the crisis," Milton Slater wrote to the *New York Times* in 1992, as the Hoover Presidential Library prepared events to commemorate its thirtieth anniversary. Slater's memories of the 1930s would have resonated with countless Americans: "I saw the empty, pleading eyes of the unemployed men wearing sandwich boards asking for a job—any job. And there were the shacks made of old cartons for the homeless on many empty city lots. These were dubbed Hoovervilles." Like many people of his generation, Slater found Hoover's speeches, and leadership, lacking: "If there were good ideas buried in that deluge of verbiage, they were obscured by his dreary monotone."[117]

Popular culture proved unkind to Hoover's legacy, especially during the 1970s, a period of hard times and uninspiring presidential leadership. Hoover's responsibility for the Depression took center-stage in the Broadway musical *Annie* (1977). In one scene, shantytown dwellers lament their lot by sarcastically singing: "We'd Like to Thank You, Herbert Hoover."[118] Hoover is an off-screen foil to FDR (Edward Herrmann) in the television drama *Eleanor and Franklin: The White House Years* (1977); Eleanor Roosevelt (Jane Alexander) hears about the contrasting styles of the two presidents following a visit with survivors of the Bonus March, one of whom had quipped: "Hoover sent the Army, Roosevelt sent his wife."[119] In *Backstairs at the White House* (1979), NBC's miniseries about interactions between the domestic staff and first families, Hoover (Larry Gates) regrets the Bonus March fiasco and his own political shortcomings. Pithy pronouncements by Lou Hoover (Jan Sterling) puncture the portrait of Hoover as dour and aloof. Lou at one point assures Bert, "Half the children in this world would be dead if you hadn't gone where you were needed."[120] Despite a friendly nod to Hoover in its theme song, the situation comedy *All in the Family* did little to advance his reputation. When asked the whereabouts of a houseguest named Herbert Hooper, Archie Bunker (Carroll O'Connor) perplexedly replies: "He died in California after inventing the Depression."[121] In 2019, *CBS Sunday Morning* tried to correct the record in an eight-minute-long segment entitled "The Real Herbert Hoover," during which Margaret Hoover nominated Leonardo DiCaprio to play her great-grandfather on the big screen.[122] The suggestion underscored the fact that Hoover has never been the subject of a feature film or documentary.

Specific institutions, spread across the United States, have endeavored to keep Hoover alive in memory and history. Visitors to Oregon's Hoover-Minthorn House, where the orphaned Bert lived with an uncle, can learn about Hoover's early struggles. In 2019, the Stanford-based institution bearing his name marked its first century, during which it had hosted such leaders as Margaret Thatcher, Mikhail Gorbachev, Henry A. Kissinger, and Condoleezza Rice. The Hoover Presidential Library has focused attention on his life and legacy. Schoolchildren have found the site illuminating, as have scholars who began researching its papers in 1966.[123] During the 1970s and 1980s, newly opened documents enabled revisionist writing on Hoover to flourish. Historians of leftist outlook, such as Joan Hoff Wilson, praised Hoover's "anti-interventionist" foreign policy, while conservatives, such as George H. Nash, chronicled his achievements over several decades.[124] The revisionists, according to the political scientist Stephen Skowronek, "have dispelled the myth of an intransigent, laissez faire ideologue hostaged to business interests and impervious to the plight of the American people. The Hoover we know about today is more like the Hoover of the memoirs. He was indeed the leading political innovator of the 1920s and a worthy heir of the progressive legacy of Roosevelt and Wilson."[125] Reassessments continued with the recent publication of two thoroughly researched biographies favorable to Hoover.[126]

Yet these books, like those of the early revisionists, failed to find a mass audience, and unflattering impressions of Hoover have persisted. The Presidential Library's foundation, for its part, has organized events to honor him, although the celebration to mark the centenary of his birth, on August 10, 1974, proved a tad disappointing.[127] The speaker on that date was Secretary of the Interior Rogers C. B. Morton, a genial party hand but not the invited star: President Nixon. The unfolding Watergate scandal had forced Nixon to send his regrets. Indeed, Nixon resigned from office one day before Hoover turned one hundred.[128] Bad luck and bad timing again beset Hoover.

Retrospect

Hoover's effort to restore his reputation bore mixed results. At one level, some public awareness of him has endured due to his international significance, his eponymous institutions, and his ties to specific locales. His name stretches across the globe: on a street sign in Warsaw, schools in Germany, and a house-turned-inn in Western Australia, where he resided as a young mining engineer.[129] At another level, however, Hoover remains unfamiliar to most people. The Hoover Presidential Library's distance from large population centers has hindered visitor turnout, along with lingering perceptions of Hoover as a failed president.[130]

Hoover's bid for his rehabilitation, his funeral, and the mourning and memorialization of him shaped a bifurcated legacy, aptly summarized by the *Wall Street Journal* in 1974: "Hoover's presidency, as a whole, was an unfortunate detour in an otherwise brilliant career."[131] Scholars friendly to him have agreed. "As an ex-president, Hoover sought historical vindication," Glen Jeansonne averred, but "it never fully restored his place in presidential history."[132] This quest, according to Richard Norton Smith, a biographer and former director of the Hoover Presidential Library, took on "the trappings of Greek tragedy."[133] Hoover's policies, Smith argued—in a book that ranked him thirty-sixth out of forty-three presidents—"failed to arrest the economic death spiral forever after linked to his name."[134] Never to be acclaimed as a great president, he nevertheless earned veneration as a great nonpresidential actor. That Hoover accomplished that much bears noting in a life marked by accomplishment before, and beyond, the White House.

Notes

1. Robert A. Taft to Herbert Hoover, May 15, 1942, folder: Hoover, Herbert 1941–48, box 1286, Robert A. Taft Papers, Manuscript Division, Library of Congress, Washington, DC (hereafter LC).

2. "Joe Garagiola Broadcast on NBC," October 22, 1964, folder: Hoover Funeral, box 182, Herbert Hoover Post-Presidential Papers: Subject File (hereafter HHPP: Subject File), Herbert Hoover Presidential Library (hereafter HHPL), West Branch, IA.

3. *Kansan* (Lawrence), October 23, 1964, folder: 1964 October 23, box 301, Herbert Hoover Clippings Files, HHPL.

4. "For Herbert Hoover, an Historic Tribute," *New York Herald Tribune*, October 23, 1964, folder: Hoover Death USA—Region 2—*New York Herald Tribune* Scrapbook Oct. 1964, box 3, Herbert Hoover Death and Funeral Collection (hereafter HDFC), HHPL.

5. Dean Kotlowski, "The President's Club Revisited: Herbert Hoover, Lyndon Johnson, and the Politics of Legacy and Bipartisanship," *The Historian* 82, no. 4 (2020): 463–91.

6. R. W. Apple, "Democrats vs. Hoover," *New York Times*, October 9, 1970, 43.

7. *London Daily Telegraph*, October 21, 1964, folder: Clips Europe British Isles, box 1, HDFC.

8. Kenneth Whyte, *Hoover: An Extraordinary Life in Extraordinary Times* (New York: Alfred A. Knopf, 2017), 219, 234–35.

9. William E. Leuchtenburg, *Herbert Hoover* (New York: Times Books, 2009), 71.

10. "Herbert Hoover's Ordeal," *Birmingham Post-Herald*, October 23, 1964, folder: Hoover Death Clips USA Region 4, box 3, HDFC.

11. Gary Dean Best, *Herbert Hoover: The Postpresidential Years 1933–1964*, vol. 1: *1933–1945* (Stanford, CA: Hoover Institution, 1983), 46.

12. Joan Hoff Wilson, *Herbert Hoover: Forgotten Progressive* (New York: HarperCollins, 1975), 276.

13. Leuchtenburg, *Herbert Hoover*, 155.

14. John D. M. Hamilton, "Visit with Mr. Hoover," March 9, 1956, folder: Visit with Mr. Hoover 7/27/55, 3/9/56, and 6/8/60, box 15, John D. M. Hamilton Papers, LC.

15. Herbert Hoover, *The Memoirs of Herbert Hoover: The Great Depression, 1929–1941* (New York: Macmillan, 1952), 2–28, 161–66.

16. John Morton Blum, *A Life with History* (Lawrence: University Press of Kansas, 2004), 138.

17. Press: Craig Lloyd, *Aggressive Introvert: A Study of Herbert Hoover and Public Relations Management, 1912–1932* (Columbus: Ohio State University Press, 1973), xii; unprecedented: Douglas B. Craig, *Fireside Politics: Radio and Political Culture in the United States, 1920–1940* (Baltimore: Johns Hopkins University Press, 2000), 150.

18. Hamilton, "Visit with Mr. Hoover," June 8, 1960, folder: Visit with Mr. Hoover 7/27/55, 3/9/56, and 6/8/60, box 15, Hamilton Papers, LC; Whyte, *Hoover*, 604; "A Conversation with Mr. Hoover," November 6, 1955, 29–31, folder 9, box 230, HHPP: Subject File.

19. Hulda Hoover McLean statement, October 20, 1964, folder: Condolences—Responses, 1964–65 (3 of 6), box 4, HDFC.

20. Whyte, *Hoover*, 612 (quotation); Booklet, "Dedication of the Herbert Hoover Building," October 18, 1960, folder: Herbert Hoover, box 1, Loretta Camp Frey Papers, HHPL.

21. "These Days: Hoover Dam," *New York Sun*, May 3, 1947, folder: Herbert Hoover Correspondence, 1939–47, box 1, Frey Papers, HHPL; "Hoover Dam: The Story of Hoover Dam," undated, Bureau of Reclamation Website, https://www.usbr.gov/lc/hooverdam/history/articles/naming.html.

22. "Most Admired Men and Women: 1948–1998," December 13, 1999, https://news.gallup.com/poll/3415/most-admired-men-women-19481998.aspx.

23. William E. Pemberton, "Struggle for the New Deal: Truman and the Hoover Commission," *Presidential Studies Quarterly* 16 (Summer 1986): 513.

24. Robert F. Kennedy to Hoover, [1954], folder: Kennedy, Robert F. Correspondence—1954, and handwritten comment on Edward M. Kennedy to Hoover, October 13, 1964, folder: Kennedy, Edward M. Correspondence—1964, box 110, Herbert Hoover Post-Presidential Papers: Individual File (hereafter HHPP: Individual File), HHPL.

25. John F. Kennedy to Hoover, March 2, 1961; Hoover to JFK, March 4, 1961, folder: Kennedy, John Fitzgerald Correspondence—1951–61, box 110, HHPP: Individual File.

26. Hamilton, "Visit with Mr. Hoover," June 8, 1960, folder: Visit with Mr. Hoover 7/27/55, 3/9/56, and 6/8/60, box 15, Hamilton Papers, LC.

27. Hoover to Richard Nixon, October 31, 1957, and note for the file, November 4, 1957, folder: Nixon, Richard M. Correspondence—1957–59, box 165, HHPP: Individual File.

28. Hoover to Lyndon B. Johnson, August 23, 1958, folder: Johnson, Lyndon B.—1955–64, box 101, HHPP: Individual File.

29. George H. Nash, *Herbert Hoover and Stanford University* (Stanford, CA: Hoover Institution Press, 1988), 86.

30. Hoover to Cordell Hull and Hoover to Henry L. Stimson, both July 3, 1944, folder: Hoover, Herbert May 20–July 20, 1944, box 47, John Callan O'Laughlin Papers, LC.

31. "The Hoover Library on War, Revolution, and Peace," undated brochure, folder: Hoover Institution Correspondence General 1960–61, box 182, HHPP: Subject File.

32. Witold Sworakowski to Hoover, November 19, 1958, folder: Hoover Institution Correspondence General 1951–59, box 182, HHPP: Subject File.

33. "Hoover Gave F.R. an Idea," *Palo Alto Times*, September 30, 1939, folder: Hoover Institution Clippings 1928–54, box 183, HHPP: Subject File.

34. Show place: Frank T. Nye, *Doors of Opportunity: The Life and Legacy of Herbert Hoover* (West Branch, IA: Herbert Hoover Presidential Library, 1988), 167; Cottage: Hoover quotation on gatepost at the birth cottage (author's photograph, December 16, 2019).

35. Nye, *Doors of Opportunity*, 171.

36. Nash, *Herbert Hoover and Stanford University*, 143.

37. Nye, *Doors of Opportunity*, 203–14, 225–36.

38. Hoover to William B. Anderson, May 21, 1958, folder: Correspondence May-June 1958, box 8, William Anderson Papers, HHPL.

39. Good friend: Nye, *Doors of Opportunity*, 351; selfless devotion: Press release, address by Wayne C. Grover, August 10, 1962, folder: Correspondence August 14–31, 1962, box 8, Anderson Papers, HHPL.

40. "The Herbert Hoover Presidential Library and Museum," undated pamphlet, folder: Hoover Library Museum Pamphlets ca. 1970s, box 1, Ross Sayles Collection, HHPL.

41. Neil MacNeil to Anderson, August 14, 1962, folder: Correspondence August 14–31, 1962, box 8, Anderson Papers, HHPL.

42. William B. Anderson Oral History with Raymond Henle, October 6, 1966, 28, HHPL.

43. Allan Hoover to William J. Wagner, September 29, 1961, folder: General Correspondence 1960–63, box 1, William Wagner Papers, HHPL.

44. Wagner to John Fitzsimmons, June 27, 1961, folder: General Correspondence 1960–63, box 1, Wagner Papers, HHPL.

45. Wagner to Allan Hoover, August 25, 1961, and Allan Hoover to Wagner, September 29, 1961, folder: General Correspondence 1960–63, box 3, Wagner Papers, HHPL; Anderson to L. D. Vickers, February 27, 1961, folder: Correspondence January–February 1961, box 6, Anderson Papers, HHPL.

46. Wagner to Allan Hoover, June 19, 1963, folder: General Correspondence 1960–63, box 1, Wagner Papers, HHPL.

47. "Description of State Funeral," undated, folder: HH Death Funeral Official Plans for Ceremonies, box 5, HDFC.

48. B. C. Mossman and M. W. Stark, *The Last Salute: Civil and Military Funerals, 1921–1969* (Washington, DC: Department of the Army, 1991), 400–401.

49. "Description of State Funeral," undated, folder: HH Death Funeral Official Plans for Ceremonies, box 5, HDFC.

50. Mossman and Stark, *The Last Salute*, 264–65.

51. Mossman and Stark, *The Last Salute*, 203, 229, 268, 270–72, 275.

52. "Last Rites: Silence, Simplicity," *Cedar Rapids Gazette*, October 26, 1964, 10A.

53. "Memorable Rites for Hoover," *Iowa City Press-Citizen*, October 26, 1964, 1.

54. Hamilton, "Visit with Mr. Hoover," June 8, 1960, folder: Visit with Mr. Hoover 7/27/55, 3/9/56, and 6/8/60, box 15, Hamilton Papers, LC.

55. "Campaign Fury Stilled for Hoover Funeral," *Hartford Courant*, October 23, 1964, 8.

56. "Family Statement," *Iowa City Press-Citizen*, October 26, 1964, folder: 1964 October 26–27, box 301, Hoover Clippings Files, HHPL.

57. "A Boy from Iowa," *Iowa City Press-Citizen*, October 26, 1964, folder: 1964 October 26–27, box 301, Hoover Clippings Files, HHPL.

58. British Pathé, "Herbert Hoover. The Nation's Last Tribute," 1964, Film ID: 3113.21, https://www.britishpathe.com/video/herbert-hoovers-funeral/ .

59. "The Long Chain," *New York Times*, October 25, 1964, E10.

60. "Herbert Hoover," *Philadelphia Inquirer*, October 21, 1964, folder: Hoover Death Clips USA Region 2 [DE, NJ, PA], box 3, HDFC.

61. "Herbert Hoover," *Dallas Morning News*, October 21, 1964, folder: Hoover Death Clips USA Region 7, box 3, HDFC.

62. "Grief and Gratitude," *Chicago Tribune*, October 21, 1964, folder: Hoover Death Clips USA Region 5, box 3, HDFC.

63. "Mirror of Americans," *Arizona Republic*, October 21, 1964, folder: Hoover Death Clips USA Region 9, box 3, HDFC.

64. These columns can be found in date-specific folders in box 301, Hoover Clippings Files, HHPL: Russell Kirk, "The Dignity of Herbert Hoover," *Danville [VA] Register*, October 29, 1964; William F. Buckley Jr., "Hail to the Chief," *Leavenworth [KS] Times*, October 22, 1964; Richard Wilson, "Hoover Ideas Still Have Currency," *Washington Star*, October 23, 1964.

65. "Today and Tomorrow . . . Herbert Hoover," *Washington Post*, October 22, 1964, A21.

66. "The Fate of Herbert Hoover," *St. Louis Post-Dispatch*, October 21, 1964, folder: Hoover Death Clips USA Region 6; "Herbert Hoover," *New York Post*, October 21, 1964, folder: Hoover Death Clips USA Region 2 [NY], box 3, HDFC.

67. "The Voice of an Honorable Man," *Wall Street Journal*, October 21, 1964, 18.

68. "Hoover Gained Back Respect," *Kokomo [IN] Tribune*, October 22, 1964, 5.

69. "Hoover Grappled with a Dying Era; He Bore His Burden without Bitterness," *Atlanta Constitution*, October 21, 1964, folder: Hoover Death Clips USA Region 4, box 3, HDFC.

70. Alonzo L. Hamby, *Man of the People: A Life of Harry S. Truman* (New York: Oxford University Press, 1996), 635.

71. "Herbert Clark Hoover," undated, folder: Condolences 1963–66, box 4, HDFC.

72. "Grade 5 People," Sparta, Wisconsin, to Mr. Hoover, October 22, 1964, folder: Condolences 1963–66, box 4, HDFC.

73. R. E. Carey to Herbert and Allan Hoover, October 26, 1964, folder: Condolence Correspondence to Allan Hoover 1, box 5, HDFC.

74. Martha Cordes, "Herbert Hoover," undated, folder: Cordes, Martha R., box 5, Manuscript Biographies Collection, HHPL.

75. Willard Boellner to Herbert Hoover Jr., November 5, 1964, folder: Condolences October–November 1964, box 4, HDFC.

76. "Herbert Hoover," *Hartford Courant,* October 21, 1964, 20.

77. Herbert Hoover Jr. to Her Majesty the Queen, November 19, 1964; Herbert Hoover Jr. to Generalissimo and Madame Chiang Kai-shek, November 24, 1964; Konrad Adenauer to Herbert Hoover Jr., October 20, 1964, folder: Condolences—Responses, 1964–65 (1 of 6) and the Duke and Duchess of Windsor to Richard E. Berlin, October 22, 1964, folder: Condolences, 1963–66, box 4, HDFC.

78. Herbert Hoover Jr. to Urko Kekkonen, November 23, 1964, folder: Condolences—Responses, 1964–65 (1 of 6); Herbert Hoover Jr. to Stanislaw Mikolajcyzk, December 29, 1964, folder: Condolences—Responses, 1964–65 (3 of 6); Baudouin to Allan Hoover, October 21, 1964, folder: Condolences—Responses, 1964–65 (6 of 6), box 4, HDFC.

79. "Tributes to a Great Citizen," *Commission for Belgian Relief Alumni News* (December 1964), 5–7. News clipping, "M. Herbert Hoover n'est plus," undated, folder: Clips Europe Belgium, box 1, HDFC (quotation).

80. Great friend: "Herbert Hoover gestorben," *Deutsche National Zeitung und Soldaten-Zeitung,* undated; and sated: "Er stillte den Hunger von Millionen," *Herrenberg Gäubote,* October 21, 1964, folder: Clips Europe Germany, box 2, HDFC.

81. "Krispresidenten Hoover," *Goteborgs Handels-Och Sjofartstidning* [Stockholm], October 21, 1964, folder: Clips Europe General, box 2; "L'homme de las crise de 1929 est mort," unidentified, undated clipping, folder: Clips Europe France, box 1, HDFC.

82. "Hoover and the Depression," *Cork Examiner,* October 21, 1964; "Herbert Hoover," *Irish Independent,* October 22, 1964, folder: Clips Europe British Isles, box 1, HDFC.

83. "Mr. Herbert Hoover," *Times* of London, October 21, 1964; "Mr. Herbert Hoover," *Nottingham Guardian-Journal,* October 21, 1964, folder: Clips Europe British Isles, box 1, HDFC.

84. *Canberra Times,* October 22, 1964, 20; "The Non-Political President," *Vancouver Sun,* October 21, 1964, folder: Clips Canada Alberta and British Columbia, box 1, HDFC.

85. Donald J. Lisio, *Hoover, Blacks, and Lily-Whites: A Study of Southern Strategies* (Chapel Hill: University of North Carolina Press, 1985), xviii.

86. "Hoover, Depression, Made Negroes Flee GOP in '32," *Chicago Defender,* October 21, 1964, 2.

87. S. Edward Peal to Herbert Hoover Jr. and Allan Hoover, October 20, 1964, folder: Condolences—Responses 1964–65 (3 of 6); Herbert Hoover Jr. to the Ambassador of South Africa, December 2, 1964, folder: Condolences—Responses 1964–65 (4 of 6), box 4, HDFC.

88. "Herbert Clark Hoover," *La Nacion* [San Jose, Costa Rica], October 21, 1964, 51; "El Fallecimiento del ex Presidente Hoover," *La Prensa* [Buenos Aires, Argentina], October 21, 1964, 2; Juan Bautista de Lavalle to Herbert Hoover Jr., November 17, 1964, folder: HH Death Condolence Correspondence Special, box 5, HDFC (quotation).

89. "Good Neighbor Herbert Hoover," *Lethbridge Herald,* October 21, 1964, folder: Clips Canada Alberta and British Columbia, box 1, HDFC.

90. Hayato Ikeda to Herbert Hoover Jr. and Chung Yul Kim to Herbert Hoover Jr., both October 21, 1964, folder: Condolences—Responses, 1964–65 (2 of 6), box 4, HDFC.

91. Joseph Kajeckas to Herbert Hoover Jr., October 22, 1964, and Stanislaw Mikolajcyzk, October 24, 1964, 4, folder: Condolences—Responses, 1964–65 (3 of 6); Yury V. Solovieff to Herbert Hoover Jr., October 20, 1964, folder: Condolences, October–November 1964, box 4, HDFC.

92. Wagner to Lewis L. Strauss, November 25, 1964, folder: Hoover Library Commemorative Stamp 1962–68, box 1, Wagner Papers, HHPL.

93. Wagner to H. R. Gross, December 14, 1964, folder: Hoover Library Commemorative Stamp 1962–68, box 1, Wagner Papers, HHPL.

94. Ira Kapenstein to Gross, February 12, 1965, folder: Herbert Hoover Foundation Topical Files National Park Service (Hoover Stamp) 1964–67, box 5, Robert Goodwin Papers, HHPL.

95. William J. Petersen, "The Hoover Memorial Stamp," *The Palimpest* 46 (August 1965): 418–23.

96. Post Office Department news release, August 10, 1965, folder: August 10, 1965, Murphy, Richard J. Address HH Commemorative Stamp, box 128, Reprint File, HHPL.

97. Robert Goodwin to Gross, May 28, 1965, folder: Herbert Hoover Foundation Topical Files National Park Service (Hoover Stamp) 1964–67, box 5, Goodwin Papers, HHPL.

98. John Henry Kyl to Goodwin, January 13, 1965, folder: Herbert Hoover Foundation Topical Files National Park Service (Hoover Stamp) 1964–67, box 5, Goodwin Papers, HHPL.

99. "Bill Signing Stirs Up a Tea Party," *Washington Post*, August 13, 1965, B1.

100. "LBJ Comes to West Branch," *Iowa City Press-Citizen*, February 21, 1969, 10B.

101. James A. Farley to Allan Hoover, March 5, 1965, folder: Condolences—Responses, 1964–65 (6 of 6), box 4, HDFC.

102. Truman to W. Glenn Campbell, July 20, 1965; Eisenhower to Campbell, July 16, 1965; Goldwater to Campbell, July 23, 1965; Nixon to Campbell, July 14, 1965; "Hoover Memorial Dedicated," *Palo Alto Times*, July 21, 1965, folder: Hoover Institution Dedication of the Hoover Memorial Room 7/20/65, box 184, HHPP: Subject File.

103. Elmer H. Vermeer to Richard J. Jacobs, March 14, 1969 (plus attachment "House File 95"), folder: Hoover Day 1969, box 182, HHPP: Subject File.

104. "Memorial Service for Herbert C. Hoover," October 23, 1964, October 21, 1964, folder: Condolences—Responses, 1964–65 (6 of 6), box 4, HDFC; "Briefing," *New York Times*, December 28, 1981, B10 (quotation).

105. "The Herbert Hoover Presidential Library and Museum," undated pamphlet, folder: Hoover Library Museum Pamphlets ca. 1970s, box 1, Sayles Collection, HHPL.

106. Whyte, *Hoover*, 613.

107. S. Con. Res. 1418, 93rd Congress, 1st sess., March 29, 1973, folder 7, box 110; S. Con. Res. 79, 93rd Congress, 2nd sess., April 1, 1974, *U.S. Congressional Record*, April 9, 1974, S-5470 and April 23, 1974, S-6052, folder 8, box 107, Robert A. Taft Jr. Papers, LC.

108. Goldwater to Robert A. Taft Jr., April 2, 1974, folder 8, box 107, Robert A. Taft Jr. Papers, LC.

109. "Shriver, in Baltimore, Assails Nixon," *Washington Post*, November 3, 1972, A2; "Nixon Policy Hit," *Washington Post*, March 10, 1973, A4.

110. "Carter Pledges Restoration of 'Strength, Hope,'" *Washington Post*, September 7, 1976, A7.

111. "Mondale Aims Pitch at Party's Unfaithful," *Washington Post*, October 12, 1984, A20.

112. "Remembering Herbert Hoover," *New York Times*, August 10, 1992, A16.

113. "Julie Charms Hoover's Hometown," *Iowa City Press-Citizen*, August 11, 1972, 4A.

114. "Thanks to Reagan, Coolidge Fans Can Let Their Love Be Known," *Washington Post*, December 17, 1981, F6.

115. Tom Wicker, "In the Nation," *New York Times,* May 26, 1970, 39; George Will, "The Tired Party," *Washington Post,* November 16, 1980, L7; "Remembering Herbert Hoover," *New York Times,* August 10, 1992, A16.

116. "Hoover, We Hardly Knew Ye," *Washington Post,* August 23, 1992, C2.

117. "Some Recall the Apple Sellers and Hoovervilles," *New York Times,* August 29, 1992, 18.

118. "We'd Like to Thank You, Herbert Hoover," from *Annie,* music by Charles Strouse, lyrics by Martin Charnin, https://www.youtube.com/watch?v=cqvYNoiPDKw.

119. *Eleanor and Franklin: The White House Years,* DVD (HBO Home Video, 2007).

120. *Backstairs at the White House,* DVD (Acorn Media, 2005).

121. "Unequal Partners," October 23, 1977, *All in the Family: The Complete Fifth Season,* DVD (Los Angeles: Sony Pictures Home Entertainment, 2005).

122. "The Real Herbert Hoover," *CBS Sunday Morning,* October 20, 2019, https://www.cbs .com/shows/cbs-sunday-morning/video/TU_AMLxwdl765VQoHQikoRln7aJ5J6Bm /the-real-herbert-hoover/.

123. Brian Weisman to Ross Sayles, December 13, 1971, and Judy Franenhotlz to Sayles, December 10, 1971, folder: Hoover Library Museum Thank You Letters 1971 and Undated, box 1, Sayles Collection, HHPL.

124. Hoff Wilson, *Herbert Hoover,* 269; George H. Nash, *The Life of Herbert Hoover,* 3 vols. (New York: W. W. Norton, 1983–96).

125. Stephen Skowronek, *The Politics Presidents Make: Leadership from John Adams to Bill Clinton* (Cambridge, MA: Belknap, 1997), 261.

126. Whyte, *Hoover,* ix–xvii, 608–14; Glen Jeansonne (with David Luhrssen), *Hoover: A Life* (New York: New American Library, 2016), 1–6.

127. Hoover Presidential Library Association *News* (May 1973), folder: Hoover Presidential Library Association 1971–75, box 32, Walter Trohan Papers, HHPL; John T. McCarty to Maury Travis, December 7, 1941, folder: Travis, Maury M., box 22, Manuscript Biographies Collection, HHPL.

128. Nye, *Doors of Opportunity,* 413–15.

129. Author's photograph, Warsaw, Poland, Summer 2014; Principal of the Herbert Hoover *Schule* to Allan Hoover, November 4, 1964, folder: Condolences October–November 1964, and Heinrich Knappstein to Herbert Hoover Jr., October 20, 1964, folder: Condolences—Responses, 1964–65 (2 of 6), box 4, HDFC; "History of Hoover House," Gwalia Ghost Town and Museum website, http://www.gwalia.org.au/hoover-house/history/.

130. Anthony Clark, *The Last Campaign: How Presidents Rewrite History, Run for Posterity, and Enshrine Their Legacies* (North Charleston, SC: CreateSpace, 2015), 47.

131. "The Restoration of Herbert Hoover," *Wall Street Journal,* August 5, 1974, 10.

132. Jeansonne, *Hoover,* 5.

133. Richard Norton Smith, *An Uncommon Man: The Triumph of Herbert Hoover* (New York: Simon & Schuster, 1984), 25.

134. Brian Lamb, Susan Swain, and C-SPAN, *The Presidents: Noted Historians Rank America's Best—and Worst—Chief Executives* (New York: PublicAffairs, 2019), 5.

"Crushed by the Burdens of War"

THE DEATH AND LEGACY OF FRANKLIN D. ROOSEVELT

David B. Woolner

Great men have two lives: one which occurs while they work on this earth; a second which begins at the day of their death and continues as long as their ideas remain powerful. In this second life, the conceptions earlier developed exert influence on men and events for an indefinite period of time. Now, only a month after his death, we are seeing the beginning of his second, and perhaps greater life. None of us can prophesy what its results will be; but few will deny that there is a continuing and beneficent spirit which will not cease to speak to a world in pain, with a voice of confidence, hope, and wise and humorous counsel.

—Adolf Berle reflecting on the death of Franklin Roosevelt, May 6, 1945[1]

O N JANUARY 20, 1945, at approximately 11:59 a.m., US president Franklin D. Roosevelt took the oath of office for the fourth time. Unlike his previous three inaugurals, the fourth was designed to be a simple, uncomplicated affair. There would be no inaugural parade or other major festivities, and the swearing-in would take place not in front of a huge crowd at the Capitol but on the south portico of the White House, just few short steps from the Blue Room at the rear of the building.

The simplicity of the ceremony was determined in large part by the circumstances of the moment. With the nation at war, FDR felt it would be inappropriate to host the usual revelry that accompanies the start of a new presidential term. But FDR's desire to keep the ceremony simple also stemmed from the fact the he was tired; tired of the ceremonial burdens of office; tired of the pain and discomfort caused by the steel braces that made it possible for him to "walk" a few short paces and stand at a lectern; worn out by what Frances Perkins called "the terrible, unceasing strains of wartime demands" and the "constant need" to make decisions that would have far-reaching consequences.[2]

At this critical moment, on the eve of his historic journey to Yalta, what was foremost in FDR's mind was the need to maintain Allied unity in the face of the ever-increasing strains that had crept into the alliance as the war in Europe approached its climax. One major concern centered on the degree to which the British and American governments could secure a measure of independence for the Polish people now that the Soviet Army was firmly lodged in the region. A second involved American distress over Great Britain's determination to establish a conservative pro-British regime in Greece—even at the cost of armed conflict with Britain's former allies, the antimonarchist and largely communist Greek resistance. These and other political issues had led to a great deal of speculation in the American press about "the gravity of the international situation" and the extent to which the Allies were actually fighting the war as a means to uphold the principles first articulated in the Atlantic Charter.[3]

FDR was deeply alarmed about the impact these anxieties might have on the willingness of the American people to abandon their isolationist tendencies, live up to their global responsibilities, and embrace the establishment of the United Nations. Nor was the war by any means over. Thanks to the shocking and unexpected German counteroffensive in the Ardennes that began in mid-December, the euphoria that had accompanied the sudden Allied breakout in Normandy in August had long since vanished. There would be no quick victory over Germany and by the time the Battle of the Bulge ended in early February 1945, approximately 19,000 Americans had been killed, nearly 50,000 were wounded, and more than 23,000 were missing.[4]

It was with all this in mind that FDR delivered what turned out to be the shortest of his inaugural addresses. He began by reminding his fellow citizens that the challenges before the American people and their allies at this vital moment represented what he called "a supreme test—a test of our courage—of our resolve—of our wisdom—of our essential democracy." If the American people met this test "successfully and honorably," he said, "we shall perform a service of historic importance which men and women and children will honor throughout all time." But he also cautioned that although "we shall strive for perfection, we shall not achieve it immediately." He then recalled what "his old schoolmaster," Dr. Endicott Peabody, said "in days that seemed to us then to be secure and untroubled," that "things in life will not always run smoothly. Sometimes we will be rising toward the heights—then all will seem to reverse itself and start downward. The great fact to remember is that the trend of civilization itself is forever upward; that a line drawn through the middle of the peaks and the valleys of the centuries always has an upward trend."

He then urged the American people not to abandon but to profit from the fearful lessons that the long years of war had wrought: "We have learned that we cannot live alone, at peace; that our own well-being is dependent on the well-being of other Nations, far away. . . . We have learned to be citizens of the world, members of the human community. We have learned the simple truth, as Emerson said, that, 'The only way to have a friend is to be one.'"

FDR closed with an observation that echoed his first inaugural when he insisted that "we can gain no lasting peace if we approach it with suspicion and mistrust or with fear. We can gain it only if we proceed with the understanding and the confidence and the courage which flow from conviction."[5]

Having lived through the failures of the Wilson administration, FDR was determined to avoid what he called "the disillusionment" that rendered a lasting peace impossible at the end of the First World War. In this sense, his fourth inaugural—and the State of the Union Address he delivered a few weeks before—represent a warning to the American people not to repeat the mistakes of the past and like the previous generation "give up the hope of gradually achieving a better peace because we had not the courage to fulfil our responsibilities in an admittedly imperfect world." FDR understood that the transition from war to peace would not be easy, but as he said in the address he delivered to a joint session of Congress upon his return from the Yalta Conference six weeks later, the defeat of the Axis powers and the understandings achieved among the British, American, and

Soviet governments during the Crimean summit represent not an end, but a beginning, the chance to fashion "a permanent structure of peace upon which we can begin to build, under God, that better world which our children and grandchildren—yours and mine, the children and grandchildren of the whole world—must live, and can live."[6]

It was FDR's determination to see the war through to its conclusion and secure the successful establishment of the United Nations that led to his fateful decision to seek a fourth term in office. Given the precarious state of his health, there is no question that this decision helped precipitate his death. But as Eleanor Roosevelt remarked to a friend on March 25, 1945, FDR knew—even as early as 1940—that his determination to seek a third and fourth term in office "must shorten his life." He made that choice, she said, in the belief that "if he can set out to accomplish what he set out to do, and then dies, it will have been worth it. I agree with him."[7]

In the end, much as Eleanor had predicted, the demands of the war proved to be too much for FDR's frail body and after struggling to maintain a supreme effort to secure that lasting peace he fell victim to a massive cerebral hemorrhage on April 12, 1945—less than two weeks before the start of the San Francisco Conference that would see the United Nations established, roughly four weeks before the defeat of Germany, and less than four months before the successful use of the atomic bomb—that he had rendered possible—brought the war against Japan to its abrupt and dramatic conclusion.

Hence, FDR did not live long enough to witness the victories he had worked so hard to achieve. Yet, like Abraham Lincoln, the timing and circumstances of his death helped contribute to and define his legacy. In this sense, FDR's "second life," as Adolf Berle put it, may be just as important, if not more important, than his first.

To fully understand why the timing and circumstances of FDR's death proved so significant we must first consider the simple fact that he had been in office for twelve years. For many Americans—especially those in uniform—this meant that FDR was the only president that they had ever known. Equally important, this was the president who had steered the nation through the two great crises of the twentieth century—the Great Depression and the Second World War. We must also remember that FDR—again, like Lincoln—was a war president; the commander-in-chief at the time when more than sixteen million American men and women were under arms and when virtually every family in the nation was touched in some way by the gargantuan struggle that the United States and its allies were waging against fascism. Finally, we must not overlook the extent to which FDR's efforts to prove to the American people that he possessed the energy and vitality to lead that nation through these trying times affected the public's perception of this highly unusual president: the only man to be elected to the White House four times and only president who could not stand or walk or get out of bed in the morning without the assistance of others. This is not to say that the public was totally unaware that FDR had a disability. They knew "that his legs were not much good to him," as a team of sympathetic physicians reported at the start of the 1932 campaign.[8] But his exuberant personality and determination to do whatever it took to get the nation out of the Great Depression convinced most Americans that FDR was a man of action. A leader who could race against speeding trains or leap across the Grand Canyon—as he was often depicted in editorial cartoons—a man who loved life as much as he loved being president. As such, the possibility that he might leave the world stage at the very moment at which the most terrible war in human history reached its conclusion seemed utterly impossible, even to those who knew in their heart of hearts that this was a dying man.

FDR's second life began on a warm spring day in Georgia, at his much-adored "Little White House," the modest cottage he had constructed just outside the tiny hamlet of Warm Springs, where, more than two decades earlier, he had first taken "the waters" associated with a rundown old resort known as the Meriwether Inn in a forlorn attempt to recover his ability to walk. FDR was so taken with the experience—and with the seemingly healing qualities of the warm mineral waters that were pumped into the resort's pools—that he purchased the property in 1926 and within a year had turned it into a hydrotherapeutic center for the treatment of polio. From this moment on Warm Springs became a symbol of hope for the thousands of American men, women, and children who had lost the full use of their limbs as a result of this disease.

As had so often been the case, FDR had traveled to Warm Springs at the end of March 1945 to get some rest; to quit the frantic environment of Washington for the quiet and relative isolation of rural Georgia, so that he might recover his strength in the wake of the arduous 14,000-mile journey he had undertaken to Yalta and the hectic schedule he had maintained since his return.

By this point, FDR's health had become a major item of concern among those who were closest to him. In the first few months of 1944, following his return from the Tehran Conference, FDR had struggled with a lengthy bout of flu and bronchitis. It was during these months that FDR's daughter, Anna, who had recently moved back into the White House, began to express alarm about the state of her father's health. This led to two extensive medical workups by a team of physicians in March and again in May of 1944. These examinations revealed that FDR was suffering from severe hypertension and the early stages of congestive heart failure.[9]

That the president of the United States was suffering from heart disease unleashed a fierce debate between Vice Admiral Dr. Ross McIntire, FDR's surgeon general and long-serving White House physician, and the other specialists brought in to examine him: Dr. James A. Paullin, former head of the American Medical Association; Dr. Frank Lahey, director of the Lahey Clinic in Boston and widely regarded as one of the most prominent surgeons in the country; and Dr. Howard Bruenn, the young naval cardiologist tasked by Dr. McIntire to carry out the initial cardiac examination. It was Dr. Bruenn who determined that FDR had heart disease and who was the most disturbed by the state of the president's health. He insisted that FDR's condition was serious enough to warrant aggressive treatment, including extensive rest as well as the administration of digitalis and two other medications.[10]

But McIntire was initially incredulous. Nor were Paullin and Lahey convinced that such treatment was necessary—in part, because they disagreed with Bruenn about the extent of the president's cardiac disease, but also out of concern that the sudden administration of a number of medications might cause the president distress. Thus they concurred with Dr. McIntire's more conservative assessment and, according to Bruenn, "grudgingly" agreed to support a compromise proposal put forward by the young cardiologist at the end of March: the president would take digitalis, go on a low-fat diet, cut the number of cigarettes he smoked to six per day, avoid stress and significantly reduce the number of hours he worked—not an easy task for a man charged with the responsibility of running a global war.[11]

By the time FDR had decided to run for a fourth term, however, the fragile consensus the team of physicians had reached over the state of FDR's health and treatment had broken down. Indeed, just days before FDR made his historic July 11 announcement to seek reelection, Lahey telephoned Admiral McIntire to inform him that the second round of tests they had conducted on the president in late May had convinced him that the president's heart condition was worse than he initially suspected and that he thus did not believe that the president "had the physical capacity to complete [a fourth] term." He insisted that it was the admiral's duty—as surgeon general and FDR's primary physician—to inform the president about the likelihood that he would not survive the strain of another four years in office and, in a clear indication of the gravity of the situation, argued that if the president did accept another term, "he had a very serious responsibility concerning who is Vice President."[12]

According to a memo that Lahey drew up recording his conversation with McIntire, the latter "was in complete agreement" about the state of FDR's health and had "informed the President" about the nature of his condition. There is no way to confirm definitively whether or not this is true, but the balance of the evidence suggests that neither McIntire nor Bruenn—who would go on to become FDR's attending physician under the supervision of McIntire—ever provided FDR or his family with a blunt warning about the risks involved in his decision to seek another term. Nor was the public fully informed. The standard line taken by Dr. McIntire—an ear, nose, and throat specialist—was that FDR was in fine health for a man his age. This was the mantra that was repeated to the press whenever the issue of the president's health came up, and despite all the evidence to the contrary, it appears that the surgeon general clung to this view right up until FDR's death.[13]

Still, FDR understood that he had "some trouble with [his] heart," and was well aware of his physicians' insistence that he had to cut back on his workload. Moreover, the weight loss that accompanied FDR's treatment, along with the ever more frequent bouts of fatigue brought on by his coronary disease and the gray pallor brought on by the digitalis, made it increasingly difficult for McIntire and other senior aides to simply brush aside both the private and public expressions of concern over the state of FDR's health. As the 1944 campaign intensified, these expressions broke out into the open. On October 17, the *Chicago Daily Tribune* insisted that the president's health be regarded as "one of the principal issues of the campaign" and two weeks later editorialized that "A Vote for F.D.R. May Be a Vote for Truman."[14]

FDR managed to dispel these alarums through his famous "Fala Speech" to the International Brotherhood of Teamsters on September 23, 1944, by engaging in a campaign swing through all five boroughs of New York City in an open car and a driving rain in mid-October, and by making whirlwind tour of seven states in the final days before the election. But the state of his health remained a serious concern for those who worked with the president on a day-to-day basis or were part of his small inner circle, and like the president, they shared the hope—or illusion—that the few weeks spent in the warm Georgia sun would provide him with the respite he needed to "bounce back" as they had seen him do so many times before.

But it was not too be. After a morning reading the papers, taking his breakfast in bed, getting dressed, and then working through his correspondence with his official secretary, William Hassett, which was his usual routine in Warm Springs, FDR remarked that he had "a terrific pain" in the back of his head. He then suddenly slumped forward unconscious. Roughly two hours later, his heart stopped, and despite the valiant efforts of his physicians to revive him, he was pronounced dead at 3:35 p.m.[15]

The death of any leader always comes as a shock, but in this case, the most powerful man in the world had just died in the midst of a global war. In Washington, the first task was to inform Eleanor Roosevelt that her husband had died. Vice President Truman also had to be notified. Equally important, it was critical not to let the news of the president's death leak out before these two tasks were accomplished. As such, it fell to Stephen Early, FDR's long-serving press secretary, to carry out these responsibilities and to coordinate how the news of the president's demise would be passed on to the world.

Eleanor, who had already been informed that her husband had fainted but had been urged by Dr. McIntire to continue with a public appearance she had been scheduled to make that afternoon, was quickly called back to the White House. Eleanor received the news that her husband "had slipped away" in her second-floor study and by all accounts took it with a great deal of dignified solemnity. She thanked Early and asked him to place a call to Harry Truman.

She then composed a somber, straightforward message to her four uniformed sons, who were scattered all over the world by the demands of war.[16]

Truman, who arrived shortly thereafter, recalled later that his first reaction upon entering the study was that something unusual had happened. Eleanor immediately stepped forward and placed her arm gently around Truman's shoulder. She then said quietly, "Harry, the President is dead."

Shocked, Truman found himself unable to speak for a moment. Then he asked Mrs. Roosevelt if there was anything he could do for her, to which she famously replied, "Is there anything we can do for *you?* For you are the one in trouble now."[17]

Truman and Secretary of State Edward Stettinius, who entered the study just moments later, decided that a cabinet meeting should be called at once and that the chief justice of the Supreme Court should be summoned to administer the oath of office. It wasn't long before the West Wing of the White House bustled with activity and apprehension as reporters, photographers, members of Congress, Secret Service agents, and other staff and officials converged from all directions.[18]

At 7:09 p.m., using an inexpensive Gideon Bible that had been retrieved from the desk drawer of the White House's head usher, Harry S. Truman took the oath of office to become the thirty-third president of the United States. He had already asked the cabinet to remain so that they could hold a brief meeting following his swearing-in, but before the new president had the chance to speak, Stephen Early entered the room to say that the press wanted to know if the San Francisco Conference on the United Nations would meet as planned on April 25. Truman answered with an emphatic yes. Thus, the first official order that the new president issued was to proceed with the endeavor that FDR had described in a recent interview with the journalist Anne O'Hare McCormick as the one project that would secure "his success in life and immortality in history"—the establishment of the United Nations.[19]

FDR's reference to the importance he attached to the United Nations, and how he would want to be remembered by future generations, was not the first time during his final months in office that he referred to his own mortality. As his fourth inaugural approached, FDR indicated to Eleanor and his aides that he wanted his eldest son James to be present. James had assisted his father in his first three inaugurals, and though in January 1945 he was serving as a marine combat officer in the Philippines, FDR insisted he do the same for his fourth. To accomplish this, FDR issued a special order for his return to Washington. His ostensible reason was his desire to keep up this tradition. But in the private conversations he held with James immediately following the inaugural ceremonies, FDR intimated that there was a second, equally important reason he wanted to see James, and that was to discuss his will.[20]

FDR informed James that he had selected him as one of three trustees and executors, and that he was the only family member among them. James said he would be honored to serve in such a capacity but hoped it would "not be a long time yet." FDR smiled and went on to tell James about a letter addressed to him, in his White House safe, that had instructions regarding his funeral, which were to be used only if he were to die in office. These included first, "a service of utmost simplicity in the East Room of the White House." Second, "No lying in state anywhere." Third, "that the Army bring his body to the Capitol for a simple service in the Rotunda for the Congress, the Judiciary and the Diplomatic Corps." That this service run about twenty minutes with two hymns and "no speaking." Fourth that "a funeral train" carry his body to Hyde Park the same day, and that "the Navy be in charge of this part of the burial." Fifth, that a brief evening service be held at St. James Church in Hyde Park "for old neighbors." Sixth, that "the casket be brought back to the house and be placed in front of east fireplace for the night." Seventh, that the burial should occur the next morning where "the sun dial stands in the [rose] garden, and that his casket be carried by men who work on the nearby estates." And finally, that a "gun carriage, not a hearse, be used throughout," that "the casket be of absolute simplicity, dark wood, [and] that the body be not embalmed or hermetically sealed."

He also indicated his hope "that my dear wife will on her death be buried there also, and that the monument contain no device or inscription except the following . . .

FRANKLIN DELEANO ROOSEVELT

1882–19—

ANNA ELEANOR ROOSEVELT

1884–19—"[21]

As Eleanor recounts in her memoirs, she and FDR had had conversations about how much they disliked the practice of a person lying in state after death so that crowds could go by to view the body in an open coffin. She was also aware of his desire to be buried in the center of the Rose Garden on his estate in Hyde Park, and there is some evidence to suggest that they discussed the idea of a service in the East Room of the White House. But she was completely unaware of the letter that her husband had addressed to James and as such proceeded with his funeral on the basis of what she thought her husband would have wanted.[22]

She had already informed Anna that she wanted a service of some sort in the White House. Eleanor was not sure what day or hour this would occur, but she wanted Anna, her secretary Malvina Thompson, and Edith Helm, the White House staff person who had helped plan all four of FDR's inaugurations, to work out the details, and draw up the guest list.

As for the more public aspects of FDR's funeral, here, we must remember that FDR was not only the nation's head of state and government. He was also the nation's commander-in-chief and the key figure in the wartime alliance that was still locked in a deadly struggle against the German army in Europe and the Japanese army in the Pacific. As such, it is perhaps not surprising that the public display of grief that followed his death took on a military bearing, not unlike the funeral arrangements for Abraham Lincoln that had taken place almost eighty years to the day before.

To help ensure that the president and commander-in-chief received all the respect that he deserved, Eleanor turned to the one man within the US military command structure who, like her husband, had served in the same post from the first day of the war, General George C. Marshall, the chief of staff of the United States Army. It was Eleanor's cable to her four sons that first alerted senior officers in the Pentagon that the president had passed away. Knowing that General Marshall would want to be informed, his aide-de-camp, Colonel Frank McCarthy, rushed out to the general's home at Fort Myer to deliver the news in person.[23]

Upon learning of the commander-in-chief's death, General Marshall and his wife hurried over to the White House to offer their sympathy and help. Eleanor promptly asked General Marshall to assume responsibility for all details of the journey north from Warm Springs, the funeral service at the White House, and for the final trip and burial in Hyde Park. Almost immediately, the great machinery of the Pentagon was put into action. From Fort Benning, Georgia, two thousand men were ordered to Warm Springs, guards of honor were to be placed along the route FDR's funeral train would take northward, and thousands more troops were to line the streets in Washington as the president's body was borne from Union Station to the White House.[24]

It was not long after Eleanor held this conversation with General Marshall that she departed for Warm Springs on a military aircraft, accompanied by Dr. McIntire and Press Secretary Early. By this point, word had already gone out to the nation and the world that the president had died. As planned, this was accomplished by a joint announcement issued by Early in Washington and Hassett in Warm Springs at 5:45 p.m., Eastern War Time, followed by a press conference in both locations, at which Early released a statement attributed to Mrs. Roosevelt, but most likely drafted by the press secretary, that said: "I am more sorry for the people of this country and of the world than I am for ourselves."[25]

This may have been the case, but it was also true that a long and difficult night lay ahead for Eleanor Roosevelt. Finally reaching the Little White House at 11:00 p.m., her first inclination was to comfort the president's grieving staff, before entering FDR's bedroom to spend five minutes alone with her deceased husband. She then had to approve the hastily arranged final preparations for her husband's body, including his being embalmed, the choice of a heavy bronze coffin, and the dark blue suit that Arthur Prettyman had selected to dress the president for the last time. That night Eleanor also learned that Lucy Mercer Rutherfurd, the woman with whom FDR had carried out an alleged affair in 1918—and had pledged never to see again—was at Warm Springs visiting her husband on the day he died. Eleanor never revealed what went through her mind in the wake of this stunning revelation, but years later, reflecting on what her husband had accomplished and meant to her, she wrote that men and women who live together for decades not only get to know each other's failings, "they also come to know what is worthy of respect and admiration in those they live with and in themselves."[26]

It was shortly after 9:00 a.m. the next morning that the public ritual of mourning for Franklin D. Roosevelt began. For those who lived through this trying era, the moving image of FDR's hearse leaving Warm Springs in front of a throng of wheelchair-bound residents, while a distraught Graham Jackson played "Going Home" on his accordion, seemed to capture the grief of the moment more than any other of the countless scenes of anguish that marked FDR's final journey as his funeral train made its way from Georgia, to Washington, and on to Hyde Park. It wasn't just that African American Chief Petty Officer Jackson had lost his president, he had lost his friend; the man who, despite his wealthy upbringing and position of privilege, seemed to understand the troubles and aspirations of each and every American, no matter what their status, race, or creed.

What makes this bond all the more remarkable is that it came about in an era when much of the rest of the world had turned its back on democracy and instead embraced the tenets of fear; fear of the other, of the unknown; fear that led millions to embrace what FDR sometimes referred to as the ideology of hate; fear that led to the most destructive war and unspeakable crimes in human history.

From the moment he took the oath of office, on March 4, 1933, FDR made it clear that his goal was not to embrace fear but to banish it; to overcome the "nameless, unreasoning, unjustified terror" brought on by the Great Depression with the full confidence that the nation would not just endure "the dark hour" that confronted it but would "revive and prosper."

Given the hope and confidence he inspired as the nation struggled through depression and war, the public outpouring of sorrow that accompanied FDR's final journey becomes all the more understandable. Thousands upon thousands of ordinary Americans lined the tracks as FDR's funeral train as it made its way from Warm Springs to Washington. Thousands more—estimates run as high as 500,000 people—lined the streets of Pennsylvania Avenue to witness the extraordinary military honors that General Marshall

FIGURE 7. Franklin D. Roosevelt's funeral procession with horse-drawn casket, Pennsylvania Avenue, Washington, DC, April 14, 1945. (Prints and Photographs Division, Library of Congress, Washington, DC, LC-USZ62-67439, https://www.loc.gov /item/96522968/)

bestowed on his chief as his body was carried from Union Station to the White House. This included a marine and army band followed by a squadron of forty-eight scout cars, and an armed escort consisting of a battalion of field artillery, a battalion of infantry, a battalion of marines, a battalion of sailors, and a composite battalion of WACs, WAVES, and female marines, all of whom began their march in front of the president's flag-draped coffin as a squadron of B-24 Liberator bombers thundered overhead.[27]

After the slow procession finally reached the White House, FDR's casket was carried to the East Room and placed before a French door banked ten feet high with lilies, roses, and other flowers. Outside, a large group of mourners lingered, seemingly unable to overcome the shock of what had just transpired, while inside five members of the armed services stood guard next to the coffin.[28]

At 4:00 p.m., the hour at which the services in the East Room were set to begin, the nation—and much of the world—paused for a moment of silence in tribute to the late president. In an extraordinary display of national unity virtually everything came to a sudden halt at the appointed moment. Throughout New York City, millions stood in utter silence or knelt on the pavement in what the *New York Times* reported as "an outpouring of mass sorrow and reverence seldom witnessed in American life." In the tunnels beneath the throng and on the elevated tracks above, all trains came to a stop, while passengers rose to their feet, or bowed their heads. In Chicago, Los Angeles, and other major cities, the normally bustling inner-city streets became deathly quiet; radios everywhere went silent; war production halted in defense plants; Western Union ceased transmitting telegrams; newspaper presses stopped printing—even telephone service was momentarily interrupted.[29]

Overseas, soldiers, sailors, and airmen—many of whom recorded that loss of FDR was like losing one's own father—paused for five minutes of silent prayer. Theaters and cabarets closed in France; pubs went silent in the United Kingdom; while in the Soviet Union, ordinary citizens wept as they viewed special newsreels featuring the late president. Indeed, the loss of the president stirred similar emotions in virtually every country around the world, from Brazil's Rio de Janeiro, where the Sociedade Amigos de America immediately resolved to erect a monument to commemorate "the passing of a great friend of humanity" to war-ravaged Manila, where thousands of ordinary Filipinos poured into the streets to weep and mourn the leader who had been unswerving in his advocacy of their right to liberty.[30]

Back in the White House, the Right Reverend Angus Dun, bishop of the National Cathedral, officiated in the short service that was in keeping with what FDR would have wanted. It consisted of two of his favorite hymns— "Eternal Father Strong to Save" and "Faith of Our Fathers"—readings of psalms and lessons from the scriptures, and at Eleanor Roosevelt's private suggestion, a reference to FDR's first inaugural. As such, after Bishop Dun offered a prayer in which he thanked God for "the qualities of heart and mind" that FDR brought to the service of the nation and of the world, he closed the ceremony with a reiteration of the sage counsel that FDR delivered to the American people more than twelve years earlier and which he frequently repeated in different forms during his long tenure in office, including the short address he delivered to the nation on the south portico of the White House just three months before.

"In his first inaugural address," the bishop said, "the President bore testimony to his own deep faith; so, first of all, let me assert my firm belief that 'the only thing we have to fear is fear itself.'"

"As that was his first word to us," he continued, "I am sure he would want it to be his last. We should go forward in the future as those who go forward without fear, without fear of our Allies or friends, and without fear of our own insufficiencies."[31]

A few hours later, FDR's coffin was carried back to Union Station for the president's last journey up the Hudson River to his beloved home in Hyde Park, accompanied by Eleanor and other members of the family, including his son Elliott, President Truman, members of his cabinet and the Congress, and a host of other dignitaries. There, the next morning, his worn-out body was lowered into its final resting place. Not everything about his burial was in keeping with his wishes. It was the army and not the navy that officiated at his internment, and his casket was carried into the Rose Garden—not by men who worked on the nearby estates—but by uniformed members of the armed services. Still, FDR would no doubt take satisfaction in knowing that his grave had been dug by William Plog, the faithful superintendent of the Roosevelt estate who had been hired by FDR's father more than fifty years before, and that it was located just as he wished: where the sundial once stood, at the center of the Rose Garden, not more than 250 yards from the home where he was born.[32]

Winston Churchill described receiving the news of FDR death late on the evening of April 12, 1945, as a "physical blow" and in the emotional tribute Churchill delivered to the House of Commons a few days after FDR's burial, observed that the timing and circumstances of FDR's death may well contribute to the fulfillment of his legacy.[33] Churchill acknowledged that while the president's passing represented a "bitter loss to humanity," he had died what Churchill considered "an enviable death." He had brought his country "through the worst of its perils and the heaviest of it toils" and had "died in harness . . . battle harness, like his soldiers, sailors, and airmen," at the very moment when "victory had cast its sure and steady beam upon him."[34]

Churchill was not alone in this observation. Countless editorials, press pieces, and radio commentaries made the same argument. On April 16, for example, Mayor Fiorello LaGuardia of New York delivered a radio address in which he said the passing of FDR meant the American people bore "a responsibility for maintaining a united front" in support of "his program for world peace and economic security for the common man." And, in words that presaged what Adolf Berle would say some four weeks later, insisted that "Franklin Roosevelt is not dead. He is keeping his rendezvous with destiny."[35]

Perhaps the most salient observation about the impact that FDR's death would have on future developments came from Anne O'Hare McCormick in an editorial she wrote days after the president died entitled, "His 'Unfinished Business'—and Ours." The article was based on an extensive interview she held with FDR on March 23, 1945—less than three weeks before he passed away. McCormick observed that while some might argue that with victory assured Franklin Roosevelt had died at the moment when his "great work was done, he would not have said so," she wrote, because the president was looking beyond victory to the meeting that was to take place in San Francisco on April 25, where the nations of the world were set to draft the final charter of the United Nations. Indeed, McCormick reported that she found the president's normally discursive mind singularly focused on the United Nations and the inaugural conference that was about to take place.[36]

She also detected his sense of urgency. "If he desired one thing more than any other in the last days of his life," she continued, "it was to see the Grand Alliance enlarged and reshaped into an armed security system while the forge of war was still hot enough to fuse the nations of the world together. . . . The San Francisco Conference is the unfinished business of the Roosevelt Administration," McCormick argued. FDR "may not be present at the conclave he called, but in the most literal sense he will be conspicuous by his absence. His voice will be the loudest there . . . [his] vacant seat will overshadow all of the occupied chairs. It may well be," she concluded, "that the speech he does not deliver—the speech his mind was full of when he fell—will be far more effective in carrying his dream toward reality than anything he could say in person."[37]

One example of how FDR's sudden death had a direct influence on coming events can be found in Soviet Premier Joseph Stalin's reaction. Not long before his passing, FDR and Stalin had been involved in a bitter dispute over a false attempt by the commander of the German forces in Italy to surrender. As a consequence, Stalin had decided to forgo sending his foreign secretary, Vyacheslav Molotov, to the San Francisco Conference, which FDR feared would be interpreted as an indication that the USSR did not take the creation of the UN seriously. The shock of FDR's death led Stalin to reverse this decision with the remark that "President Roosevelt has died but his cause must live on."[38]

In many respects, then, Churchill's and McCormick's observations about the timing of FDR's death proved accurate. FDR had died at an opportune moment, and had not, as he himself feared he might, lingered on to fight the battle over the creation of the United Nations and the establishment of the peace in an incapacitated state, as had Woodrow Wilson decades earlier.[39]

One person who certainly would have agreed was the longstanding Roosevelt associate Benjamin Cohen. Cohen was the one administration official who had the temerity to argue in the spring of 1944 that FDR's running for a fourth term would be a mistake. It would, Cohen feared, lead to a kind of apathy or intellectual and political fatigue among the American public that risked leaving "Rooseveltian ideas, like Wilsonian ideas . . . discredited for a considerable period, not because they are basically unsound but because political conditions will not permit them to be accepted or even understood." If, on the other hand, FDR were to end his career in 1944 on what could only be described as a high point, the influence of his ideas "may be greater," as the people will always remember that at no moment and in no crisis did Roosevelt ever let them down. Thus, whoever succeeds FDR will be under great pressure to follow his example in fighting for and watching out for "the common people's interests."[40]

Cohen's reasoning reinforces the argument that the circumstances of FDR's death played a critical part in cementing and defining his legacy. In his determination to provide economic security for the average American, for example, through Social Security, unemployment insurance, worker's rights, and the regulation of the financial sector, not to mention a massive investment in infrastructure, FDR not only helped save liberal capitalist democracy at the moment it was under siege in much of the rest of the world, but also fundamentally altered the relationship between the American people and their government.

With Eleanor Roosevelt's help, FDR also helped usher in an America that was far more inclusive of racial and religious minorities. This is not to say that he rid the country of racism, anti-Semitism, or other forms of bigotry and religious intolerance, but FDR's habit of "including the excluded" and paying attention to the needs of the marginalized helped lay the foundation for the all-important Civil Rights Movement that followed. As Mary McLeod Bethune once noted, the Roosevelt years represented "the first time in the history" that African Americans felt that they could communicate their grievances to their government with the "expectancy of sympathetic understanding and interpretation." By 1936, over 90 percent of African American voters—most of whom had supported the Republican Party in the past—were voting for Roosevelt and the Democrats.[41]

FDR's leadership had an equally strong impact on the relationship between the United States and the rest of the world. As with his social and economic reforms, the most transformative aspect of this came about in the minds of the American people, who, by the time of FDR's death—and inspired by it—had largely accepted the idea that the so-called isolationism of the 1930s, or what might better be defined as unilateralism, was a failed policy. To a large extent this conviction stemmed from the lessons FDR and his contemporaries gleaned from the experience of the Great Depression, which included stark recognition of the link between the global economic crisis of the 1930s and the concomitant rise of fascism in Europe and parts of Asia. Commenting on this in his famous Economic Bill of Rights speech in January 1944, FDR said, "We have come to a clear realization of the fact that true individual freedom cannot exist without economic security and independence. 'Necessitous men are not free men.' People who are hungry and out of a job are the stuff with which dictatorships are made."[42]

In light of this, FDR firmly believed—as he said in his fourth inaugural— that the security and well-being of people on distant continents was directly linked to the security and well-being of the American people. It is for this reason that he launched the wartime effort to secure a new postwar multilateral order that rejected the economic nationalism and unilateralist tenets of such organizations as the America First movement. In place of high tariffs and restrictive trade practices, his administration embraced the free movement of capital and freer trade, and by the summer of 1944 had created the basis for this new world order through the successful negotiation of the Bretton Woods Accords, which gave us the World Bank and International Monetary Fund.

Another consequence of this transformation can be seen in the willingness of the American people to maintain and expand the transatlantic ties to Great Britain that emerged during the war under the so-called "special relationship." Here, FDR's emphasis on the importance of the Atlantic to national security would find new life in the creation of the North Atlantic Treaty Organization (NATO) that emerged in April 1949, just four years after his sudden collapse.[43]

Of course, it was the establishment of the United Nations that FDR would have regarded as his greatest contribution to the world that emerged after his death. The UN Charter that was signed on June 26, 1945, stands as a fitting testament to FDR's vision. Its emphasis on human rights and the establishment of a human rights commission would eventually lead—under the skillful leadership of Eleanor Roosevelt—to the adoption of the Universal Declaration of Human Rights in 1948. Its call for the establishment of "international machinery for the promotion of the economic and social advancement of all peoples" echoes FDR's 1941 call for "Freedom from Want" in his Four Freedoms address, and closely mirrors the Atlantic Charter's appeal for the "fullest collaboration between all nations in the economic field with the object of securing, for all, improved labor standards, economic advancement and social security." The creation of the Trusteeship Council, which was established to supervise the UN's Trust Territories and facilitate the charter's goal of the right to "self-determination," helped initiate the postwar process of decolonization. Finally, the establishment of the Security Council, while imperfect, has nevertheless helped avert the outbreak of what FDR feared most—a Third World War.[44]

These accomplishments certainly place FDR among the ranks of our most effective presidents. Yet we must also acknowledge that FDR was not without his critics—both during and after his presidency. His government intervention in the economy and expansion of federal powers was deeply opposed by a coalition of conservative Democrats and Republicans in Congress whose opposition to his leadership rendered further New Deal reforms all but impossible by the end of 1938. Nevertheless, FDR still hoped that further reform might be possible as the nation made its transition from war to peace. The first indication that FDR was intent on enlarging the New Deal came with his January 1944 announcement of the need for the nation to embrace the "economic Bill of Rights," noted above. These included the right to a useful and remunerative job; to adequate food, clothing, and recreation; to a decent home; to adequate medical care; and to a good education.[45]

Even though not all of these goals would be achieved, in the decades following FDR's death—and in part because of it—a majority of Americans agreed that the federal government had a special responsibility in trying to maintain the social and economic well-being of the nation. This New Deal consensus began to unravel in the 1960s and 1970s, however, thanks in part to the disillusion over the government's handling of the Vietnam War, the Watergate crisis, and the issue of race, the last of which drove many white Americans out of the ranks of the Democratic Party following the political victories that Black America achieved via the Civil Rights Act of 1964, the Voting Rights Act of 1965, and the subsequent push for desegregation and affirmative action.

By 1980, Ronald Reagan converted the discontent many Americans felt about these issues into an attack on New Deal government with a call for the "restoration of individualism, family values, states' rights and patriotic pride."[46] The conservative assault that Reagan led against the New Deal— which mirrored the attacks of the 1930s—proved very effective, with the result that by the end of the century, the self-proclaimed "New Democrats," led by President Bill Clinton, had all but abandoned the word "liberal," openly renounced "big government," and joined many of their conservative colleagues in the dismantling much of the regulatory structure of the New Deal in favor of the seemingly rationality and fairness of "free markets."

The subsequent collapse of the US economy in the Great Recession of 2008–9, coupled with the onset of the climate crisis and growing wealth disparity between the top 1 percent and the average American, has resulted in a resurgence of the ideas behind the New Deal, however. This has led a new generation of "progressive Democrats" to call for the establishment of a Green New Deal and other programs not unlike those championed by FDR roughly eight decades ago. It has also led President Joe Biden to repeatedly invoke the legacy of Roosevelt in his campaign and as president, where in his push for a massive federal investment in social and economic infrastructure has been likened to FDR's policies.[47] The unprecedented Russian attack on Ukraine, in February 2022, has also led Congress to invoke FDR's wartime legacy through the passage of the Ukraine Democracy Defense Lend-Lease Act of 2022, a law that mirrors FDR's decision to support Great Britain as the country stood alone against the Nazis in the spring of 1941.[48]

There are other aspects of FDR's legacy that have shifted with the changing times. The decision of the FDR Memorial Commission to acquiesce in the disabled community's demand to include the now famous statue of FDR in his wheelchair at the FDR Memorial in Washington, DC, has altered the nation's collective memory of FDR—from a man of action, who had largely recovered from polio to our nation's only "wheelchair president."[49] FDR has thus become a champion of the disability rights movement in a way that he could not have imagined at the time of his passing.[50] The onset of the COVID-19 pandemic reminds us of FDR's association with the March of Dimes and the development of the polio vaccine that was released ten years to the day after he died.

The very existence of the beautiful memorial along the tidal basin—which was initiated by Congress in 1955 and was signed into law by President Reagan in 1982—is also something that FDR might not have anticipated, as the only memorial he envisaged for himself involved a simple block of stone roughly the size of his presidential desk that he wanted placed in "the little green triangle" in front of the National Archives Building.[51]

That FDR chose this site for this monument raises another largely unrecognized aspect of his legacy: his love of history and ardent determination to preserve and protect the records of the past. It was this zeal that led FDR to create the nation's first presidential library—a concept that he initiated as a means to house his own massive collection of books, prints, historic manuscripts, personal and official papers, as well as the papers of those who served in his administration.[52] The creation of the FDR Library and Museum served as the precedent for all the presidential libraries that followed and has played a critical role in preserving and protecting the records of every subsequent administration.[53]

This would have pleased the president. For as he remarked at the opening of the FDR Library on June 30, 1941, in words that echoed what Bishop Dun said at the close of the president's memorial service, and that might serve as a fitting epitaph to this remarkable leader:

> The dedication of a library is in itself, an act of faith.
>
> To bring together the records of the past, and to house them in buildings where they will be preserved for men living in the future, a nation must believe in three things.
>
> It must believe in the past
>
> It must believe in the future
>
> It must, above all, believe in the capacity of its people so to learn from the past that they can gain in judgment for the future.

And then, in reference to the terrible war that was raging in Europe, and would soon break out in the Pacific, he insisted that "this latest addition to the archives of America is dedicated at a moment when government of the people by themselves is everywhere attacked. It is, therefore, proof—if any proof is needed—that our confidence in the future of democracy has not diminished in this nation and will not diminish."[54]

As we struggle in our own time to overcome the fear and uncertainty that has led some Americans to question the very efficacy of democracy, even in the wake of the Russian assault on Ukraine, perhaps this is the most important lesson that FDR has imparted to us: his fundamental faith in democracy, and his confidence in the ability of the American people "so to learn from the past that they can gain in judgement for the future." FDR may well have been "crushed by the burdens of war" as he struggled on in the final months of his life, but he refused to give up on the idea that a suffering humanity could fashion a better world out of the ruins of depression and war.[55] It was this capacity never to give in to despair that helped inspire the generation that lived through those difficult years to find renewed determination to carry his vision forward even in the wake of his death. Perhaps the most fitting tribute we might offer the late president, therefore, is to take heed of the observation he made in the final hours of his life, when he wrote that "if civilization is to survive, we must cultivate the science of human relationships—the ability of all peoples, of all kinds, to live together and work together, in the same world at peace."[56]

Notes

1. Adolf A. Berle, *Navigating the Rapids,* ed. Beatrice Bishop Berle and Travis Beal Jacobs (New York: Harcourt Brace Jovanovich, 1973), 535

2. Frances Perkins, *The Roosevelt I Knew* (New York: Penguin, 1982), 372.

3. Lansing Warren, "Hatch and Ball See Danger in United Nations Disunity," *New York Times,* December 24, 1944, 1.

4. Rebecca Erbelding, *Rescue Board: The Untold Story of America's Efforts to Save the Jews of Europe* (New York: Doubleday, 2018), 231.

5. Franklin D. Roosevelt, Fourth Inaugural Address of the President, January 20, 1945, Master Speech File, box 85, FDR Presidential Library (hereafter FDRL), Hyde Park, NY.

6. Franklin D. Roosevelt, "Message to Congress re: State of the Union," January 6, 1945, Master Speech File, box 85, FDRL; Franklin D. Roosevelt, Message to Congress re: the Yalta Conference, March 1, 1945, Master Speech File, box 86, FDRL.

7. Margaret Fayerweather, Diary, March 25–28, 1945, Eleanor Roosevelt Papers, box 1559, FDRL.

8. Earle Looker, "Is Franklin Roosevelt Physically Fit to be President?" *Liberty Magazine,* July 25, 1931.

9. Vice Admiral Ross T. McIntire, *White House Physician* (New York: Putnam's Sons, 1948), 183–87; Clinical Notes on the Illness of the President, Dr. Howard G. Bruenn Papers, box 1, 1944–46, FDRL.

10. David B. Woolner, *The Last 100 Days: FDR at War and at Peace* (New York: Basic Books, 2017), 5.

11. Woolner, *The Last 100 Days,* 5.

12. Memorandum by Dr. Frank Lahey, July 10, 1944, Lahey Clinic, Burlington, MA, as cited in Steven Lomazow, MD, and Eric Fettmann, *FDR's Deadly Secret* (New York: Public Affairs, 2009), 119–21.

13. Memorandum by Dr. Frank Lahey; Woolner, *The Last 100 Days,* 6.

14. Margaret "Daisy" Suckley Diary, May 5, 1944, reel 2, FDRL; Woolner, *The Last 100 Days,* 6–7; "President's Health," *Chicago Daily Tribune,* October 17, 1944, 14; "A Vote for FDR May Be a Vote for Truman," *Chicago Daily Tribune,* October 28, 1944, 10.

15. This included Dr. Bruenn, who, from the moment FDR's cardiac disease was discovered, accompanied the president whenever he traveled.

16. Linda Lotridge Levin, *The Making of FDR: The Story of Stephen T. Early, America's First Modern Press Secretary* (Amherst, NY: Prometheus Books, 2008), 426–27.

17. Harry S. Truman, *Memoirs,* vol. 1: *Year of Decisions* (Garden City, NY: Doubleday, 1955), 5.

18. David McCullough, *Truman* (New York: Simon & Schuster, 1992), 346.

19. McCullough, *Truman*, 346; Truman, *Year of Decisions*, 9; "His Unfinished Business—and Ours," *New York Times*, April 22, 1945, SM3.

20. Woolner, *Last 100 Days*, 26.

21. FDR to James Roosevelt, December 26, 1937, Burial Instructions, PSF Subject File, Box 160, FDRL.

22. Eleanor Roosevelt, *The Autobiography of Eleanor Roosevelt* (New York: Da Capo, 1992), 276–77. Eleanor was in fact handed the envelope upon her return to the White House, on April 14, but refused to open it as it was addressed "To James Roosevelt—Burial Instructions."

23. Thomas Parrish, *Roosevelt and Marshall: Partners in Politics and War* (New York: William and Morrow, 1989) 506–507.

24. George C. Pogue, *George C. Marshall: Organizer of Victory, 1943–1945* (New York: Viking, 1973), 557–58.

25. Woolner, *The Last 100 Days*, 283.

26. Eleanor Roosevelt, *Autobiography*, 279.

27. "500,000 Line Capital Streets to Bid Roosevelt Farwell: Funeral," *Washington Post*, April 15, 1945, M1; Pogue, *Organizer of Victory*, 559.

28. "Rites at Capital: War Leader's Fearless Faith Called by Bishop Dun a Bequest to All," *New York Times*, April 15, 1945, 1.

29. "Millions in City in City Ignore Rain to Pay Honor to Roosevelt," *New York Times*, April 15, 1945, 1; "City's Silence Signals Grief for Roosevelt," *Los Angeles Times*, April 15, 1945; Bernard Absell, *When FDR Died* (New York: Holt, Rinehart, and Winston, 1961), 178–79.

30. David B. Woolner, "Epilogue: Reflections on Legacy and Leadership—the View from 2008," in *FDR's World: War, Peace, and Legacies*, ed. David B. Woolner, Warren F. Kimball, and David Reynolds (New York: Palgrave Macmillan, 2008), 226; "Nations Set Aside Days of Mourning," *New York Times*, April 15, 1945, 1; "Latin-Americans Mourn President," *New York Times*, April 14, 1945, 6; "As News of President Roosevelt's Death Travelled across the Seas," *New York Times*, April 14, 1945, 5.

31. "Rites at Capital," *New York Times*, April 15, 1945, 1.

32. Woolner, *Last 100 Days*, 289–290. FDR's sons John and Franklin Jr. were unable to attend. His son James rushed back to New York from the Philippines, but he arrived too late to attend his father's burial.

33. Churchill to King George VI, April 13, 1945, Winston S. Churchill Papers, CHAR 20/193B/185–86, Churchill Archives, Cambridge, UK.

34. "Churchill Eulogizes Roosevelt as Best US Friend to Britain," *New York Times*, April 18, 1945, 5.

35. "Mayor Asks Nation to Prove Faith by Finishing Roosevelt's Program," *New York Times*, April 16, 1945, 10

36. Anne O'Hare McCormick, "His Unfinished Business—and Ours," *New York Times*, April 22, 1945, SM3.

37. McCormick, "His Unfinished Business—and Ours."

38. David Reynolds and Vladimir Pechatnov, *The Kremlin Letters: Stalin's Wartime Correspondence with Churchill and Roosevelt* (New Haven: Yale University Press, 2018), 585.

39. Woolner, *The Last 100 Days*, 22.

40. Woolner, *The Last 100 Days,* 293; Benjamin Cohen, "Confidential Memo Concerning a Fourth Term," sent to FDR March 8, 1944, Benjamin C. Cohen Papers, box 12, LC.

41. Alan Brinkley and David B. Woolner, "Franklin Roosevelt and the Progressive Tradition," in *Progressivism in America: Past Present and Future,* ed. David B. Woolner and John M. Thompson (New York: Oxford University Press, 2016), 21.

42. Franklin D. Roosevelt, State of the Union Address, January 11, 1944, Master Speech File, box 77, FDRL.

43. David B. Woolner, "Churchill and the Birth of the Anglo-American Special Relationship," in *Winston Churchill: Politics, Strategy and Statecraft,* ed. Richard Toye (London: Bloomsbury Academic, 1017), 153.

44. Woolner, *The Last 100 Days,* 298–99.

45. Ronald Edsforth, *The New Deal: America's Response to the Great Depression* (Malden, MA: Blackwell, 2000), 2.

46. Edsforth, *The New Deal,* 4.

47. David B. Woolner, "Biden Wants to Go Big on Infrastructure. History Says That's the Right Call," *Washington Post,* April 7, 2021.

48. David B. Woolner, "What FDR Would Have Said about the Unfolding War in Ukraine," *Smerconish.com,* March 10, 2022.

49. For more on the question of "collective memory," see David Reynolds, "FDR's Foreign Policy and the Construction of American History, 1945–1955," in *FDR's World,* 5.

50. "Disabled Protest Memorial to FDR," *Los Angeles Times,* February 28, 1997.

51. Notes of Conversation with Franklin D. Roosevelt, September 27, 1941, Roosevelt Memorial Commission, Felix Frankfurter Papers, LC.

52. Robert "Bob" Clark, "FDR: Archivist: The Shaping of the National Archives," *Prologue Magazine* 38, no. 4 (Winter 2006).

53. Clark, "FDR: Archivist."

54. Franklin D. Roosevelt, Remarks at the Dedication of the Franklin D. Roosevelt Library, June 30, 1941, Master Speech File, box 61, FDRL.

55. Arthur Krock, "End Comes Suddenly at Warm Springs," *New York Times,* April 13, 1945, 1.

56. Franklin D. Roosevelt, Draft of Jefferson Day Dinner Speech, (not delivered) April 11, 1945, Master Speech File, box 86, FDRL.

"He Gave His Life for Us"

THE CIVIL RIGHTS MARTYRDOM OF JOHN F. KENNEDY

Sharron Wilkins Conrad

O N NOVEMBER 22, 1963, news of President John F. Kennedy's assassination in Dallas, Texas, circulated with extraordinary speed. Within moments of its announcement, word spread around the globe that the forty-six-year-old leader died from an assassin's bullet at the tail end of an otherwise routine motorcade, part of a five-city campaign swing through the Lone Star State. The world responded with shock and grief, and Americans turned to their television sets to confirm the initial reports. The pace of communication meant that most Americans learned the essential details quickly: at 12:30 p.m. local time, while riding in an open limousine, Kennedy suffered a fatal shot to the back of the head and crumpled onto the lap of First Lady Jacqueline Kennedy, seated next to him. Secret Service agents whisked him to Dallas's Parkland Hospital, where doctors failed to revive him. Officials pronounced the president dead at 1:00 p.m.

Among those most shattered by Kennedy's death were his African American supporters. Black voter affection had deepened for the thirty-fifth president over the course of that year, and their grief reflected the magnitude of what they viewed as a personal blow. Even so, the intensity of their sorrow, the unconventional explanations to which they attributed his death, and the community traditions that sprang up to acknowledge Kennedy's significance in Black households remains underscrutinized.[1] Like other groups, African American mourners processed the assassination through the filter of their experience, but Black observers linked Kennedy's demise to the fate of the Civil Rights Movement, believing that his death foretold the collapse of their social justice hopes.

Mrs. Andrew Burril of Mattoon, Illinois, expressed this sentiment well. Composing a condolence letter on the assassination's one-year anniversary, Burril offered Jacqueline Kennedy a theory on "why [her late husband] . . . is sleeping in Arlington National Cemetery to day." In her view, Kennedy's fate was linked to his call for a Civil Rights Act. "The Enemys [sic] of my people slew him, because he was fighting and working that we might have our just rights and freedom too [sic] live and dwell like all the rest." Acknowledging the president's supreme sacrifice, Burril professed to his widow, "he gave his life for us."[2] The belief that President Kennedy martyred himself for civil rights—and fell victim, not to the leftist arrested for the crime, Lee Harvey Oswald, but to right-wing extremists—took hold in Black communities.[3]

This view circulated and proliferated quietly. African Americans honored Kennedy in their most sacred space: the family living room. There, away from a society that too often judged and found them wanting, Black families celebrated President Kennedy's contributions by placing his portrait alongside those of other leaders admired for their commitment to African American social justice, a tradition tied to how Abraham Lincoln's likeness appeared in Black residences following his assassination in 1865. Connecting Kennedy's appearance in private memorials to the memorialization of Lincoln illuminates the depth of feeling African Americans felt for John Kennedy, and highlights how Black citizens established their own understanding of what defined a civil rights presidency, a classification often at odds with scholarly interpretation.

African Americans React to the News

Pollsters at the time of John Kennedy's assassination understood the importance of documenting public reactions to the news, and a few recognized the value of including African American responses in their findings. A summary of studies examining media coverage of the assassination, how Americans learned about the event, and the ways adults and children behaved after hearing of the tragedy showed that African Americans reacted significantly more intensely than whites.[4] After examining twenty-five reports from sociologists, psychologists, social psychologists, political scientists, and communications specialists, researchers concluded that "Negroes showed more sorrow, a greater sense of personal loss, and more physical symptoms." Furthermore, their concerns persisted far longer than those of whites. Black interviewees "continued to feel unsafe, to perceive considerable unrest, to see prejudice and hatred around them, and to be more concerned about lack of leadership" long after white respondents. The authors noted that "for some time after the assassination Negroes were the only segment of the population that continued to be afraid."[5] The studies made clear that Black citizens felt uniquely traumatized by President Kennedy's violent death.

A poll conducted by the University of Chicago's National Opinion Research Center (NORC) the week following the assassination documented the scope of that trauma for Black mourners. Of the total 1,384 people asked to determine if they were "more upset than most people" following President Kennedy's death, 30 percent believed that to be the case. However, pollsters found that an appreciably higher 49 percent of the study's 165 African American respondents felt their dismay exceeded that of others.[6] Indeed, Black participants in the weeks-long study maintained that their symptoms of grief—insomnia, fatigue, nervousness—lasted longer than white participants' symptoms. Researchers calculated that while 75 percent of those asked indicated that their symptoms disappeared in the days immediately following the funeral, two-thirds of African Americans admitted they still suffered one or more symptoms days after the service.[7] These answers, although self-reported and wholly unscientific as a measure of real physiological distress, registered the intensity of the Black community's response to the tragedy.

These findings corresponded to the written expressions of heartbreak that poured into the White House mailroom from Black mourners all over the country. In less than two months following the assassination, some 800,000 pieces of condolence mail found their way to the newly widowed Jacqueline Kennedy.[8] The official collection ballooned to 1,250,000 pieces of correspondence by 1965.[9] The letters, cards, and other expressions of grief from African Americans offered an unusual degree of poignancy and urgency.

Writing exactly one week after the murder, Ethel C. Williams of Detroit, Michigan, explained in her letter to Mrs. Kennedy that the president "made

me proud of being colored, by the lov'ing enterest [*sic*] he took in my people."[10] Another Ethel, this one Ethel M. Robinson of Norristown, Pennsylvania, offered a similar rationale for her admiration of the thirty-fifth
president. She divulged in a letter dated December 7, 1963, "I am a negro
mother and grandmother, poor in the material things of life, but rich from
the thought that to-day and to-morrow, the American negro can breathe a
little freer and hold his head a little higher, because of a great young man of
courage."[11] A similar message arrived from Mr. and Mrs. Speed Ross Jr. of
Los Angeles in January 1964. The Ross family wanted "The First Lady of the
World," to understand that "President Kennedy did many things for many
people, but we the Negroes will remember that it was Mr. Kennedy who took
giant steps against great odds to help depressed mankind everywhere."[12] The
correspondents' pride in the president's accomplishments and deep reverence for his sacrifice punctuated every line.

The NORC study offered quantitative evidence to support these anecdotes.
Pollsters found that, of the small percentage of respondents who believed ideology was a motivation of the president's assassin, one-quarter maintained
that the shooter held leftist views and was probably a communist supporter
of Cuba's Fidel Castro. However, when researchers extracted the responses of
African Americans from this grouping, they found Black interviewees much
more likely to say a segregationist or white supremacist killed President Kennedy. Researchers highlighted the exception, noting, "of the one-third of all
Negroes who suspected an ideological motive for the assassination, 2 out of
3 blamed a segregationist; whites, whether North or South, pro-Kennedy or
anti-, were much more likely to attribute the deed to a Communist or Castro
supporter."[13] Thus, even in the week immediately after the death and funeral,
African Americans harbored the suspicion that hatred of the president's
social justice commitment provoked his assassination. That association likely
derived, in part, from the June assassination of NAACP organizer Medgar
Evers outside of his Jackson, Mississippi, home. Evers's murder occurred the
day after the dramatic integration of the University of Alabama, and hours
after President Kennedy's televised call for civil rights legislation.

Black mourners also related Kennedy's sacrifice to the martyrdom of
Jesus Christ. Alfred Duckett, a contributor to the *Chicago Defender* newspaper, anointed Kennedy as "John the Just" in a column published two

weeks after the assassination. In Duckett's view, segregationist politicians, ministers, housewives, and shopkeepers "crucified" Kennedy because he "hailed mankind as the children of God and therefore as brothers." Duckett promised that Kennedy, like Jesus, would "arise in resurrection" only when America acknowledged its sins and lived in accordance with Jesus'—and by extension, Kennedy's—teachings on tolerance and acceptance.[14]

Henry J. Langdon, a Black expatriate living in Montreal, Quebec, made a similar connection in a letter published by the *Pittsburgh Courier* the same week Duckett's column appeared. Langdon declared that "the betrayal of this truly great American leader ranks highly in the minds of every Negro as we compare the fate of this outstanding man to that of the 'Prince of Peace,' Jesus Christ." Furthermore, Langdon prophesized that Kennedy's legacy would live on even though he had been "sacrificed on the altar of inhuman brutality."[15] These links between Kennedy's murder and the crucifixion of Christ reflected the Black community's view that the president's death by segregationists ennobled him. For many, associations with Jesus Christ elevated Kennedy—like Lincoln before him, and Martin Luther King Jr. and Robert Kennedy later—to the status of "secular saint," a transformation made possible by his selfless actions in life and his tragic death.[16]

High school student Edward Harris certainly understood the Kennedys' significance to his community in religious terms. Although still young in the early 1960s, he recalled that "Black people throughout the country were really inspired by the Kennedys, because we as a people have always looked upon the Kennedys as saviors, so to speak."[17] Others concurred with his memory. Dallas activist Betty Culbreath admitted, "I sort of thought this man was the Messiah" due to how he carried himself in office.[18] Opal Mitchell Lee, originally of Malone, Texas, found Kennedy's White House tenure liberating. She explained how to her "President Kennedy represented a way out, he was hope for the future. He gave me reason to believe that we were finally going to be free. In a sense he was my savior, and a savior to my people."[19]

While several episodes during Kennedy's short presidency sparked the sense of possibility that made some consider him a liberator, his televised remarks on June 11, 1963, generated the most sustained outpouring. The same day the Justice Department orchestrated the successful integration of the University of Alabama by exerting federal authority to override Governor George Wallace's infamous "Stand in the Schoolhouse Door" attempt to prevent James Hood and Vivian Malone from enrolling, President Kennedy spoke directly to the nation on civil rights. In the address, he articulated the moral case for African Americans' right to full equality. The president looked directly into cameras and reasoned with the American people: "We are confronted primarily with a moral issue. It is as old as the scriptures and is as clear as the American Constitution. The heart of the question is whether all Americans are to be afforded equal rights and equal opportunities, whether we are going to treat our fellow Americans as we want to be treated . . . the time has come for this Nation to fulfill its promise."[20] For African American viewers, the moment—and the explicit affirmation of their struggle—engendered lifelong loyalty.

Given the city's association with the president's major civil rights address and the hope inspired by that summer's March on Washington, it is unsurprising so many Black mourners found their way to the nation's capital for the president's extended funeral services. *Jet* magazine correspondent Larry Still estimated that one-third of the 300,000 people who stood in line to pay respects as Kennedy's casket reposed in the Capitol Rotunda were Black.[21] In the crowd at the Capitol was army sergeant James L. Felder, an African American member of the Honor Guard Ceremonial Unit in Washington, DC. Felder served as ranking sergeant of the casket bearers' platoon, the team of eight servicemen from every military branch who acted as pallbearers for President Kennedy's casket that weekend.[22] The sergeant and his fellow bearers accompanied Kennedy's remains from the time the casket arrived from Texas until the burial at Arlington National Cemetery. "For four days, that body was never out of our sight. . . . I got maybe six hours of sleep from Friday until Monday. . . . I witnessed the autopsy, I witnessed the embalming, I witnessed the changing of the casket."[23] Reporting to Feldman was 3rd Class Seaman Hubert Clark of the US Navy, another Black casket bearer.[24] One of the first inquiries a newly inaugurated President Kennedy made in 1961 was to ask why the honor guard at his inaugural parade remained segregated.[25] Three years later, an integrated Ceremonial Unit led by a Black sergeant and aided by a Black seaman ensured the commander-in-chief a dignified funeral service.

Honoring Kennedy's Memory

The most prominent sign of Kennedy's elevation among Black mourners appeared in Black households. Almost immediately, African American families installed images of the martyred president in their homes alongside portraits of Jesus Christ and Martin Luther King Jr. in a triangular formation I refer to as "the Trinity."[26] Arranging Kennedy's likeness beside two of the most revered figures in the Black community showcased his stature to family members, guests, and the next generation. Kennedy completed the religious triad, with Jesus at the top, Dr. King below and to the right, and the president on the left. The Trinity tradition likely started organically and spread quickly through a variety of means.

Friends Trudie Kibbe and Oneida Graves grew up in South Dallas and attended James Madison High School together in 1963, but they recalled alternate origins for their families' Trinity wall images. Kibbe's family purchased commemorative portraits of its heroes at the H. L. Green variety store, and in Black-owned shops along the city's Second Avenue.[27] Graves's parents and grandparents also obtained images at small variety stores in the community, but she remembered, "lots of people back in the day bought pictures from a peddler." In her recollection, "the Broom Man"—a blind peddler who visited the neighborhood regularly—walked the streets and drummed up business for his housewares by yelling "Broom Man!" repeatedly.[28] Peddlers marketed and sold the ubiquitous mementos that Black homemakers used to decorate their homes, and they probably helped spread the popularity of Trinity displays.

In addition to peddlers, Black insurance and funeral homes distributed calendars that included portraits that could be repurposed for Trinity walls. Fort Worth, Texas, native Bob Ray Sanders explained that his family installed "two or three" photos of President Kennedy in their home. "Certainly one . . . was on a calendar or something like that. Kennedy quickly became a hero in our family."[29] A photo of a woman seated in her Halifax, North Carolina, bedroom features multiple calendars on the wall, one of which exhibits an image of Jesus Christ. A cutout of President Kennedy hangs nearby. The image of Christ with his arms outstretched was produced by the Metropolitan Funeral Home, as indicated in large print just above the calendar. Kennedy's portrait

FIGURE 8. A woman in Halifax, North Carolina, sits below images of Jesus Christ and President Kennedy displayed in her bedroom in 1971. (https://alex -harris.com)

is displayed above a framed picture of a bouquet of flowers. The floral tribute demonstrates that the woman continued to tend to the fallen leader eight years after his death. In some cases, the Trinity tradition persisted well into the 1980s, and in the case of one family, until the early 1990s.[30]

Another source for Trinity imagery came from the pages of the Black press. Since the nineteenth century, African American publications offered readers a vehicle for documenting inequality, celebrating successes, and informing subscribers about issues of concern. In the months following the assassination of President Kennedy, Black newspapers and magazines promoted the importance of showing fealty to the "martyred president" by installing his portrait in one's home. The *Pittsburgh Courier* and the *Chicago Defender*—two of the most prominent and widest circulated newspapers of the era—and *Jet* and

Ebony magazines found ways to monetize reader interest in memorializing Kennedy by selling portraits, busts, keychains, record albums, photo books, and other items. An early advertisement appeared just seven weeks after the president's funeral. The *Pittsburgh Courier* advertised a Kennedy bust priced at four dollars, promising an "unbreakable—antique bronzed finish—felted base" to honor "one of the greatest men of our time."[31] Weeks later, the same newspaper marketed commemorative oil-on-canvas portraits for one dollar, which would become "a treasure you will cherish forever."[32] An ad placed by the Illinois Federal Savings and Loan Association, a Black-owned bank in operation since the 1930s, encouraged *Chicago Defender* readers to open a new account in exchange for a "free, free, free John F. Kennedy coin bank."[33]

The ads described above were placed by private companies, but soon African American publishers recognized how lucrative the Kennedy commemoration business could be; when this became evident, Black publications started promoting their own memorabilia to Black readers. The *Pittsburgh Courier's* July 1964 advertisements relied heavily on the community's deep desire to celebrate Kennedy as a champion of civil rights. The newspaper adopted an emotional appeal in its sale of memorial portraits of the president, inquiring, "Have you a picture of our martyred President in your home? The story of his fight for freedom for all men everywhere will inspire your children and your grandchildren. This is a cherished keepsake, an official Presidential portrait, reproduced in full color splendor. . . . It deserves the finest frame."[34] Insinuating that only an official portrait displayed sufficient admiration and acknowledgment of President Kennedy's sacrifice, the promotional ad cultivated guilt to guarantee the sale.

Magazines, as well as newspapers, understood the financial rewards behind celebrating Kennedy's civil rights legacy. Johnson Publishing Company developed a line of memorial merchandise, which it sold in its magazines, *Jet* and *Ebony*. The magazines, in addition, marketed recordings and coffee table books that highlighted the late president's words and image. The *John F. Kennedy and the Negro* record album reproduced seven of Kennedy's most celebrated civil rights speeches, offering it in memory of "a leader in the Lincoln and Roosevelt tradition," mourned by African Americans "not only as the death of a friend but [as] the desecration of a dream." Furthermore, the producers offered the LP as "a living memorial to a great president, and as a testament to the cause for which he gave his life."[35] The emphasis on the album as a living memorial presented listeners with a means of keeping Kennedy's memory alive through his voice as well as his words.

Determined not to miss an opportunity to capitalize on wide interest in the imagery of Kennedy's Camelot mythology, the publishers likewise developed a visual dedication to accompany its audio offering. The 160-page, glossy photo book, *The Kennedy Years and the Negro: A Photographic Record*, featured an introduction by Kennedy's associate press secretary, Andrew Hatcher, the first African American to serve in the White House Press Office. Hatcher's essay noted that Kennedy deployed every tool to ensure equality, declaring that African Americans revered him because he was "accessible to Black citizens and their ideas."[36] Both the book and album were promoted in "Ebony Bookshop" ads that showcased "books by, about, and related to the Negro" for years after President Kennedy's death.[37]

There were many different ways of honoring Kennedy. Even as records and photo books showed admiration, Trinity displays could be adjusted for personal preference. The tradition took on many forms and might aptly be referred to as a "Trinities" ritual. In addition to the typical orientation with Jesus at the top of the triangle, Dr. King on the right, and Kennedy on the left, others could be added to the triumvirate. Edward Harris, an activist who traveled the South as part of his work with the Student Nonviolent Coordinating Committee (SNCC), recalled seeing President Kennedy's image in Black homes everywhere he went. According to his recollection, though, instead of Jesus Christ positioned alongside the president and King, the president's brother Robert Kennedy held the third position. In fact, Harris observed, "most African American households back then and even . . . up through the '70s . . . had pictures of Dr. King and Robert and John Fitzgerald Kennedy."[38]

Cleveland, Mississippi, activist Mary Dora Jones would have concurred with Harris on both timing and substance. In the early 1970s she welcomed an oral history interviewer into her "spotlessly clean" home, and the observant historian noted that "on the living room wall is a tapestry of the Last Supper. Grouped around the tapestry are photographs of John F. Kennedy, Martin Luther King, Jr., and Robert Kennedy." Jones must have been asked about the display because Jones revealed that "Robert Kennedy's photograph is in the center and higher than the others, because once, on a tour of the Delta, he visited the home of her friend [fellow activist] Amzie Moore."[39] Dallas County, Texas, commissioner John Wiley Price agreed that Robert Kennedy often found his place in the typical tableau, and expanded the number in the grouping further still. Price explained, "There were three pictures . . . that all Black homes had, maybe four. They always had a picture of Jesus, and they always said that the three disciples were President Kennedy, his brother Robert, and Martin Luther King. . . . It didn't matter what their economic social status was. Those four pictorials were going to be in Black homes: Jesus . . . Robert and John, and Martin."[40] Thus, while Jesus and King featured most prominently in Trinity imagery, other worthy figures recognized for their dedication to African American rights were elevated into the pantheon.

Trinity memorials included various personnel and served multiple purposes. As indicated by the language found in advertisements promoting the purchase of Kennedy's image, the displays functioned as daily reminders to family and guests of the devotion the martyred president deserved. It helped that many of these displays were arranged in Black families' living rooms. Poet Elizabeth Alexander characterizes the Black living room as the space where—both literally and metaphorically—authentic Black life happens beyond the gaze of the white world that too often stereotypes it. The Black interior represents the physical place where "complex Black selves, real and enactable Black power, rampant and unfetishized Black beauty" emerges.[41] The African American living room, then, became a sacred space where Black families could push back against society's pressures, and do so through pictorial honor walls.

Fort Worth, Texas, native Eddie Griffin affirmed that the tumultuous times demanded the strength, fortitude, and safety afforded within the Black home. Connecting this to the complex messaging of the Trinity wall, Griffin maintained that the tableaux represented more than a simple homage. For Griffin, the Trinity signaled veiled defiance to segregation and the Jim Crow status quo. He suggested how, after the assassination, "you did not want to get too close to the memory of John F. Kennedy, 'cause even after he was assassinated, there were still people who were hostile to the Kennedy family, Martin Luther King, civil rights. . . . And it was dangerous."[42] Given the real or perceived threat, hanging President Kennedy's image in one's home communicated tenacity and rebellion, as well as hope.

If, as Griffin indicated, displaying Kennedy's portrait could be deemed a challenge to the segregated white world, its power was embraced by businesses and institutions that served the Black community. Black-owned funeral homes from Oklahoma to Washington, DC, invoked images of the Kennedys as well as Martin Luther King's on printed, hand-held fans distributed in churches and funeral homes. The funeral fans served the dual purpose of cooling mourners or worshippers during the summer months and acknowledging the efforts of three men viewed as "Freedom Fighters" who "Died for Freedom." The objects also reminded parishioners that the president and his brother merited recognition alongside King.[43] Similarly, when Chicago's nonprofit American Negro Public Opinion Service designed a felt banner to promote efforts to reduce crime in the Black community by collecting and sharing data, it showcased King's image on one side with the message, "We Shall Overcome." On the reverse, the institution's founder, Jesse Glass—an African American who retired from the Chicago Police Department—included President Kennedy's portrait under the declaration, "We Mourn Our Loss."[44]

African Americans honored the president's memory in other unique ways, including using service and activism as signs of their devotion. Writing in the *Chicago Defender*'s "Younger Set" section the week after the assassination, high school student Judith Smith challenged others of her generation to live up to the president's high ideals. She argued that, because "this man whose firm stance on civil rights was . . . the main factor in his death," therefore "it is also up to us, the young people, especially Negroes to go to school, and to strive to match the dreams he had for us. Most important, let it not be said that our President died in vain."[45] For contributors to the issue's youth section, the best way to celebrate Kennedy's sacrifice was to live according to his example.

Texas activist Clarence Broadnax also turned to Kennedy's inaugural message of service for inspiration. Twenty-three years old in June 1964, Broadnax traveled to Dallas to meet a US Air Force recruiter about enlistment. When he stepped into a local Piccadilly Cafeteria for a meal, the manager refused him service because Broadnax was Black. After declining when

FIGURE 9. Clarence Broadnax honors John Kennedy's sacrifice by linking his activism to Kennedy's legacy. (Dallas County Sheriff's Department Collection. Courtesy of the Sixth Floor Museum at Dealey Plaza, Dallas, TX)

asked to leave, he was arrested. What started as an impromptu decision to take a stand on segregated facilities turned into a month-long demonstration against the cafeteria when members of the National Association for the Advancement of Colored People (NAACP), SNCC, and other civil rights organizations joined the effort. A Dallas County Sheriff's Department surveillance photograph of the protest showed Broadnax outside the eatery, confronting the restaurant's manager.

Broadnax wears a fedora, suit jacket, tie, and sunglasses as he explains his position. His right hand is pressed against his chest as the two men debate. In his other hand, Broadnax holds a hand-painted sign he made to illustrate the inspiration for his actions. The sign includes an official portrait of President Kennedy on one side and the words, "Did J.F.K. Die in Vain" on the other. Broadnax holds the sign so that the manager can read and contemplate its message. To Broadnax, Kennedy's death resulted from his fight for racial equality; therefore, it was up to him and all those alive after the assassination to fulfill the president's legacy through action. He determined, "the best thing to do is not let his name die in vain. You know, his old saying is 'Ask not what your country can do for you. Ask what you can do for your country,' and . . . so I decided, well, his name must live on. And from then on, I would have my signs . . . I would go home, and just think of the words I could put on the sign to keep his name alive. So, that's what I did."[46] Joining Broadnax's protest was a recent Southern Methodist University Divinity School graduate, the Reverend Earl Allen, who viewed Broadnax's sign as an indictment of Dallas's lack of remorse following the president's death. Allen believed true repentance required the city to abolish Jim Crow facilities.[47] The demonstrations concluded when the Piccadilly's manager complied with the Civil Rights Act of 1964, signed on July 2, 1964. For Kennedy supporters involved in the protest, the result offered a fitting tribute to the president who had fought for the legislation and been gunned down a few blocks away as retribution.

In addition to using Kennedy's memory as a call to service, some African American families taught their children about the late president's legacy. Magdalene Holsey, writing to Jacqueline Kennedy on March 24, 1964, explained that she and her husband recently welcomed a baby girl into the world. Holsey expressed minor disappointment because she "was hoping to have a boy to name after your dear husband . . . [whom] we all loved. . . . [H]e had done so much for our race and all the people I wanted to let his name go from generation to generation in my family." She continued by revealing that, because the expected child was a girl instead of the boy they planned for, the couple named their daughter Jacqueline Fitzgerald. Holsey included a photograph of herself holding baby Jacqueline. Behind the sofa on which they sit, a photograph of President Kennedy surrounded by his fellow presidents hangs proudly.[48] Mr. and Mrs. Speed Ross of California did not name their daughter after the president, but they enclosed her photograph inside a condolence letter mailed to the first lady. The picture shows the toddler standing next to a framed portrait of President Kennedy in the family living room, precariously posed between what appears to be a rocking horse and a television set. Yolanda Ross suggested that, although the child could not talk yet she would probably declare that the man in the framed picture "is one who has made this a better world for her to live in."[49] Both Holsey and Ross promised to convey to their daughters President Kennedy's significance to their community and to the girls' future aspirations.

Despite the many examples of how indebted African Americans felt to their martyr-president, not everyone agreed with that portrayal of him. Several Black writers, leaders, and activists expressed concern about the unquestioning embrace of Kennedy as a civil rights icon. When the Nation of Islam's provocative spokesman, Malcolm X, ignored his leader Elijah Muhammad's request that ministers remain silent about President Kennedy's death, it ignited a firestorm. The trouble started when Malcolm X responded to a reporter's request for comment on the assassination. He answered, stating that he believed Kennedy's death was a case of "chickens coming home to roost," an activity that never made him sad, but in fact always made him glad. The disobedience culminated in his immediate censure, a ninety-day silencing, and his eventual break with the Nation, but Malcolm X never retracted the statement. "I said . . . that the hate in white men had not stopped with the killing of defenseless Black people, but that hate, allowed to spread unchecked, finally had struck down this country's Chief of State. I said it was the same thing as had happened with Medgar Evers."[50] For Malcolm X, the president presided over a nation that allowed hate and violence to fester, and therefore, merited some blame for the consequences.

As someone who sparred with Malcolm X about the movement's strategies, the Congress of Racial Equality's (CORE) director James Farmer seemed unlikely to back the minister's concern about the community's disproportionate response to Kennedy's death. Even so, Farmer freely admitted his frustration about the flood of adoration that African Americans directed at the late president. CORE had tangled with the Kennedy administration from the very beginning, specifically over the organization's 1961 Freedom Rides campaign challenging segregated interstate travel. Speaking to writer Robert Penn Warren in 1964 about Kennedy's legacy, Farmer acknowledged that although the president eventually supported civil rights, the display of over-the-top reverence following his death was excessive. He confessed that he had grown "nauseated by the current deification . . . because it is not accurate. The president did intellectualize the issue, but it was a cold intellectual issue and political issue with him."[51] To Farmer, Kennedy's deification elided the fact that his attention to civil rights happened only because activists made it happen. Farmer's concerns echoed those raised by one of King's key advisors in the Southern Christian Leadership Conference (SCLC), Andrew Young. Young expressed ambivalence about the Kennedys' mystique and the Black community's unquestioning loyalty to them. He confessed, "I was always both attracted to the Kennedys and afraid of them" because he doubted that affection was returned with equal measure and good faith.[52]

The Trinity's Antecedents

The debate surrounding whether the assassinated president merited the outpouring of grief that followed his death echoed analysis of Abraham Lincoln's evolving views on Black social and political rights prior to his death. African Americans immediately drew parallels between Kennedy's death and Lincoln's. *Ebony* magazine's Washington, DC, bureau chief, Simeon Booker, made that link in an article that ran along with an eight-page pictorial essay of President Kennedy's funeral. In "How JFK Surpassed Abraham Lincoln," Booker suggested that "Kennedy died, as had President Abraham Lincoln, a martyr to the cause of freedom." He continued, "President Kennedy did more than any other chief executive to advance the Negro—and simultaneously, America's—cause."[53] In Booker's estimation, Kennedy went even further than the Great Emancipator because he promoted social, as well as political equality for Blacks.

The connection Booker drew between the two presidents resonated with African American labor leader A. Philip Randolph. Randolph explained in a eulogy for Kennedy that "the call of history in this hour of trial by fire is for Negroes in particular and America in general to march forward toward the goal of human dignity and social and racial justice, to honor this man whose place in history will be next to Abraham Lincoln—the greatest president this country has ever known."[54] For Randolph, Kennedy and Lincoln were inexorably linked by how they lived their lives and by the way they died.

The tradition of honoring a president by hanging his portrait in African American homes also bonded these leaders. The first documented president invited into a Black living room was Abraham Lincoln. Formerly enslaved Blacks showed their affection by displaying his portrait, evident in interviews conducted by the federal government's Works Progress Administration (WPA) in the 1930s (later renamed the Work Projects Administration). Seventy years after his death, Black octogenarians in Georgia, North Carolina, Ohio, and Oklahoma shared their feelings about Lincoln. Going beyond past remembrances of the assassinated leader, they described their lingering affections and identified visual evidence of Lincoln's presence in their daily lives. Freedmen and women pointed enthusiastically to Lincoln's picture exhibited in places of honor in their homes. Eighty-year-old Matilda Poe of McAlester, Oklahoma, boasted to her WPA interviewer that "Abe Lincoln was a good man, everybody liked him. See, I got his picture."[55] Residing an hour north of her in Muskogee, Oklahoma, William W. Watson echoed Ms. Poe's pride when describing Lincoln: "I was treated mean in slave times, glad to the Lord I'm free and serving the Lord and Abe Lincoln's spirit, that's how much I love that man. I got his picture here too."[56] And while he was not mentioned specifically by Ellen Campbell, her interviewers remarked on Lincoln's presence in Campbell's tiny Augusta, Georgia, cabin: "When she took us into the crowded, but clean room, she showed us proudly the portrait of [her] . . . grandson, now dead. All the walls were thickly covered with framed pictures of different members of her family, most of whom are now dead. In their midst was a large picture of Abraham Lincoln."[57] Lincoln earned a place alongside Campbell's cherished family members, just as John Kennedy did in the 1960s. The abiding admiration for Abraham Lincoln mirrored the reverence with which many African Americans responded to John Kennedy's death a century later.

Conclusion

Kennedy's appeal among African Americans has maintained a staying power, even as time and deeper scrutiny of his civil rights record tempers its intensity. A 1966 Harris Poll asked African American respondents to indicate which of the last five presidents—from Eisenhower to Johnson—did the most for Black civil rights. Sixty-nine percent chose Kennedy, compared to the 15 percent who selected Johnson, despite his recent signing of the Civil Rights Act and Voting Rights Act into law.[58] More than fifty years later, a 2020 study conducted by UMass Amherst asked Black voters to select the president who had done the most for African Americans in US history. Lyndon Johnson and Dwight Eisenhower came in second and third, respectively, with Abraham Lincoln ranking first overall.[59] Kennedy had been omitted as a choice, signaling the skeptical way scholars, journalists, and other critics have come to assess his civil rights legacy.[60]

The half century between those public opinion polls saw African Americans coming to terms with the distance between Kennedy's elevation as a martyr and the limitations of his brief presidency. On the ten-year anniversary of the assassination, the *Washington Afro-American* ran an editorial acknowledging that although many criticized President Kennedy's inaction on civil rights, he "set a tone and helped create a progressive challenge during his thousand days in the White House, which endeared him to minority citizens." The Black newspaper concluded that, despite the fact that Lyndon Johnson accomplished many of the things Kennedy only talked about, "millions of Americans, especially black and poor people" remained deeply connected to the Kennedy family.[61]

Residents of Baltimore, Maryland, also asked to consider their memories of President Kennedy in 1973, rued his loss and still held racists responsible. Fifty-six-year-old trucker Ralph Jackson complained, "[The president] was out there trying to do something for our people. And then they killed him. Every time you get somebody, black or white, who's concerned about improving conditions for our people, they kill him."[62] On the thirtieth anniversary in 1993, *Baltimore Afro-American* editor James D. Williams examined the event with more historical objectivity. Williams cited Kennedy biographer Richard Reeves's recent book as he recounted instances where President Kennedy fell short on civil rights and acknowledged that Lyndon Johnson had more claim to the title "the great Civil Rights President."[63] Despite this, William continued, "the manner of his death, of course, had much to do with the making of the Kennedy legend, which . . . endured over these past three decades."[64]

Williams closed by remembering his own experience with the Trinity tradition. Some years before he had visited a Mississippi lumber company town and entered the humble home of a Black worker. With respectful amazement Williams noted that "the people, despite working every day, lived in poverty. Yet, in every Black home, in a place of honor, hung two pictures—Dr. Martin Luther King, Jr. and John F. Kennedy. . . . If that town still exists, those pictures are probably still there—a mark of the Kennedy mystic [sic] that exists these many years on the other side of his grave."[65] John Kennedy's memory was still likely to be tended in Black communities, he believed, thirty years after the president's death.

Even as some have criticized Kennedy's civil rights achievements or disparage them as more symbolic than substantive, positive sentiments toward him linger in the Black community. The symbolic actions enacted by the telegenic leader made lasting impressions on African Americans desperately in need of them at the time, and they communicated his value to generations born after long after his passing. Speaking to a group about Kennedy's 1960 presidential campaign, the African American newspaperman, Kennedy aide, and the unofficial "Godfather of Black Politics" Louis Martin reflected on the disconnect between those who believed Kennedy's contributions were largely symbolic and undeserving of the affection they generated among Black voters and the majority of African Americans. Martin suggested, "[T]here are times . . . when symbolism becomes substance and . . . [Kennedy] made a difference in black thinking about whether they are acceptable or not."[66] To Martin, and for many African American observers, Kennedy's symbolism *was* the substance, and that substance proved worthy of honor.

Notes

1. Important scholarship has touched upon the affinity many African Americans felt for President Kennedy, but none examines the mourning rituals in detail or connects them to the distinctive relationship Black citizens developed with select presidents before or since. See Carl M. Brauer, *John F. Kennedy and the Second Reconstruction* (New York: Columbia University Press, 1977), 312–20; Nick Bryant, *The Bystander: John F. Kennedy and the Struggle for Black Equality* (New York: Basic Books, 2006), 458–59; Peniel E. Joseph, "JFK's 1963 Race Speech Made Him an African-American Icon," *McCall.com*, November 21, 2013, https://www.mcall.com/opinion/mc-xpm-2013-11-21-mc-jfk-race -web-20131121-story.html.

2. Ellen Fitzpatrick, *Letters to Jackie: Condolences from a Grieving Nation* (New York: HarperCollins, 2010), 104.

3. Despite the fact that Oswald once publicly praised President Kennedy's leadership, he was a proud Marxist and a member of the communist advocacy organization, Fair Play for Cuba. He was far from being right-wing. There is no indication Oswald opposed the Civil Rights Movement or Kennedy's support for new legislation.

4. Bradley S. Greenberg and Edwin B. Parker, "Social Research on the Kennedy Assassination: A Summary," in *The Kennedy Assassination and the American Public: Social Communication in Crisis,* ed. Bradley S. Greenberg and Edwin B. Parker (Stanford, CA: Stanford University Press, 1965), 361–82.

5. Greenberg and Parker, "Social Research on the Kennedy Assassination," 377, 378.

6. Paul B. Sheatsley and Jacob J. Feldman, "The Assassination of President Kennedy: A Preliminary Report on Public Reactions and Behavior," *Public Opinion Quarterly* 28, no. 2 (Summer 1964): 194. I contextualize this polling data and its implications in "More Upset Than Most: Measuring and Understanding African American Responses to the Kennedy Assassination," forthcoming in the June 2023 edition of *American Quarterly.*

7. Sheatsley and Feldman, "Assassination of President Kennedy," 199–200.

8. Fitzpatrick, *Letters to Jackie,* xiii.

9. Jay Mulvaney and Paul De Angelis, *Dear Mrs. Kennedy: A World Shares Its Grief, Letters November 1963* (New York: St. Martin's Press, 2010), 8.

10. Fitzpatrick, *Letters to Jackie,* 100.

11. Fitzpatrick, *Letters to Jackie,* 268.

12. Mr. and Mrs. Speed Ross Jr., "Letter to Mrs. John F. Kennedy, First Lady of the World," accompanying photograph dated January 14, 1964, Papers of John F. Kennedy, Condolence Mail, box R001, John F. Kennedy Library and Museum, Boston.

13. Sheatsley and Feldman, "Assassination of President Kennedy," 195.

14. Alfred Duckett, "The Crucifixion of John the Just," *Chicago Defender,* December 7–19, 1963, 8. Interestingly, Duckett casts Jacqueline Kennedy in the role of the pious Mary for cradling "John the Just's" bleeding head in her arms.

15. Henry J. Langdon, quoted in "JFK Death Invokes Outpouring of Grief in Letters and Poems," *Pittsburgh Courier,* December 14, 1963, 9.

16. James Swanson, *Chasing King's Killer: The Hunt for Martin Luther King, Jr.'s Assassin* (New York: Scholastic, 2018), 228. Swanson uses the term "secular saint" to denote how John and Robert Kennedy, along with Martin Luther King, were honored as martyred saints in memorial triptychs that appeared in American homes after their deaths.

17. Edward Harris, interview by Stephen Fagin, February 6, 2006, transcript, Sixth Floor Museum at Dealey Plaza Oral History Project, Dallas, TX, 10.

18. Betty Culbreath, interview by Stephen Fagin, April 26, 2011, transcript, Sixth Floor Museum at Dealey Plaza Oral History Project, Dallas, TX, 8.

19. Opal Mitchell Lee, interview with Stephen Fagin, June 29, 2011, Sixth Floor Museum at Dealey Plaza Oral History Project, Dallas, TX. NB, Believe it or not, this is not the same Opal Lee from Texas who is known as the Grandmother of Juneteenth. There are two African-American activists born in Texas by that name. Opal Mitchell Lee, quoted here, passed away in 2017.

20. John F. Kennedy, "Televised Address to the Nation on Civil Rights—June 11, 1963," John F. Kennedy Presidential Library and Museum, https://www.jfklibrary.org/learn/about-jfk/historic-speeches/televised-address-to-the-nation-on-civil-rights/.

21. Larry Still, "May Have Learned History's Greatest Lesson Too Late," *Jet,* December 12, 1963, 8.

22. James L. Felder, *I Buried John F. Kennedy* (Columbia, SC: Lee Books, 1994), 33–34.

23. "I Buried John F. Kennedy—Interview with James Felder," *WACH-Fox News* 57, November 21, 2013, www.youtube.com/watch?v=6lRmfc71TIU.

24. Carol Ann Benanti, "As Camelot Died, a Staten Islander Bore Kennedy's Broken Body," *Staten Island Live*, www.silive.com/news/2013/11/as_camelot_died_a_staten_islan.html.

25. Roy Wilkins and Tom Mathews, *Standing Fast: The Autobiography of Roy Wilkins* (New York: Viking, 1982), 281. Felder, *I Buried John F. Kennedy*, 12.

26. Swanson calls the later ritual of hanging photos of the Kennedy brothers alongside one of King a "religious triptych" in his book, *Chasing King's Killer*, 228. However, the use of the phrase "the Trinity" to fully contextualize the tradition to include Jesus imagery is mine.

27. Trudie Kibbe Reed, telephone interview by the author, March 2, 2020.

28. Oneida Graves Bailey, telephone interview by the author, March 9, 2020.

29. Bob Ray Sanders, interview by Stephen Fagin, September 10, 2007, Sixth Floor Museum at Dealey Plaza Oral History Project, Dallas, TX.

30. A 1984 photograph taken by Louie Psihoyos shows a Chicago woman in her bedroom beneath the Trinity. It appears in *National Geographic* 166, no. 1 (July 1984): 37. Another woman recalled Kennedy's portrait hanging in her home in the 1990s. See Gwendolyn McMillan Lawe, interview by Stephen Fagin, June 6, 2016, Sixth Floor Museum at Dealey Plaza Oral History Project, Dallas, TX.

31. John Fitzgerald Kennedy bust advertisement, *Pittsburgh Courier*, January 11, 1964, 12.

32. John F. Kennedy memorial portrait advertisement, *Pittsburgh Courier*, February 1, 1964, 12.

33. Illinois Federal Savings and Loan Association coin bank advertisement, *Chicago Defender*, March 9, 1964, 8.

34. Advertisements, *Pittsburgh Courier*, July 11, 1964, 11.

35. *John F. Kennedy and the Negro* (recorded 1962–63), LP (Johnson, 1964).

36. Doris E. Saunders, ed., *The Kennedy Years and the Negro: A Photographic Record* (Chicago: Johnson, 1964), ix.

37. Ebony Bookshop advertisement, *Ebony: Special Issue*, August 1967, 69.

38. Harris, interview, 11.

39. Howell Raines, *My Soul Is Rested: The Story of the Civil Rights Movement in the Deep South* (New York: Penguin Books, 1983), 279.

40. John Wiley Price, interview by Stephen Fagin, July 3, 2013, transcript, Sixth Floor Museum at Dealey Plaza Oral History Project, Dallas, TX, 4.

41. Elizabeth Alexander, *Toward a Black Interior* (Saint Paul, MN: Graywolf, 2004), x.

42. Eddie Griffin, interview by Stephen Fagin, January 30, 2013, transcript, Sixth Floor Museum at Dealey Plaza Oral History Project, Dallas, TX, 6.

43. *Handheld Church Fan*, 1970, paper, wood, metal, 12 1/8 x 7 1/2 x 1/8 in., National Museum of American History, Washington, DC, americanhistory.si.edu/collections /search/object/nmah_214151/. *Advertising Fan for Funeral Home*, circa 1975, paper and wood. 12 x 7 in., Henry Ford, Dearborn, MI, https://www.thehenryford.org/collections -and-research/digital-collections/artifact/312567/.

44. The *American Negro Public Opinion Service Banner* is in the collection of the Sixth Floor Museum at Dealey Plaza, Dallas, TX.

45. Judith Smith, "The Nation Died as Kennedy Died," *Chicago Defender—The Younger Set Section*, November 30–December 6, 1963, n.p.

46. Clarence Broadnax, interview by Stephen Fagin, August 14, 2006, transcript, Sixth Floor Museum at Dealey Plaza Oral History Project, Dallas, TX, 9.

47. Earl E. Allen, interview by Stephen Fagin, June 23, 2007, transcript, Sixth Floor Museum at Dealey Plaza Oral History Project, Dallas, TX, 9.

48. Reprinted in Fitzpatrick, *Letters to Jackie*, 355, and back endpaper, middle.

49. Mr. and Mrs. Speed Ross Jr., "Letter to Mrs. John F. Kennedy, First Lady of the World."

50. Malcolm X, *The Autobiography of Malcolm X as Told to Alex Haley* (New York: Ballantine Books, 1997), 347.

51. Quoted in Robert Penn Warren, *Who Speaks for the Negro? With an Introduction by David W. Blight* (New Haven: Yale University Press, 2014), 202.

52. Young is actually referring to his fears that the Kennedys would take Black votes for granted, but his point about their inordinate sway over African Americans voters merits attention. Andrew Young, interview by Thomas H. Baker, June 18, 1970, transcript, LBJ Library Oral History Collection, Austin, TX, 14.

53. Simeon Booker, "How JFK Surpassed Abraham Lincoln," *Ebony*, February 1964, 25, 27.

54. Quoted in William Brink and Louis Harris, *Black and White: A Study of U.S. Racial Attitudes Today* (New York: Simon & Schuster, 1967), 94.

55. Matilda Poe, quoted in *The WPA Oklahoma Slave Narratives*, ed. T. Lindsay Baker and Julie P. Baker (Norman: University of Oklahoma Press, 1996), 326.

56. William W. Watson, quoted in *The WPA Oklahoma Slave Narratives*, ed. Baker and Baker, 457.

57. "Ellen Campbell," Library of Congress, Federal Writers' Project, vol. 4, Georgia, Pt. 4, Telfair-Young (with combined interviews of others), http://hdl.loc.gov/loc.mss/mesn .044/.

58. "Black and White: A Major Survey of U.S. Racial Attitudes Today," *Newsweek*, August 22, 1966, 38. A more comprehensive report of these findings was published the following year in Brink and Harris, *Black and White*.

59. Tatishe Nteta, "Abraham Lincoln Decisively Tops University of Massachusetts Amherst Poll as Most Impactful U.S. President for African Americans," *UMass.edu*, November 2, 2020, https://www.umass.edu/news/article/abraham-lincoln-decisively-tops -university/.

60. Among the harshest critiques is journalist Nick Bryant. In *The Bystander*, Bryant argues that Kennedy's cautious approach to civil rights led to the radicalization of the Civil Rights Movement and was directly responsible for the race riots of the late 1960s (465).

61. "Tragedy Remains Kennedys Comrade," *Washington Afro-American*, November 27, 1973, 16.

62. Charles Roberts, "Readers Remember President John F. Kennedy," *Baltimore Afro-American*, November 24, 1973, A5.

63. James D. Williams, "30th Anniversary of Assassination Recalls Kennedy's Civil Rights Record," *Baltimore Afro-American*, November 27, 1993, A6.

64. Williams, "30th Anniversary."

65. Williams, "30th Anniversary."

66. Louis Martin, "Organizing Civil Rights," in *The Kennedy Presidency: Seventeen Intimate Portraits of John F. Kennedy*, ed. Kenneth W. Thompson (Lanham, MD: University Press of America, 1985), 96.

The Long Goodbye

MOURNING AND REMEMBERING RONALD REAGAN

Chester Pach

T HE NEWS CAME LESS than two hours before post time for the Belmont Stakes in New York, in which Smarty Jones was trying to become horse racing's first Triple Crown winner in more than a quarter century. The record crowd of more than 120,000 people looked away from the tote boards and observed a moment of silence. A few miles away at Yankee Stadium, the seventh-inning stretch became a somber interlude in the baseball game between the New York Yankees and the Texas Rangers when public address announcer Bob Sheppard relayed the news. Millions of viewers got the same information when ABC interrupted its regular television programming at 4:42 p.m. (EDT) on June 5, 2004, and CBS did the same thing eight minutes later. ABC anchor Elizabeth Vargas told viewers that former president Ronald Reagan, age ninety-three, had died at his home in Los Angeles.[1]

These brief factual announcements on a Saturday afternoon began a week in which Americans mourned and remembered Reagan. Millions watched and thousands participated in the most elaborate and scripted presidential funeral in US history. "This is a legacy-building event," declared Jim Hooley, the former White House director of presidential advance who helped carry out the plans for Reagan's funeral. The goal was to use every opportunity to "evoke the rugged individual spirit, limited government," and to say "to the world [that] Ronald Reagan has gone home."[2] But even though Reagan's final goodbye was made for TV, his death also inspired spontaneous and passionate tributes from ordinary citizens. "When I think of him, I think of

America," said one California mourner. "What's that saying—American like Mom and apple pie? He should be in that, too. Because he represented what this country is all about."[3]

Reagan's death was hardly unexpected. As President George W. Bush declared at the state funeral in the nation's capital, "We lost Ronald Reagan only days ago, but we missed him for a long time."[4] Almost ten years earlier, Reagan had told the American people that he suffered from Alzheimer's disease and then retired from public life. He returned in June 2004 as an iconic figure, remembered more for his optimism, patriotism, and decency than for his tax and budget cuts, soaring deficits, antipathy toward big government, defense buildup, anticommunism, response to the AIDS crisis, misrepresentations about negotiating with terrorists during the Iran-Contra scandal, or unexpected but essential contributions to the end of the Cold War. The fortieth president's death provided a chance to remember when it was Morning in America, when the United States was dynamic, righteous, and victorious—or so it seemed. "I think people are still looking for a real hero in America," said one of the mourners at the Reagan Library. "He was one and is one."[5]

Farewell

Reagan had bid farewell to the American people a decade earlier when he revealed that he was suffering from Alzheimer's disease. On November 5, 1994, he released a short, handwritten letter, which he hoped would raise awareness about Alzheimer's and contribute to "a clearer understanding of the individuals and families who are affected by it." He declared that he was feeling fine and intended to spend his remaining years enjoying the outdoors, keeping in touch with friends and supporters, and sharing "life's journey with my beloved Nancy and my family."[6] An accompanying statement from Reagan's physicians explained that tests during the previous year showed that the former president was "entering the early stages of this disease."[7]

Reagan released this simple, moving letter so that he could reveal the news of his illness on his own terms. Nancy Reagan knew that the Alzheimer's diagnosis would not remain a secret, especially since the former president's recent public appearances had provided unsettling indications that something was wrong. At the celebration of his eighty-second birthday in February 1993, Reagan offered two identical lengthy toasts to former British prime minister Margaret Thatcher, unaware that he was repeating himself.[8] At the funeral of Richard Nixon in April 1994, his conversations with the other former presidents aroused concerns. Jimmy Carter thought the Great Communicator didn't sound right; Gerald Ford worried that Reagan seemed "hollowed out." Politicians and journalists who learned about Reagan's deteriorating condition participated in "a gentle conspiracy" of silence: they tacitly decided to "let Reagan talk about it when and if he wanted to."[9] But Reagan's inner circle learned that some journalists who knew about the former president's decline were unwilling to join the conspiracy. Nancy Reagan told her husband, "We're going to have to deal with this. Word is going to get out." Reagan went to his desk and returned fifteen minutes later with a two-page letter. Many newspapers published the letter in their Sunday editions the following day.[10]

The announcement renewed speculation about whether early symptoms of dementia had affected Reagan during his presidency. His personal physician, John Hutton, maintained that Reagan showed no evidence of cognitive decline during his White House years.[11] The president's younger son, Ron Reagan, however, thought he saw early indications of the affliction while his father was in office. He recalled that his father became alarmed in 1986 when he could not remember the names of familiar canyons near Los Angeles. Public observers also worried about Reagan's mental acuity. The president's fumbling performance during his first debate in October 1984 with Democratic presidential nominee Walter Mondale produced widespread speculation that age had taken its toll.[12] During the Iran-Contra scandal, Reagan's detachment, confusion, and inability to recall basic facts led some aides to consider invoking the Twenty-fifth Amendment concerning presidential disability.[13] Even though no physician diagnosed Reagan with any cognitive disability while he was president, Ron Reagan maintained that the physiological and neurological deterioration associated with Alzheimer's could begin "years, even decades, before identifiable symptoms arise." In view of those medical realities, the younger Reagan concluded that "the question . . . of whether my father suffered from the beginning stages of Alzheimer's while in office more or less answers itself."[14] Speech scientists corroborated that judgment several years later when their analysis of Reagan's news conferences found changes in the president's speaking patterns associated with the onset of Alzheimer's.[15]

Nancy Reagan believed that a horseback riding accident was the cause of her husband's cognitive decline. In July 1989, while visiting a friend's ranch in Mexico, Reagan's mount reared and threw him to the ground. An examination revealed a subdural hematoma near his brain that required surgery. Though Reagan recovered quickly from the operation, his wife later asserted, "I've always had the feeling that the severe blow to his head . . . hastened the onset of Ronnie's Alzheimer's."[16] Reagan's younger son, however, maintained that the accident proved that his father was already suffering from the disease. He claimed that the surgeons saw signs of Alzheimer's even though they made no formal diagnosis of that illness.[17]

After further testing enabled doctors to confirm the onset of Alzheimer's, Reagan made his exit from public life with uncommon grace and plain-spoken eloquence. He thanked the American people for the honor of serving as president. He expressed no regrets save for wishing that he could spare his wife the heavy burden of caring for him as the disease progressed. Despite his grim prognosis, he looked ahead with undiminished hopefulness. "I will leave with the greatest love for this country of ours and eternal optimism for its future," he declared. "I now begin the journey that will lead me into the sunset of my life. I know that for America there will always be a bright dawn ahead."[18]

World leaders and thousands of citizens praised Reagan for his candor and courage. President Bill Clinton, who was campaigning in Oakland, California, on the final weekend before the midterm elections, told a Democratic rally that Reagan's announcement "touched my heart."[19] George H. W. Bush praised Reagan's forthrightness in "sharing this private matter with the American people." Gerald Ford, former Canadian prime minister Brian Mulroney, and Thatcher telephoned to express their sympathy and support. Phones lines to Reagan's office were jammed. Thousands of letters deluged Reagan's office during the following weeks. An official with the Los Angeles chapter of the Alzheimer's Association called Reagan's announcement "a transforming moment" and said his office had been inundated with telephone calls seeking information and assistance. At the time of Reagan's diagnosis, Alzheimer's afflicted four million Americans and claimed 100,000 lives each year.[20]

The Long Goodbye

"It's a long goodbye," Nancy Reagan explained in a speech in 1995, as she watched Alzheimer's rob her husband of recollections of their life together.[21] "No one can really know what it's like unless they've traveled this path," she wrote of her experience with Alzheimer's. "You know that it's a progressive disease and there's no place to go but down, no light at the end of the tunnel. You get tired and frustrated, because you have no control and you feel helpless. . . . There are so many memories that I can no longer share."[22] She was no longer sure in 2002 that her husband knew her.[23]

The public saw nothing of Reagan's decline after the release of his poignant letter. "He wanted people to remember him as they had known him," recalled Frederick Ryan, Reagan's first postpresidential chief of staff. "Maybe because of his old days in Hollywood he knew when it was the right time to exit the stage." Occasionally, the public would get a glimpse of Reagan walking in a park or entering a restaurant—but only at a distance. He also continued going to his office in Century City, but only staff members, friends, or veterans of the Reagan administration saw him for more than a smile and a handshake.[24] Edmund Morris, his authorized biographer, dropped by on December 9, 1994, and the conversation consisted of awkward, one-sided, small talk. The only time the former president seemed sure of himself was while describing a painting of the Rock River in Dixon, Illinois, where for seven summers he had been a lifeguard and saved seventy-seven people from drowning. When they parted, Morris knew that Reagan "had stopped recognizing me." Painfully, he added, "Now I no longer recognize him."[25]

Alzheimer's relentlessly compressed the circles of Reagan's life. Soon after releasing his public letter about Alzheimer's, Reagan stopped going to his ranch in the Santa Ynez Mountains near Santa Barbara. Since 1975, Rancho del Cielo—the ranch of the sky—had been the Reagans' rustic retreat. "I thought the ranch was a place that would always make him happy, no matter what," wife Nancy had believed.[26] But the two-hour drive from the Reagan home in the Bel Air neighborhood of Los Angeles became onerous. There was also less reason to visit because Reagan had to relinquish one of the pleasures that made the ranch so attractive: he could no longer ride safely on horseback. Nancy Reagan put the ranch up for sale in August 1996, and it became the property of the Young America's Foundation, a conservative group that has preserved it as "a lasting monument" to Reagan's "accomplishments and ideas."[27]

Visits to the office became more difficult as Reagan's capabilities declined. The former president said little to the few visitors who were allowed to see him. Son Ron noted the irony that the Great Communicator found that "facility with language was among the first of his faculties to desert him."[28] When she called on her father in his office in August 1997, daughter Patti Davis found him sitting at his desk with "nothing on it, . . . his hands folded, . . . his eyes focused on nothing. . . . My heart hurts for him."[29] On one occasion, Reagan returned home clutching a small object. He opened his hand and showed his wife a ceramic model of the White House that had been in the office aquarium. He explained that although he didn't know what it was, he had brought it home because it had "something to do with me."[30]

At home, his activities diminished as the disease stripped away his vigor, independence, and awareness. His wife sometimes showed him scrapbooks or videos, hoping that he could remember his presidency or their life together. Yet the memories that most often returned were of his youthful days as a high school and college football player. "There's a game. They're waiting for me," he would insist as he awakened in the early morning and tried to surge through the bedroom door.[31] Yet along with these jarring episodes, there were also poignant, heartbreaking moments. On a walk with a Secret Service agent, he tried to open the gate to a house with a flower garden. The agent told Reagan he couldn't walk into someone else's yard. "I know," he replied, "but I just wanted to pick a rose for my love."[32]

Family members spoke in public for the former president who no longer could. Nancy Reagan addressed the 1996 Republican National Convention in San Diego as the party honored its most popular living former president. As Mrs. Reagan spoke about her gratitude for the cards and letters that sustained her and "Ronnie" through the "terrible pain and loneliness" of Alzheimer's, some convention delegates wiped away tears. Claiming that she wasn't the speechmaker in the family, she quoted from her husband's remarks to the Republican convention four years earlier, which he had foreseen as his last such address. "Whatever else history may say about me when I'm gone," he had declared, "I hope it will record that I appealed to your best hopes not your worst fears, to your confidence rather than your doubts." She closed her bittersweet remarks with an assurance that "Ronnie" still saw America as "the shining city on the hill, a place full of hope and promise for us all."[33]

Although she appeared at the convention that nominated Bob Dole for president, Mrs. Reagan avoided partisan comments at that event. She did not hesitate to speak out, however, to protect her husband or advance his interests. She denounced Oliver North, a major figure in the Iran-Contra scandal, as someone who had "lied to my husband and about my husband." Her blunt criticism was a major reason that North lost the election for US senator from Virginia in 1994. She was no less determined in calling for the use of tissue from aborted fetuses in stem-cell research to find a cure for Alzheimer's disease, a position that social conservatives generally opposed.[34] Daughter Maureen Reagan also became a fervent advocate for improved care for Alzheimer's patients and further research about the disease.[35]

Daughter Patti had little patience with Republican presidential aspirants who invoked Reagan to boost their own candidacies. As he sought the Republican presidential nomination, Dole had declared, "I'm willing to be another Ronald Reagan if that's what you want me to be."[36] "As if this were possible," Davis sneered in her memoir of her father's last illness. She thought Dole didn't "get it." No one could "manufacture my father, put him together like a paint-by-number drawing, and then imitate him." Although her own liberal political views had long been at odds with her father's and she had been estranged from her mother before her father's Alzheimer's diagnosis, Davis resented ambitious Republicans "co-opting" her father's "legacy for their own self-consumed goals at a time when he couldn't speak up for himself."[37]

"My father is getting smaller," Davis wrote painfully as his decline accelerated during his last years. Reagan was shorter, his once athletic legs thinner, "his essence" progressively "whittled down, trimmed, reshaped by a disease that has its own blueprint."[38] He could no longer carry on a coherent conversation. In January 2001, he fell and broke his hip. An ambulance took him to the same hospital where Maureen was receiving cancer treatment. He did not understand that his daughter was only a few floors away or that malignant melanoma claimed her life in August 2001. Reagan returned home a week after successful hip surgery.[39] The accident, however, forced another difficult adjustment. The former president spent the rest of his life sleeping alone in a hospital bed with rails to prevent another accident.[40] "For more than forty years," Patti reflected, "my mother ha[d] rolled into my father in the gray stillness of dawn, waking to the scent of his skin, the heat of his body beside her. . . . It's almost unfathomable to me, the loss she must be wrestling with."[41]

Reagan clung to life for three more years. In October 2001, at age ninety, he became the oldest former president in US history, surpassing John Adams's record for longevity. In March 2002, he and Nancy spent their fiftieth wedding anniversary together. Confined to the hospital bed in what had once been his home office, his life seeped away in spring 2004. Mrs. Reagan sorrowfully acknowledged that "Ronnie's long journey has finally taken him to a distant place where I can no longer reach him."[42] His eyes were usually closed, his breathing shallow and irregular. Nancy and Patti along with an Irish nurse, Laura, who had been a source of comfort to the former president, hovered near him. Son Michael visited as the end approached, but traffic prevented him from reaching the Bel Air home in time on the day that his father drew his last breath. Ron and wife Doria cut short a Hawaiian vacation and arrived at Reagan's bedside in the early morning of June 5. Somehow Reagan summoned the will and the strength to do the unexpected. At 1:00 p.m., he turned his head toward his wife and opened his eyes. As Patti recollected, his eyes were wide open, focused, and bluer than they had been in more than a year. After looking directly at his wife, he stopped breathing. He uttered no final words, but they were unnecessary. "That's the greatest gift you could have given me," Mrs. Reagan said softly.[43]

Into the Sunset

Nancy Reagan's simple, two-sentence statement announcing her husband's death and expressing appreciation for "everyone's prayers" began a week in which Ronald Reagan commanded national attention.[44] Reporters had gathered outside the gate of the Reagans' home even before the formal announcement of the former president's passing. Ordinary people soon joined them, arriving to pay tribute or participate in an historic event.

Helicopters provided aerial shots of the Reagan residence and the hearse's journey along streets lined with well-wishers and curiosity-seekers.[45]

ABC and CBS interrupted Saturday afternoon sports coverage for special reports, while cable news channels suspended their usual programming and concentrated exclusively on Reagan. There was little to report about Reagan's death, other than the official cause was pneumonia as a complication of Alzheimer's. Instead, the coverage provided a remembrance—and, often, a celebration—of Reagan's life and career. The news channels had had a long time to prepare obituaries and video compilations of Reagan's life. His career in Hollywood and his made-for-TV presidency gave the networks a rich video legacy on which to draw. Highlight reels included Reagan's most famous lines—"Win just one for the Gipper," from *Knute Rockne, All American;* "Mr. Gorbachev, tear down this wall" from his speech in Berlin on June 12, 1987. Sometimes there was no audio, just the iconic moments that everybody could recognize—riding a horse at the ranch or walking with Soviet president Mikhail Gorbachev in Red Square in 1988.[46] The pervasiveness of video was an indication that Reagan had made indelible impressions as much with his style and image as with his words and deeds.

The assessments of Reagan's presidency on that first day were laudatory, even effusive. On ABC, biographer Lou Cannon explained that "Reagan's greatest asset was that he was underestimated." People often failed to appreciate that Reagan "was a very smart guy and a very masterful politician. And he . . . knew what he wanted to accomplish."[47] On Fox, Rudolph Giuliani, whom Reagan had appointed as US attorney for the Southern District of New York, declared that Reagan's presidency had defined the last half of the twentieth century just as Franklin D. Roosevelt's had defined the first half. Richard Allen, the former special assistant for national security affairs, insisted that Reagan, despite his reputation for inattention to details, understood public policy as well as any president. The praise on Fox—not as unfair and unbalanced as it later became—was no greater than on the other networks.[48]

The most adulatory assessments on that first night were not on Fox, and they came from two unlikely sources. David Stockman, the former director of the Office of Management and Budget, had written a tell-all memoir in which he criticized Reagan's ignorance of supply-side economics and the president's inability to carry out sweeping changes in economic policy. On

CNN, however, Stockman called Reagan "the greatest president of the twentieth century." What had been deficiencies in Stockman's earlier reckoning—an inability to grasp specifics and provide leadership—became assets—a gift for rising above detail and the vision to grasp the moment for far-reaching change.[49] Similar encomiums came from Edmund Morris, who had written an authorized biography that the president's family and inner circle detested, partly because Morris had concluded that Reagan "remained a mystery to me, and worse still . . . an apparent airhead."[50] On CBS, however, Morris paid tribute to Reagan as "the greatest [president] since Harry Truman."[51]

Interspersed with these assessments were statements of world leaders, past and present. President George W. Bush was in France for the commemoration of the sixtieth anniversary of D-Day. Twenty years earlier, Reagan had given one of his most inspiring speeches as he saluted the "boys of Pointe du Hoc," the Allied troops that landed on the beaches of Normandy to liberate Europe from Nazi occupation.[52] Because of the time difference, Bush read a statement to reporters and TV cameras after midnight in France in which he praised Reagan for winning "America's respect with his greatness" and "its love with his goodness." Margaret Thatcher remembered Reagan for winning the Cold War without firing a shot. Former president Bill Clinton hailed Reagan "for the way he personified the indomitable optimism of the American people, and for keeping America at the forefront of the fight for freedom for people everywhere."[53]

The most engaging and enjoyable TV recollection on the day of Reagan's death was a panel discussion on CNN's *Larry King Live*. The participants chatted about Reagan's notable achievements—rejuvenating the economy, diminishing Cold War tensions, restoring American confidence in the future. But the best conversation was about Reagan the man, who could talk to anybody, lift their spirits, and make them laugh. Walter Cronkite recalled how in the first weeks of his presidency Reagan granted him an interview just before he retired as anchor of the *CBS Evening News*. Pleasure followed business, as the president took Cronkite to his private office for champagne, cake, and two hours of swapping stories that left both doubled over in laughter. CBS reporter Mike Wallace, renowned for his hard-hitting interviews on *60 Minutes*, believed Reagan "was a man we all admired, no matter what our politics." He added, "There's a quality about that man."[54]

Wallace understood that what touched so many people was Reagan's humanity, humor, hopefulness, and homespun authenticity. Video essays on the broadcast networks and cable news channels emphasized those themes along with Reagan's successes or failures in Hollywood and Washington. The TV networks also looked back at the love affair of Ronald and Nancy Reagan, which lasted more than half a century and proved more resilient than the scourge of Alzheimer's. The TV news coverage of the last chapter in Reagan's public career and the first in his afterlife was as much about the man as his achievements. Indeed, only hours after the former president's death, CNN's John King presciently predicted that the week ahead would be full of "statements of condolences and sadness, but also a celebration of [Reagan's] optimism, a celebration of his spirit."[55]

Most Sunday newspapers had Reagan's death as their lead story, often with banner headlines and large photos or drawings, as well as editorial assessments and even special pull-out sections. The headlines alone provide a glimpse of the emotional impact of Reagan's passing and the ways that journalists conveyed the significance of his life and career: "Goodbye, Gipper" (*Sacramento Bee*); "America's Warrior: He Promised U.S. Would Stand Tall Again" (*St. Petersburg Times*); "'The Great Communicator' Was Architect of an Era" (*Kansas City Star*); "Reagan Dies at 93: Popular President Changed the Political Landscape" (*Los Angeles Times*); "An American Original" (*Lewiston [Maine] Sun Journal*); "Mourning in America: 40th U.S. President Left Legacy as Model of Courage" (*Cincinnati Enquirer*); "Passing into History" (*Portland Oregonian*).[56]

Obituaries and editorials provided more detail and nuance, but also varying assessments. One of the most favorable came from the *Chicago Tribune*, which praised Reagan as a "revolutionary" who "could turn a slogan into reality." His influence lived on in "the Supreme Court's rediscovery of the powers of the states, . . . the proliferation of conservative commentators in the news media, . . . and the continuing spread of freedom and democracy."[57] The *Washington Post* published the most thorough and thoughtful obituary, written by reporter Lou Cannon, who covered Reagan from Sacramento to Washington and wrote what is still widely regarded as the best Reagan biography. Cannon emphasized that Reagan was an ordinary man with exceptional political skills and a leader who exceeded expectations, reshaped the conservative movement, and connected with the American people as few others had.[58] The *Post* editorial writers echoed Cannon's view that Reagan was "more than capable" of reaching his fellow citizens and fulfilling "one of the most important functions of the presidency"—reaffirming "the basic beliefs of people in the words he spoke." But that admirable talent had to be balanced against "his intermittent denigration of government, and of people who depended on government services, [which] fed into and bolstered hurtful and unfair stereotypes."[59]

Other newspapers reached more critical conclusions. The obituary in the *Los Angeles Times*, Reagan's hometown newspaper, emphasized his "tangled legacy"—a stronger economy with record deficits, the success of an historic nuclear arms control agreement with the Soviet Union, along with the debacles of the marine barracks bombing in Lebanon in 1983 that killed 241 US troops and the Iran-Contra scandal.[60] The *New York Times* also mixed criticism with praise, including a theme often neglected by obituary writers—the Reagan administration's retreat from civil rights enforcement. The *Times* editorial writers agreed that Reagan left a "complicated legacy," but attributed some of his success to "good timing and good luck."[61] Jimmy Carter's "dour pedantry" made Reagan a welcome change; Gorbachev, rather than his intransigent predecessors in the Kremlin, was the ideal negotiating partner.[62]

"An immensely popular and polarizing figure," is how the *New York Daily News* summarized Reagan's White House years. Reagan's economic policies had created "a staggering divide between rich and poor" and "gutted more than 50 years of social programs." While Reagan achieved "his greatest triumph" during his second term—an arms control deal with Moscow—he also endured "his greatest shame"—the Iran-Contra scandal. Nevertheless, the editorial writers at the *Daily News* judged Reagan as one of "the 20th century's three most presidential presidents," along with the two Roosevelts. He "ended a nightmarish Cold War pretty much all by himself"—they were apparently oblivious to Gorbachev's role—and he retired from office "as beloved an elder statesman as the country has ever known."[63] Like so many commentaries, the *Daily News* editorial praised Reagan for a simple, essential virtue that couldn't be taken for granted: he knew how to be president. "Central Casting could have supplied no one more presidential."[64] As these obituaries and editorials suggested, most Americans liked Reagan even if they had very different views about his presidency and its legacies.

The news media reported about the plans for Reagan's funeral, which were elaborate and precise, with some events timed "down to the minute." A 300-page document, known as "The Book," covered every detail of the ceremonies. The planning had begun in 1981, with many revisions and updates, the last just ten days before Reagan's death. The Military District of Washington oversaw the preparations and drew on the traditions of previous state funerals, especially those for Abraham Lincoln and John F. Kennedy. The specifics, though, reflected the preferences of the president and Mrs. Reagan. The former first lady did much of the fine-tuning with help from Michael Deaver, the peerless stage director of Reagan's most memorable public appearances. "It is an American service, and it is as American as Ronald Reagan," declared former assistant Frederick Ryan. As aides helped implement these plans, they thought about HPS—headline, picture, story. The overall goal was to portray "Ronald Reagan as a man who won the Cold War, who brought back America's faith in itself."[65]

What made Reagan's funeral distinctive was that it spanned the country, beginning with ceremonies at the Reagan Library in Simi Valley, then services in Washington, and finally burial in California on the grounds of the library as the sun set behind the mountains. Reagan chose the place and time for his burial. "He said dusk is the time to do this," recalled Kenneth Duberstein, the president's last White House chief of staff. "He understood that this would be his closing scene."[66]

There were similarities between the ceremonies for Reagan and the state funerals for Lincoln—the nation's first—and for Kennedy—the first televised presidential rite. Reagan, for example, lay in state in the Capitol Rotunda, his casket on the catafalque constructed for Lincoln's ceremony and used again for Kennedy's. But there was a fundamental difference. Kennedy and Lincoln died from assassin's bullets while in office. Reagan had left the White House fifteen years before his passing; his public life had been over for a decade; his death after a long, cruel illness came as no surprise. There were many tears for Reagan as there had been for Kennedy and Lincoln, but none of the horror arising from sudden violence or the shock of a life abruptly cut short. Dignitaries as well as common citizens celebrated Reagan as much as they mourned him; they smiled even if they cried. Some people felt a sense of relief that the end had finally come for Reagan and that his wife, his primary caregiver, no longer had to carry such a heavy burden. As family spokesperson Joanne Drake acknowledged, "While it is an extremely sad time for Mrs. Reagan, there is definitely a sense of relief that he is no longer suffering and that he has gone to a better place."[67]

The memorial services began on Monday, June 7, when a military honor guard carried Reagan's casket from the Santa Monica funeral home to a waiting hearse for the forty-mile drive to the Reagan Library. Mrs. Reagan, escorted as she would be all week by Commanding General Galen B. Jackman of the Military District of Washington, received a round of applause when she appeared in public for the first time since her husband's death. Throughout the weekend, people had gathered outside the mortuary to pay tribute to Reagan and leave tokens of their admiration, including flags, flowers, cowboy hats, and jellybeans—a presidential favorite. Mrs. Reagan and the children paused at one of these makeshift memorials, where son Michael—adopted during Reagan's previous marriage to Jane Wyman— read one of the many notes and shed a tear. During the drive, the motorcade passed hundreds of onlookers who waved or saluted. Some of the expressions of patriotism and celebration, however, were not entirely spontaneous. Reagan aides distributed 50,000 flags to crowds along the motorcade route. At the Reagan Library, there was a brief, private service in which the Reverend Dr. Michael Wenning, the former senior pastor of the Bel Air Presbyterian Church where the Reagans had worshiped, led the family and a few close friends in prayer. Television cameras showed Mrs. Reagan touching her cheek to the casket at the end of the ceremony.[68]

After the Reagan family departed, throngs of citizens began filing by the casket in the lobby of the library. NBC's Brian Williams called them Reagan's "American family." Traffic overwhelmed local roads. The backup on one expressway extended for more than four miles.[69] More than 100,000 people—far more than planners had anticipated—viewed Reagan's casket before the library closed its doors on Tuesday evening.[70] Many came to honor the man they saw, in the words of NBC Nightly News anchor Tom Brokaw, "as their shining hero on the hill."[71]

The ceremonies shifted to the nation's capital on Wednesday after a cross-country flight that departed from Point Mugu Naval Air Station in California and landed at Andrews Air Force Base in suburban Maryland on a steamy afternoon. Thousands along the National Mall watched the funeral procession move solemnly toward the Capitol even though the heat was so intense than more than one hundred people required medical attention.[72] "It's a once-in-a-lifetime experience," exclaimed Susie Beatty of Vienna, Virginia, "a moment in history."[73] The daylong journey of Reagan's body from a jumbo jet, to a hearse, and then a horse-drawn caisson was "a trip back in time, technological progress in reverse" for a man born during the presidency of William Howard Taft.[74] Reagan appropriately made his final entrance into the Capitol through the West Front, since he had been the first president to be inaugurated on that side of the building in 1981. While a band played "The Battle Hymn of the Republic," military pallbearers, working in shifts because of the wilting heat, carried the 700-pound casket up 116 steps and placed it on the Lincoln catafalque in the Rotunda. During the short evening ceremony, Republican leaders of Congress—Ted Stevens, the president pro tempore of the Senate, and Dennis Hastert, the Speaker of the House—delivered eulogies. So, too, did Vice President Dick Cheney, who extolled Reagan as "a graceful and a gallant man." Mrs. Reagan gently rubbed the flag on the casket before departing. In their own ways, the hundreds of international dignitaries, members of Congress, and justices of the Supreme Court who attended this ceremony paid their respects.[75]

Following this private event, the Rotunda opened to the public at 9:00 p.m. that evening. First in line was Carol Williams, a professor at Strayer University, who arrived sixteen hours earlier and expressed pleasure that in death Reagan had accomplished what was harder to achieve in life—getting the American people to set aside their political differences, if only for a while.[76] The Rotunda stayed open continuously through Wednesday and Thursday nights, a total of thirty-four hours, while 105,000 people filed past Reagan's coffin.[77] "They all seem to have a story, a reason, a personal tug that has brought them here," NBC's Brian Williams declared. One man flew in from Florida with his son, Reagan Jonathan, named after the former president.[78] Some mourners thought Reagan represented the promise of America—the son of a modest, midwestern family who became president. "In no other country is that going to happen," said Frank Halecki, who drove from New Jersey to apologize to Reagan "for not voting for him in 1980."[79]

The viewing at the Capitol Rotunda and the Reagan Library "was intended to allow ordinary citizens to pay their respects."[80] Even this most elaborate funeral included the average person. "People want to see it" and witness it, explained one expert on death and mourning. "We are helpless before death. . . . When all we can do is show up, then that is what we do."[81] Each of them left with a commemorative card, which read "in final tribute from a grateful nation."[82]

While ordinary citizens celebrated Reagan's simple virtues, journalists and commentators continued to assess Reagan's legacies. Their appraisals ran the gamut from "Reagan's Recipe for Presidential Greatness" to "Rosy Outlook Hid Ugly Facts from Reagan"; from "An Optimist's Legacy" to "Critics See a Reagan Legacy Tainted by AIDS, Civil Rights, and Union Policies."[83] Columnist David Ignatius lauded Reagan as "a master of combining pragmatism and principle" "in a way that eventually toppled the Soviet Union," while Stephen J. Hedges emphasized that "some of his most ambitious military initiatives became costly misadventures."[84] There were antipodal judgments of his economic policies. Robert J. Samuelson praised Reagan's "overlooked" achievement of helping to lower double-digit inflation, but Paul Krugman dismissed Reagan's contribution while crediting Federal Reserve chair Paul Volcker as "the architect of America's great disinflation."[85]

The NBC Nightly News ran a week-long series on Reagan's legacy. In addition to analyzing familiar subjects—Reaganomics, lessening US-Soviet tensions—it examined Reagan's role as the "godfather of a powerful conservative movement and a new generation of conservative activists." Among those zealots were radio talk-show host Laura Ingraham, who as a high school student cheered Reagan's victory in the election of 1980 and became an ardent supporter, and Senator Lindsey Graham (R-SC), who praised Reagan for replacing "the scowling face of conservatism with an easy smile, a common touch, and a sense of humor." In a 1996 interview that NBC anchor Tom Brokaw agreed to hold until after Reagan's death, Patti Davis hoped that her father's legacy would be "beyond politics" and that he would "inspire people . . . about what was possible." For many ordinary Americans Reagan did indeed transcend politics.[86] But in death as in life, Reagan's policies continued to provoke considerable disagreement.

Security was elaborate and extensive during the ceremonies in Washington, far more than for the last state funeral for a president, Lyndon Johnson's, in 1973. Three decades later with the September 11, 2001, attacks a vivid memory and the divisive war in Iraq a provocation for opponents of US intervention who promised vengeance, terrorism was a major concern. Security measures multiplied with the arrival of dozens of world leaders, past and present, for the Friday morning funeral service at the National Cathedral. More international dignitaries, including 25 heads of state and 180 foreign ministers and ambassadors, came to Washington than for any event since John F. Kennedy's funeral. Among the mourners were British prime minister Tony Blair, German chancellor Gerhard Schroeder, South African president Thabo Mbecki, United Nations secretary general Kofi Annan, former Soviet president Gorbachev, and Great Britain's Prince Charles. Also attending the Friday ceremonies were the four living former US presidents—Ford, Carter, George H. W. Bush, and Clinton—as well as President George W. Bush and Vice President Cheney. Anxiety about a terrorist attack triggered the evacuation of the Capitol on Wednesday afternoon, just two hours before the arrival of Reagan's casket. "This is not a drill. Get out as fast as you can," police officers shouted to members of Congress, staff personnel, and former Reagan aides awaiting the evening ceremonies. Men removed suit jackets and women high heels as they ran to safety. The reason for the evacuation was a communications breakdown with a small plane headed toward restricted Washington airspace. The plane, it turned out, carried not a hijacker, as air traffic controllers feared, but the governor of Kentucky; a broken transponder halted transmission of flight data. Despite the panic, the events at the Capitol went precisely according to schedule, as did the remainder of the ceremonies until Reagan made his final journey to California on Friday afternoon.[87]

Federal offices were closed on Friday, June 11, which President Bush had designated a national day of mourning, and rain fell as the hearse arrived for the late-morning funeral service. National Cathedral could accommodate 4,000 mourners, and most seats were reserved for members of Congress and foreign leaders or diplomats. The former first lady allocated 1,000 tickets, a small number for all the Reagan friends and former administration officials. Guests found their seats according to a color code on their tickets, yellow dots for those in front, black for those in the rear.[88]

They witnessed some stirring moments. Irish tenor Ronan Tynan sang Franz Schubert's "Ave Maria." Justice Sandra Day O'Connor read from John Winthrop's sermon in 1630 urging the Puritan settlers of Massachusetts Bay to make their colony an example to the world or "a city upon a hill." Reagan embellished that phrase, making it "a shining city on a hill" and using it in many speeches to express his vision of American exceptionalism. The Reagan family selected the four eulogists. Margaret Thatcher recorded her tribute earlier because she had given up public speaking after a series of small strokes. She was vibrant and eloquent in her video, lauding Reagan for his role in ending the Cold War. "With the lever of American patriotism," she exclaimed, "he lifted up the world. And so today the world—in Prague, in Budapest, in Warsaw, . . . and in Moscow itself . . . mourns the passing of the Great Liberator." Former Canadian prime minister Brian Mulroney fondly remembered Reagan as "the leader we respected, the neighbor we admired, and the friend we loved." Former president George H. W. Bush made up his lack of eloquence with affecting emotion. "I learned more from Ronald Reagan than from anyone I encountered in all my years of public life," Bush declared as his voice quavered. "I learned kindness. . . . I also learned courage." After his father's tribute, the younger President Bush proclaimed, "Ronald Reagan belongs to the ages now, but we preferred it when he belonged to us." There were closing prayers from clergy of several faiths and a homily from John Danforth, the former Republican senator from Missouri and ordained Episcopal priest who officiated at the ceremony at Mrs. Reagan's request when health problems incapacitated the Reverend Billy Graham. As the Reagan motorcade prepared to depart for Andrews Air Force Base and the return trip to California, the cathedral's Bourdon Bell tolled forty times for the fortieth president.[89]

Reagan's final scene that Friday evening may have been his most memorable. The departure from Washington was timed perfectly so that Reagan's services would conclude in the California evening. The setting was the west lawn of the Reagan Library with the president's casket on a platform near the edge of a hill. An earlier plan was to show the burial site in the background but changing the camera position provided a more dramatic image. In the background were the Santa Susana Mountains, with a sinking sun painting the sky and the hills in serene hues of yellow and orange. There were no more political tributes from world leaders or Washington officials. Seven hundred invited guests, including Hollywood celebrities, political figures, and international dignitaries, instead heard the three surviving Reagan children provide affectionate remembrances of their father. Michael, the oldest, described himself as "the chosen one . . . the lucky one. In all his years, he never mentioned that I was adopted." Patti recounted how her father taught her as a child that "new life always comes out of death" by holding a funeral service for her expired goldfish and explaining it was swimming in "the clear blue waters in heaven." Ron was humorous, recalling his father's fondness for grasping ear lobes and explaining how his thumbs-up signal inspired a protester to approach the president's limousine with "an entirely different hand gesture" involving "an entirely different digit." The youngest Reagan child closed his tribute with touching eloquence: "Those of us who knew him well will have no trouble imagining his paradise. Golden fields will spread beneath the blue dome of the western sky. Live oaks will shadow the rolling hillsides. . . . Across those fields he will ride a gray mare he calls Nancy D. . . . He will rest in the shade of the trees. Our cares are no longer his. We meet him now only in memory. But we will join him soon enough. All of us. When we are home, when we are free."[90]

The end was majestic and moving. As an honor guard carried the casket to the burial site only yards away, a bagpiper played "Amazing Grace," as Reagan had requested years earlier during the funeral planning.[91] The Reverend Wenning's benediction preceded a twenty-one-gun salute and then another. A bugler played taps, and fighter aircraft flew overhead in one more military tribute. The commander of the USS *Ronald Reagan* presented Mrs. Reagan with the flag that had draped the coffin—the same flag that had flown over the Capitol on the day of Reagan's first inauguration. Only as the former first lady approached the casket for the last time did grief finally overwhelm her. She had endured five days of ceremonies with grace, fortitude, and dignity. "I can't leave him here," she sobbed as she rubbed the casket. The three Reagan children gently led her away. She held the arm of her military escort, General Jackman, one more time.[92]

After Mrs. Reagan departed, aides lifted glasses at gatherings inside the Reagan Library until after midnight. Each of the handful of mourners who drank the final toasts threw a cup of dirt on the casket.[93] Workers closed the crypt that contained Reagan's body at 3:00 a.m.[94] Two days later, the library reopened, and the first public visitors walked by the gravesite

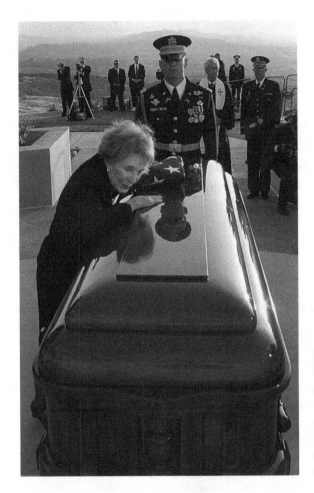

FIGURE 10. Nancy Reagan says a final goodbye to President Ronald Reagan after services at the Reagan Library, Simi Valley, California, June 11, 2004. (US Navy)

inscribed with words from Reagan's speech at the dedication of his library, "I know in my heart that man is good, that what is right will always eventually triumph, and there is purpose and worth to each and every life."[95]

Remembering Reagan

Reagan's passing inspired a flurry of proposals to honor the fortieth president. Illinois governor Rod Blagojevich used his executive authority to name part of Interstate 88 near Reagan's boyhood home of Dixon after the former president. In Washington, members of Congress debated redesigning coins and currency. One Florida House member introduced legislation to put Reagan's likeness on the half dollar, but there were competing suggestions to do the same with the twenty or hundred-dollar bill.[96]

The most popular idea was to substitute Reagan for Alexander Hamilton on the ten-dollar bill, a proposal favored by conservative activist Grover Norquist, the founder of the Ronald Reagan Legacy Project. Since its establishment in 1997, the project has aimed at establishing a Reagan memorial in each state as well as naming a park, public building, or road after the former president in each of America's 3,140 counties. Among the most notable successes of these boosters was the naming of National Airport in Washington after Reagan in 1998 and the commissioning of an aircraft carrier in 2003 that bore the former president's name. Norquist, however, didn't see the fulfillment of his dream to add Reagan to Mount Rushmore. In the days after Reagan's death, Senate Democratic Leader Tom Daschle brushed aside the frantic efforts to honor Reagan. He said, "I think we have to allow historians and others with some thought to consider how we might best remember President Reagan officially."[97]

Historians' assessments of Reagan's presidency had become more favorable in the years preceding his death. During his White House years, Reagan usually had strong support in public opinion polls, although his standing sank during the recession of 1981–82 and the Iran-Contra scandal. Reagan's reputation with scholars was another matter. A poll of historians in 1997 ranked him as an "average" president. But that overall assessment concealed wide divisions: seven of the scholars considered him "near great," while nine thought he was "below average" and four deemed him a "failure."[98] A *Wall Street Journal* ranking five years later, however, found him "near great." The release of documents in the Reagan Library and the publication of volumes of Reagan's letters and other writings destroyed the myth that Reagan was an "amiable dunce," in Clark Clifford's caustic phrase. Those documents showed that Reagan could write a speech as well as deliver it; that he was an engaged rather than detached chief executive; and that he was hardly an "airhead" but instead had a set of principles that guided him in office. Among those fundamental beliefs was a determination to shrink "big government" and defeat international communism, a deep trust in the fairness of the American people, and a certainty that the United States—the "shining city on a hill"—was an inspiration to freedom-loving people around the world. Even historians who reached critical judgments about his administration's policies recognized Reagan's significance. Writing a few years after the fortieth president's death, the historian Sean Wilentz, no fan of Reagan, concluded, "If greatness in a president is measured in terms of affecting the temper of the times, whether you like it or not, Reagan stands as second to none among the presidents of the second half of the twentieth century." The title of his book is *The Age of Reagan*.[99]

The plaudits for Reagan reached a high point during the centennial celebration of his birth in 2011. Republicans praised Reagan effusively as he was still the single most important influence on their party, and they often found in his words or deeds something to advance their own political interests. For example, Speaker of the House John Boehner of Ohio, contending with Tea Party critics who doubted his conservative zeal, insisted that Reagan's "promise of a smaller, less costly, and more accountable government" appealed to "small-town, small-business people like me who were fed up with intrusive government and indecisive leadership."[100]

Democrats joined this chorus of praise. President Barack Obama, then adjusting to Republican congressional majorities after the recent midterm elections, commended Reagan for his ability "to compromise on issues as contentious as Social Security and tax cuts . . . and work with leaders of all political persuasions to advance the cause of freedom, democracy, and security around the world." Reagan even received plaudits from a most unlikely source, the Congressional Progressive Caucus, which urged the Republicans who controlled the House and Senate to "take President Reagan's message to heart and put what's best for America's economy ahead of gaining a short-term advantage."[101] By 2011, Reagan had become part of the American political pantheon. Democrats as well as Republicans could invoke his words or example whenever they discovered a politically convenient part of his legacy. Reagan probably would have smiled.

Reagan's week-long journey beyond the sunset was a compelling event for millions of Americans. The cable news channels—CNN, Fox, and MSNBC—made Reagan the main story for an entire week. The broadcast networks limited their coverage mainly to live events in California and Washington. The ratings increased for the cable news channels, especially during the live ceremonies. "This is a perfect example of what cable news is for," declared CNN anchor Aaron Brown. "We are in these moments the corner square. It's an opportunity to come and share the common experience." TV provided a sense of involvement, even if viewers never left their living rooms. TV coverage of Reagan's funeral gave them an opportunity, as one expert on grief declared, to participate in a "sacred community theater."[102]

There's no doubt that the Reagan family and their astute media advisors used the ceremonies to shape the memory of the former president. As one news executive explained, "The Reagan administration always knew about the power of imagery."[103] But no amount of stage direction or spin could have created the long lines at the Reagan Library and the Capitol Rotunda or the makeshift memorials with gifts and letters to a president so many people revered. Those who honored Reagan were hardly a cross-section of America. *ABC News* anchor Peter Jennings noted, for example, how few people of color paid tribute to Reagan at the public events.[104] Yet while Reagan's appeal was hardly universal, he may have touched even more people in death than in life. "He encompassed what it is to be an American," said one woman who traveled from New York to watch the funeral procession in Washington. "He symbolizes the American Dream."[105] Reagan lived what he called in his autobiography an American life.[106] It continued even after his death.

Notes

1. "Smarty Jones Is Run Down at Belmont," *Washington Post* (hereafter *WP*), June 6, 2004; "Rangers Rookie Cools Off Yanks," *Associated Press*, June 6, 2004; "Special Report" introduction, *ABC News Transcripts*, June 5, 2004.

2. Jacob M. Schlesinger, "Operation Serenade: Laying Groundwork for Reagan's Funeral," *Wall Street Journal*, June 10, 2004, https://www.wsj.com/articles /SB108681419310032998/.

3. "A Nation and the World Pay Tribute to Reagan," *WP*, June 7, 2004, A1.

4. "Curtain Falls on 'a Great American Story,'" *WP*, June 12, 2004, A27.

5. "Hail, Farewell to the Chief," *WP*, June 8, 2004, A1.

6. "Reagan's Letter Announcing His Alzheimer's Diagnosis," November 5, 1994, Ronald Reagan Presidential Library (hereafter RRPL), https://www.reaganlibrary.gov/reagans /ronald-reagan/reagans-letter-announcing-his-alzheimers-diagnosis/.

7. "Physician's Explanation of Ronald Reagan's Alzheimer's Diagnosis," November 5, 1994, RRPL, https://www.reaganlibrary.gov/reagans/ronald-reagan/physicians-explanation-ronald-reagans-alzheimers-diagnosis/.

8. Edmund Morris, *Dutch: A Memoir of Ronald Reagan* (New York: Random House, 1999), 656.

9. Hugh Sidey, "The Sunset of My Life," *Time*, November 14, 1994, 65.

10. Michael K. Deaver, *Nancy: A Portrait of My Years with Nancy Reagan* (New York: William Morrow, 1994), 190–91; Morris, *Dutch*, 664–66.

11. Transcript, oral history interview, Dr. John Hutton, April 15–16, 2004, "Ronald Reagan Oral History Project," Miller Center for Public Affairs, https://millercenter.org/the-presidency/presidential-oral-histories/john-hutton-md-oral-history/.

12. "Reagan Criticizes Comments on Age," *New York Times* (hereafter *NYT*), October 11, 1984, A1.

13. Morris, *Dutch*, 622–23.

14. Ron Reagan, *My Father at 100: A Memoir* (New York: Viking, 2011), 217–18.

15. "In Reagan's Speeches, Early Clues to Dementia," *NYT*, March 31, 2015, D3.

16. Nancy Reagan, *I Love You, Ronnie: The Letters of Ronald Reagan to Nancy Reagan* (New York: Random House, 2000), 179–80.

17. Ron Reagan, *My Father*, 217.

18. "Reagan's Letter Announcing His Alzheimer's Diagnosis," November 5, 1994, RRPL, https://www.reaganlibrary.gov/reagans/ronald-reagan/reagans-letter-announcing-his-alzheimers-diagnosis/.

19. William J. Clinton, "Remarks at a Rally for Democratic Candidates in Oakland, California," November 5, 1994, American Presidency Project, https://www.presidency.ucsb.edu/node/288323/.

20. "Reagan's Illness Triggers Support: Letters Inundate California Office," *St. Louis Post-Dispatch*, November 7, 1994, 1A; "Reagan Praises Sung: People Laud His Candor in Revealing That He Has Alzheimer's Disease," *Los Angeles Times* (hereafter *LAT*), November 7, 1994, OCA3; "Old Allies Comfort Reagan," *The Advertiser*, November 9, 1994; "Reagan Discloses His Alzheimer's," *NYT*, November 13, 1994, E2; Bob Spitz, *Reagan: An American Journey* (New York: Penguin Books, 2018), 754; "Reagan's Church Prays for Him; Office Overwhelmed by Well-Wishers," *Associated Press*, November 7, 1994.

21. "Reagan's Cloudy Days," *WP*, June 8, 1995, D1.

22. Nancy Reagan, *I Love You Ronnie*, 184.

23. "The Reagans' Long Goodbye," September 24, 2002, *CBS News*, https://www.cbsnews.com/news/the-reagans-long-goodbye/.

24. Transcript, interview with Frederick J. Ryan Jr., Ronald Reagan Oral History Project, Miller Center for Public Affairs, http://web1.millercenter.org/poh/transcripts/ohp_2004_0525_ryan.pdf.

25. Edmund Morris, "This Living Hand," *New Yorker*, January 16, 1995, 66–69.

26. Deaver, *Nancy*, 202.

27. Spitz, *Reagan*, 755; Ron Reagan, *My Father*, 220; "Nancy Makes a Sad Choice," *Newsweek*, September 2, 1996, 6; "Preserving Rancho del Cielo," Young America's Foundation, https://reaganranch.yaf.org/.

28. Ron Reagan, *My Father*, 221.

29. Patti Davis, *The Long Goodbye* (New York: Alfred A. Knopf, 2004), 179–80.

30. *Reagan,* directed by Eugene Jarecki, aired on HBO, February 7, 2011, DVD (Ro*Co Films Educational, 2011).

31. Ron Reagan, *My Father,* 141–42.

32. Deaver, *Nancy,* 202, 207–8; Davis, *Long Goodbye,* 182.

33. Republican Convention Evening Session, August 12, 1996, C-SPAN, https://www.c -span.org/video/?74304-1/republican-convention-evening-session; "A Bittersweet Moment Brings Tears," *NYT,* August 13, 1996, A14.

34. James G. Benze Jr., *Nancy Reagan: On the White House Stage* (Lawrence: University Press of Kansas, 2005), 163–65.

35. "Former First Daughter Maureen Reagan Dies," *WP,* August 9, 2001, B7.

36. "GOP Candidates Trade Barbs at Summer Conference," *LAT,* July 16, 1995, A24.

37. Davis, *Long Goodbye,* 116–19, 172.

38. Davis, *Long Goodbye,* 146.

39. "Reagan Falls at Home, Breaks His Right Hip," *WP,* January 14, 2001, A21A; "Reagan Recovering at Hospital after Surgery for Broken Hip," *WP,* January 14, 2001, A2; "Reagan Goes Home after Hip Surgery," *WP,* January 21, 2001, A10; Deaver, *Nancy,* 204.

40. Deaver, *Nancy,* 203–5.

41. Davis, *Long Goodbye,* 13.

42. "Nancy Reagan Calls for Stem Cell Research," *WP,* May 10, 2004, A2.

43. Davis, *Long Goodbye,* 184–94; Reagan, *My Father,* 222.

44. "Former President Reagan Dies at 93," *LAT,* June 6, 2004, A1.

45. Davis, *Long Goodbye,* 194.

46. "Death of President Ronald Wilson Reagan (4:50 PM E.T.–10:00 PM E.T.)," CNN, June 5, 2004, YouTube, https://www.youtube.com/watch?v=HxtQSBv24_g&t=313s.

47. "Special Report" introduction, *ABC News Transcripts* (7:00 PM ET), June 5, 2004.

48. *Fox News,* June 5, 2004.

49. "Death of President Ronald Wilson Reagan."

50. Morris, *Dutch,* 579.

51. "Death of Former President Ronald Reagan," *CBS News Transcripts* (4:50 ET), June 5, 2004.

52. *Public Papers of the Presidents of the United States: Ronald Reagan, 1984,* I (Washington, DC: Government Printing Office, 1986), 817.

53. "Death of President Ronald Wilson Reagan."

54. *Larry King Live,* CNN, June 5, 2004, https://www.youtube.com/watch?v=7ORxyZ8oOSI.

55. "Reagan Dies," CNN Transcripts, June 5, 2004.

56. "'Goodbye Gipper': How U.S. Newspapers Covered the Death of Ronald Reagan," *WP,* June 5, 2014, https://www.washingtonpost.com/news/post-nation/wp/2014/06/05 /goodbye-gipper-how-u-s-newspapers-covered-the-death-of-ronald-reagan/.

57. "Ronald Reagan, Revolutionary," *Chicago Tribune* (hereafter *CT*), June 6, 2004, 8.

58. Lou Cannon, "Actor, Governor, President, Icon," *WP,* June 6, 2004, A1.

59. "Ronald Wilson Reagan," *WP,* June 6, 2004, B6.

60. "Former President Reagan Dies at 93," *LAT,* June 6, 2004, A1.

61. "Ronald Reagan Dies at 93," *NYT,* June 6, 2004, N1.

62. "Ronald Reagan," *NYT,* June 7, 2004, A26.

63. "After a Long Struggle, Gipper Is Dead at 93," *New York Daily News,* June 6, 2004, 2.

64. "Ronald Wilson Reagan, 1911–2004," *New York Daily News,* June 6, 2004, 42.

65. Schlesinger, "Operation Serenade"; "Down to the Last Detail, a Reagan-Style Funeral," *NYT,* June 8, 2004, A1; Craig Shirley, *Last Act: The Final Years and Enduring Legacy of Ronald Reagan* (Nashville: Nelson Books, 2015), 64–66, 74.

66. "Down to the Last Detail, a Reagan-Style Funeral"; "LBJ's 1973 Funeral to Be Model for Farewell to 40th President," *WP,* June 6, 2004, A32.

67. "The Reagan Legacy," *LAT,* June 7, 2004, A1.

68. "A Nation and the World Pay Tribute to Reagan," *WP,* June 7, 2004, A1; "First a Private Farewell, Then a Public Outpouring," *NYT,* June 8, 2004, A23; "Funeral Home Departure," *CBS News,* June 8, 2004, https://www.cbsnews.com/pictures/funeral-home -departure/; Schlesinger, "Operation Serenade."

69. *NBC Nightly News Reports*–Death of President Reagan, June 7, 8, 2004, YouTube, https://www.youtube.com/watch?v=OzFNCP6iLbE&t=1640s.

70. Shirley, *Last Act,* 112.

71. *NBC Nightly News Reports*–Death of President Reagan.

72. "Washington Heat Wilts the Waiting," *NYT,* June 10, 2004, A20.

73. "A Somber Procession of Present and Past," *WP,* June 10, 2004, A21.

74. "An American Journey," *WP,* June 10, 2004, VAB9.

75. "The Capital Pays Homage to 'a Graceful and Gallant Man,'" *NYT,* June 10, 2004, A20; Reagan State Funeral Ceremony, June 9, 2004, C-SPAN, https://www.c-span.org/video /?182164-1/reagan-state-funeral-ceremony.

76. "The Capital Pays Homage to 'a Graceful and Gallant Man.'"

77. "Lying in State for Former President Reagan," June 11, 2004, U.S. Capitol Police, https://www.uscp.gov/media-center/press-releases/lying-state-former-president -reagan; Shirley, *Last Act,* 239.

78. *NBC Nightly News Reports*–Death of President Reagan.

79. "An American Journey," *WP,* June 10, 2004, VAB9.

80. "100,000, One by One, Pay Tribute to a President," *NYT,* June 9, 2004, A1.

81. "A Tangible Grief," *WP,* June 8, 2004, C1.

82. "After Long Distances and Long Waits, Everyday Admirers Say Their Goodbyes," *NYT,* June 11, 2004, A24; "Showing Their Affection One Final Time," *WP,* June 11, 2004, A28.

83. Kathleen Parker, "Reagan's Recipe for Presidential Greatness," *CT,* June 9, 2004, 1: 31; Marc Fisher, "Rosy Outlook Hid Ugly Facts from Reagan," *WP,* June 8, 2004, MDB1; George F. Will, "An Optimist's Legacy," *WP,* June 6, 2004, B7; "Critics See a Reagan Legacy Tainted by AIDS, Civil Rights, and Union Policies," *NYT,* June 9, 2004, A20.

84. David Ignatius, "Protean Leader," *WP,* June 8, 2004, A23; Stephen J. Hedges, "His Military Successes Had a Price," *CT,* June 10, 2004, 1, 19.

85. Robert J. Samuelson, "Unsung Triumph," *WP,* June 9, 2004; Paul Krugman, "An Economic Legend," *NYT,* June 11, 2004, A27.

86. *NBC Nightly News Reports*–Death of President Reagan.

87. "With Fears about Terrorism, Security Measures Multiply," *NYT,* June 8, 2004; "The Capital Pays Homage to 'a Graceful and Gallant Man'"; "False Alarm Over Unidentified Plane Tested Emergency Response," *WP,* June 11, 2004, A28; "Reagan Team, a Bit Grayer, Gathers Again," *NYT,* June 10, 2004.

88. "Reagan Team, a Bit Grayer, Gathers Again"; "Reagan Hailed as Leader for 'the Ages,'" *WP*, June 12, 2004, A1.

89. "Reagan Hailed as Leader for 'the Ages'"; "An Era's Icons Fill Cathedral to Mourn," *NYT*, June 12, 2004, A1; The State Funeral of Ronald Reagan, CNN, June 11, 2004, https://www .youtube.com/watch?v=FhIxybSILTw; "Presidential Funerals," Washington National Cathedral, https://cathedral.org/history/prominent-services/presidential-funerals/.

90. Private Funeral of Ronald Reagan, June 11, 2004, CNN, https://www.youtube.com /watch?v=cAaBKhSg6m8; "Reagan Buried at His Library," *LAT*, June 12, 2004, A1; Schlesinger, "Operation Serenade."

91. "Down to the Last Detail, a Reagan-Style Funeral."

92. Private Funeral of Ronald Reagan; Davis, *Long Goodbye*, 197.

93. Shirley, *Last Act*, 284, 294–96.

94. "Reagan Is Entombed in California," *NYT*, June 13, 2004, N36.

95. "A Sunset Ceremony Filled with Memories," *NYT*, June 12, 2004, A10; "Reagan Presidential Library Dedication," November 4, 1991, C-SPAN, https://www.c-span.org/video /?22610-1/reagan-presidential-library-dedication/.

96. "Second Highway Named for Reagan," *CT*, June 9, 2004, 1.22; "Have You Got Two Reagans for a Twenty?" *NYT*, June 9, 2004, A20.

97. Iwan Morgan, *Reagan: American Icon* (London: I. B. Taurus, 2016), 324–35; About the Ronald Reagan Legacy Project, http://www.ronaldreaganlegacyproject.org/about/; "Have You Got Two Reagans for a Twenty?"

98. Chester Pach, "How Do Historians Assess Ronald Reagan?" History News Network, https://historynewsnetwork.org/article/341/.

99. Chester J. Pach, "Reputation and Legacies: An American Symbol," in *A Companion to Ronald Reagan*, ed. Andrew L. Johns (Malden, MA: Wiley Blackwell, 2015), 629, 637–40; Sean Wilentz, *The Age of Reagan: A History, 1974–2008* (New York: Harper, 2008), 286.

100. Pach, "Reputation and Legacies," 626.

101. Pach, "Reputation and Legacies," 627.

102. "Networks Fear Burnout of 'Wall to Wall' Story," *CT*, June 9, 2004, 1, 24; "Day after Day, Funeral Filled the Small Screen," *NYT*, June 12, 2004, A10.

103. "Day after Day, Funeral Filled the Small Screen."

104. "Special Report" introduction, June 9, 2004, *ABC News Transcripts;* Shirley, *Last Act*, 235–36.

105. "An American Journey," *WP*, June 10, 2004, VAB9.

106. Ronald Reagan, *An American Life* (New York: Pocket Books, 1990).

Mourning the Death of
George H. W. Bush

→ • ←

Warren Finch

THE PASSING OF FORMER presidents occurs with some frequency yet remains a significant historical event in the United States, especially when the individual lived a meaningful life after leaving office. The country shifts focus for a few days to remember their service and accomplishments, while historians and commentators discuss their legacy. Smaller communities to which the former president belonged often play a personal role in the mourning process. For former president George H. W. Bush, the communities in Houston, Texas; Kennebunkport, Maine; and Bryan/College Station, Texas, had become important parts of his postpresidential life. Although President Bush and former first lady Barbara Bush passed several years ago, those of us who were so privileged to have worked with them still miss them. I arrived in College Station in 1993 as planning for the future presidential library and museum was under way and for the next twenty-five years worked as an archivist, deputy director, and director.

The Love of a Community

As he considered a site for his presidential library, a special relationship developed between President Bush, Texas A&M University, and the greater Bryan/College Station area. President Bush was not a graduate of Texas A&M; he never lived in the community nor was the region in his congressional district when he served in Congress.[1] However, as he often said, he loved the "spirit of the place." The community and the university's enthusiastic reception of his presidential library contributed to this goodwill. Bush did not want the same experience as President Ronald Reagan—for years Reagan and those tasked with finding a home for the museum discussed and planned a presidential library for him at Stanford University, but ultimately the Reagan Foundation selected a site elsewhere.[2]

Over the years, College Station became President and Mrs. Bush's second home in Texas. They had their own apartment and offices in the Presidential Conference Center space adjacent to the museum. Mrs. Bush walking their dogs was the first sign that they had arrived on campus. For a university whose highest-ranking cadet, Reveille, happens to be a dog, it was a natural fit. The Bushes frequently visited the Texas A&M campus after his presidency ended, up to several times a month during the fall and winter, before their sojourn to Kennebunkport, where President Bush spent each summer of his life, save one.[3]

They attended football, basketball, and baseball games and the president used the university recreation center. An intern at the Bush Library shared once that when she was on an elliptical machine and "in the zone," she looked over to see the President Bush exercising next to her and nearly fell off her machine. The former first couple also walked the campus, and, in their later years, often used Segways or scooters. They loved to dine in local restaurants and to this day, there are pictures of them all over town in their favorite places, like Christopher's and Koppe Bridge, enjoying a meal.

Then there were the events. President Bush always had an idea for an event. Jean Becker, his postpresidential chief of staff, said that the words she feared hearing the most were "Jean, I have an idea." A long list of friends, former leaders, and people still involved in politics and public life visited the Presidential Library Center and presented programs or visited classes at the Bush School of Government and Public Service, including President Mikhail Gorbachev of the Soviet Union, British Prime Ministers Tony Blair and John Major, President Barack Obama, Senator Edward Kennedy, and Congresswoman Nancy Pelosi. Many were recipients of an award created by the president, the George Bush Award for Excellence in Public Service.[4]

The president also became well known for his parachute jumps. President Bush parachute jumped at the library for his seventy-fifth and eightieth birthdays, and for the tenth anniversary of the opening of the museum in 2007. As Mrs. Bush once said, it was a great way to go "one way or another." He enjoyed skydiving, but there was also a serious reason for his first jump at age seventy-two. During World War II, while bailing out of a crashing Avenger, he pulled his chute too soon and hit his head on the tail of the aircraft as the chute caught wind and dragged him out. He always wanted a chance to do it the right way and kept on making jumps to prove that "old guys didn't just have to sit around drooling."

Mrs. Bush was also a beloved figure in both local and national spaces in the years after her husband's presidency. She was widely celebrated and is still remembered for her contribution and fierce dedication to the literacy movement. The Barbara Bush Foundation for Family Literacy raised millions to promote literacy for both children and adults. As Mrs. Bush pointedly told me after I once mistakenly introduced her as a promoter of children's literacy, it was just as important that parents and adults learn to read so that they could pass along the skill to their children in the home.

Every year she hosted a program at the Bush Library promoting literacy for local schools. Usually, a famous children's author read a book and then several children read to each other on stage, followed by a question-and-answer session for Mrs. Bush. In addition to the 600-plus students, teachers, and parents in the audience, it was not uncommon to have hundreds of schools across the country connected via a teleconferencing network. Typically, over one hundred thousand people joined live, and many more watched the program recordings. One year, a group of schoolchildren from Guinea in western Africa connected and asked Mrs. Bush a question.

Locating the Library

In 1988, shortly after the election, President-elect Bush summoned many friends to the White House to discuss energy policy, and the idea of putting the Library and Museum in College Station was born. Michel T. Halbouty, a Texas oilman and a graduate of Texas A&M (and whose name the Petroleum Engineering Department Building bears), was present at the meeting. Halbouty proposed that the president-elect locate his future presidential library

and museum at Texas A&M. Bush responded that that decision was prema-
ture as he was not even president yet. Halbouty offered to see what the folks
at the university thought of the idea and asked for permission to pursue
it. President Bush gave a qualified yes to this proposal, if the administration at Texas A&M understood that it was too soon to make a definite decision. Halbouty agreed and traveled to College Station—where the university
embraced the idea.

A committee, including Halbouty, was formed by the Texas A&M University chancellor to begin work on a proposal and the president was invited
to give an address for the Texas A&M University Spring Commencement.
By the time President Bush arrived in College Station in May 1989, a three-
dimensional model of the future presidential library and museum was on
display at the Memorial Student Center for him to consider. Halbouty had
an ace in his coat pocket and took out the presidential election box returns
for the three universities in Texas vying for the Bush Library.[5] Only at Texas
A&M had a majority voted for Bush. Halbouty asked President Bush if that
made a difference and the president responded that it did indeed.[6]

In the second year of his administration, President Bush decided to place
his future presidential library at Texas A&M, which was earlier in his term
than any of his predecessors. In 1992 President Bush lost his bid for reelection to Bill Clinton, and the National Archives scrambled to prepare to
transport the artifacts and records to College Station. As the materials were
housed in a temporary facility in College Station, plans for the future library
and museum began to materialize.

Universal Exhibits was hired to design and install the museum exhibits
that interpreted the Bushes' impressive life of public service, in consultation
with the National Archives staff at the library. Universal Exhibits decided
and the library staff agreed to interpret their lives in a linear fashion beginning with the president's early life and family, to his service in World War II,
and through his very active life after his presidency. The staff consulted the
Bushes as staff developed exhibit plans, but typically they deferred to the
experts and made corrections to text and exhibits as necessary. The only
hiccup was a TBM Avenger, the same model Bush had flown in the war,
which was donated to the museum after the building was almost completed.
The staff of the Bush Library, riggers from the Naval Aviation Museum in

Pensacola, and the structural engineer were unsure that the plane would fit into the building, and that it could be safely hung from the ceiling. Fortunately, the structural engineer proclaimed that the roof would support the weight and it would deflect one-quarter of an inch. When asked what would happen if the roof buckled more than a quarter inch, there was silence.

Later, an Oval Office was also added to the museum. The original plans didn't include an Oval Office; the former president felt that it was unnecessary as every other presidential museum had a replica Oval Office. Bush opted instead to include his office at Camp David which he had used extensively to meet world leaders. He preferred a more relaxed and intimate setting, but an Oval Office was eventually added at visitors' requests.

President and Mrs. Bush immediately felt at home in College Station. Originally, the Bushes were going to be buried near their church in Kennebunkport, Maine. They picked out plots, but after they attended the funeral of President Richard Nixon in 1994, at his childhood home and presidential library in Yorba Linda, California, they decided they wanted to be buried at their Presidential Library.[7] They made the decision three years before the Bush Library was completed, so their wishes were incorporated into the landscaping of the grounds of the library. A secluded spot across a stream and footbridge, about a five-minute walk from the museum entrance, was chosen for the gravesite. A few years after the Bush Library opened, the President and Mrs. Bush had the remains of their daughter Pauline Robinson "Robin" Bush, who had died of leukemia just before her fourth birthday, moved from her burial place in Connecticut to the family gravesite in College Station.[8] In a private burial, she was reinterred between what would be the final resting places of her mother and father.[9] Over the years, the Barbara Bush Garden was created around the pond. The garden incorporated antique roses and became a place to visit and reflect.

The Funeral Plan

As the former president and first lady's health began to deteriorate, planning for their funerals accelerated.[10] The three entities of the Bush Center, the Bush Library, and the Bush Foundation, as well as Texas A&M, were involved in this planning process. Logistics staff from Union Pacific were also included in those conversations. The US Military District of Washington, an organization tasked with planning and executing the official state funeral events for former presidents, coordinated this planning.

These plans were added to a huge binder. The binder contained the details for what would happen every day for the seven days immediately following the president's death. This plan was premised on the president's wishes and the needs of his family, friends, and the public to mourn his passing, as well as the protocols dictated by the Military District for a state funeral. The plan called for a small service at St. Anne's Episcopal in Kennebunkport if he died in Maine, followed by his body lying in state in the Capitol Rotunda, a service at the National Cathedral in Washington, DC, and then another service in Houston at St. Martin's Episcopal, where the president and Mrs. Bush were longtime members, and finally burial at the Bush Center gravesite.

In the early years, there were periodic meetings about these funeral plans.[11] As the pair aged, and especially after the president developed a case of bronchitis in early 2017 and spent several days in the hospital, these meetings became more frequent. The plan for the president's passing spelled out what would happen each day of the funeral, and what we needed to do to prepare. Details ranged from the seemingly mundane—feeding everyone who would be working the days leading up to the burial—to the very important, such as security for former presidents and other VIPs who would attend some or all funeral services.

One of the most interesting elements of the funeral planning centered on a train that had originally come to the Bush Library as part of a museum exhibit. In 2004, the library and museum planned an exhibit on American railroads, and the impact of railroads on the United States' culture and economy. The exhibit was the brainchild of Dr. Robert Holzweiss, the Bush Library's supervisory archivist, who had completed a PhD dissertation on the Penn Central Railroad. I traveled to Omaha, Nebraska, with Holzweiss and Roman Popaduik, the Bush Foundation director, to obtain Union Pacific's support and artifacts for the exhibit, and a caboose for display outdoors. Richard Davidson, then CEO at Union Pacific, not only offered a caboose but also a new locomotive. He proposed that the locomotive be painted in the color scheme of *Air Force One*, numbered 4141 after the forty-first president, and unveiled in a ceremony near the library for the opening of the exhibit. It was displayed on a sidetrack near the football field during the exhibit, and later traveled the country as part of the Union Pacific fleet as a rolling billboard for the museum. President Bush was thrilled with the locomotive and had the idea of using the locomotive to pull a funeral train from Houston to College Station for his interment. Union Pacific agreed and after a year on the tracks, the 4141 locomotive was put into storage at a UP facility in Little Rock, Arkansas, for what would become a long wait.

At this point, much of the focus was on President Bush's funeral plans; then Mrs. Bush's health began to deteriorate rapidly. After their return from Kennebunkport in the fall of 2017, it was clear that she was not well, but she continued to keep up a reduced schedule of events and was at the Bush Center in March 2018, just a month before her death on April 17. In the middle of a Bush Center event that evening, key people in the theater received calls from the Bush staff in Houston and exited the theater. The program continued and those who had left rejoined the postprogram dinner. The dean of the Bush School, Mark Welsh, made the announcement that Mrs. Bush had died and gave a short tribute to her, and the dinner continued as Mrs. Bush would have wanted. Behind the scenes, her funeral plan commenced. As the doors opened the next day, the last touches were placed on her memorial exhibit in the museum rotunda. Visitors streamed through the doors for the next two days and signed the condolence books, after which the Bush Library was closed for two days. The first day of closure permitted the Secret Service to secure the facilities and permit a run-through of the funeral movements without the public and the media present to photograph or record the practice. On the second day, the library remained closed for Mrs. Bush's interment.

One of the highlights of Mrs. Bush's (and later, her husband's) funeral were the scrapbooks that she had kept since the very early years of their marriage. In 100 books of various sizes, Mrs. Bush had created a sizable record of every aspect of their lives, both public and private. These scrapbooks and the memories they contained appeared in news stories across the country. They provided insight on seventy-three years of marriage and were an uplifting reminder during the periods of mourning that the two had enjoyed a very long and happy life together. They also documented their impressive public life. Mrs. Bush preserved programs from White House events, state dinner menus signed by those who had sat at Mrs. Bush's table, and other historic mementos.

Mrs. Bush was quick to tell you she had created the scrapbooks herself and the evidence on the page spoke for itself. She had annotated each page by hand, and many of photos were her own, especially those from the later years. Mrs. Bush was famous for carrying around a small digital camera and snapping pictures. One of the more poignant reminders of their great love story captured in the scrapbooks was the wishbone from one of their first Thanksgivings together as a married couple. She had sealed it in an envelope and written the names of the small group of guests who had attended the meal in 1946 while they were still at Yale.[12]

Mrs. Bush laid in repose on April 20, at St. Martin's Episcopal Church in Houston, where President Bush would have his own Houston funeral later that year. Then on April 21, after the funeral at St. Martin's, the casket and body made their way to College Station where a private burial took place on the grounds of the Bush Presidential Center. All along the highway from Houston to College Station, large groups of people gathered to mourn the former first lady. As the family followed the hearse in several vehicles, they waved at the crowds and were visibly moved by the outpouring of emotion. Once the hearse arrived in College Station, the roads along the way to the Bush Library were flanked with local people saying their last goodbyes.

From a practical standpoint, Mrs. Bush's death served as a trial run for the president's funeral—albeit with fewer days, no train, and no funeral in DC. For us at the Bush Library and Museum, we corrected mistakes and oversights for which we had not prepared.

The arrival of many media personnel was the biggest surprise. The Bush Library staff assumed that much of the preparation by the media was completed ahead of time but did not account for the number of live stories covered by news crews in town. Nearly two of the museum's parking lots were taken up entirely by media trucks and a photo and camera platform constructed for the event.[13] Because the Bushes had been public figures for many years, and had been active after they left office, there was great interest in their lives and deaths.

The Bushes had been a part of so many communities, Kennebunkport in Maine, Houston, Midland/Odessa, and College Station in Texas, that media from Maine to Kuwait arrived. During the president's days in office, networks and CNN existed, but the increase in other news outlets and the twenty-four-hour news cycle increased funeral coverage. To meet the media demand, the audiovisual archivist spent two days preparing additional audiovisual materials and showing Mrs. Bush's scrapbooks to reporters. For the president's funeral, we revamped the media plan.

The Death of President Bush

The next month, the former president's health began to fail, and when he left Houston for Kennebunkport, Maine, his doctors told Jean Becker, the president's chief of staff, that they did not believe he would leave Maine alive. Toward the end of summer, Becker and Evan Sisley, President Bush's aide, sat down with him to ask about his wishes. They explained that they could remain in Maine if he wished. The president astutely inquired if they were asking him where he wanted to die, and then stated that he was going to go home. He had made the decision to die in Houston, Texas—his adopted home—which he did on November 30, 2018.[14]

On December 3, his body was transported from Houston to Washington, DC, aboard *Air Force One*. The tradition of transporting the body of the former president aboard *Air Force One* began with former President Lyndon Johnson. President Richard Nixon sent the presidential aircraft to bring Johnson's body back to Washington for his state funeral in 1973. Former Presidents Ronald Reagan and Gerald Ford were also transported to Washington for their funerals; however, Presidents Nixon and Harry Truman opted not to have state funerals.[15]

Mike Wagner, the chief of national planning, called on the Department of Defense for the use of the plane. The ceremonial arrivals and departures of the casket were conducted by a joint military escort. Not all the people who had worked with President Bush in various jobs throughout his career in business and politics could attend the actual funerals, but these movements gave them a special opportunity to bid farewell, including Bush's Secret Service detail and the Golden Knights parachute team. The Golden Knights had trained the president for his first parachute jump in Arizona on March 25, 1997, and had participated in each jump thereafter.

The president lay in state in the Capitol Rotunda from the evening of December 3 through the morning of December 5. Thousands of people paid their respects to President Bush, but none were more moving than Senator Robert Dole, who at times had been a political rival of the former president. With some help from his aide, Senator Dole stood up from his wheelchair and saluted President Bush. The poignant scene was replayed repeatedly in the days to follow—two old soldiers, each returned from World War II scarred. One was a veteran of the European Theater, who lost the use of his right hand, and the other of the War in the Pacific, who was forever traumatized by the loss of his two crewmen at Chichi-Jima. Dole and Bush had last seen each other in College Station on December 7, 2016, the seventy-fifth anniversary of the attack at Pearl Harbor. Dole had been the president's choice to receive the George Bush Award for Excellence in Public Service that year and it was the last award ceremony the president attended before his death. They reminisced about old times and joked about their past and cried next to each other, both in wheelchairs on stage.

All through the night into the next day visitors arrived, from President Donald Trump and First Lady Melania Trump to former cabinet members, friends, family, and the public. Public esteem for the former president had grown in the years since he left office. He had become the elder statesman and people wanted to mourn, to say goodbye, thank him, and pay their respects. He had not been reelected for a second term, having been turned out by a newer generation that had not served in World War II. But as time went on, his accomplishments had been recognized and treated with greater admiration, including the North American Free Trade Agreement, which was passed shortly after he left office in 1993. During his time in office the Cold War ended peacefully, the Berlin Wall fell, Germany was reunified, and the first Gulf War was a success. Perhaps his most his enduring legacy is the Americans with Disabilities Act. Although not always harmonious, the Bush administration worked with a Congress that was controlled by the opposition party to reach these accomplishments. Bush knew and counted among his friends politicians from both sides of the aisle. Bush entered Congress at a time when politicians did not fly home each weekend, and the political community was much more intimate. As one former member of Congress said, "It was hard to call your fellow member a SOB when you were both leaders of the local Boy Scout group which included your sons."[16]

Bush had worked with Bill Clinton, the man who had defeated him in 1992 and denied him a second term, on important humanitarian missions. Bush put any hard feelings about the defeat behind him, and he and Clinton became good friends, providing an example to Americans and observers across the globe that politics could be set aside for the greater good. They helped raise millions of dollars in aid for hurricane relief, earthquake relief, and they traveled to Asia after the tsunami that devastated coastal areas. This friendship across political lines, in contrast to the polarizing political climate at the end of Bush's life, inspired a feeling of nostalgia. People longed for the time when the two parties could work together, and governing officials appeared capable of getting things done. By embracing this bipartisan spirit, Bush became what Jon Meacham titled the prologue of his biography of President Bush, "The Last Gentleman."[17]

On the morning of December 5, President Bush's body was transported to Washington National Cathedral for the national funeral service. The Office of George Bush worked to seat as many as possible. Although the National Cathedral has a capacity of 4,000 seats, many of those seats were already claimed. Protocol required that a certain number of seats went to members of the House and Senate. Only former senior members of Bush's White House staff received a seat in the church. The president had such a large family, and so many friends and former colleagues, that there were not enough places in either church to hold everyone that should be invited. Staff decided that those east of the Mississippi would go to the service at the National Cathedral and those west of the Mississippi would attend the funeral in Houston.

President Bush had selected the service and speakers. Several grandchildren offered readings. Ronan Tynan, who had often been called on to entertain guests for the former president and had sung at the president's eightieth birthday, sang several of the hymns. A delegation of the crew from the USS *George H. W. Bush,* including all the captains of the ship and the admirals of the Bush Strikeforce, were the honorary pallbearers.

The speakers chosen for the funeral were people who had been close to President Bush and gave attendees and those watching on television a sense of the magnitude of the man. Historian Jon Meacham and President George W. Bush delivered the eulogies. Dr. Russell J. Levenson, the rector of St. Martin's in Houston, offered the homily. Brian Mulroney, one of his closest friends, who served as prime minister of Canada while Bush was president, gave a moving tribute.

Former senator Alan Simpson's tribute may have best summed up how the president's family and friends felt about his death.[18]

> You would have wanted him on your side. He never lost his sense of humor. Humor is the universal solvent against the abrasive elements of life. That's what humor is. He never hated anyone. He knew what his mother and my mother always knew. Hatred corrodes the container it's carried in.
>
> The most decent and honorable person I ever met was my friend George Bush, one of nature's noblemen. His epitaph, perhaps just a single letter: the L for loyalty. It coursed through his blood, loyalty to his country, loyalty to his family, loyalty to his friends, loyalty to the institutions of government and always, always, always a friend to his friends.
>
> He was a man of such grace, humility, those who travel the high road of humility in Washington, DC, are not bothered by heavy traffic.

After the emotional service at the National Cathedral, the body was transported from Washington, DC, to Andrews Air Force Base for the final journey back home to Texas aboard *Air Force One*. Family and friends joined the former president's body on the plane. On its way to Houston, *Air Force One* made an unplanned, slow low circle around the Bush Center where a crowd waved goodbye. The president's body arrived in Houston on the evening of December 5 and was taken to St. Martin's Episcopal Church to lay in repose overnight. Thousands passed through St. Martin's to pay their respects that night.

Texas Says Goodbye

The funeral at St. Martin's took place the next morning. Dr. Levenson conducted the traditional Episcopalian service and gave the homily. James Baker, "Bake" as Bush called him, eulogized the president. Baker and Bush were longtime friends, beginning in the 1960s.[19] Baker spoke of their friendship and President Bush's many accomplishments. George P. Bush, President

Bush's oldest grandchild and Texas land commissioner, also gave a moving tribute. He said that the man he knew as Gampy "was the most gracious, most decent, most humble man that I will ever know." Several granddaughters of President Bush also shared readings and prayers. The Oak Ridge Boys sang "Amazing Grace" and Reba McEntire sang "The Lord's Prayer." The honorary pallbearers included officials from Texas A&M and the dean of the Bush School, the Bush Foundation director, and myself as the director of the Presidential Library and Museum.

After the funeral, a hearse transported President Bush's body to Spring, a town near Houston, where Union Pacific had a railhead and yard. Union Pacific brought the 4141 locomotive, along with several passenger and service cars, from its heritage fleet in Omaha, Nebraska. The passenger cars carried close family and friends on the approximately ninety-mile journey to a prepared railroad crossing in College Station on the university campus. Union Pacific had modified a baggage car and painted it in a red, white, and blue color scheme and cut large windows on each side. The president's flag-draped coffin sat on a raised pedestal in the car and was clearly visible to all along the way.

President Bush had loved traveling by train and did a couple of whistle-stop tours on a train during the 1988 and 1992 campaigns. In 1988, he traveled through Missouri and Illinois with a stop in St. Louis, and in 1992 he campaigned in Wisconsin, Michigan, Ohio, Georgia, and North and South Carolina.[20] After his presidency, he organized a train trip though the West Coast at the invitation of Union Pacific and brought his grandkids Gigi and Robert. He used a sleeper car because he believed everyone should spend the night on a train. The staff always tried to work a train into major events whenever possible.[21] Prior to his passing, Bush told his chief of staff Jean Becker that it would be a perfect way to go to the funeral. "They could all eat lunch on the train," the president said, but as Becker pointed out to him, "you won't be eating lunch." Well, he responded, he'd "still be there."[22] Dick Davidson, the CEO of Union Pacific, helped fulfill one of the president's final wishes.

The train departed Spring for the slow journey to College Station. Tens of thousands of mourners greeted this unique procession. In small towns like Magnolia and Hempstead, mourners placed coins on the tracks so that when the 4141 rolled over them they would be flattened as mementos of the

FIGURE 11. Funeral of President George H. W. Bush in College Station, Texas, December 6, 2018. (Photo by Grant Miller. Courtesy of the George and Barbara Bush Foundation)

day. Others carried with them American and Texas flags and sat on horse-back along the tracks in the fields in between towns as the train passed. I was with the group of honorary pallbearers and Texas A&M officials who had attended the Houston service, and we took a bus to College Station so we could meet the train when it arrived. The bus paralleled the train tracks in many places along the route. We were amazed by the size of the crowds and the homemade banners. The crowds held signs of all kinds, which said things like "Thank you," "God Bless You," "Texas Loves You." As the procession approached College Station, the crowds grew even larger.

Once the train pulled into College Station, a joint military guard removed the casket onto a platform specially constructed for the occasion. Members of the Ross Volunteers, an elite unit within the Texas A&M Corps of Cadets, stood at attention in their crisp white uniforms as the body was transferred to a hearse. The Singing Cadets, the renowned university chorus, sang several hymns. Due to the somberness of the moment, the audience was shocked when the University Band struck up the very upbeat "Aggie War Hymn." The hymn broke the tension and thousands of attendees spontaneously cheered—a sight the president would have loved.

After the body was loaded into the hearse, it made the short trip to the George Bush Presidential Library and Museum for the private burial. Media coverage showed the procession entering the grounds and down the driveway flanked by members of the Corps of Cadets standing at attention. The coverage ended as the hearse stopped and the procession moved toward the gravesite. An unprecedented flyover of twenty-one Navy F-18 Hornets was performed at the conclusion of the ceremony to honor the president as a former Navy pilot. It was the largest single flyover ever performed at a funeral. The aircraft also performed a missing man formation. The band played "Taps," and the soldiers fired a twenty-one-gun salute. The president was officially laid to rest next to his wife and daughter with a simple service cross. It was inscribed "George Bush, LTJG 17344, 41st President of the United States."[23]

Mourning at the George Bush Presidential Library and Museum

The George Bush Presidential Library and Museum was a focus of the public's mourning of both the president and the first lady. Long before their deaths, the planning for a memorial exhibit for each of them in the rotunda got under way. A collection of large portraits hung from the ceiling around the rotunda to document their lives. Many of Mrs. Bush's photos illustrated her life of service, her work advocating for literacy, and her love of family. The portraits of the former president highlighted his extensive resumé including photos of him as a child, in his Navy uniform, a congressional photo, at the United Nations, as head of the Republican National Committee, as US liaison to China, as director of Central Intelligence, as vice president, and as president.

Instead of black mourning bunting, staff decorated the rotunda with red, white, and blue bunting, much like what you might see on the Fourth of July. A large American flag hung in the center of the rotunda. A portrait stood on a base in the rotunda, flanked by flowers with and large condolence books in front of the portraits to give mourners an opportunity to leave condolence messages.

The portrait chosen for Mrs. Bush had been painted by Chas Fagan and was one of her favorites.[24] For President Bush, we chose the portrait by Ron

Sherr, which normally hung next to Mrs. Bush's at the beginning of the museum's permanent gallery. He liked this portrait, and it was similar to the one hanging in the Hall of Presidents at the National Portrait Gallery in Washington, DC.

For the first two days following the president's death, the Bush Library and Museum were open and overwhelmed with visitors. Each visitor received a poster-sized copy of the president's official portrait, and the pallet of photos was quickly depleted. The next day, the research room and museum closed to prepare for the president's burial on December 6.[25] Over five thousand people visited the museum itself on December 8, and countless more traveled to the gravesite to pay their respects. The memoriam exhibit with the condolence books and portrait stayed in the rotunda for several months. The Bush Foundation contracted with a media company to compile coverage of the funeral services into a ten-minute video, which focused on the arrival ceremony in College Station. The film was placed in the rotunda of the museum with the rest of the exhibit and played on a loop.

Extensive audiovisual materials were loaded onto the library's and the Bush Foundation's webpages and social media pages in anticipation of an onslaught of media attention after the president's death. Over the years larger newspapers, such as the *New York Times* and the *Houston Chronicle,* contacted the library for materials on which to build obituaries and articles for publication. Leading up to their deaths, various networks and news channels also requested both textural and audiovisual materials of the president and former first lady. Camera crews visited frequently in these later years to shoot B-roll footage. Learning from Mrs. Bush's funeral, the library staff was better prepared for the onslaught of media requests.

A New Exhibit

The museum staff collected memorabilia from the various funerary services as work began on a permanent exhibit to document the presidential funeral and national grieving process. In the following weeks, materials arrived at the library from all over the country, illustrating the various tributes to the president, including shell casings from the twenty-one-gun salutes fired by military units across the country, the empty shell casings from the twenty-one-gun salute performed during the private burial at the museum gravesite, the condolence books from Blair House signed by President and Mrs. Trump, and the condolence books from Washington National Cathedral and St. Martin's in Houston. These books joined the museum's condolence books, which had been placed in the rotunda for visitors to sign.[26] The crew of the USS *George H. W. Bush* made a ship's wheel and presented it to the museum, and it was also placed in the exhibit. In April of 2019, the United States Postal Service announced the issuing of a George H. W. Bush commemorative stamp. The exhibit also included the artwork for the stamp, as well as a sheet of stamps once they were released.[27]

Shortly after Mrs. Bush's death in spring of 2018, President Bush had received a yellow Labrador retriever, Sully, for use as a service dog. Sully was supplied by American VetDogs, an organization that supplies dogs to veterans though a partnership with Walter Reed Army Medical Center. A photo of Sully lying in front of the president's casket made the national news during the funeral.[28] That photo, along with Sully's service vest, was included in the exhibit. On December 2, 2019, a life-sized bronze statue of Sully created by sculptor Susan Bahary was unveiled at the museum and placed in the exhibit. Other items included the drum light from the UP 4141, a cross-section of the track over which the UP 4141 had traveled, and the American flags that had flown over the White House and Capitol during the state funeral.

Thousands of people wrote letters expressing their condolences to the family. Many of those notes came directly to the museum and were forwarded to either the Office of George H. W. Bush in Houston, or the Office of George W. Bush in Dallas. Later, many of these letters were returned to the Bush Library and Museum and a sample was added to the permanent collection. Staff collected hundreds of artifacts left either at the gravesite or in front of the museum building and included them in the exhibit, including a photo of a large group of mourners greeting the president's train in Tomball, Texas.

In July 2019, the Bush Library and Museum curated the first exhibit since the president's death, entitled "Wit and Humor: American Political Cartoons." The exhibit included political cartoons from Thomas Nast, Bill Mauldin, Herbert Block (Herblock), Garry Trudeau, and Patrick Oliphant, and two cartoons by Marshall Ramsey, a nationally recognized syndicated cartoonist.[29] When Mrs. Bush died, he drew a cartoon of her entering heaven and being greeted by their daughter Robin. When President Bush died, Ramsey created a new cartoon of President Bush flying an Avenger to heaven, awaited by both Robin and Mrs. Bush.[30] After the exhibit closed, the two cartoons were added to the memorial exhibit.

Looking Forward

The mourning process continues at the Bush Center. With both Bushes now gone, we embarked on a new chapter in the life of the George Bush Presidential Library and Museum. Much of the orientation film that played for visitors and the audio tour of the museum featured their words. As we move forward, we are creating a new orientation film, which will use some of the archival footage we have recorded of President and Mrs. Bush over the years. The new film will reflect on their lives and include video from the funeral ceremonies and the burials in College Station, but it will also look forward and include their "legacies." The locomotive 4141 that brought the president to College Station for interment will have a place on the grounds of the museum as a permanent display. Much of the narrative around the 4141 will be about the funeral, but it will also be joined by one of the *Marine One* helicopters that the president flew. It was after exiting *Marine One* that the president uttered those now-famous words, "this aggression will not stand," and set into motion the events of the first Gulf War.

The president hated what he called the "L" word, which stands for legacy. Once, he had come home from a soccer game as a child and told his mother that he had scored three goals. She had scolded him, telling him that the "me word" was not important, it was how the team had performed. "George," she had told him, "no-one likes a braggadocio!" That lesson made a mark on his psyche. An early version of the museum did not include enough photos or speeches of the president. When we redesigned the museum for the tenth anniversary, we included more of the former president in his own words and photos. Much of the content came from the scrapbooks that Mrs. Bush had lovingly kept during their many years of marriage. Upon reopening the museum, the president walked through and commented that his mother would not approve because it was too much about him. Too much about his legacy.

Yet President Bush's legacy is a significant one. During his time in office, he had great successes in foreign policy. The Berlin Wall fell, Germany was reunified, and the Soviet Union dissolved without an international confrontation. He created a coalition of disparate nations to fight the first Gulf War. He worked with Democrats to make bipartisan deals on the federal budget, strengthen the Clean Air Act Amendments of 1990, and pass the Americans with Disabilities Act, a sweeping piece of legislation. In an age when many view politics as having become too confrontational, many Americans reflect on the Bush presidency as "a kinder and gentler" political era.

President Bush's life and legacy will continue to be interpreted through the millions of records and holdings at his presidential library. As archivists first began processing those records, President Bush requested that they open as soon as possible. He believed that these materials would be critical for an objective analysis of his presidency, and accessibility to those materials would benefit his legacy. The Bush archives includes thirty-eight million pages of textual records, two million photographs, and ten thousand video and film recordings. For more than twenty-five years, a dedicated team of archivists have processed and made these records available so that students, authors, documentary filmmakers, and others have access to a nearly complete account of the Bush Administration—warts and all. As director of the George Bush Presidential Library and Museum, it is my responsibility to make these records accessible to all, but it will be up to future historians and scholars to assess and evaluate the legacy of the forty-first president.

Notes

1. President Bush served as congressman for the Texas 7th Congressional District, which included sections of Houston and Harris County, from 1967 to 1971.
2. The Reagan Library and Museum is located in Simi Valley, CA, north of Los Angeles.
3. This exception was the year he served as a naval pilot in the Pacific during World War II.
4. President Bush created the George Bush Award for Excellence in Government Service shortly after the opening of the library. The award was given annually to world leaders, politicians, and others noted for public service.

5. In addition to Texas A&M, Rice and the University of Houston (both located in the president's adopted hometown of Houston) had shown interest in hosting the library.

6. Michel T. Halbouty, "Visions and Leadership in the Creation of the George Bush Library Center," John Miles Rowlett Lecture Series, Texas A&M University, College Station, TX, February 10, 1998.

7. Jean Becker, former Bush chief of staff, 1994–2018, telephone interview with author, January 18, 2021.

8. The family plot in Connecticut is where Prescott Bush Sr. and Dorothy Bush would later be buried.

9. Robin was reinterred on May 4, 2000.

10. Staff and family assumed that the president would die first, as his health seemed more precarious than hers.

11. Shortly after the president left office, the Washington Military District, which is the military division tasked with planning and executing presidential funerals, began visiting College Station periodically.

12. Barbara Bush donated the entire collection of scrapbooks to the Bush Library.

13. Every news crew wanted to do a live stand-up of their reporters and the archivist going through the scrapbooks.

14. Becker interview.

15. President John F. Kennedy's body was also transported to Washington, DC, from Dallas on *Air Force One* after his assassination.

16. Author's conversation with former congressman Chet Edwards, College Station, TX, 2008.

17. Jon Meacham, *Destiny and Power: The American Odyssey of George Herbert Walker Bush* (New York: Random House, 2015).

18. Simpson and Bush had been friends since Simpson's father Milward moved into the Senate office vacated by Bush's father Prescott.

19. Peter Baker and Susan Glasser, *The Man Who Ran Washington* (New York: Penguin Random House, 2020).

20. Union Pacific, "A Brief History of Trains and the U.S. Presidency" (2017), https://www .up.com/cs/groups/public/@uprr/@newsinfo/documents/up_pdf_nativedocs/pdf_up _media_rr_presidents.pdf. William McKinley, Theodore Roosevelt, William Howard Taft, Woodrow Wilson, Franklin Roosevelt, and Harry S. Truman all campaigned by train. Dwight Eisenhower was the last president to use trains for campaigning as Mamie was afraid to fly. However, President Johnson had Lady Bird campaign from Washington, DC, to New Orleans on the "Lady Bird Special" in 1964.

21. Jean Becker and Michelle Whelan, telephone interview with author, January 18, 2021.

22. Becker interview.

23. LTJG = Lieutenant Junior Grade. Photo of George Bush Presidential Gravesite, Flickr, https://www.flickr.com/photos/georgebushlibrary/50693509977/.

24. Mrs. Bush's portrait by Fagan was unveiled at the library's tenth anniversary.

25. The museum closed to allow for security preparations and to allow military units to rehearse and work though logistics.

26. The museum condolence books, which were large format, contained 591 pages of signatures.

27. The first day of issue was June 12, 2019, which would have been Bush's ninety-fifth birthday.
28. In February 2019, Sully was assigned to Walter Reed Military Hospital's Facility Dog Program.
29. "Wit and Humor: American Political Cartoons," exhibition at George H. W. Bush Presidential Library and Museum, July 15, 2019–January 5, 2020, https://www.bush41.org /exhibits/single-past?id=45.
30. Ramsey came to speak at the Bush Museum about the cartoons and his work and donated both originals to the collection.

Conclusion

Jeffrey A. Engel

MORTALITY BINDS US ALL. Even presidents of the United States, preponderantly powerful in most other circumstances, die. This point should not surprise, especially having read to this volume's conclusion. The Constitution imbues presidents with tremendous responsibility and authority. They are at once the federal government's chief executive, military commander-in-chief, principal diplomat, and most essential patronage dispenser, capable of shaping federal policy and the judiciary. The Constitution even enables presidents to pardon federal crimes, and thus to mete out justice.

Presidents cannot, however, overcome death. They wield the power to take life in a manner most societies throughout history would have considered supernatural, especially in the nuclear age. It wasn't always so. James Madison, one of the country's early presidents, could not safeguard his own capital from marauding foreign troops. Abraham Lincoln, its sixteenth, feared enemy soldiers might parade down Pennsylvania Avenue as well. That possibility was hard to fathom a century later, when American power in the world grew apace into the imperial presidency, whose nuclear war plans called for global annihilation well before a foreign invasion. "We are in the era of the thermonuclear bomb that can obliterate cities and can be delivered across continents," President Dwight Eisenhower explained in 1956. The world would likely burn before enemy boots touched the streets of Washington, DC, Eisenhower warned, even though he feared such concentration of power in one frail human's hands. "With such weapons," he said, "war has become, not just tragic, but preposterous."[1]

The breadth and scope of this unrivaled power helps explain why the reverence and remembrance of past presidents has taken on if not religious than at least imperial qualities far from the plain republican (please note the lower-case *r*) funeral the nation's first president desired. George Washington's successors could destroy the world. Yet they could not save themselves from death's inevitable toll. Indeed, death stalks every hall of the White House through the portraits of the president's predecessors. The more thoughtful minds engaged within its walls took time to contemplate the meaning of morality and time itself. "Death is always and under all circumstances a tragedy," Theodore Roosevelt opined mere months before an assassin's bullet elevated him to the presidency. It was also unavoidable. "But it is well to live bravely and joyously," Roosevelt thus concluded, "and to face the inevitable end without flinching when we go to join the men and tribes of immemorial."[2]

Living well meant, for the historically minded Roosevelt at least, living with an eye always cocked toward how future scribes might recall their current deeds, including their deaths. TR well understood that the length of a single life pales next to the lifespan of nation-states and civilizations, leaving any person a fleeting chance to make their mark. While some presidents might have found the realization of their puny importance unsettling, even despairing, Roosevelt found it motivating. He argued that "our history contains no name worth remembering of any man who led a life of ease."[3]

We remember and can name the two-score and more men who have held the title of president of the United States, and most have passed from this life. George H. W. Bush was the last one laid to rest, and our most recent data-point for evaluating how the nation mourns its lost leaders. Imperfect, Bush nonetheless lived as TR implored, pushing aside the ease of his lofty birth in pursuit of greater challenges. The last World War II veteran to occupy the Oval Office and the last president to oversee the Cold War, the congenitally optimistic Bush lived well into his ninth decade, yet rarely found time to ponder the past.

Six months after the Japanese attack on Pearl Harbor, Bush volunteered for military service, midway through his senior year of high school, far in advance of what his age, and his family's status, required. The war would last years, experienced mentors, including the sitting secretary of war, told

Bush. Boys like him should go to college, at least for a few years, before taking on responsibilities no child should bear.[4]

That wasn't fast enough for Bush. He could have frolicked on Yale University's leafy New Haven campus, but instead joined up for war in the South Pacific. A naval aviator, one of the youngest in the entire Pacific theater, he'd lost friends and comrades, and wrote too many condolence letters by September of 1944. He nearly required one himself. Shot down by enemy fire while on a bombing mission over the Japanese-held island of Chichi-Jima, Bush looked in vain for his two crewmates once he pulled himself, bloodied but alive, from the ocean into the small life-raft that inflated along with his parachute. He made it. They didn't. "The fact that our planes didn't seem to be searching anymore showed me pretty clearly that they had not gotten out," he wrote his parents after his rescue. "I'm afraid I was pretty much of a sissy about it cause I sat in my raft and sobbed for a while . . . I feel so terribly responsible for their fate."[5] He had just turned twenty-one.

After the war, he could have lounged through college, yet pursued an accelerated course, which led to a Phi Beta Kappa key in three years' time and inclusion in the university's most venerable secret society. He could have accepted a cushy job in his father's New York City investment firm but set out for the West Texas oil patch with a frenetic energy to crowd out quieter thoughts and memories. "George lives his life in chapters, like a lot of Bushes do," his sister once remarked of her brother's attitude after leaving the navy at World War II's end. "The war was over, and he left it behind. Some people had trouble doing that. George didn't."[6] He'd seen enough of death during his combat tours and sat next to enough empty chairs at dinner that had been occupied the breakfast to know that comfort was fleeting. He rarely talked about the war later, leaving it to others to remind voters of his military record, and leaving his own biographers grasping for details when he clammed up about this part of his past.

Those painful war memories resurfaced once American pilots flew into combat under his command during the first Gulf War in 1991. "I see the faces of the young pilots [saying] 'Let us go; let us do our job; we can do it,'" Bush wrote in his diary. "Then the Marines and the Army guys—young, young, so very young." He read letters that came into the White House as the military conflict loomed, especially those written by parents with children in harm's way. "All of them saying, 'take care of my kid'; some saying, 'please don't shoot'; some saying 'it's not worth dying for gasoline,' and on and on it goes; but the cry is, 'Save my boy, save my boy.'"[7] He'd seen the look in parents' eyes before. When he left for his own basic training fifty years before he saw his father cry for the first time.[8]

Such stories from Bush's wartime service rebounded after his 2018 death, flattening his personal narrative while allowing commentators to glide over its more controversial moments. Arguably no one, perhaps save Dwight Eisenhower, assumed the Oval Office with a better political resumé than Bush. After military service, an Ivy League degree, and success in business, he'd been a congressman, Senate candidate, US ambassador to the United Nations, Washington's chief envoy to the People's Republic of China, head of the Republican National Committee, head of the Central Intelligence Agency, and vice president for two terms before winning the presidency. Both the Cold War and the Gulf War ended on his watch. A storied and full career indeed.

Yet no part of his career seemed to matter as much to Bush's eulogists as his military service. Television news networks focused programming on the events and ceremonies instigated upon his death, showing "live" shots of his lying-in-state in the US Capitol, and then broadcasting his (two) formal funerals in their entirety. Bush's military record echoed throughout each service, and the punditry that followed. His thirteen pallbearers were all current or former naval officers, and whereas other former presidents lie beneath eternal flames or marble obelisks, a simple military headstone adorns Bush's gravesite, noting that the man buried below had been the forty-first president and a lieutenant (JG) in the United States Navy, serial number 173464.

The focus on Bush's youth should not surprise. Twenty-first-century Americans look back longingly to a seemingly less-partisan era, one in which service and sacrifice transcended divisive party lines. Their gaze often settles on the era of the Second World War, the country's last "good war," whose participants derive from the largely self-anointed "greatest generation." Who could critique the story of a young man who volunteered to risk his life to liberate the world from tyranny? Praising Bush as a member of the generation of the 1940s was, in 2018, political safe space. A eulogist who recalled Bush's civil rights record, his potential connection to the Iran-Contra scandal of the 1980s, or the unpleasant racial tone of his own 1988 presidential campaign, each signature moments in his political life, would undoubtedly have raised the ire of someone in the room. Similar qualms simply do not arise when describing a nineteen-year-old willing to join the nation's great international crusade against evil.

Yet there was more embedded within praise of Bush's wartime years than future generations may realize because the timing of those comments mattered. Bush died during Donald J. Trump's unpopular presidency, whose dearth of military service—indeed, his active avoidance of it in his own youth—offered critics an easy angle of attack. "Private Bone-Spurs," Trump was derisively called by opponents who found his doctor's note excusing him from Vietnam less than satisfying.[9] It was easy for pundits commenting on Bush's passing to raise Bush's profile while diminishing Trump's merely by mentioning the former's military record. Trump had none. "He [Bush] was America's last great soldier-statesman," Bush's official eulogizer noted.[10]

Cameras panned to Trump. There is no reason to suspect every posthumous reference to Bush's wartime years contained an embedded swipe at the man who sat in the front row of Washington National Cathedral with arms crossed. Yet no thinking person could have heard the speech without noting the distinct difference between the two men: Bush called for a "kinder and gentler nation" and a "new world order" built on international cooperation and civility. Trump, whose vitriolic rhetoric ushered in a particularly nasty political environment, promised to "Make America Great Again," by rejecting anything that did not, in his mind, put "America First." Bush's funeral, as already noted, was the nation's last goodbye to a former president as of the time of this writing, and like presidents before, he yearned to shape his legacy. Bush worked with aides throughout his retirement years to script the event, routinely reworking everything from the funeral's list of attendees to its seating chart. Ironically, the greatest boost to Bush's reputation, and that of his presidential son as well, was Trump himself, whose brash style helped elevate both Bushes in both popular and academic rankings of past presidents.[11]

The aforementioned Theodore Roosevelt similarly yearned to control his political fate. Yet, by failing to control his post-mortem narrative, his example wonderfully illustrates how a president's legacy can morph, wobble, and even appear repugnant long after his time. Once celebrated as a statesman for his enthusiastic yet judicious use of force in Latin America and praised for his thoughtful critiques of national and racial qualities, later generations considered him the archetypical *yanqui* bully, and worse. In 2021, New York's American Museum of Natural History—an institution largely founded with his family's money—asked city officials to remove its iconic statue of the country's twenty-sixth president for its (accurate) representation of Roosevelt's imperialist views. The sculpture featured Roosevelt astride a mighty stallion, confidently staring into the distance as though daring the future to come fight. Two figures on foot flank Roosevelt's bronze figure, designed by the sculptor to appear African and Native American.

The artist's message could not be clearer. Roosevelt, and by implication the white force of civilization, lead others toward a new world order. First unveiled to the public in 1940, at a moment when nations around the world and across the Atlantic Ocean looked to the United States for inspiration and salvation, the statue celebrated American leadership. Divorced of that context, it appears far more pernicious and paternalistic by today's standards. Caught in the wave of racial reckoning that washed over the United States in the first decades of the twenty-first century, its protectors and the museum's administrators finally consented to the statue's removal. Even his descendants concurred with the decision. "The world does not need statues, relics of another age, that reflect neither the values of the person they intend to honor nor the values of equality and justice," Theodore Roosevelt IV explained of his support for removing his great-grandfather's likeness.[12] Much had changed between 1940 and 2020, but Roosevelt's actual record did not.

Presidents stop contributing to their records at their last breath, but their impact, on the other hand, reaches far beyond their last day. That story continues to unfurl long after their death. Innumerable books have explored what presidents did during their time in office, and a fair number have explored their exploits once their tenure in office expired. The question at hand for this volume, however, a consideration of how a democratic republic mourned its lost leaders, is not, therefore, really about presidents at all. Their accomplishments and failures, in and out of office, are of course interesting and important. Yet they are not the real subjects here.

We are. Names like Jefferson, Lincoln, and Reagan adorn each chapter, but for this volume's historians, the details of each president's actual deaths pale in importance to what came next. *Mourning the Presidents* is ultimately a book about how these men are commemorated and remembered, at first, and then over ensuing generations. Someday, hopefully soon, women shall join the litany of presidents, but they too will be bound by three unavoidable facts. The first is that the United States Constitution currently bars presidents from holding the office for more than ten years minus one day, or, most often, two full terms if a president first came to power via an election rather than as a vice president elevated upon the current occupant's passing.

The second is that newly sworn-in presidents may know the end date of their time in office, but not when their own personal constitution might fail. They know when their own contribution to presidential history begins and is *supposed* to end, but cannot say when exactly the story of their time in office will be complete. For some, like Kennedy and the prospect of nuclear disarmament for example, this meant unfinished business. For other leaders, especially those with small dreams, even a short time in office might have been plenty enough to leave the legacy they desired. As Camille Davis demonstrates within this volume, President Zachary Taylor's eulogist argued that their fallen leader would not have acted differently if he had known the date of his death. Unremarkable as a president, Davis concludes, Taylor was nonetheless respected for his record and virtue. "Taylor admirably served as a general yet struggled to master the political questions that dominated his time in office," Davis concludes. "Most assuredly, his legacy would be remembered differently had Taylor ended his public service after the Mexican-American War and avoided the presidency. Taylor's ascension to the presidency resulted in a blot from which his legacy never recovered."[13]

The third unavoidable fact of presidential life and death illustrated throughout this volume is that presidents cannot control how they are remembered. Some found this third fact haunting. Others, liberating. Bush worked and reworked his funeral and plans for his burial plot until the end. But he believed it was better to let others make the case for you. "I want somebody else to define the legacy," George H. W. Bush told his granddaughter during his final months. "I've kind of banned the use of the L-word. . . . I think history will point out the things I got wrong, and perhaps some of the things we did right."[14] Having made history across the length of his career, Bush wasn't about to write his own. "Things change, often and rapidly," his authorized biographer explained of Bush's attitude toward historical judgments. "So why bother worrying about it?"[15] "I had already faced death, and God spared me," Bush wrote years after his ill-fated September 1944 flight. "I had this very deep and profound gratitude and a sense of wonder. . . . I was being spared for something on earth."[16] A few words written in an obscure book by an even more obscure historian mattered quite little in the end.

Not every White House occupant felt so sanguine about history's decree. Some feared its ultimate assessment and tried during their time in office to alter the way future generations perceived their efforts and deeds. To cite one infamous example, Andrew Jackson's obsession with refuting accusations of misconduct during the Seminole War led him to spend a considerable amount of time as president writing his own history of the affair. Jackson wrote a good story, so long as one is not too concerned with the facts. Jackson "had a more than common ability to rearrange facts and adjust his memory to suit his purposes," one biographer offered, "to convince himself that what he needed at the moment to assert was really true."[17] Presidential time is precious and limited. What might Jackson have accomplished in office had he not been so obsessed with controlling the story?

In office and during retirement, Harry Truman similarly exaggerated when justifying his decision to drop atomic bombs on Japanese cities in World War II's waning days. Truman insisted that incinerating tens of thousands of civilians to shorten the bloodiest war in human history was the right thing to do. Yet, he also felt moral haunting that it was simultaneously terribly wrong. In 1946, Truman claimed the use of the atomic bomb, which killed at least 150,000 Japanese, avoided a full-scale invasion of the Japanese home islands, saving 250,000 American lives. Two years later, it was a quarter-million Americans and "an equal number of Japanese young men." By 1949, the number had grown to half a million, while after a decade more, Truman claimed the bombs saved "millions of lives." On one occasion his staff urged him, when pressed by a journalist to give his own account of the fateful decision, to employ the one million casualties figure his secretary of war had recently offered, albeit with no corroborating evidence.

"Dropping the bombs ended the war, saved lives, and gave the free nations a chance to face the facts," he subsequently wrote.[18]

Those are hard points to dispute, and in truth, subsequent historians have spent more time investigating the various contributing factors that led to Truman's fateful decision than vilifying it. Yet the vigor and frequency of Truman's self-defense makes one wonder precisely why he felt the need to raise exculpatory points so often. Guilt is one potential answer. Fear of God's ultimate judgment another. Fear of history's judgment seems more likely. We do not know if God exists, and it is not hard to fashion a life without pondering, or at least, fretting, the question. Historians, however, are unavoidable.

Presidents interested in shaping their legacy thus frequently cast the events of their time in more favorable light—unsurprisingly, as these are people ambitious enough to climb the highest rung of American politics, and willing to assume responsibility for enough weaponry to exterminate humanity itself. They are likely to believe themselves capable of shaping future perceptions, too. "You'll be here in the year 2000," Richard Nixon told a reporter soon after becoming the first—and only—president ever to resign the office. "We'll see how I'm regarded then."[19] Nixon lived a full twenty years in retirement, offering advice to both Republican and Democratic successors and arduously rehabilitating his reputation. No one ever doubted his foreign policy savvy, not even those who considered him a war criminal following revelation of his policies toward Southeast Asia, and a common criminal following the Watergate scandal that forced him from office. Even a generation of hard work, however, never fully rehabilitated his reputation. "Two hundred years from now, when he will get only a paragraph or two in a high school American history text," a noted Nixon biographer concluded, "the first sentence will [still] begin: 'Richard Nixon, thirty-seventh president, resigned his office.'" There is nothing the thirty-seventh president could do, in retirement or even beyond the grave, to change that defining sentence.[20]

Well, perhaps nothing. Employees and guards at the Richard Nixon Presidential Library have reported seeing a spectral figure entering Nixon's (locked) childhood home on the site; heard knocking noises emanating from the museum's Watergate exhibit; and perhaps most poignantly, found the machines that played the audio of the infamous Oval Office tapes that proved his political demise working perfectly well at closing time, only to discover them mysteriously malfunctioning the next day.[21]

Dead presidents are just that, yet, as historian David Greenberg noted, nearly every novel, film, or cartoon depicting Nixon in the years after his death included at least one moment of the former president striving to rehabilitate his image. "The common denominator to the postmortem analyses," Greenberg wrote, "was that Nixon was again constructing and doctoring his public identity: coming back, fighting for rehabilitation, rolling out this year's model of the new Nixon."[22] Hardly a model of presidential virtue while in office, one could easily conjure the image of his fellow presidents nonetheless seeking his advice for rehabilitating their own reputations once all gathered in the afterlife.

This book is therefore about presidential memories shaped and reshaped over time, and about presidential attempts to influence that process, but also about the act of mourning itself. Presidents may hope to control this process but cannot. Even the first president, from whom all subsequent presidential precedents flowed, would have been pained by how quickly his own wishes were ignored. "It is my express desire that my Corpse may be interred in a private manner," George Washington instructed his family, "in a private manner, without parade or funeral oration." As Mary Thompson writes, little more than a day passed since Washington's last breath before "things began to go wrong, at least in the sense that plans for the small private service George Washington wanted, began to go off the rails."[23]

Washington's experience in death set another precedent. The plain funeral he desired never took place, replaced instead by one more useful to those he left behind. So too with every president to follow, albeit with varying depths of sorrow and growing spectacle as the nation itself grew into its superpower role, until by the onset of the twenty-first century, the ceremonies used to lay a former president to rest looked strikingly like the funerals for kings against whom the original American revolutionaries ousted. Seeking a similar homespun effect, Ronald Reagan's descendants and acolytes yearned to make him once more appear a common man of the people when they rejected a speaking role for any political leaders, foreign or domestic, at his 2004 state funeral. Some touches are hard to pass up, however. Common people rarely have 700 attendees at their graveside. Neither do most funerals include twenty-one-gun salutes or military jet flyovers.

Presidential funerals, like so much of the office's day-to-day requirements, are political theater, designed not only to say goodbye, but also to cast the former leader in the best light—one last act to shape public memory and ensure a positive legacy. Yet, legacies are not a fallen president's to ensure, and neither is history's positive assessment. Thomas Jefferson's descendants continue to gather two centuries after his death, as Andrew Davenport explained, linked not by the former president's death but by the accidents of their births. Theirs is less an annual celebration of Jefferson's life, than a rite filled with mourning for the pain his abusive and thoughtless treatment of the enslaved community at Monticello continues to inflict across ensuing generations.

Jefferson's death meant an end to families and friendships, as those he owned and those whose blood mingled with his were sold to pay his earthly debts. Birth is always accidental to a newborn. Jefferson's descendants had no say in the matter. They have, however, shaped how his death is remembered. So too with every president mourned, whose passing generates the first full reviews of their legacy, but in no case the last.

Notes

1. For Eisenhower, see Public Papers of the Presidents, "Address at the Cow Palace on Accepting the Nomination of the Republican National Convention," August 23, 1956, https://www.presidency.ucsb.edu/documents/address-the-cow-palace-accepting-the -nomination-the-republican-national-convention/. For Eisenhower's broader assessment, and his fear of nuclear weapons, see Campbell Craig, Destroying the Village: Eisenhower and Thermonuclear War (New York: Columbia University Press, 1998); Richard Immerman and Robert R. Bowie, Waging Peace: How Eisenhower Shaped an Enduring Cold War Strategy (New York: Oxford University Press, 2000).
2. Stephen Gwynn, The Letters and Friendships of Sir Cecil Spring Rice (Boston: Houghton Mifflin, 1929), 317.
3. President Roosevelt, Concord, NH, [October 31, 1902?], Library of Congress Prints and Photographs Division, https://www.theodorerooseveltcenter.org/Research/Digital -Library/Record?libID=0274423. Theodore Roosevelt Digital Library. Dickinson State University.

4. Jeffrey A. Engel, *When the World Seemed New: George H. W. Bush and the End of the Cold War* (New York: Houghton Mifflin Harcourt, 2017); Jon Meacham, *Destiny and Power: The American Odyssey of George Herbert Walker Bush* (New York: Random House, 2015).

5. George Bush, *All the Best: My Life in Letters and Other Writings* (New York: Touchstone, 1999), 51.

6. Engel, *When the World Seemed New,* 29.

7. Meacham, *Destiny and Power,* 454.

8. Meacham, *Destiny and Power,* 46.

9. William Cummings, "Podiatrist's Daughters Say Bone Spur Diagnosis That Helped Trump Avoid Vietnam Draft Was 'Favor,'" *USAToday,* December 27, 2018.

10. Jon Thune, "Remembering 41," https://www.thune.senate.gov/public/index.cfm/2018 /12/remembering-41/.

11. Philip Rucker, "Trump Sits with Fellow Presidents but Still Stands Alone," *Washington Post,* December 5, 2018.

12. Robin Pogrebin, "Roosevelt Statue to Be Removed from Museum of Natural History," *New York Times,* June 20, 2020.

13. Quotation on p. 95.

14. Jamie Ducharme, "George H. W. Bush on Death, the After Life and Almost Dying in World War II," *Time,* December 1, 2018.

15. Meacham, *Destiny and Power,* 524.

16. Engel, *When the World Seemed New,* 29.

17. Daniel Feller, "A Crisis of His Own Contrivance: Andrew Jackson's Break with John C. Calhoun," in *When Life Strikes the President: Scandal, Death, and Illness in the White House,* ed. Jeffrey A. Engel and Thomas J. Knock (New York: Oxford University Press, 2017), 32.

18. J. Samuel Walker, *Prompt and Utter Destruction: Truman and the Use of Atomic Bombs against Japan,* 3rd ed. (Chapel Hill: University of North Carolina Press, 2016), 103.

19. Paul West, "Nixon's Final Campaign," *Baltimore Sun,* December 15, 1991.

20. West, "Nixon's Final Campaign."

21. David Greenberg, *Nixon's Shadow: The History of an Image* (New York: W. W. Norton, 2003), 338.

22. Greenberg, *Nixon's Shadow,* 346.

23. Quotation on p. 15.

CONTRIBUTORS

LINDSAY M. CHERVINSKY is a senior fellow at the Center for Presidential History at Southern Methodist University and a professorial lecturer at the School of Media and Public Affairs at George Washington University. She received her BA from George Washington University, her master's and PhD from the University of California, Davis, and her postdoctoral fellowship from Southern Methodist University. Her writing has appeared in many forums, including the *Wall Street Journal, Ms. Magazine, USA Today, CNN,* and the *Washington Post.* Dr. Chervinsky is the author of the award-winning book *The Cabinet: George Washington and the Creation of an American Institution* (2020).

SHARRON WILKINS CONRAD is an associate professor of history at Tarrant County College, and a senior fellow at Southern Methodist University's Center for Presidential History. Prior to these appointments, she served as director of education and programs at the Sixth Floor Museum at Dealey Plaza, interpreting the assassination and legacy of John Kennedy. Her work has been supported by the John F. Kennedy Presidential Library and the Lyndon Johnson Foundation. She received her BA in history and anthropology from Penn State University, an MA in public history from Howard University, and a PhD from the University of Texas at Dallas. Her book, *The Trinity: John Kennedy, Lyndon Johnson, and Their Civil Rights Legacies in African American Imagination,* is currently under development.

MATTHEW R. COSTELLO is vice president of the David M. Rubenstein National Center for White House History and senior historian for the White House Historical Association. He received his PhD and MA in American history at Marquette University, and BA from the University of Wisconsin–Madison. He has published articles in the *Journal of History and Cultures, Essays in History,* and *White House History Quarterly.* His first book, *The Property of the Nation: George Washington's Tomb, Mount Vernon, and the Memory of the First President* (2019), was published by University Press of Kansas and was a finalist for the George Washington Book Prize. He has interviewed with media outlets including *CNN, Fox News,* the *Washington Post,* and the *New York Times* on a wide variety of historical and presidential topics.

ANDREW M. DAVENPORT is the public historian at the Thomas Jefferson Foundation and director of the Getting Word African American Oral History Project. He is a PhD candidate in US history at Georgetown University. Davenport has published in *Lapham's Quarterly, Los Angeles Review of Books,* and *Smithsonian Magazine.* He also serves on the Board of Directors of the American Agora Foundation (*Lapham's Quarterly*). He earned a BA in English from Kenyon College, an MA in American studies from Fairfield University, and an MA in US history from Georgetown University.

CAMILLE DAVIS is the inaugural H. Ross Perot Sr. Postdoctoral Fellow at the Center for Presidential History at Southern Methodist University. She holds a PhD in history from Southern Methodist University, a BA in journalism from Baylor University, and an MA in history from the University of North Texas. She is an alum of the Institute on Political Journalism at Georgetown University, and she has received research support from the Winterthur Museum and the Smithsonian National Portrait Gallery.

JEFFREY A. ENGEL is founding director of the Center for Presidential History at Southern Methodist University and a professor in the Clements Department of History. He received his BA from Cornell University and his MA and PhD in American history from the University of Wisconsin–Madison, before holding a John M. Olin Postdoctoral Fellow in International Security Studies at Yale University. Engel has authored or edited thirteen books on American foreign policy, including *The China Diary of George H. W. Bush: The Making of a Global President* (2008); *The Fall of the Berlin Wall: The Revolutionary Legacy of 1989* (2009); and *When the World Seemed New: George H. W. Bush and the End of the Cold War* (2017). Engel is also a frequent media contributor on international and political affairs on venues including MSNBC, Fox News, CNN, National Public Radio, and the BBC.

TODD ESTES is professor of history at Oakland University in Rochester, Michigan. He earned his PhD from the University of Kentucky and is the author of the book *The Jay Treaty Debate, Public Opinion, and the Evolution of Early American Political Culture* (2006; paperback 2008). He edited *Founding Visions: The Ideas, Individuals, and Intersections That Created America* (2014) and has published many articles, book chapters, and essays on early national political history and other topics. Estes has won several teaching prizes including the 2001 Oakland University Teaching Excellence Award. Since 2009, he has been a Distinguished Lecturer as selected by the Organization of American Historians (OAH).

WARREN FINCH received a Bachelor of Arts degree from the University of South Alabama in June 1983 and an MA in history from Auburn University. Finch is the director of the George Bush Presidential Library and Museum in College Station, Texas. He was detailed to the Bush White House as part of the National Archives team that handled the transition of Bush presidential materials. He has served at the Library and Museum as archivist, supervisory archivist, and deputy director prior to being appointed director in 2004.

MARTHA HODES, professor of history at New York University, is the author of *Mourning Lincoln* (2015), winner of the Lincoln Prize, awarded by the Gilder Lehrman Institute of American History, and the Civil War and Reconstruction Book Award from the Organization of American Historians. Hodes is also the author of *The Sea Captain's Wife: A True Story of Love, Race, and War in the Nineteenth Century* (2006) and *White Women, Black Men: Illicit Sex in the Nineteenth-Century South* (1997). She has received numerous fellowships, including from the John Simon Guggenheim Memorial

Foundation, the Cullman Center for Scholars and Writers at the New York Public Library, the National Endowment for the Humanities, the American Council of Learned Societies, the Fulbright Commission, and the Whiting Foundation. She is an elected fellow of the Society of American Historians.

DEAN J. KOTLOWSKI is a professor of history at Salisbury University. He is the author of *Nixon's Civil Rights: Politics, Principle, and Policy* (2001) and *Paul V. McNutt and the Age of FDR* (2015) and the editor of *The European Union: From Jean Monnet to the Euro* (2000). He has published over forty articles and book chapters, including in such journals as *Diplomatic History, Pacific Historical Review, Journal of Policy History,* and *Business History Review.* He has been a Fulbright Scholar four times, in the Philippines (2008), Austria (2016), and Australia (2020, 2022), the last of which was a distinguished chair. He has served as an historical adviser to the National Archives, Richard Nixon Library, and U.S. Mint. His next book, *Toward Self-Determination: Federal Indian Policy from Truman to Clinton,* is under contract with University of North Carolina Press.

CHESTER PACH is a member of the Department of History at Ohio University, where he has been the winner of the Jeanette G. Grasselli Brown Faculty Teaching Award in the Humanities. He holds an AB from Brown University and MA and PhD degrees from Northwestern University. He has received fellowships from the National Endowment for the Humanities and the Fulbright Scholar Program. He is the author or editor of four books, including *Arming the Free World: The Origins of the United States Military History Program, 1945–1950* (1991); *The Presidency of Dwight D. Eisenhower* (rev. ed., 1991); and *A Companion to Dwight D. Eisenhower* (2017). He is finishing *The Presidency of Ronald Reagan* for publication by the University Press of Kansas.

BRANDON A. ROBINSON is an attorney and independent historian based in Durham, North Carolina. A seventh-generation native of North Carolina's Piedmont Triad Region, Robinson earned his BA degree in European history (minor in philosophy) and MA degree in American history, both from Western Carolina University; he also earned a JD degree from North Carolina Central University School of Law. Robinson is a past member of the North Carolina

Bar Association Board of Governors, and currently serves as president of the Conservation Trust for North Carolina and Durham County Bar Association.

COLLEEN J. SHOGAN is senior vice president of the White House Historical Association and the director of the David M. Rubenstein National Center for White House History. Shogan previously worked for over a decade at the Library of Congress in various senior management positions. She received her BA from Boston College (Phi Beta Kappa) and her PhD in political science from Yale University, where she was a graduate fellow with the National Science Foundation.

MARY V. THOMPSON is the emerita research historian at the Fred W. Smith National Library for the Study of George Washington at Mount Vernon, where she has worked since 1980. A graduate of Samford University (BA in history, with a minor in folklore), she received an MA in history from the University of Virginia. She is the author of *"In the Hands of a Good Providence": Religion in the Life of George Washington* (2008); *A Short Biography of Martha Washington* (2017); and *"The Only Unavoidable Subject of Regret": George Washington, Slavery, and the Enslaved Community at Mount Vernon* (2019).

DAVID B. WOOLNER is a professor of history at Marist College; senior fellow and resident historian of the Roosevelt Institute; and senior fellow of the Center for Civic Engagement at Bard College. He is the author of *The Last 100 Days: FDR at War and at Peace* (2017), and is editor/coeditor of five books, including *Progressivism in America: Past, Present, and Future* (2016), *FDR's World: War, Peace, and Legacies* (2008), and *FDR, the Vatican, and the Roman Catholic Church in America* (2003). Woolner served as historical advisor to the Ken Burns film *The Roosevelts: An Intimate History* and for numerous special exhibitions at the FDR Presidential Library and Museum. He earned his PhD and MA in history from McGill University and a BA in English literature and history from the University of Minnesota.

INDEX

Miller Center Studies on the Presidency

The Peaceful Transfer of Power: An Oral History of America's Presidential Transitions
DAVID MARCHICK AND ALEXANDER TIPPETT, WITH A. J. WILSON

Averting Doomsday: Arms Control during the Nixon Presidency
PATRICK J. GARRITY AND ERIN R. MAHAN

The Presidency: Facing Constitutional Crossroads
MICHAEL NELSON AND BARBARA A. PERRY, EDITORS

Trump: The First Two Years
MICHAEL NELSON

Broken Government: Bridging the Partisan Divide
WILLIAM J. ANTHOLIS AND LARRY J. SABATO, EDITORS

Race: The American Cauldron
DOUGLAS A. BLACKMON, EDITOR

Communication: Getting the Message Across
NICOLE HEMMER, EDITOR

American Dreams: Opportunity and Upward Mobility
GUIAN MCKEE AND CRISTINA LOPEZ-GOTTARDI CHAO, EDITORS

Immigration: Struggling over Borders
SIDNEY M. MILKIS AND DAVID LEBLANG, EDITORS

Crucible: The President's First Year
MICHAEL NELSON, JEFFREY L. CHIDESTER, AND
STEFANIE GEORGAKIS ABBOTT, EDITORS

The Dangerous First Year: National Security at the Start of a New Presidency
WILLIAM I. HITCHCOCK AND MELVYN P. LEFFLER, EDITORS

The War Bells Have Rung: The LBJ Tapes and the Americanization of the Vietnam War
GEORGE C. HERRING